**Architecture
against
Democracy**

Architecture against Democracy

Histories
of the Nationalist
International

Reinhold Martin and
Claire Zimmerman
Editors

University of Minnesota Press
Minneapolis
London

Copyright 2024 by the Regents of the University of Minnesota

"Hints on Whiteness and American Public Architecture" copyright 2024 by Mabel O. Wilson

All rights reserved. No part of this publication may be reproduced, stored in a retrieval system, or transmitted, in any form or by any means, electronic, mechanical, photocopying, recording, or otherwise, without the prior written permission of the publisher.

Published by the University of Minnesota Press
111 Third Avenue South, Suite 290
Minneapolis, MN 55401-2520
http://www.upress.umn.edu

ISBN 978-1-5179-1675-6 (hc)
ISBN 978-1-5179-1676-3 (pb)

A Cataloging-in-Publication record for this book is available from the Library of Congress.

Printed in the United States of America on acid-free paper

The University of Minnesota is an equal-opportunity educator and employer.

33 32 31 30 29 28 27 26 25 24   10 9 8 7 6 5 4 3 2 1

Contents

Editors' Note — vii

Introduction: Architecture and the Nationalist International — 1
Reinhold Martin and Claire Zimmerman

Part I. Hegemony: Coercion with Consent — 17

1. Hints on Whiteness and American Public Architecture — 19
Mabel O. Wilson

2. The Photographic Mythology and Memory of Hitler's Destroyed New Reich Chancellery — 37
Naomi Vaughan

3. DIY Fascism: Architecture and the Autarchic Exhibition of Italian Minerals — 59
Ruth W. Lo

4. The Concrete Politics of Housing: Assembling Cecap Guarulhos in Authoritarian Brazil — 82
José H. Bortoluci

5. Freehold/Freedom: Exurban Existence in the United Arab Emirates — 98
Kishwar Rizvi

Part II. Technocracy: Ideologies of Expertise — 119

6. Germanizing Krakow: The Political Complexity of Architecture under Nazi Occupation — 121
Paul B. Jaskot and Eve Duffy

7. Afro-Caribbean Migration and Detention at Ellis Island — 140
Itohan Osayimwese

8. Curtain Wall Inside-Out: Technocracy, Theocracy, and 163
Technoaesthetic Formations of Cold War Fascism
María González Pendás

9. Sert Goes South: Planning South America 185
Ana María León

10. Albert Speer, Ernst Neufert, and the Modularization of the World 211
Nader Vossoughian

Part III. Democracy: Perennially Deferred? 233

11. "The Fairness of Our Demands": Ecclesiastical Architecture, 235
Bureaucracy, and Resistance in the Prussian Rhineland, 1815–1840
Laura diZerega

12. Metropolis against the State: Architectures of Violence 257
after the Paris Commune
Peter Minosh

13. The Racial Allegories of Frank Lloyd Wright's Prairie Style 279
Charles L. Davis II

14. Democracy and War: The University of Baghdad 299
between Collaboration and National Competition
Esra Akcan

15. The Aesthetics of Resistance: Istanbul's Standing Man 321
between the Body Politic and Bare Life
Can Bilsel

Conclusion: Democracy Now? 343
Reinhold Martin and Claire Zimmerman

Contributors 353
Index 357

Editors' Note

This project would not have been possible without the collaboration of many who are not named in its pages. The project originated in the spring of 2017 with a series of workshops hosted by Columbia University's Temple Hoyne Buell Center for the Study of American Architecture, directed by Reinhold Martin, on infrastructure and emergency powers. These workshops belonged in turn to a multiyear project, "Power: Infrastructure in America," documented on a website of the same name. The last workshop concluded on March 8, 2020, as Covid-19 shuttered the world.

The guiding hypothesis of the emergency powers workshops was that the antidemocratic tendencies made especially visible by the 2016 presidential election in the United States were reproduced in the built environment by longer-term developments in neoliberal governance at the state and municipal levels centered on a politics of infrastructure. The suspension of the right to infrastructure, we argued, was an overlooked aspect of urban political ecology, whereby emergency management became a vehicle for consolidating unaccountable executive power in a newly reconfigured partnership with capital. This had been the case in New Orleans in the aftermath of Hurricane Katrina in 2005 and in the Flint, Michigan, municipal water crisis since 2014; it would recur in Puerto Rico in the aftermath of Hurricane Maria in 2017, among numerous other instances. Public programs hosted by the Buell Center that brought together academics and activists to discuss each of these three cases formed a backdrop for the current volume, which developed more directly out of a scholarly workshop on nationalism, aesthetics, and emergency powers focused on historical examples held at Columbia University in spring 2018.

But in many ways the origins of *Architecture against Democracy* also lie in a workshop co-organized by the Buell Center that same spring in collaboration with Andrew Herscher and Claire Zimmerman at the University of Michigan and Louise Seamster then at the University of Tennessee, Knoxville, held on the Michigan campus with an opening panel and community discussion at the Cass Corridor Commons in Detroit. The workshop, on austerity, race, and the "legacies of emergency management," focused on the politics of infrastructure around the Flint water crisis. Activists led the conversation, and much of the aftermath involved detailed reflection on what academic institutions might responsibly contribute. In this context we began to discuss the need for a more robust scholarly literature that acknowledged, explained, and interpreted the historical reality that our collaborators faced daily: an antidemocratic politics of the built environment. And, as academic relations continually intertwine, this sense of need was also catalyzed by work on *Visualizing Fascism: The Twentieth-Century Rise of the Global Right* (Duke University Press, 2020), a volume then in development and edited by Julia Adeney Thomas and Geoff Eley. The current volume, then, is intended as another contribution to such a literature. The cases our authors consider represent a vanishingly small sample of a vast archive; nevertheless, we hope that they might help frame future work, centered on sites around the world where the antidemocratic project continues to gain ground, as the convulsions that have shaken the United States in the years since 2016 amply demonstrate.

All of this, and much else besides, was in turn made possible by the daily work of two colleagues: Jacob R. Moore, associate director of the Buell Center, and Jordan Steingard, Buell Center program manager. Their contributions, both institutional and intellectual, to the Buell Center's work cannot be measured. Likewise, Lucia Allais, who now directs the Buell Center, has offered instant, steadfast support in seeing this project through. We also thank Taubman College at the University of Michigan for early support of the project. At the University of Minnesota Press, Pieter Martin has responded to this unwieldy undertaking with an extraordinarily open mind. His thoughtful guidance has been invaluable, as has Anne Carter's care together with her colleagues, especially Rachel Moeller, in steering the volume through production. To which we add our gratitude to Rob Hill for his expert copyediting and to the incomparable Kitty Chibnik for her exceptional proofreading and the index. We also thank our anonymous peers who reviewed the manuscript for their constructive suggestions, which have surely made the volume stronger. And finally, to our contributors one and all, we convey once again our sincere thanks for your patience and understanding but, most especially, for the work that you do.

Introduction

Architecture and the Nationalist International

Reinhold Martin and Claire Zimmerman

In 1816 on the island of Saint Helena, Napoléon Bonaparte articulated his failed vision of a pan-European empire, with himself at its helm: "I felt myself worthy of this glory!"[1] By 2016, a group of ersatz Napoléons had assumed leadership positions in governments across the globe, with the threat of an antidemocratic alliance of nationalist authoritarians replacing outright imperialism. *Architecture against Democracy* investigates the aesthetic, social, and technological dimensions of antidemocratic formations throughout the intervening two centuries. The political moves toward fascism and its likenesses related to modernization have assumed particular patterns in architecture and are therefore susceptible to spatiotemporal, cultural, and material analysis. From what the historian Christopher Bayly called the "wreck of nations" after 1815 to our own day, concentrating on the politics of nationalism, white supremacy, protofascism, and fascism, this volume offers an architectural history of this recent *nationalist international*.[2]

When they consider the subject at all, histories of modern architecture and politics typically treat democracy as a norm to which architecture idealistically aspires, or from which it tragically deviates. We propose the opposite: that, regardless of authorial intent, the built environment has provided a fast track to antidemocratic praxis, with structural alliance with democracy an unreliable exception, especially in the creation of public architecture. For centuries, architects have knowingly supplied antidemocratic powers with technical knowledge and adaptable symbols, sometimes accompanied by magical thinking—that architecture could "improve" the political scene in one way or another—and sometimes shrouded in the agnosticism of expertise. But even when buildings themselves explicitly "speak of" or otherwise exhibit manifestly democratic values, they do so most commonly in a univocal manner that accepts as unexamined doctrine the idea that democracy can be conjured formally or symbolically rather than as hypotheses contributing to a shared conversation. This volume highlights these and related contradictions, suggesting a more focused attention to and discourse on architecture and politics. We choose *democracy* as our political benchmark rather than some other, more radical measure to acknowledge the generally liberal milieux within which architecture and architects have circulated globally since around 1800, including in the socialist world. Such a benchmark ("democracy") also resonates broadly, even with those who doubt whether it can really exist. We track the absence of convincingly democratic architecture, not to expose all modernisms as reactionary, but to gain a counterfactual understanding of what replacing the preposition with a conjunction—architecture *and* democracy—might actually entail. Some of the authors gathered here make the positive case, although not always in the places one might expect.

Three themes have proved especially useful guides in understanding this process and organizing the chapters: *hegemony, technocracy,* and *democracy* itself. Overlapping and interdependent, each concept identifies a way of governing that has found notable articulation in architecture, urbanism, and other aspects of the built environment during the modern era. None describes this era fully, nor do all three summarize the many conflicting dimensions of modern political life, its institutions, or its forms. Still, whether taken separately or together, these three themes enable what this volume sets out to do: to explore the history of architecture globally during the modern era as a form of political history, inclusive of economic relations but not reducible to these, by providing a viable, open framework that may be extended and modified with further study.

The many scenes of architecture's antidemocratic public appearance may also be grouped heuristically into three overlapping and unequal periods for the purposes of this volume: that from around 1815 to 1918, in which liberal nationalist and republican tendencies developed and combined worldwide as empires clashed; the transitional interwar period, during which the totalitarian threat loomed largest even as internationalisms flourished and anticolonial resistance grew; and the period after 1945, when different versions of anticolonial nationalism struggled amid Cold War polarities to gain a foothold against technocratic developmentalism and global neoliberalism. Although the essays collected in this volume are arranged thematically rather than chronologically, each may be read into this loose succession of political orders, if only to deepen (and sometimes contradict) the narrative we offer here. We expand on these historical phases here and in our Conclusion.

Before engaging our three conceptual themes, some general notes about writing on architecture and politics reveal a few recurrent patterns. Those writing from within the field of architectural history often turn to theory drawn from other disciplines to provide context and argumentation about the relationship between the built environment and political events. Frequently overlooked, however, is political history, most notably the history of fascism, but also histories that focus on the three orders that organize this volume: hegemony, technocracy, and democracy. We note that historical arguments about the conditions under which state-sanctioned fascism developed provide crucial foundations for theorizing the relationship between state building programs and fascist politics more generally. Historians have debated related issues for decades, beginning with the famous *Historikerstreit* in Germany in the 1980s that coincided with related architectural debates about classical form and the recent past. Architectural historians have much to learn from these debates, including the important revisions that actual, built environments offer to the abstraction of much historical writing in other fields.

Similarly, a recent work edited by political scientists Duncan Bell and Bernardo Zacka, *Political Theory and Architecture,* engages selectively with architectural history, its methods, and conclusions.[3] While that volume's introduction defines architecture quite broadly, architectural writers of the past several decades have made significant progress in articulating the field—both empirically and by developing methodologies and drawing conclusions on which others build. Political theorists (like historians) might therefore benefit from existing debates about the built environment as well as discourse around urban design and planning, architecture, and historic preservation. Indeed, part of our point here is that even in its most esoteric forms, architecture is a public practice, and its modes might be much better understood across multiple constituencies. This reiterates the challenge of interdisciplinary scholarship: to be conversant in the literature of more than one discipline on any given topic or period and to make one's own work relevant to other fields. Perhaps the longevity of Barbara Miller Lane's classic study of architecture and politics reflects how well Miller Lane did her work in the fields of political *and* architectural history.

In 1968, Miller Lane published a detailed study of the problem of attaching political meaning to architecture that remains a standard for scholarship on the topic. In *Architecture and Politics in Germany, 1918–1945,* Miller Lane reconstructs the complex continuities and transformations, from the Weimar period to the Third Reich, by which a disparate array of cultural and political figures, from architects to party leaders to bureaucrats, sought an elusive synthesis of architecture and political ideology. The book's concluding chapter, on "Nazi Architecture," makes the point most explicitly. In fact, Miller Lane argues, the Nazi program comprised three distinct components: an internally contradictory state ideology, an opportunistic (not to say fraudulent) propaganda campaign, and an ideologically inconsistent state-building campaign.[4] That these rarely coincided and often seemed at odds may be less an indication of the skin-deep character of Adolf Hitler's conception of the National Socialist state as an artwork (as Miller Lane implies) than of the deceptive shape-shifting of totalitarian rule itself, reliant as it is on entropy and chaos to indemnify the power of its leaders.

Fearful of this power, Nazi officials often spoke in coded euphemisms when claiming that a particular architectural style, from a bloated neoclassicism to *Volkisch* town planning, best embodied the will to power of "blood and soil." Observing the compensatory imbalance between propagandistic publicity campaigns and actual building, Miller

Lane concludes that the Nazi regime did not get very far in "establishing 'totalitarian' control of architectural style."[5] Instead, the regime redirected efforts to attach political meaning to architecture derived from highly charged debates of the Weimar period. The intensity of Nazi propaganda, according to Miller Lane, opportunistically reproduced the Weimar-era "belief in the symbolic meaning of architecture" while draining the prior contest over form and meaning of whatever ideological consistency it may have had.[6] Such a redirection took particular forms in architecture and aesthetic production as a whole; the films of Leni Riefenstahl provide eloquent testimony of the mutability of film and architecture to a transposition of meaning from left-avant-gardist to right.

Two other possibilities shadow Miller Lane's subtle exposition. First, that the properly totalitarian project was to attach meaning to itself, independent of political content, as a bulwark against the perceived depthlessness of modern life (through appeals to ethnicity and nationhood); and second, that the architecture–propaganda relation was in fact reversed. That is, rather than the surrounding ambience of exhibitions, publications, and parades papering over the buildings' stylistic inconsistencies with trite, ideological slogans, that very inconsistency served as a most effective medium to construct an elaborate theater of political meaning, with buildings as stage sets and the furnishings of civic life as props.[7] Correspondingly, the artfulness of Nazi propaganda may well have consisted not in deceit but in a perverse sort of truth-telling, where there was no question of mistaking the part for the whole—the partially realized fragment never signaled a coherent state ideology. Rather, the Potemkin village of the totalitarian artwork staged an intense, contradictory aesthetics of willful, *knowing* participation in a grotesque and genocidal fiction—and of assenting to it nonetheless.

Interwar Totalitarianism and the *Historikerstreit*

Although many essays in this volume address very different contexts, to date the German as well as the Italian case have remained somewhat paradigmatic in the architectural literature. Miller Lane argues that there was no coherent ideology to represent, only a grotesquely hollow shell, in the architecture of National Socialism. This was also the thesis of Hannah Arendt's controversially revisionist interpretation, captured famously in her stark observations at the trial of Adolf Eichmann, on the "banality of evil." Against this backdrop, Arendt's spatiopolitical reflections on the lives of the *demos* remain a useful benchmark for thinking historically about architecture and/against democracy.[8] Arendt evaluated totalitarian lies, fictions, and propagandistic representations on the basis of their repetition ad absurdum rather than for their twisting of the truth per se. What sustains these lies is the "totalitarian movement," an entire "fictitious world" that, when defeated, causes its members to "quietly give up the movement as a bad bet and look around for another promising fiction or wait until the former fiction regains enough strength to establish another mass movement."⁹ The totalitarian world's forms of organization—its institutions and its conventions—back up the fiction with a reality suited to it rather than the other way around. Thus in the National Socialist case, Roman classicism, built out of readily available stone quarried by enslaved laborers, provided just the right kind of "fictitious world." Its demise appears complete in Alexander Kluge's film *Brutalität im Stein* of 1961, pendant to Riefenstahl on the other side of World War II, and part of the "coming to terms with the past" that followed 1945 in West German society.¹⁰

Both Arendt's and Kluge's work preceded the controversial *Historikerstreit* of the second half of the 1980s in the Federal Republic. As conservative politicians and historians sought an exit from histories of the Nazi past by affirming the sufferings of *Schutzstaffel* (SS) soldiers under Hitler, German national identity, "communities of fate," and the need to "move on" from National Socialist history, the philosopher Jürgen Habermas sounded the alarm.¹¹ In response to Ronald Reagan's 1985 visit to Bitburg cemetery to honor fallen SS soldiers and the opinion pieces that supported the rehabilitation of German soldiers in World War II, Habermas decried a growing apologism for Hitler. History in the public sphere became a battleground between "German Germans and non-German Germans" (to quote Dirk Moses), one that has hardly been cleared today. The continuance of this debate in the wake of reunification has taken different forms, most notably in a public memorial culture dedicated to "coming to terms with the German past" (*Vergangenheitsbewältigung*). As current events at the time of writing attest, the recent and unfolding history of Germany is equally as important for students of democracy as is the past that continually gnaws on that history.¹²

Publicly, a reunited Germany engaged in collective anamnesis in its many memorials to the recent past before and after World War II, yet it also took on the trappings of unrestrained capitalist urban development. The former was the province of the state, the latter that of private capital (although frequently with state support). Anamnesis gave rise to Holocaust memorials and other acts of contrition throughout the land. Yet in the same span of time, Berlin's imperial *Schloss* (palace) was reconstructed, Potsdamer Platz was rebuilt as an eclectic mixture of neotraditionalist and neomodernist design for international brand-name retailers and hotel chains, and a new capital complex prepared the ground for reinvigorated free-market capitalism supported by state policies, starting with a glass-domed Reichstag. A haunting image: the old Großmarkthalle of Frankfurt, constructed to modernize the city's food distribution network in the late 1920s and later used as a gathering point for those en route to concentration camps, now punctured by a glass and steel tower for the European Central Bank, designed by former bad-boy avant-gardists Coop Himmelb(l)au. Germany is awash in purported democratic symbols built for the public—as well as their opposite. In this it exaggerates (but also basically aligns with) postwar economic developments elsewhere that have similarly left their mark in buildings. Hence the need to tighten the analytic frame.

Hegemony: Coercion with Consent

As we use it here, the concept of *hegemony* was most cogently formulated by the political philosopher Antonio Gramsci as a relationship of domination in which coercion combines with consent in varying degrees of contingency, a concept closely linked to capitalism as it floats free of the legal architecture of representative democracy.[13] The historian Ranajit Guha explained the concept succinctly: *"hegemony stands for a condition of Dominance (D), such that... Persuasion (P) outweighs Coercion (C)."* Yet, "there can be no hegemonic system under which P outweighs C to the point of reducing it to nullity."[14] The built environment can be a powerful instrument of hegemony, or coercion persuasively naturalized, in part because it exists without concrete alternatives. There is no control case for a city or a building, only that which exists or which once existed.

On the question of hegemony in and through constructed environments, the bibliography of works that directly reference the term is relatively slim. To a certain extent, recent critical histories of architecture and development, mostly in the global South, have shown how discourses and practices associated with modernization reproduce hegemonic dispositions. Many of these histories also utilize the tools of ideology critique, explicitly or implicitly, to decode the neocolonial paternalism of modernist planners and architects. Effective as such unmaskings are, the difficulty of distinguishing the making and remaking of hegemonies among the governed from the ideological projections of the governors poses a perennial challenge to scholars who seek to repair the epistemological and material damage wrought by Western colonialism, or indeed by white supremacy. So too for those who, in recent years, have sought to give historical texture to the term "neoliberalism" as both an ideologeme and a set of material and discursive practices.[15]

Here we place the accent on politics. Architecture and the built environment, as many of our authors show, can be a compelling instrument of coercion, with consent generally neutralized by the process of construction (it can be withheld only with difficulty once a building is complete). The first group of case studies in this volume traces the material conditions of specific localities to show how they distribute power through constructed environments—often inhibiting or opposing but also occasionally enabling democratic spatial practices. This group includes Mabel O. Wilson on the racial contradictions of early public architecture in the United States; Naomi Vaughan on the technical production and reproduction of the *Führer* myth in Nazi Germany; Ruth W. Lo on the imbrication of construction materials, modernization, and nationalism in Fascist Italy; José H. Bortoluci on housing and enforced political consensus in Brazil; and Kishwar Rizvi on homeownership as a form of political belonging in Dubai. Like the others in this volume, these chapters focus on the built environment as a vehicle for political relations.[16] They showcase moments when architects and urbanists were hailed by forces of democracy, sometimes successfully, but also when material sites were active contributors to disenfranchisement and antidemocratic practices.[17] In some of these cases, capital was the coercive agent of nation-states; in others, something closer to the reverse was true. Still other cases find citizens pursuing their interests in cities, towns, and enclaves, with little regard for democracy at all. Among our goals is to articulate this spectrum of political concerns; to show acts of omission as much as acts of commission; and to highlight the rare synergies that suggest possible exit ramps leading to better routes ahead.

Technocracy: Ideologies of Expertise

The technical challenge of making something and rationalizing it provides a ready set of procedures where domination hides behind pragmatic orderliness and specialized expertise. If *hegemony* designates coercion with consent, *technocracy* is intimately linked, insofar as the term has come to mean "the exercise of power by means of, or justified by, specialist knowledge."[18] The critique or defense of technocracy does not feature prominently in Western political theory or in the political science literature. Most common are historical references to the sociologist Thorstein Veblen's advocacy of government by technical experts—in his case engineers, and for other social scientists, managers.[19] By the 1970s, the historian of science Langdon Winner had introduced the concept of "autonomous technology" to suggest that means and ends had reversed, as technological systems began to acquire a governing logic of their own, one that unduly shaped the values of technocrats empowered to govern through them. Twenty years ago, referring to the work of Michel Foucault and others, the historian and political scientist Timothy Mitchell influentially described a "rule of experts" in colonial North Africa as central to the logic of Western imperialism, to which scholars have added numerous other cases.[20] In political theory, Jeffrey Friedman's controversial 2019 *Power without Knowledge: A Critique of Technocracy* animated debates about the political functions of technocratic systems; his invocation of an "exitocracy" to counter technocracy only deepens questions about the political effects of rationalist or technocratic decision-making in public life (and does *not* describe the kind of exit strategy we seek).[21]

Technocracy finds a ready home in built environment practices of the post–World War II period, by which time the Veblenian model had been well established in the profession. Second-wave industrialization advanced technocratic architectural production in industrial sectors; these connected closely to large professional practices that specialized in high-rise office design, hospitals, or other institutional building types. Curtain wall design, for example, reflects a pattern throughout the field: narrow specialization on autonomous building components, such that the provision of a single system was effectively divorced from considerations of its use or public impact, or used as ideological cover.[22]

Architectural historians, ourselves included, have often engaged the study of technocracy without necessarily invoking the term as such.[23] This volume addresses that omission, and a second group of essays suggests a larger effort to explore architecture as a technocratic instrument. This group includes Paul B. Jaskot and Eve Duffy on techniques used by National Socialist planners to dehumanize Jews in Krakow; Itohan Osayimwese on the preemptive and racially based detention of immigrants to the United States; María González Pendás on theocratic governance through modular, modernist design in Franquista Spain; Ana María León on modernist planning and neocolonialism in Latin America; and Nader Vossoughian on the rationalization of design and construction as an afterimage of National Socialist ideology in postwar Germany. Some studies of architecture and technocracy build on recent work centered on the everyday technics of "governmentality," a term borrowed from Foucault.[24] Earlier work like Miller Lane's, however, reminds us that political ideology and the rule of technical experts (or in the case of architects, generalists) often go hand in hand. This, in turn, recalls the fierce, oppositional critique of industrial and postindustrial technocratic rule carried out by Manfredo Tafuri. In the oft-overlooked penultimate chapter of *Architecture and Utopia* (1973), for example, the Italian historian characterized even structuralist semiology as a networked "ideology of communication" symptomatically disclosed, in urbanism, by the thought of the German cybernetician Max Bense.[25] To the extent, then, that the Foucauldian study of governmentality has offered a pathway out of the structuralist double bind, we may now find ourselves on the other side of that bind, ready to return—with or without Tafuri—to the critique of ideology by another name. That is, to the critique of technocracy.

Democracy: Perennially Deferred?

Somewhat counterintuitively, the political theorist and historian Jan-Werner Müller has called the European twentieth century after the First World War an "age of democracy."[26] That is not to say that all political forms of the period were democratic—on the contrary. Rather, Müller suggests, *democracy* had become a discursive figure by which political ideologies were measured, a point he illustrates with the words of the Italian Fascist philosopher Giovanni Gentile: "the Fascist State . . . is a people's state, and, as such, the democratic state *par excellence.*"[27] Under fascism, all have rights—except that some have more rights than others.

This generalization of *democracy* as a semantically flexible term had its roots in the previous century, which saw numerous republican experiments arise amid and across two types of imperial formations—territorial (Austro-Hungarian, Ottoman, Russian, but also China) and maritime (Great Britain, France, Germany)—during and after Eric Hobsbawm's "age of revolution" in Europe and in the Americas.[28] At the start of the First World War these empires were largely still governed by what Max Weber called "the charisma of blood."[29] In Europe by war's end, the institutionalized charisma of the monarch had effectively been displaced into that of the masses given form as a "people"—a "sleeping sovereign" born, according to Richard Tuck, in early modern Europe, to whom both parliamentarians and authoritarians would henceforth address themselves.[30] Partha Chatterjee has explained further how this ultimately liberal logic, of a people "sovereign without exercising sovereign power," was challenged by populisms of both the left and the right during those years, the legacy of which remains today.[31]

In this way, democracy was naturalized as the rule of the masses. But nowhere were those masses uniform, defined as they were by the conflict among social and economic classes on the one hand and among cultural groups, or "nations," on the other. Ironizing the identification of formal democratic government with white supremacy in the United States during the Jim Crow era, Weber's transatlantic colleague, W. E. B. Du Bois, described instead the unfinished project of Reconstruction as that of establishing an "abolition democracy."[32] This concept, which premised government by the people upon social, racial, and economic equality among those people, rewrote "democracy" as a political-economic term, the meaning of which is not limited to the political forms by which a people governs or is governed.

Recent architectural scholarship has begun to respond to Du Bois's challenge, in particular with collaborative efforts that address the history of what he called the "color line" as a spatial as well as a social phenomenon.[33] Whereas architectural modernists frequently drew parallels with democratic ideals—see the words and works of Frank Lloyd Wright, or postwar calls for a civic-minded "new monumentality," to cite just two well-known examples—critical architectural scholarship has struggled to address political concepts directly. In one notable exception, Timothy Hyde, writing on republican Cuba, has identified what he calls "constitutional modernism" as the product of a liberal civil society, for which some architects worked to secure a political order through the symbolic and practical mediation of the law.[34] Aside from the left-ideological critique of a figure like Tafuri and his Venice School cohort, political thought per se has offered architectural scholars minimal traction.[35] A third group of essays collected here thus takes up specific historical features of democracy as leverage in design and planning projects. This group includes Laura diZerega on the decentralization of sovereignty in early nineteenth century Prussia; Peter Minosh on radically democratic "architectures" of the Paris Commune; Charles L. Davis II on Wright's architecture and the intimacies of racialization; Esra Akcan on the U.S. export of democracy-as-ideology in postcolonial Iraq; and Can Bilsel on the performative "aesthetics of resistance" in contemporary Turkey. Like the other contributions to this volume, these chapters suggest preliminary steps toward bringing political thought out from under the historiographical shadows in architecture. Conversely, the chapters in the preceding two sections place an irreducibly political concept—*democracy*—at the center of their inquiry, but one modified by hegemonic, or technocratic practices and regimes.

The Architecture of Compliance

In the West, popular discourse often links democratic governance with capitalism, singling out the United States to demonstrate just how intertwined these political and economic systems are thought to be.[36] More cautiously, *Financial Times* commentator Martin Wolf has articulated the concept of "democratic capitalism." Capitalism without democratic governance or democracy in a failed capitalist state, he argues, both tend to lead to instability, plutocracy, demagogy, and autocracy—and, by inference, fascism. Tensions between the two—democracy and capitalism—result in part from their differing spatial effects. "Democracy," Wolf writes, "is local. It is based on a tie between a particular location and the people who live there."[37] It is similarly *situated* aspects of architecture and building that concern us here, although in a manner more attentive to the contradictions entailed by such a formulation.

National capitalist democracy combined with international capitalist domination is one trademark of empire. But if capitalism and democracy work best when combined, as Wolf argues, what are the implications of threats to the latter today, when patterns of the built environment are increasingly shared around the globe? The terms' inside–outside dualism posits democracy as an ideal for the "inside" of the nation-state, or for its enfranchised citizens (often these are not the same). Imperial capitalism similarly designates power exercised over allies, adversaries, or subalterns externally or internationally.[38] Perhaps unsurprisingly, the twentieth-century architectural imaginary of these relations, of which afterimages persist in being built today, associates monumental public architecture with imperial expansion, whether in the U.S. embassy in Athens (arch. W. Gropius) or the headquarters of the British Raj in New Delhi (archs. E. Lutyens and H. Baker). Both building complexes showcased the modernity of the regimes they represented, as those regimes attempted to tighten the bonds of empire in the post–World War II Mediterranean basin (from the United States) and in South Asia around World War I (from the United Kingdom), respectively. The U.S. embassy-building program likewise yielded mostly modernist buildings throughout the global sphere of influence of the United States after World War II, substituting the language of international modernism for the hybridized classicism of the colonial capital.[39]

Yet if Western imperial ambitions abroad do somehow depend on democracy "at home," as Wolf implies, how does this dependency affect the architecture or built environments of either case? There seems little easy correlation between buildings as material things and the politics that unfold through their action. Imperial formations also unfold internally as state-affiliated capitalism extends its reach and persuades consumers within any given nation-state to comply with market guidance. And while this kind of architecture of compliance might differ from that of government administration, both act hegemonically, declaiming as irrevocable fact what is really just fiction—that there is no alternative to liberal (or neoliberal) state-aligned capitalism. Thus, while there may be little architecture of democracy per se, a generous array of antidemocratic architecture abounds. Indeed, built environments that impede democratic praxis have proliferated under neoliberalism, where the consent to be coerced has gradually developed into powerfully addictive patterns that weaponize capital in the guise of "free choice."[40]

Organization of the Book

As noted, the contributions to *Architecture against Democracy* fall under three subject headings: Hegemony, Technocracy, and Democracy. Although clearly overlapping, these distinct figures highlight particular aspects of any given antidemocratic conjuncture, grounding the analysis in specific practices and locating its theoretical substance in cities and buildings. As the basis of thematic groupings, they draw widely varying case studies together through practices of de-democratization rather than through chronology or geography.

A further aim of the thematic groupings (which are by no means exclusive—others might be found) is to emphasize architecture's active role in the development and maintenance of political concepts, ideologies, and practices beyond simply servicing or otherwise representing historically defined political projects such as National Socialism or Fascism. Those seeking to understand antidemocratic tendencies in the making or to track authoritarian politics at levels other than that of the nation-state will find thought-provoking case studies in this volume's pages. Furthermore, repositioning architecture and urbanism as variables in the construction of democracy introduces new actors into the historical equation, from civil society and elsewhere. We hope that this approach will allow scholars to reconstruct the architecture–politics relation not only in terms of manifest ideological positions but also within everyday (though no less antidemocratic) social and spatial practices. We hope that the framework we offer will provide students with a useful basis on which to build their own understanding of such practices and processes.

The three thematic categories also describe distinct activities and formations. To better gauge their interaction, each part of the book is introduced with a brief summary that details the contributions within it. The first traces the emergence of antidemocratic, racist, or authoritarian social norms, ideologies, and practices and their diffusion throughout civil society, which provides industrial and postindustrial capitalism with competing forms of coercion with consent ("Hegemony"). Second, technobureaucratic instruments and procedures build, sustain, and reproduce these forms for the coercive or administrative maintenance of political order, as well as its symbolic representation ("Technocracy"). The volume concludes with the reconfiguration, appropriation, or suppression of representation or of a popular will ("Democracy"), pivoting to the category most immediately open to public intervention in the form of protest, strike, or revolt. Each essay in these three parts demonstrates, in implicit dialogue with the others, what kinds of objects, figures, and processes critical historical scholarship in architecture might take up to study these underexamined problems in depth, how this might be done, and why doing so might matter.

Notes

1. The Count de las Cases, *Memoirs of the Life, Exile, and Conversations of the Emperor Napoléon*, vol. 4 (London: Henry Colburn, 1836), 104.
2. On the "wreck of nations," see C. A. Bayly, *The Birth of the Modern World, 1780–1914: Global Connections and Comparisons* (Malden, Mass.: Blackwell Publishing, 2004), 125ff. By *nationalist international* we mean to recognize the shifting alliances and ideological affinities, as well as rivalries, that arose around 2016 among nationalist leaders such as Donald Trump in the United States, Vladimir Putin in Russia, Narendra Modi in India, Viktor Orbán in Hungary, Recep Tayyip Erdoğan in Turkey, and later, in 2018, Jair Bolsonaro in Brazil, among others.
3. Duncan Bell and Bernardo Zacka, *Political Theory and Architecture* (London: Bloomsbury Publishing, 2020).
4. Barbara Miller Lane, *Architecture and Politics in Germany, 1918–1945*, 2d ed. (Cambridge, Mass.: Harvard University Press, 1985 [1968]), 187.
5. Miller Lane, *Architecture and Politics in Germany*, 216.
6. Miller Lane, *Architecture and Politics in Germany*, 215.
7. On the theatricality of National Socialist architecture, see Dieter Bartetzko, *Zwischen Zucht und Ekstase: Zur Theatralik von NS-Architektur* (Berlin: Mann, 1985).
8. In the *New Yorker* articles on which the book bearing this subtitle, the "banality of evil," was based, Arendt circled around her more famous formulation with reflections on Eichmann's nearly compulsive tendency to repeat clichés. What she later called "banality" was a certain mendacious emptiness, which was all the more inclined to operate the ruthlessly bureaucratic mechanization of death by faithfully rehearsing a million vacant little lies, rather than aspire to the ideological plenitude of what today is called the "big lie," or a coherent system of belief calculated to deceive. Hannah Arendt, *Eichmann in Jerusalem: A Report on the Banality of Evil* (New York: Viking Press, 1963), originally published (slightly abbreviated) as Arendt, "Eichmann in Jerusalem I–V," *New Yorker* (February 8–March 16, 1963). On the "big lie," see Timothy Snyder, "The American Abyss," *New York Times* (January 9, 2021), available at https://www.nytimes.com/2021/01/09/magazine/trump-coup.html. Arendt proposes that the "true goal" of totalitarian propaganda is "not persuasion but organization," for which purpose "originality in ideological content can only be considered an unnecessary obstacle." Hannah Arendt, *The Origins of Totalitarianism*, 2nd ed. (New York: Harcourt, Brace, Jovanovich, 1973 [1951]), 361.
9. Arendt, *The Origins of Totalitarianism*, 363.
10. The literature on *Vergangenheitsbewältigung* and the "Historikerstreit" of the late 1980s in the Federal Republic is immense. For one synthetic summary of events up to 2007, see A. Dirk Moses, "The Non-German German and the German German: Dilemmas of Iden-

tity after the Holocaust," *New German Critique* 34, no. 2 [101] (Summer 2007): 45–94, https://doi.org/10.1215/0094033X-2007-003. On German stone construction in the Nazi period, see Paul Jaskot, *The Architecture of Oppression: The SS, Forced Labor and the Nazi Monumental Building Economy* (New York: Routledge, 2000).

11. Jürgen Habermas, "Eine Art Schadensabwicklung: Die apologetischen Tendenzen in der deutschen Zeitgeschichtsschreibung," *Die Zeit*, 18 July 1986. Reprinted in Habermas and Leaman, "A Kind of Settlement of Damages (Apologetic Tendencies)," *New German Critique* 44 (1988): 25–39, https://doi.org/10.2307/488144.

12. We refer here to the recent coup attempt by a gang surrounding the improbably named Heinrich XIII, https://www.bbc.com/news/world-europe-63885028. See Moses, "The Non-German German and the German German," 45–94. See also the disturbing events at Documenta 15, from the opposite end of the spectrum: "Germany Has Cancelled Us," *Art Newspaper*, September 22, 2022, https://www.theartnewspaper.com/2022/09/22/documenta-15-closes-curators-ruangrupa-exhibition-kassel.

13. Note "Gramsci's definition of hegemony as something different than sheer domination . . . hegemony is the *additional* power that accrues to a dominant group by virtue of its capacity to *lead* society in a direction that not only serves the dominant group's interests but is also perceived by subordinate groups as serving a more general interest . . . If subordinate groups have confidence in their rulers, systems of domination can be governed without resorting to force. But if that confidence wanes, they no longer can. By the same token, Gramsci's notion of hegemony may be said to consist of the 'power inflation' that ensues from the capacity of dominant groups to present their rule as credibly serving not just their interests but those of subordinate groups as well. When such credibility is lacking or wanes, hegemony deflates into sheer domination, that is, into what Ranajit Guha has called 'dominance without hegemony.'" Giovanni Arrighi, *Adam Smith in Beijing: Lineages of the Twenty-First Century* (London: Verso, 2007), 149–50. Also see Perry Anderson, *The H-Word: The Peripeteia of Hegemony* (Brooklyn: Verso, 2017); Antonio Gramsci, *Prison Notebooks* (New York: Columbia University Press, 1992); Ernesto Laclau and Chantal Mouffe, *Hegemony and Socialist Strategy: Towards a Radical Democratic Politics* (London: Verso, 1985).

14. Ranajit Guha, "*Dominance without Hegemony* and Its Historiography," in *Subaltern Studies* 6 (1989): 231–32. Italics in original.

15. For a recent example, see Aggregate Architectural History Collaborative, eds., *Architecture in Development: Systems and the Emergence of the Global South* (London: Routledge, 2022). For a nuanced case, see Farhan Karim, *Of Greater Dignity Than Riches: Austerity and Housing Design in India* (Pittsburgh: University of Pittsburgh Press, 2019). On hegemonic constructions of race in and through the built environment, see the essays collected in Irene Cheng, Charles L. Davis II, and Mabel O. Wilson, eds., *Race and Modern Architecture: A Critical History from the Enlightenment to the Present* (Pittsburgh: University of Pittsburgh Press, 2020). On neoliberalism, see Kenny Cupers, Catharina Gabrielsson, and Helena Mattsson, eds., *Neoliberalism on the Ground: Architecture and Transformation from the 1960s to the Present* (Pittsburgh: University of Pittsburgh Press, 2020). A landmark work of cultural history that remains relevant is Victoria de Grazia, *Irresistible Empire: America's Advance through Twentieth-Century Europe* (Cambridge, Mass.: Harvard University Press, 2005).

16. For studies of architecture and capitalism, see Peggy Deamer, ed., *Architecture and Capitalism, 1845 to the Present* (London: Routledge, 2014); Linda Clarke, *Building Capitalism: Historical Change and the Labour Process in the Production of the Built Environment* (London: Routledge, 1992); Carol Willis, *Form Follows Finance: Skyscrapers and Skylines in New York and Chicago* (New York: Princeton Architectural Press, 1997).

17. For an additional legal case study, see Sarah Schindler, "Architectural Exclusion: Discrimination and Segregation through Physical Design of the Built Environment," *The Yale Law Journal* 124, no. 6 (2015): 1934–2024.

18. Robert Putnam, "Elite Transformation in Advanced Industrial Societies: An Empirical Assessment of the Theory of Technocracy," *Comparative Political Studies* 10, no. 3 (1977): 383–412; Alfred Moore, "Architects and Engineers: Two Types of Technocrat and Their Relation to Democracy," *Critical Review* 32, no. 1-3 (2020): 164–81.

19. Thorstein Veblen, *The Engineers and the Price System* (New York: B. W. Huebsch, 1921). Also see William H. Smyth, "Technocracy: National Industrial Management," *Industrial Management* 57 (March 1919): 208–12. See also Joanna Merwood-Salisbury, *Barbarian Architecture: Thorstein Veblen's Chicago* (Cambridge, Mass.: MIT Press, forthcoming 2024).

20. Timothy Mitchell, *Rule of Experts: Egypt, Techno-Politics, Modernity* (Berkeley: University of California Press, 2002).

21. Jeffrey Friedman, *Power without Knowledge: A Critique of Technocracy* (Oxford: Oxford University Press, 2019).

22. For industrial construction, see R. M. E. Diamant, *Industrialised Building*, 3 vols (London: Iliffe Books, 1964); for complex curtain wall design see Alexandra Quantrill, "The Value of Enclosure and the Business of Banking," *Grey Room* 71 (Spring 2018), https://doi.org/10.1162/grey_a_00244, as well as González Pendás in this volume.

23. See, for example, the essays collected in Aggregate Architectural History Collaborative, eds., *Governing by Design: Architecture, Economy, and Politics in the Twentieth Century* (Pittsburgh: University of Pittsburgh Press, 2012). See also Ijlal Muzaffar, *The Periphery Within: Modern Architecture and the Making of the Third World* (Austin: University of Texas Press, forthcoming); Aggregate Architectural History Collaborative, eds., *Architecture in Development*; Michael Osman, *Modernism's Visible Hand: Architecture and Regulation in America* (Minneapolis: University of Minnesota Press, 2018); Arindam Dutta, *A Second Modernism: MIT, Architecture, and the 'Techno-Social' Moment* (SA+Press, Department of Architecture, MIT, 2013); John Harwood, *The Interface: IBM and the Transformation of Corporate Design, 1945–1976* (Minneapolis: University of Minnesota Press, 2011); Arindam Dutta, *The Bureaucracy of Beauty: Design in the Age of Its Global Reproducibility* (Routledge, 2007); Felicity D. Scott, *Architecture or Techno-Utopia: Politics after Modernism* (Cambridge, Mass.: MIT Press, 2007); Reinhold Martin, *The Organizational Complex: Architecture, Media, and Corporate Space* (Cambridge, Mass.: MIT Press, 2003); Claire Zimmerman, *Albert Kahn Inc.: Architecture, Labor, Industry, 1905–1961* (Cambridge, Mass.: MIT Press, forthcoming 2024).

24. As members of the Aggregate Architectural History Collaborative have put it, referring to Foucault, governmentality entails "the combination of protocols, rules, structures, and institutions through which our desire to be governed is cultivated and channeled." Aggregate Architectural History Collaborative, eds., *Governing by Design*, vii.

25. Manfredo Tafuri, *Architecture and Utopia: Design and Capitalist Development*, trans. Barbara La Penta (Cambridge, Mass.: MIT Press, 1976), 166.
26. Jan-Werner Müller, *Contesting Democracy: Political Ideas in Twentieth-Century Europe* (New Haven: Yale University Press, 2011), 4.
27. Müller, *Contesting Democracy*, 4. The quotation is from Giovanni Gentile, "The Philosophic Basis of Fascism," *Foreign Affairs* 6, no. 2 (January 1928): 302.
28. Eric J. Hobsbawm, *The Age of Revolution: Europe 1789–1848* (London: Weidenfeld and Nicolson, 1962). See also Jürgen Osterhammel, *The Transformation of the World: A Global History of the Nineteenth Century* (Princeton: Princeton University Press, 2014), 593–94.
29. Max Weber, cited in Müller, *Contesting Democracy*, 9.
30. Richard Tuck, *The Sleeping Sovereign: The Invention of Modern Democracy* (Cambridge: Cambridge University Press, 2015).
31. Partha Chatterjee, *I Am the People: Reflections on Popular Sovereignty Today* (New York: Columbia University Press, 2020), especially 73–122.
32. W. E. B. Du Bois, *Black Reconstruction: An Essay Toward a History of the Part Which Black Folk Played in the Attempt to Reconstruct Democracy in America, 1860–1880* (New York: Russell & Russell, 1935). See also Robert Gooding-Williams, *In the Shadow of Du Bois: Afro-Modern Political Thought in America* (Cambridge: Harvard University Press, 2009).
33. Cheng, Davis, and Wilson, eds., *Race and Modern Architecture*. See also (among others) Charles L. Davis II, *Building Character: The Racial Politics of Modern Architectural Style* (Pittsburgh: University of Pittsburgh Press, 2019) and Wilson, *Negro Building: Black Americans in the World of Fairs and Museums* (Berkeley: University of California Press, 2012).
34. Timothy Hyde, *Constitutional Modernism: Architecture and Civil Society in Cuba, 1933–1959* (Minneapolis: University of Minnesota Press, 2012). Another exception, on "organic" architecture and democratic ideals related to Wright's discourse, is Jonathan Massey, "Organic Architecture and Direct Democracy: Claude Bragdon's Festivals of Song and Light," *Journal of the Society of Architectural Historians* 65, no. 4 (December 2006): 578–613.
35. In particular, see Tafuri, *Architecture and Utopia*.
36. For example, Jonathan Levy, *Ages of American Capitalism: A History of the United States* (New York: Random House, 2021).
37. Martin Wolf, "The Crisis of Democratic Capitalism," Neubauer Collegium, April 5, 2021. https://neubauercollegium.uchicago.edu/events/uc/directors_lecture_with_martin_wolf/.
38. "Thus, the metropolitan bourgeoisie who professed and practised democracy at home were happy to conduct the government of their Indian empire as an autocracy." Guha, "*Dominance without Hegemony* and Its Historiography," 213.
39. Jane C. Loeffler, *The Architecture of Diplomacy: Building America's Embassies* (New York: Princeton Architectural Press, 1998); Annabel Jane Wharton, *Building the Cold War: Hilton International Hotels and Modern Architecture* (Chicago: University of Chicago Press, 2001).
40. For one compelling example, see Natasha Dow Schüll, *Addiction by Design: Machine Gambling in Las Vegas* (Princeton: Princeton University Press, 2012). For architecture and neoliberalism, see Douglas Spencer, *The Architecture of Neoliberalism: How Contemporary Architecture Became an Instrument of Control and Compliance* (New York: Bloomsbury Academic, 2016) and Cupers, Gabrielsson, and Mattsson, eds., *Neoliberalism on the Ground*.

Part I

Hegemony
Coercion with Consent

Scholars have understood the built environment as an instrument of hegemony across a spectrum that ranges from enforcing domination to imposing an oppressive common sense; the spectrum, in other words, of coercion with consent. The essays in the first part of the book explore this range and more. In different ways they ask what to make of claims that an architecture of democracy has been realized, or that enhanced democratic freedoms are available through architecture and urbanism. Are such claims mere ideological cover for soft power, or docile, everyday compliance? In what ways does the technical expertise of the architect and urbanist contribute to these processes?

In "Hints on Whiteness and American Public Architecture," Mabel O. Wilson probes how the figures of the African American and the Native American were rendered as countersubjects in efforts to construct European Enlightenment on North American soil, for which buildings supplied hegemonic force. Through the slave economy in the United States, the doctrine of Manifest Destiny, and the making of public institutions like the Smithsonian Institution in Washington, D.C., those efforts became constitutive of U.S. nationhood. Reading the debates over the design of the Smithsonian by James Renwick and under the supervision of U.S. Representative Robert Dale Owen, son of socialist reformer Robert Owen, Wilson finds architectural style doubly coded by both racial ideologies and the myth of national character. She thereby shows how building construction embodies hegemonic force.

Naomi Vaughan's essay "The Photographic Mythology and Memory of Hitler's Destroyed New Reich Chancellery" reconsiders the monumental architecture of National Socialist Berlin. There the persona of Adolf Hitler was embodied and amplified in a building, the New Reich Chancellery, conceived almost entirely as a set of spectacular effects—whether in photographs that continue to reverberate historically or in the impact the constructed building had on its few occupants and visitors. Here fascist subjectivity, carefully constructed in architecture and technologically reproduced through photography, persists long after the building has disappeared. The incoherence of the monument as built, in contrast to the mythic coherence of the photographs, adds further weight to Vaughan's argument, emblematizing hegemonic power as it fails to provide for public welfare.

Similarly, in an essay that adds much to our understanding of fascist subjectivity as spectacle in direct service of hegemonic rule, Ruth W. Lo probes the combined effects of Italian fascism and autarchy in the wake of international sanctions following Italy's 1935 invasion of Ethiopia. In "DIY Fascism: Architecture and the Autarchic Exhibition of Italian Minerals," Lo portrays Italian nationhood as derived from the economic mandate of autarchy and the ideology of autochthonous creation, shaped from the soil and substrata of Italy itself. Disarticulated through its representation in machine exhibits, photo murals, and full-scale mockups, a complex of Italianness, Mussolini, and the Italian public was represented as a matter of faith to be reproduced technologically in the scattered buildings and monuments of the fascist state.

In a related vein but a different context, José H. Bortoluci's "The Concrete Politics of Housing: Assembling Cecap Guarulhos in Authoritarian Brazil" examines a mass housing project designed by João Vilanova Artigas, an architect with strong socialist convictions, in collaboration with a number of colleagues with varying political ties under military dictatorship in 1960s Brazil. As Bortoluci shows, the divergent, sometimes conflicting interests of distinct agents (the architects, the inhabitants, and the state) combined in the design and construction of this sprawling modernist housing complex on the outskirts of São Paulo. The design process and its realization to some extent rearticulated these agents, as it helped to assemble a "people" who were subject to the dictatorship's hegemonic power while also remaining the potential wellspring of counterhegemonic momentum. That the project never fulfilled these initial ambitions and instead became a largely middle-class investment vehicle only adds new ambiguities.

Elsewhere and more recently, the democratic promise has been explicitly withheld on arrival, as in the sharp distinction between property rights and political rights for emigrants to the United Arab Emirates that is the basis of Kishwar Rizvi's study of property development (and hegemonic persuasion) in Dubai, "Freehold/Freedom: Exurban Existence in the United Arab Emirates." Rizvi shows how economic and social freedom have been split off from political freedom in planned residential developments marketed to middle- and upper-middle-class workers from around the world who come to Dubai seeking opportunity and prosperity. Located in an intermediate zone between the luxury towers of the superrich and the indentured workers who build them, these enclaves address their inhabitants as consumers rather than citizens while, Rizvi argues, affording them the rudiments of furtive belonging. Whether this is neoliberalism's last laugh remains for readers to decide.

Chapter 1

Hints on Whiteness and American Public Architecture

Mabel O. Wilson

> Americans' fear of being outcast, of failing, of powerlessness; their fear of boundarylessness, of Nature unbridled and crouched for attack; their fear of the absence of so-called civilization; their fear of loneliness, of aggression both external and internal. In short, the terror of human freedom—the thing they coveted most of all.
>
> —Toni Morrison, *Playing in the Dark: Whiteness in the Literary Imagination*

To English writer Charles Dickens, who traveled to Washington, D.C., in 1842, the capital city had "spacious avenues, that begin in nothing, and lead nowhere; streets, mile-long, that only want houses roads and inhabitants; public buildings that need but a public to complete and ornaments of great thoroughfares, which only lack great thoroughfares to ornament." What the cosmopolitan Dickens beheld was a "City of Magnificent Intentions."[1] In the six decades after the American Revolution, the nation's capital had yet to live up to its monumental aspirations, and perhaps along a parallel trajectory the national character of the American masses had been, according to Dickens, "sadly sapped and blighted in their growth."[2] By 1846, however, plans were underway by the federal government to erect the new Smithsonian Institution on the National Mall. It would be the first institution of its kind in the United States, dedicated "to the increase and diffusion of knowledge among men."[3] In this new building with its library, museum, and art gallery and its mission to pursue physical research and host popular lectures, the Smithsonian planned to cultivate a national culture (whose absence Dickens had keenly noted) through dual, at times dueling, programs of scientific inquiry by experts and popular education of the American public. This endeavor was embarked on in the 1830s when the generation of Founding Fathers—the white merchants, farmers, physicians, naturalists, educators, lawyers, and slave owners who signed the Declaration of Independence and the Constitution—had all died.[4] With the passing of these witnesses of the republic's formation, the need to cultivate knowledge of the nation's bounty and a public narrative of its origins became an architectural, museological, and intellectual project. It was also a period when the cultivation of a national culture—its arsenal of representations and institutions—was dependent on regimes of state-sanctioned violence mobilized to keep thousands of Blacks in a dire state of enslavement as an available labor force and to displace sovereign Native American nations from land deemed necessary for future white settlement in western territories.

In this pivotal era of reform and expansion, the pleas of abolitionists to end the institution of slavery and the domestic slave trade had become more urgent and vocal. Of the seventeen million U.S. residents in 1840, an estimated 2.4 million were enslaved men, women, and children.[5] White Americans lived in fear of slave rebellions, especially those in the South where in some regions the enslaved outnumbered free whites. The fact that in 1831 Virginia's Nat Turner had rallied his fellow slaves to launch a deadly insurrection against his enslavers still terrified white communities. With 378,000 free Blacks living in all states, but mostly concentrated in the North, the rights accorded by citizenship were under threat, which by law had made freedom the preserve of white citizens. As large-scale plantation agriculture dependent on enslaved labor power continued to prosper in the Lower South and the West, tensions between northern and southern factions were exacerbated as Congress tried to settle whether a newly admitted state to the Union should allow slavery or ban it.[6] This continued push westward by white settlers, some freed Blacks, and land speculators encroached further into the territories of sovereign Native American nations. In 1830 President Andrew Jackson authorized the wholesale removal of Native Americans, along with their enslaved Africans, from southern regions to lands west of the Mississippi renamed as the Indian Territories. The violent removal of Indigenous peoples by force was typically accompanied by the legal dispossession of their territories, which undermined their sovereignty.

Because the internal presence of enslaved Africans posed a legal, moral, and material challenge to national identity and the external proximity of Indigenous sovereignty posed a threat to the lives of settlers in border territories and the national mythos of abundant wilderness for white colonists to settle, both disruptions to the racialized liberal project of American nationalism in this period exemplify the deadly violence at the core of America's Enlightenment project. The debate about the architecture of the Smithsonian Institution launched by the U.S. Representative Robert Dale Owen of Indiana concluded that rather than the Neoclassical architecture that had been typical of most buildings in the capital city, this new building dedicated to knowledge and science required a new national style like the Gothic Revival or Romanesque Revival. The construction logics of those styles were rooted in local materials with cultural roots in northern European architecture, thereby illustrating the subtle ways that national culture evidenced racial character.[7] In light of this fraught history behind the veil of American innocence and exceptionalism, it is important to understand how the creation of the Smithsonian Institution, along with the design and construction of a building to house its novel functions, sought to aesthetically represent and scientifically rationalize the ongoing process of colonization and domination. To realize the "magnificent intentions" of American Democracy held deadly consequences for "Indians," deemed a noble but degenerating civilization, and "Negroes," recognized as a necessary yet racially inferior source of labor.

"Supply to This New World an Architecture of Its Own"

In 1829 the U.S. government was notified that the English scientist James Smithson had bequeathed, in lieu of heirs, a large sum of gold to the United States to establish an institution "dedicated to the increase and diffusion of knowledge." Once the monies were transferred to the U.S. Treasury in 1838 after a lengthy discussion about whether to accept the sum and what to do with the endowment, a debate ensued in Congress about how to respond to Smithson's charge to erect an institution of research and public knowledge. When U.S. Representative Robert Dale Owen became chairman of the Select Committee on the Smithsonian Bequest in 1845, he rallied support to ensure that education would be central to the mission of the new institution and that a new building reflective of America's cultural character would be erected.

As the son of Robert Owen, a Welsh landowner, textile manufacturer, and socialist reformer, Dale Owen was familiar with architecture's importance in facilitating the reform of modern society. His father, a one-time follower of the utilitarian theories of Jeremy Bentham, advocated for an improved work environment in the factory, better living conditions in housing, and education for industrial workers (many of them children) at his mills in New Lanark, Scotland. In 1824 the senior Owen traveled to the United States, eventually followed by his four sons and a daughter, to proselytize the virtues of his philosophy and establish a new community dedicated to his socialist agenda. Like many utopian socialist groups that followed Owen, including Shakers, Moravians, and Fourierists, the reformists decided to build anew in the plains of Indiana. Owenites, as they became known, settled on lands once inhabited by the Shawnee, Wea, and Miami nations that had been forced to cede territories through a series of federal treaties and migrate to regions west of the Mississippi.[8]

The senior Owen, working with his sons Robert Dale, David Dale, and Richard, along with a host of American and European educators, scientists, and communitarians, inaugurated a social reform agenda that advocated popular education and scientific learning as fundamental programs for achieving class and gender equality. To ensure these goals, all property at New Harmony, Indiana, was communally owned. As stated in its constitution, the experimental society was "instituted generally to promote the happiness of the world" by ameliorating the exploitative conditions of industrial work and the drudgery of farming.[9] Dale Owen worked closely with his father to establish a community that espoused equality for its members. That said, the constitution also declared that freed and enslaved Blacks were welcomed not as residents but as workers: "persons of all ages and descriptions, exclusive of persons of color may become members of the preliminary society. Persons of color may be received as helpers to the society, if necessary."[10] New Harmonists espoused sentiments similar to those of abolitionists and members of American Colonization Societies who believed that Blacks should not be enslaved but could not be integrated into white society. Instead, the Harmonists suggested, emancipated Blacks should live in "associated" separate communities "in Africa, or in some other country, or in some other part of this country."[11]

At both New Lanark and New Harmony, Owen prioritized reforms in the built environment as a panacea for social ills, an early example of welfare capitalism that would become more fully developed in late nineteenth-century experimental communities like Bourneville and Port Sunlight in the United Kingdom. The design of the work, living, and social spaces was foundational to nurturing a harmonious society of virtuous individuals. To house the two thousand future inhabitants of the experimental community, the Owens envisioned an architecturally ambitious complex and solicited English architect Thomas Stedman Whitwell to design a new structure with four large gothic-like cloisters. Education, specifically the Swiss educational philosophy and pedagogical movement Pestalozzianism, which emphasized applied learning rather than theoretical study, would be the collective force to elevate the mental and material conditions of the New Harmonist community.[12] Yet despite repeated attempts by the Owen family and their collaborators to bolster New Harmony's novel social order, the community failed, although many of the educators and naturalists chose to remain in the town. Still, the experiment taught important lessons. For Robert Dale Owen, the commitment to popular education in agriculture and applied sciences as foundational to social and economic reform laid the intellectual foundation for his proposals for the new Smithsonian Institution. In debates with his fellow congressmen that took place from 1844 to 1846, Dale Owen advocated that the Smithsonian include a national normal school to train teachers.[13]

In August 1846, the U.S. Congress passed legislation to establish the Smithsonian Institution. According to a report summarizing the institution's early activities, in order to carry out Smithson's wishes, "the plan of organization should evidently embrace two objects: one, the increase of knowledge by the addition of new truths to existing stock; the other, the diffusion of knowledge thus increased, among men."[14] To achieve this goal, the bill outlined that the institution would erect a new building that would include a library, museum, art gallery, public lecture hall, and laboratories. Dale Owen's mandate was, in part, realized.

In what manner should the architecture of a public institution embody the nation's moral character and establish a unique national style appropriate for a modern society, one guided by advancements in the sciences and the arts that the new Smithsonian Institution would study and display to the public? In his 1849 treatise *Hints on Public Architecture,* Dale Owen summed up his thoughts on what kind of new building would be "suited to our own country and our own time," an answer rooted in racialized ideas of historical development.[15] Adaptable to climate, utilitarian in nature, and affordable for the American public were, observed Dale Owen, "certain conditions . . . set down as essential, in any style of architecture that shall justly obtain, in our republic, the character of national."[16] The congressman veered away from the Neoclassical and Greek Revival architecture that had defined the first fifty years of civic building in the nation's capital and instead proposed that this unique national institution needed a new style and to "supply to this New World an architecture of its own."[17] Architecture, reasoned Dale Owen, was an art of utility. His choice of the Norman style (a revival that merged late Romanesque and early Gothic from the twelfth and thirteenth centuries and is best termed "Romanesque Revival") represented a more refined and purer development of structure and form. The prosaic and practical merger of structure, form, and material of the Romanesque Revival indicated that under American genius "piloted by good taste and steering by the polar star utility, may win honor and profit by a successful voyage into unexplored regions of art."[18] Rather than choose a style of architecture like the Greek Revival, whose influences drew on techniques of construction (post and lintel) and materials (like marble) suited to warmer Mediterranean climates, the arcuated Romanesque Revival should be understood as a uniquely Northern European style adapted to the materials, climates, and cultures of Germany and England. Dale Owen's tectonic rationale tallied with aspects of arguments by architect Heinrich Hübsch, whose 1828 treatise *In welchem Style sollen wir bauen?* (In What Style Should We Build?) advocated for a nationalistic Romanesque as an architecture for the masses.[19] These cultural styles, while not native to the United States, were suitable for structural expression in local materials like sandstone and the utilitarian and economic needs of the nation. Such cultural transplantation to "graft a national style of Architecture for these States" was therefore a reasonable ambition for Dale Owen.[20]

From his experiences in New Harmony, Robert Dale Owen recognized that a new building was critical for the Smithsonian to implement its mission. Prior to the Smithsonian's congressional approval, the architect Alexander Jackson Davis proposed in 1840 a Greek Revival edifice. In 1841, Robert Mills, architect of the Washington Monument, designed a building in what Robert Dale Owen characterized as the "Anglo-Saxon" style of English educational institutions—an homage to Smithson's nationality.[21] The latter, along with Whitwell's cloistered plan for New Harmony, informed David Dale Owen's 1845 design for a three-story main building of lecture halls, libraries, museum, and galleries in what he described as the more economic "Norman Style,"

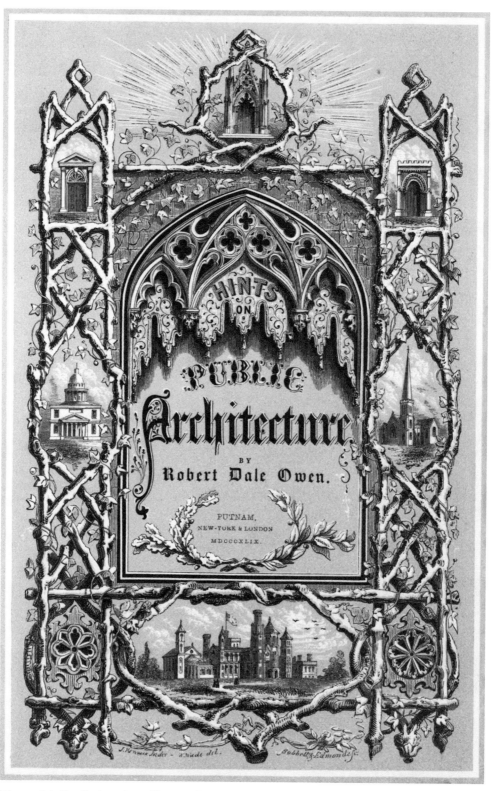

Figure 1.1. Frontispiece from *Hints on Public Architecture* by Robert Dale Owen, 1849.

Figure 1.2. James Renwick's design for the Smithsonian Institution from *Hints on Public Architecture*.

although the specific characteristics that distinguished "Norman," "Anglo-Saxon," and "Saxon" from "Lombard" were at times interchangeable in these debates.[22] Styles aside, the Owens remained committed to Pestalozzianism, and David Dale Owen's proposed design included two wings with additional lecture rooms for "common school," a recognition of his brother's desire that the building should incorporate space for a normal school.[23]

Once the Smithsonian was officially chartered in 1846, a free-for-all among architects ensued, with several architects (including Mills with his revised design) vying for the commission.[24] At the same time, a contentious debate erupted within the newly formed Board of Regents, a body composed of white politicians (including Robert Dale Owen), the vice president of the United States, the chief justice of the Supreme Court, the mayor of Washington, D.C., and learned educators and scientists. The men disagreed about which aspect of the Smithsonian's mission (pursuit of knowledge or public education) should be the central driver of the new building's design. Some regents, like Joseph Henry, the Smithsonian's first secretary, debated whether a new building was

Hints on Whiteness

even necessary, concerned that its construction would be an ostentatious undertaking that would siphon funds from scientific research.

New York architect James Renwick adopted Dale Owen's carefully argued rationale for the new institution, and in the fall of 1846 he proposed to the Smithsonian two designs: one Gothic Revival and one Romanesque Revival.[25] The Board of Regents' selection subcommittee chose one of Renwick's designs in what they called the "late Norman Lombard style," better known as the round-arched "Romanesque Revival."[26] Renwick's pragmatic design provided offices for administrators along with laboratories for natural history and chemical research. The two constituencies shared the library with researchers accessing the upper stacks and visitors gazing at the wonder of human knowledge being gathered about their nation. To carry out its public mission, Renwick's proposed building would host museum spaces for viewing new instruments and artifacts, an art gallery for sculpture and paintings, and a large auditorium for lectures. Visitors could climb one of the octagonal towers to survey the city and surrounding landscape. The prospect allowed them to behold the rich bounty of the nation's genius and natural resources. Renwick's details of wide arches, turrets, and crenellations crafted in red sandstone (a revival of German Romanesque, according to Kathleen Curran) towered over the National Mall. The building would affirm America's cultural legacy and present a new national style.[27] Renwick's Romanesque Revival edifice, built from locally quarried red sandstone, began construction in 1847 and was completed in 1855.

Home of the Oppressed

In Washington, D.C., the Washington Canal zigzagged between the two grand thoroughfares of Pennsylvania and Maryland Avenues. The canal moved barges of goods through the city and served (among other places) Center Market, a hodgepodge of buildings that fronted Pennsylvania Avenue. When the regents reviewed sites for the new Smithsonian, the mayor proposed the area around Center Market as a vehicle to improve the character of the area. This central part of the capital with its access to the canal was more than a site for commerce and civic activities; it was also the neighborhood that housed the private jails, markets, residences, taverns, and slave pens of the district's lucrative slave trade.

With tobacco farming in the Chesapeake region petering out due to soil exhaustion, slave owners sold their surplus chattel to southern plantation owners who needed slaves to build the Cotton Kingdom.[28] With President Jefferson ending U.S. participation in the transatlantic slave trade in 1808, the domestic slave trade boomed as new territories opened for settlement in the West. From 1825 to 1850, Washington, D.C., served as a key market for purchasing and transporting slaves between the busy ports of Baltimore and Richmond. From these Upper South cities, slavers transported their human cargo down the eastern coastline to Lower South markets in Charleston and New Orleans or via land and inland waterways in coffles to markets in Louisville and Natchez. In addition to slave-trading firms such as Simpson and Neal, James Birch, and William H. William, the Washington, D.C.-based firm Franklin and Armfield (which made millions of dollars by innovating forms of credit and an infrastructure of agents, depots, and slave ships) drove the trade. Their newspaper advertisements in *The Globe* and *Daily National Intelligencer* solicited "Cash for Any Number of Negroes."[29] The traders and their agents worked the taverns, markets, and hotels in full view of the U.S. Capitol and the White House.

Not everyone in the United States accepted the trade in human flesh in their capital city. A multiracial coalition of white and Black abolitionists of the American Anti-Slavery Society, based in Philadelphia, denounced the Washington, D.C., slave trade in an 1836 broadside "Slave Market of America." One of the poster's most scathing vignettes recounted the true story of a group of manacled slaves singing "Hail, Columbia!" (the first national anthem) while being marched in front of the U.S. Capitol. As the broadside's headings announced, "the land of the free" was also the antidemocratic "land of the oppressed." By 1850, the same year Congress banned slave trading (but not slave owning) in Washington, D.C., Blacks comprised one-quarter of the district's total population, with at least two-thirds of Black residents being free. The 1857 Supreme Court case of *Dred Scott v. Sandford* ruled that Blacks would never qualify for the rights and privileges associated with citizenship. Enslaved Missourian Dred Scott had sued his owner in order to purchase his and his family's freedom. Scott believed such a transaction was legal and permissible because he had resided with his owner for a few years in the free state of Illinois and in the Wisconsin territory. But Chief Justice Roger Taney, who served on the Smithsonian's Board of Regents, wrote in the majority opinion that "black Africans" were "so far inferior, that they had no rights which the white man was bound to respect; and that the negro might justly and lawfully be reduced to slavery for his benefit. He was bought and sold, and treated as an ordinary article of merchandise and traffic, whenever a profit could be made by it."[30] By comparison, Taney also argued in his opinion that "uncivilized" American Indians were "a free and independent people, associated together in nations or tribes, and governed by their own laws."[31] For scholar Jodi A. Byrd, Taney deployed "the notion of the free and independent Indian-government-as foreign-government not to recognize Indian nations but to reprehensibly secure and cohere white supremacy by distinguishing African Americans as 'a subordinate and inferior class of beings.'"[32]

Because the Smithsonian was erected in proximity to Virginia and Maryland, where slave holding was also still in practice as it was in the city, building trades employed enslaved Africans in various stages of the building's construction, as they had done for the construction of the White House, U.S. Capitol, and other regional civic buildings such as the Virginia Statehouse.[33] Enslaved men, for example, quarried and milled the red sandstone from the Seneca Quarry in nearby Montgomery County, Maryland, that was

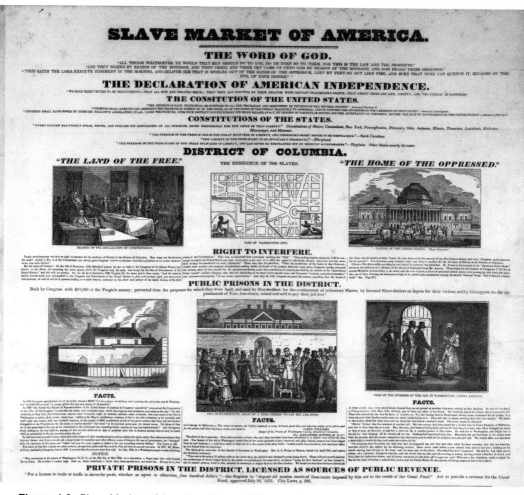

Figure 1.3. *Slave Market of America.* A broadside condemns the sale and keeping of slaves in the District of Columbia. Library of Congress Rare Book and Special Collections Division.

used for the Smithsonian's exterior.[34] Loading and transporting the stones would have most likely engaged enslaved labor. Head contractor Gilbert Cameron and subcontractors hired enslaved construction workers—bricklayers, stonecutters, carpenters, and unskilled laborers—to perform various tasks at the Smithsonian's construction site.[35]

When the first sandstone blocks were emplaced for the Smithsonian, a monument to the history and future of American civilization, whiteness defined the racial character of the public to whom that knowledge was to be disseminated. In 1851, artist and critic Horatio Greenough encountered the new Smithsonian under construction: "Suddenly, as I walked, the dark form of the Smithsonian palace rose between me and the white Capitol, and I stopped, tower and battlement, and all that medieval confusion, stamped itself on the halls of Congress, as ink on paper! Dark on that whiteness—complication on that simplicity!"[36] The aesthetic sublime associated with European architecture and art, whether stylistically Romanesque, Norman, or Gothic, nonetheless projected a deep fear, one that Toni Morrison described as "Romance, an anxiety imported from the shadows of European culture," one that "offered platforms for moralizing and fabulation, and for the imaginative entertainment of violence, sublime incredibility, and terror—and terror's most significant, overweening ingredient: darkness, with all the connotative value it awakened."[37] Greenough's Romanticist encounter conveys how a sublime blackness haunted the whiteness of the nation's capital in the mid-nineteenth century—affectively and materially. While necessary for the maintenance of every minutiae of daily life and as a source of great wealth, for white Washingtonians the proximity of Black bodies posed a threat mainly because of what Thomas Jefferson labeled as "10,000 recollections, by blacks, of the injuries they have sustained."[38] Greenough had just completed *The Rescue,* a statue that portrayed a robust frontiersman disarming a lean, seminude Indian warrior who threatened to kill a cowering pioneer woman and child representing the future of the nation. That statue was installed on the entry staircase of the U.S. Capitol in 1853.[39] The other haunting threat to whiteness loomed in the western territories.

"The Anglo-Saxon Foot Is Already on Its Borders"

The Compromise of 1850 ended the slave trade but not slave owning in Washington, D.C. In that bundle of legislation Congress included the Fugitive Slave Act, which required the return of runaway slaves captured in the North to their owners in the South. The act was passed to quell rising tensions between anti- and proslavery factions that had erupted with the contested annexation of western states. This territorial expansion annexed lands for white settlement, a movement west that Americans believed was legally justified and divinely authorized through the concept of Manifest Destiny.[40] Coined by John O'Sullivan in 1845, Manifest Destiny swept across and displaced Native American nations and left in its wake white Americans and culture: "The Anglo-Saxon foot is already on its borders. Already the advance guard of the irresistible army of Anglo-Saxon emigration has begun to pour down upon it, armed with the plough and the rifle, and marking its trail with schools and colleges, courts and representative halls, mills and meeting-houses."[41] While the Smithsonian's architectural style selected Northern European culture, whether Norman or Anglo-Saxon, as foundational to American cultural nationalism, it is important to understand how this was supplemented by its institutional mission to advance scientific research that benefited from the forced removal of Native American nations from their sovereign territories and contributed to historical, scientific, and aesthetic discourses that Native Americans were a degenerate and dying race of people clearing the land for white settlers.

To achieve these goals of building a formidable national institution dedicated to knowledge, the Smithsonian's organization had to be planned in meticulous detail. The newly formed Board of Regents conceived the Smithsonian's mission to focus primarily on three areas: the physical (the material world, including "Man"), the moral and political (the individual and the State) and literature and fine art (culture).[42] To lead this enterprise, Joseph Henry, a natural scientist at Princeton University, accepted the post as the first Secretary of the Smithsonian in the fall of 1846. Henry vehemently opposed Robert Dale Owen's proposed plans, especially the amount of area of the building that would be open for public use, and he warned against the expense of a new building for the Institute. While under construction and in the absence of Dale Owen's influential voice (the congressman left office in 1847), Henry successfully altered Renwick's designs toward his aim of an institution solely dedicated to research with the removal of the normal school, and possibly the library and museum.[43]

Under the aegis of the Smithsonian, learned white men studied how the nation's rich flora and fauna, mineral deposits, human populations, and cultural productions such as art, literature, and architecture had changed over time. Their collective work, guided by Henry, placed the nation's bounty within a historical register that measured how far American civilization, the culture that bound together its white population, had advanced. Through the collection of materials in all of these areas, it was particularly important for the emerging scientific disciplines of this period that no longer fit under the eighteenth-century rubric of natural history to identify and measure the forces that transformed humans, animals, and the Earth. There had been a long history of European naturalists launching and accompanying colonial expeditions to the New World. The same held true for the cadre of naturalists who migrated with Robert Owen to join the socialist experiment in New Harmony, Indiana. Many of these scientists and educators remained in the town after the community collapsed. Those remaining to pursue research included David Dale Owen, Scottish-American geologist William Maclure, French naturalist Charles A. Lesueur, and American zoologist Thomas Say. Because the Miami Nation and some of the Potawatomi Indians remained in the regions of Indiana and Ohio despite legislated voluntary removal (which often devolved into forced relocation), New Harmony would remain a base for scientific research amid the region's shift from settler colonial border to full-fledged state. The town also served as a waystation for expeditions such as the two-year exploration undertaken by Prussian naturalist and ethnologist Prince Maximilian zu Wied, who traveled throughout the Great Plains with Swiss artist Karl Bodmer and others from 1832 to 1834.[44]

Under the stewardship of Henry and assistant secretary Spencer Baird, the Smithsonian dispatched experts to gather materials, thus increasing the knowledge base of areas such as the study of ancient peoples, storms, historical sites, minerals, and a host of other things that had not yet been fully articulated into disciplines or fields.[45] Eventually, credentialed experts (scientists and historians) would replace the gentlemen explorers and natural historians exemplified by Thomas Jefferson. Groups of scientists joined military parties, surveyors, and engineers to explore and map uncharted lands external to the nation's western boundary. Those scientists' materials were sent back to Washington, D.C., for evaluation by experts in residence or affiliated with the Smithsonian. Documents like the Smithsonian's *Contributions to Knowledge* published their findings and circulated their reports to an international audience. Some material was placed on view in exhibitions. Public lectures hosted at the Smithsonian's new building explained these discoveries to audiences eager to learn more about the nation's resources, riches, and history.

Artists like Bodmer and the American George Catlin joined expeditions to document via sketch and watercolor the various animals, vegetation, geological formations, landscapes, and Native American nations. Intent on vivifying the exotic peoples and places of North America, these artists drew from their archives to create paintings that they put on view to the public in special exhibitions and as engravings that circulated widely in newspapers and print publications. For example, in 1852 the first exhibition of paintings in the Smithsonian Institution's newly opened galleries featured the "Indian Gallery," a taxonomic collection of 150 paintings of Native Americans by American artist John Mix Stanley, who sought to benefit financially by sharing his paintings. The Smithsonian also reproduced Stanley's paintings in its pamphlets and as stereoscope cards, thus using an emerging mass culture to make them available to the wider American public unable to visit the galleries.

Beginning his explorations in the 1830s, Stanley had traveled widely around the Great Plains, Pacific Coast, and desert Southwest. He continued working as an illustrator by joining the first of five surveys: the federally funded Northern Pacific Railroad survey of 1853–55. The survey's mission was to chart a path for a transcontinental railroad that would ferry white settlers into Northwest territories and transport raw materials from those regions to manufacturers and markets in the East. Although Baird did not make the journey, he served as the chief naturalist in charge of organizing the collection of materials by a team of scientists, including Stanley. Led by military officers and engineers, Stanley's experience proved invaluable in the process of surveying routes and with contacting nations of the Blackfoot Confederacy in the northern Great Plains.[46] As Stanley wrote in his report, artists tried to capture what they took to be the nobility of Native Americans in a realist aesthetic of ethnographic representation: "sketches of Indians should be made and colored from life, with care to fidelity in complexion as well as feature."[47] In 1857, based on his life of expeditionary travels, Stanley painted *The Last of Their Race,* which depicts a grouping of fictional Native men, women, and children on the shores of the Pacific, wearing an amalgamation of clothing from different nations. Their eventual disappearance is symbolically conveyed by the setting sun and animal carcasses strewn along the beach.[48] Not only did naturalists

Figure 1.4. Old Fort Walla Walla by John Mix Stanley, 1853. Wikimedia Commons.

and artists like Stanley collect specimens and likenesses of people, places, and things; the reports and catalogs, perhaps with no malice of intent, contributed to an archive that historicized the disappearance of a dying race. The federal government and private interests mobilized these popular narratives and images to rationalize the taking of sovereign land for railroads to encourage and facilitate further white settlement.[49]

These practices of dehumanization and dispossession paved the way for the peopling and territorial expansion of the United States. The inherently unjust ideologies of racial violence and imperialism would continue to be fundamental to the workings of American democracy well into the next century. It is important to note that in 1862 the U.S. Congress passed the Homestead Act, which granted white male settlers (many of whom were European immigrants) 160 acres of surveyed public land. This typified how domestic and international laws were mobilized to incrementally steal land from sovereign Native American nations. Through land surveys, public land was abstracted into parcels that could be sold to private interests with the intent of settlement and resource extraction.[50] By then, Native American nations had been placed in the rearguard of civilization's advance by the truths of scientific inquiry and banished to an alternative temporality—the ancient. They had also been gradually corralled by the Indian

Wars into an alternative spatiality—the reservation, which was established by Congress in 1853, the same year Greenough's *The Rescue* was installed on the steps of the U.S. Capitol. When the Civil War erupted in 1861, the flood of settlers into western territories and the sovereign lands of Native Americans was temporarily slowed. At the heart of the conflict between the U.S. government and the Confederate States of America (C.S.A.) was property: human and territorial. For the C.S.A., as the nation's boundaries moved westward, enslavement, the form of forced labor used on large-scale plantations that had created the wealth of a Southern class of oligarchs, should be adopted as each state desired. Comparatively, enslaved humans were worth more than the land. The racial project of whiteness, as Taney's *Dred Scott v. Sandford* decision supported, was fundamental to the rights and privileges of citizenship, including property ownership. Therefore, before and during the Civil War both free Blacks and enslaved persons had no future as citizens of the United States and certainly not within the Confederate States of America.

Even after bloody civil conflict, white Americans would nonetheless conjure new practices of racial violence, enforced at times by white vigilante organizations like the Ku Klux Klan, to maintain unequal and separate conditions for Black Americans. These included the curtailment of ability to vote, to hold political office, to own property, to be educated, and to be paid a fair wage. For Native American nations, the splendid galleries of the Smithsonian Institution made visible the original inhabitants who once freely roamed the lands now claimed by the United States, a condition of sovereignty that the Indian Wars of the 1870s and 1880s would eventually eradicate, as Stanley's *The Last of Their Race* predicted. By the end of the nineteenth century, schools like Hampton Normal and Agricultural Institute in Virginia were dedicated to Americanizing both the "Negro" and "Indian" through educational regimes popularized by progressive social reformers like the formerly enslaved Booker T. Washington and financed by robber baron capitalist George F. Peabody, who built his wealth from Mexican and transcontinental expansion of railroads across formerly Indigenous land. Even though many were forced to adopt respectable, civilized cultural practices, neither group was ever socially integrated into the American social fabric but instead kept distinct and distanced (by violence, if necessary) in their respective enclosures of the ghetto and the reservation. That neither Blacks nor Native Americans could receive the freedoms or be incorporated into the project of American liberal democracy was one made possible by the internal exploitation of Black labor and external expropriation of sovereign Indigenous land. The Smithsonian Institution—its Romanesque style of architecture earned it the nickname "The Castle," befitting some of its founders' desire for an Anglo-Saxon source—along with the programmatic innovation that combined research and public education, made the aesthetic and scientific argument to the American public that whiteness defined the national ethos.

Notes

1. Toni Morrison, *Playing in the Dark: Whiteness and the Literary Imagination* (New York: Vintage Books, 1993), 36–37.
2. Morrison, *Playing in the Dark*, 170.
3. The construction of a new building for the Smithsonian was immediately undertaken by the Board of Regents on its second convening on September 9, 1846. See William J. Rhees, Smithsonian Miscellaneous Collections (Smithsonian Miscellaneous Collections: Smithsonian Institution, 1880), 3–4, http://books.google.com/books?id=2AEFAAAAQAAJ&oe=UTF-8.
4. Charles Carroll, signatory of the Declaration of Independence, died in 1832; James Madison, signatory of the Constitution, died in 1836.
5. Department of State, *Compendium of the Enumeration of the Inhabitants and Statistics of the United States* (Washington, D.C.: Thomas Allen, 1841), https://www.census.gov/library/publications/1841/dec/1840c.html.
6. See Sven Beckert, *Empire of Cotton: A Global History*, 1st ed. (New York: Vintage Books, 2015). Walter Johnson, *River of Dark Dreams: Slavery and Empire in the Cotton Kingdom* (Cambridge, Mass.: Belknap Press of Harvard University Press, 2013).
7. Irene Cheng, "Structural Racism in Modern Architectural Theory," in *Race and Modern Architecture: A Critical History from the Enlightenment to the Present*, ed. Irene Cheng, Charles L. Davis II, and Mabel O. Wilson (Pittsburgh: University of Pittsburgh Press, 2020), 134–52.
8. See Irene Cheng, *The Shape of Utopia: The Architecture of Radical Reform in Nineteenth-Century America* (Minneapolis: University of Minnesota Press, 2023).
9. George Browning Lockwood, *The New Harmony Communities* (Marion, Ind.: The Chronicle Company, 1902), 105.
10. Lockwood, *The New Harmony Communities*, 105.
11. Lockwood, *The New Harmony Communities*, 105.
12. John F. Sears, "'How the Devil It Got There': The Politics of Form and Function in the Smithsonian 'Castle,'" in *Public Space and the Ideology of Place in American Culture*, ed. Miles Orvell and Jeffrey L. Meikle (Amsterdam: Rodopi, 2009), 55–56.
13. Sears, "How the Devil It Got There," 57.
14. Smithsonian Institution, "Smithsonian Contributions to Knowledge" (Washington, D.C., 1848), 5.
15. Robert Dale Owen and Smithsonian Institution, *Hints on Public Architecture, Containing, among Other Illustrations, Views and Plans of the Smithsonian Institution: Together with an Appendix Relative to Building Materials*, Publication (Smithsonian Institution) (New York: G. P. Putnam, 1849), 109.
16. Dale Owen, *Hints on Public Architecture*, 8.
17. Dale Owen, *Hints on Public Architecture*, 10.
18. Dale Owen, *Hints on Public Architecture*, 71.
19. Barry Bergdoll, "Archaeology versus History: Heinrich Hübsch's Critique of Neoclassicism and the Beginnings of Historicism in German Architectural Theory," *Oxford Art Journal* 5, no. 2 (1983): 11.

20. Dale Owen, *Hints on Public Architecture*, 89.
21. Kenneth Hafertepe and Smithsonian Institution, *America's Castle: The Evolution of the Smithsonian Building and Its Institution, 1840–1878* (Washington, D.C.: Smithsonian Institution Press, 1984), 2–8, 18.
22. As Kathleen Curran notes, Mills made the distinction of style as follows: "Saxon meant round-arched; Anglo-Saxon meant Gothic, or pointed-arches; and Norman meant a combination of round and pointed arches." See Kathleen Curran, *The Romanesque Revival: Religion, Politics, and Transnational Exchange* (University Park: The Pennsylvania State University Press, 2003), 250–51; Hafertepe and Smithsonian Institution, *America's Castle*, 3, 18–19.
23. Hafertepe and Smithsonian Institution, *America's Castle*, 19–20; Curran, *The Romanesque Revival*, 248.
24. Curran, *The Romanesque Revival*, 245–52.
25. See Hafertepe and Smithsonian Institution, *America's Castle*, 37 and Curran, *The Romanesque Revival*, 251–52.
26. As summation of the selection of Renwick described the process: "They [the Executive Committee of the Board of Regents] recommended to the Board for adoption one of these, being a design in the later Norman, or, as it may, with strict propriety be called, the Lombard style, as it prevailed in Germany, Normandy, and in Southern Europe in the twelfth century." See Smithsonian Institution, *The Smithsonian Institution: Journals of the Board of Regents, Reports of Committees, Statistics, Etc.*, ed. William J. Rhees (Washington, D.C.: Smithsonian Institution, 1879), 7.
27. Curran, *The Romanesque Revival*, 253.
28. Johnson, *River of Dark Dreams*, 8.
29. "Classified Advertisements," *Daily National Intelligencer* (Washington, D.C.) January 1, 1838, *Nineteenth-Century U.S. Newspapers*. Web. Accessed August 9, 2019.
30. Scott v. Sandford, 60 U.S. 393 (1856).
31. Scott v. Sandford, 60 U.S. 393 (1856).
32. Jodi A. Byrd, *The Transit of Empire: Indigenous Critiques of Colonialism* (Minneapolis: University of Minnesota Press, 2011), 169.
33. Bob Arnebeck, *Slave Labor in the Capitol: Building Washington's Iconic Federal Landmarks* (Charleston: The History Press, 2014). Mabel O. Wilson, "Race, Reason, and the Architecture of Jefferson's Virginia Statehouse," in *Thomas Jefferson, Architect: Palladian Models, Democratic Principles, and the Conflict of Ideals*, ed. Lloyd DeWitt and Corey Piper (New Haven: Yale University Press, 2019).
34. Mark Auslander, "Enslaved Labor and Building the Smithsonian: Reading the Stones," *Southern Spaces* (2012). https://southernspaces.org/2012/enslaved-labor-and-building-smithsonian-reading-stones/.
35. Auslander, "Enslaved Labor." Also see Garrett Peck, *The Smithsonian Castle and the Seneca Quarry* (Charleston: The History Press, 2013), 26–29.
36. Horatio Greenough, *Form and Function: Remarks on Art, Design, and Architecture*, ed. Harold A. Small, 1st paperbound ed. (Berkeley: University of California Press, 1958), 36.
37. Morrison, *Playing in the Dark*, 36–37.

38. Thomas Jefferson, *Notes on the State of Virginia* (Richmond: John A. Randolph, 1853), 149.
39. See Susan Scheckel, *The Insistence of the Indian: Race and Nationalism in Nineteenth-Century American Culture* (Princeton: Princeton University Press), 143–44, and Vivien Green Fryd, "Two Sculptures for the Capitol: Horatio Greenough's 'Rescue' and Luigi Persico's 'Discovery of America,'" *The American Art Journal* 19, no. 2 (1987).
40. For an early colonial history of the dispossession and displacement of the Indigenous nations of the Chesapeake region of Washington, D.C., see April Lee Hatfield, *Atlantic Virginia: Intercolonial Relations in the Seventeenth Century* (Philadelphia: University of Pennsylvania Press, 2004).
41. John O'Sullivan, "Annexation," *United States Magazine and Democratic Review* 17, no. 1 (July–August 1845): 9. https://books.google.com/books?id=JvE7AQAAMAAJ&printsec=frontcover&source=gbs_ge_summary_r&cad=0#v=onepage&q&f=false.
42. Smithsonian Institution, *Smithsonian Contributions to Knowledge*, 35 vols. (Washington, D.C.: Smithsonian Institution, 1848), 1: v.
43. Hafertepe and Smithsonian Institution, *America's Castle*, 126–27.
44. Maximilian Wied, Hannibal Evans Lloyd, and Karl Bodmer, *Travels in the Interior of North America* (London: Ackermann and Co., 1843).
45. See Cameron B. Strang, *Frontiers of Science: Imperialism and Natural Knowledge in the Gulf South Borderlands, 1500–1850* (Chapel Hill: University of North Carolina Press, 2018).
46. "Reports of Explorations and Surveys to Ascertain the Most Practicable and Economical Route for a Railroad from the Mississippi River to the Pacific Ocean," ed. House of Representatives (Washington, D.C.: A.O.P. Nicholson, 1855), 56, 67, 447–49.
47. United States Congress, United States Congressional Serial Set, Vol. 721 (Washington, D.C.: U.S. Government Printing Office, 1854), 15.
48. Mindy N. Besaw, "John Mix Stanley's 'The Last of Their Race' and the 'Doomed Indian' in American Culture," in *Painted Journeys: The Art of John Mix Stanley*, ed. Peter H. Hassrick and Mindy N. Besaw (Norman: University of Oklahoma Press, 2015), 95.
49. "Reports of Explorations and Surveys," 8.
50. See Alyosha Goldstein, "By Force of Expectation: Colonization, Public Lands, and the Property Relation," *Discourse—UCLA Law Review*, March 1, 2018, https://www.uclalawreview.org/by-force-of-expectation/. Also see Brenna Bhandar, *Colonial Lives of Property: Law, Land, and Racial Regimes of Ownership* (Durham: Duke University Press, 2018).

Chapter 2

The Photographic Mythology and Memory of Hitler's Destroyed New Reich Chancellery

Naomi Vaughan

In January 1948, in Berlin's Soviet sector, crews set to work demolishing Hitler's bunker, the site of his last stand, defeat, and suicide in the historic governmental quarter on Wilhelmplatz. At the same time, salvage crews were already stripping materials from the building to which it was attached: the New Reich Chancellery. Designed by Albert Speer, constructed over 1936–39, the building extended the length of Voßstraße toward the Tiergarten from the complex that previously housed the chancellors of the German Empire and Weimar Republic. A prized subject of propaganda, privileged frame for Hitler's public appearances, ridiculed in Charlie Chaplin's *The Great Dictator* (1940), and excoriated by architectural historians, less than a decade after its construction its materials were requisitioned for Berlin's reconstruction. In March, authorities declared the Führerbunker's successful destruction; in 1949, *démontage* on the main building transitioned to structural demolition, which continued into the early 1950s. As this brief account suggests, the New Chancellery's destruction was neither a singular event nor a continuous process but, rather, a staggered affair. The erasure of this notorious (and notoriously destroyed) building ultimately lasted decades—and was never fully completed.

In 1989, the fall of the Berlin Wall unearthed the site formerly occupied by its "Death-Strip," revealing the Führerbunker's bulk preserved underground, along with parts of the New Chancellery's foundation, cellar, and ground floor. City officials, however, refused to grant these fragments protected status, instead opting to sell off the sectioned lot, leaving up to the new owners what to do with the remains as they began constructing Berlin's reunified landscape.[1] If, in the early 1990s, this site near Potsdamer Platz formed one of the "voids of Berlin," it later became a void in another sense.[2] Then, an absence visualized by an empty space, its absence in New Berlin's "memorial district" is now concealed by recent construction.³ Though its fragments are scattered throughout the city, the building itself has irrevocably vanished.

Over its brief existence, the New Chancellery became a touchstone of monumental fascist building—architectural expression of Hitler's "word in stone."⁴ This impression was primarily the result of its reproduction and mythologization in propaganda. Nevertheless, repeated attempts to destroy the building, dismantle its legacy, and purge it from Berlin and from cultural memory have met with limited success. Its images surface in German films and artworks,⁵ and its site persists as a fascinating attraction for tourists. In a sense, its absence only affirms its continued, auratic power—a power generated by and preserved in its mediated archive.

This essay claims the New Chancellery's mythical status, achieved through its images, is sustained precisely because it was destroyed and because the visual memory of its demolition was suppressed. Providing a critical, historical account of the New Chancellery, this chapter compares the actual building with National Socialist (NS) architectural photographs, which form the most complete repository of its existence, and reconstructs the process of its demolition, interrogating its rubble images' significance amid Berlin's postwar reconstruction. Unpublished demolition photographs likewise offer the most comprehensive documentation of this event. They also reveal its importance to the occupying Soviet regime, highlighting strategies used to undermine the architecture's representational value by targeting the sources of its auratic power. That is, these demolition images both account for the architecture's disappearance and counter the ideological rhetoric imbued in its memory by NS propaganda. Moreover, they suggest its demolition did not respond to some inherent, "dangerous" quality but instead resulted from the routine (if unpredictable) implementation of Soviet architectural politics in newly divided Berlin. As these images were never put to public use, in closing, I consider the impact of their suppression on the building's contemporary mediation and memory in reunified Berlin.

Following Hitler's ascent to power in 1933, Germany's original chancellery buildings underwent near-continuous renovations. In 1875, the state had purchased and remodeled the Schulenburg Palace, one of the historic baroque mansions along Wilhelmstraße, as Bismarck's residence and office.⁶ To accommodate the bureaucracy's expansion, a neighboring addition, designed by Eduard Jobst Siedler, was completed in 1930.⁷ Early NS renovations consolidated and isolated the chancellor's apartments in the Schulenburg Palace and transformed and modernized its public reception halls.⁸ Hitler often claimed the building's deplorable condition necessitated renovations, but archival records contradict this assertion.⁹ Rather, alterations were "driven first and foremost by concern for the Führer's domestic image."¹⁰ Hitler's proclivities and self-stylization as architect–politician drove the National Socialists' well-known instrumentalization of architecture as a medium of state representation and a means of economic and industrial mobilization.[11] The renovation of his homes and their reproduction in propaganda were crucial to depicting and marketing his dual roles as both bourgeois everyman and demonic political force.

Though distinct from representational NS building at large, each step in the chancellery's transformation was inseparable from this project's ideology. Initial cosmetic renovations evinced Hitler's propensity to interweave politics and art, a phenomenon that would continue to ramp up in intensity. In 1935, after the Röhm Purge, the state requisitioned the Borsig Palace, adjacent to the Siedler building, to rehouse the S.A.[12] That year also saw the addition of Hitler's balcony overlooking Wilhelmplatz and a salon behind the Schulenburg Palace, providing the opportunity to install the chancellery's first bunker.[13] The simultaneous projects suggest these political and architectural designs' proleptic character, targeting the outgrowth of Hitler's authority. Plans for an entirely new chancellery were already under discussion in 1934, rendering ongoing renovations redundant at best. In 1935, Hitler sketched a design outlining the structure's main features; the plan's provisional nature notwithstanding, building acquisition and demolition along Voßstraße began immediately and was completed by 1937.[14]

This initial phase of the New Chancellery's construction is often overlooked. This is unsurprising, as it was actively concealed. Its scheduled completion by 1939/40 was inextricable from Hitler's secret plans for rearmament and war. Through 1937, widely announced plans for Berlin's redevelopment provided cover for construction, which began without the typical ostentatious groundbreaking ceremony.[15] In January, Albert Speer was named Director General for the Imperial Capital's Redevelopment.[16] Though he encountered difficulties securing materials and workers for the New Chancellery, with industries squeezed by mobilization for the Four Year Plan, Speer's connection to Hitler and the Führer's personal investment in this project afforded preference and let him circumvent ordinary channels as he competed and collaborated with other agencies to fulfill their overlapping goals.[17] Speer's position further enabled the New Chancellery's rapid completion over 1938. The unprecedented acceleration of construction was both symptom and facilitator of Hitler's consolidation of power, a turning point in Nazism's "inexorable disintegration into systemlessness."[18]

Hitler was essential to National Socialism's political order and "self-destructive dynamism."[19] As "embodiment" of the "Volk," the Führer mythos undergirded public support; as personified state, head of all government agencies, he was "the only common link between [the entire system's] various component parts."[20] Nazism can thus be viewed as a "classic 'charismatic leadership movement'" superimposed on a modern machine of "bureaucratic domination."[21] Hitler, however, was disinterested in bureaucratic details and furthermore barred from officially directing initiatives by the "inbuilt need to protect his deified leadership position."[22] Instead, "working towards the Führer" offered NS elites "endless scope for barbarous initiatives . . . institutional expansion, power, prestige and enrichment."[23] His lack of oversight left their actions unobstructed, while his sporadic interventions shaped the development of policy, resulting in "cumulative radicalisation," the dissolution of rational systems of government, with Hitler as the empty but indispensable center of sovereignty.[24] Sustaining and amplifying his representational visibility was paramount to maintaining the state's legitimacy but inimical to its operational stability.

Characteristically, the New Chancellery's construction was radically wasteful, exorbitantly expensive, improvisational, and uncoordinated.[25] Beyond diverting materials for rearmament, its implementation required demolishing a block of apartments amid a housing crisis and recommissioning forced laborers from the Westwall during the final stages of construction.[26] Most shockingly, motivating this expenditure of energy and resources was the sole intent to *temporarily* bolster Hitler's centralized authority since the building was openly acknowledged as provisional.

The New Chancellery was revealed to the public in August 1938 at its topping out ceremony. There, Hitler introduced the myth of its nine month construction.[27] His speech congratulated workers on sustaining a frantic pace over the previous five months (eliding the preceding three years) and clarified the building's purpose: to project a monumental image of Germany's reinvention as an empire, following Austria's annexation, and showcase its dynamic revival and mobilization under his leadership.[28] He further stressed the necessity of renovating Berlin's state buildings due to the expanded population and territory and corresponding growth of the bureaucracy and so the city might hold its own as a metropolitan center opposite Vienna.[29] With this achievement, he proclaimed, Germany established a center of power in which the people could "show their face" to the world—that is, his face, framed as "embodiment," architect, and driver of their resurrection.[30] Hence, even before its completion, the New Chancellery was styled as a monument to the future "Volksgemeinschaft." But, as Hitler explicitly noted, it was a provisional monument, destined for some unnamed future use by 1950.[31] Opened with the annual diplomatic welcome in January 1939, it asserted an architectural image of the "people's empire" (now including Czechoslovakia's "ethnic Germans").[32] Yet, at its dedication, Hitler again named it a "tiny stone" in Berlin's redevelopment, ushering in an exponential pace of growth that would quickly outstrip the architecture's representational capacity.[33]

Meanwhile, the New Chancellery assembled Hitler's expanded power base into an articulated structure, which appeared externally as a bureaucratic fortress. Composed of three blocks, wrapping Voßstraße's western corner, and terminating in two freestanding barracks, the imposing façade reflected the hierarchical organization of State, Party, and Führer. Physically isolated office wings, outfitted with mirroring portals, housed the Reich and Party Chancelleries, flanking the central Führer-building. The design incorporated and altered stylistic elements of its predecessors. The tripartite structure and central forecourt echoed the Schulenburg Palace, rotating its orientation to face south and laterally emphasizing its magnified monumentality. Vertical dimensions matched the previous ensemble; the articulation with the Borsig Palace, facilitated by a reduction in window lines, visually transitioned between Berlin's imperial architecture and modern NS bureaucracy.[34]

The building's bureaucratic function was decisively downplayed on the rear. There, the Führer-block appeared as single mass, with a sloping roof and temple-like portico, fronted by an enormous terrace outside Hitler's ceremonial office at the building's axial center. A recessed courtyard outside the Reich Chancellery lay to the west behind a pergola; to the east, a colonnade outside the Party Chancellery's dining hall concealed any trace of administrative function. The garden side thus gave the impression of a residential palace—Hitler's idyll in the governmental quarter—and offered a stately vista from his private apartments.[35]

The disconnect between the building's front and rear indicates inconsistencies endemic to the overall design, most evident in the relation between exterior and interior. While the front suggested an expansive, modern bureaucracy, the interior projected an image of classically styled sovereignty. An enfilade leading to Hitler's office composed the interior "diplomatic route"—the building's most iconic structure, copiously reproduced in propaganda. The visitor entered by car through the Siedler building and was dropped off at a portico at the open-air Honor Court's western end, which lead into a modest foyer. This space enhanced the dramatic transition to the cavernous Mosaic Room, surfaced with polished marble and Teutonic motifs and entirely empty of furniture save for during sensationally staged state events. Beyond the door at its far end, a museal rotunda concealed the hinge in the building's lateral axis. From there, the main event: the Marble Gallery, longer than the Palace of Versailles's Hall of Mirrors, with a central doorway to Hitler's office and a Reception Hall at its far end.[36] Viewed in isolation, the sequence appropriated the signifying elements of classical architecture.[37] Considered in context—its site plan, representational façade, and administrative function—the design ignores the organic foundations of both classical and modern architecture.

Regarding the former, the decorative elements and especially the ceremonial enfilade performed the axiality and symmetrical form of neoclassical style while abandoning its norms. The diplomatic route's processional had virtually nothing to do with the overall layout, moving parallel to the street rather than symmetrically through the building. On the other hand, contrary to modern design principles, the New Chancellery's external design elements and cladding were in no way conditioned by the structural reality or materials that lay underneath. As shall be explored in detail below, the architecture exhibited none of the transparency between exterior and interior one might expect from modern planning. Indeed, the external and internal representational wrapping of the diplomatic route invasively and aggressively disrupted the building's functionality.

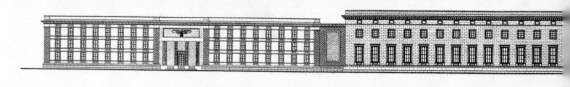

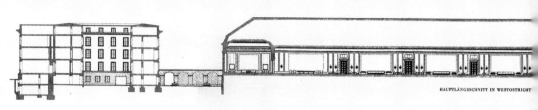

HAUPTLÄNGSSCHNITT IN WESTOSTRICHT

DIE NEUE REICHSKA

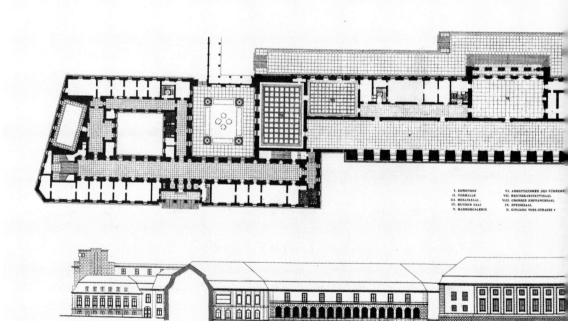

I. EHRENHOF
II. VORHALLE
III. MOSAIKSAAL
IV. RUNDER SAAL
V. MARMORGALERIE
VI. ARBEITSZIMMER DES FÜHRERS
VII. REICHSKABINETTSSAAL
VIII. GROSSER EMPFANGSSAAL
IX. SPEISESAAL
X. EINGANG VOSS-STRASSE

ANSICHT VO

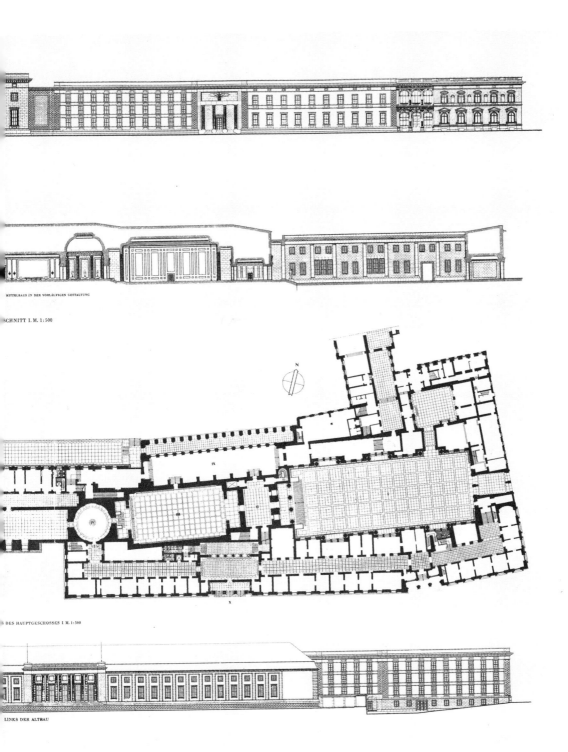

Figure 2.1. Elevation, section, and ground floor plan of the New Reich Chancellery. *Die Neue Reichskanzlei,* Müller & Sohn, 1942.

Beyond stylistic incoherence, the diplomatic route wrought chaos throughout the interior, as is evident from its few surviving floor plans.[38] The distribution of floors and offices, indicated on the front, bore little relation to their situation in the building. For example, although the Führer-block appeared functionally integrated with the adjacent wings, its first two floors contained no offices on the building front, as they were occupied by the Marble Gallery. Indeed, the majority of the ground floor was devoted to hallways.[39] The dual portals, suggesting a pathway through the building's depth, branched off laterally to accommodate the diplomatic route in the eastern tract and a courtyard and atrium to the west. The layout of the Reich Chancellery wing proved fairly rational and consistent between floors, but the layouts of the other wings were plagued by inefficiencies. On the Führer-block's rear, offices were exclusively located on the ground and second floors owing to the sloping roof and enlarged attic; on the street side, its upper floors held isolated hallways accessible only by stairwell and offices outfitted with floor-level windows and skylights. In the western half of the Party Chancellery block, a single row of ground-floor offices was tucked against the façade; on the second story, the mismatched floor height with the Borsig Palace produced another abbreviated, isolated hallway. Packing administrative spaces around the diplomatic route further resulted in varying wall thicknesses and voids honeycombing the structure. Perhaps no surprise: out of 315 offices, 130 were crowded around bunkers in the cellar, many without natural light or air circulation.[40]

Crucially, however, NS state operations aligned with these architectural affordances. The New Chancellery reflected and exacerbated the dissolution of rational systems of governance. Of 180 employees occupying the building, 14 were high-ranking officers who mediated access to Hitler or acted in his stead as he was rarely in residence.[41] The structure formed a monumental bottleneck, transmitting and articulating Hitler's authority through the anonymous bureaucracy.[42] If the fleet of guards, secretaries, and domestic and technical workers were disturbed by its problematic functionality, this was irrelevant; only provisional, its infelicities could be corrected post facto, its ill-equipped rooms later retrofitted. Further, the administrative interior, materializing the state's internal chaos, remained invisible, as it was almost categorically excluded from representation.

The architecture concealed the state's experimental (dis)organization behind an image of classical authority constructed in modern media. Reproductions of the interior "imparted a feigned public character" to inaccessible spaces, "reducing the population's desire to participate in . . . politics to viewing photographed rooms in which relevant decisions were ostensibly made."[43] The New Chancellery's essential purpose was to produce an idealized impression of state operations through its visual reproduction. It thereby offers a remarkable example of photographic architecture: a modern representational building encountered primarily through images, a structure that integrated optical elements resonant with photographic technology into its design.[44]

In 1939, iconic images of the New Chancellery's representational spaces were published in a lavish architectural monograph,[45] images subsequently reproduced in picture postcards, commemorative coins, postage stamps, and so on. Speer notably employed modernist photographers, stipulating exact camera positions for their images.[46] Photographs offered a drastically different impression from the one available onsite—for example, by downplaying the architecture's fragmented style. Speer's design sectioned the exterior into discrete structural elements, favoring reproduction in isolated points of view, dovetailing with particular photographic strategies and technologies. The front façade's lateral emphasis, for instance, prevented its full view from street level, even assisted by a wide-angle lens; evident in newsreels, it was best captured cinematically from a moving vehicle. Photographs of static design elements, in contrast, functioned metonymically, standing in for the structure, which remained hidden from view.[47] Above all, the diplomatic route itself operated as visual shorthand for the architecture. Reducing its visual identity to this representational element actively concealed its disorganized administrative spaces. Instead, the enfilade's carefully staged images constructed a sequential, spatial narrative, offering an ideologically charged impression of the building's bodily experience and idealized allegory of its alleged function.

This impression issued from photographs and optical strategies employed in Speer's design. In combination, the state's ideological order of power, "embodied" in Hitler and articulated in the bureaucracy, transformed into "bodily" domination visually translated into two dimensions. In photographs of the diplomatic route, the limited perspective and constrained views offer a "controlled" gaze as a surrogate for a disciplined body. Photographs of the Marble Gallery, for example, suggest an enforced trajectory inward, heightening intensity and anticipation along the approach to Hitler's office. Furthermore, the reflective materials and their emphasis in photographs evoke modern technologies of visual reproduction, without, however, revealing them.

The abundance of marble reflected prestige and durability—and bodies in the building.[48] In photographs, finely worked, polished surfaces appear opposite the implied visitor but, absent their reflection, reduce their presence to a disembodied gaze, approximated by the camera. Optical elements, resonant with modern photographic-architectural design practices, also paradoxically "reinsert" the body back into space.[49] Slippery surfaces meant to physically destabilize visitors also implied a *visual* asymmetry, suggestive of the hidden machinery of surveillance and control. The body's implicit, multiplied visibility operates metaphorically, suggesting it as the object of the state's technologically articulated gaze concealed behind the walls. Hence, at the end of the journey inward, Hitler's "sovereign gaze" becomes a kind of hidden camera, insinuating the visitor into an order of knowledge and power.

Positioned like a throne room, Hitler's office was the grandest chamber and the only one suggestive of an administrative function. Its most iconic photograph is taken from behind Hitler's oversized desk. Decorative elements hearken back to the diplomatic

Figure 2.2. Marble Gallery viewed from the east, with doorway to Hitler's office just right of image center. *Die Neue Reichskanzlei,* Müller & Sohn, 1942.

route, suggesting classical masculine authority.[50] The design and images are oriented around invoking the sovereign's gaze, bolstered by Bismarck's portrait above the hearth.[51] The plane of the desk dominates the frame, humanizing the exaggerated dimensions. Offset to the left, the angle of view downplays the room's symmetry, emphasizing Hitler's invisible body (signified by his chair) as producing visual order. The sovereign's gaze is likewise suggested in the wide-angle lens's subtle compression of space into an easily surveyed unity. But the conspicuous display of bureaucratic implements alters the classical conceit, identifying the space as the modern control room of the state's interior. The power implicitly attributed to Hitler is also mediated through the telephone and writing block, his connection to the state's hidden eyes and ears.

Events staged in the New Chancellery, reproduced in propaganda, reinforced the mythology of its dominating, disciplinary effects. A notable example: in 1939, Czech President Emil Hácha was summoned to the building.[52] He walked the diplomatic route, only to be left in suspense for hours before being admitted into Hitler's office

Figure 2.3. Hitler's ceremonial office viewed from behind his oversized desk, looking east. *Die Neue Reichskanzlei*, Müller & Sohn, 1942.

around one in the morning. Hitler finally arrived and unleashed a barrage of threats, accusations, and demands, so overwhelming Hácha that he passed out and had to be revived by an injection. He awoke, faced with an ultimatum: sign away his remaining territories and let German troops annex them the following day or face a violent overthrow. Hácha capitulated. While the architecture framed Hitler's totalizing control over and elevation of the Volk, it also functioned as threat, a space of coercion.[53]

The New Chancellery was employed as a backdrop for bellicose political events: signing the "Pact of Steel," staged meetings with military commanders, decoration ceremonies, and state funerals, all of which appeared across media. Typically, however, its rooms sat empty, save during occasional "Chief-Conferences" held without their commander.[54] Between 1941 and 1945 Hitler returned to Berlin only intermittently, preferring to spend time away from the front in Berchtesgaden.[55] The New Chancellery's function as the heart of NS sovereignty was thus purely symbolic, largely unused throughout the regime's waning duration, with the notable exception of its extensive bunker complex. Even as it framed and mediated Hitler's appearance, the New Chancellery primarily outlined his *absence*; a surrogate, photographically constructed image-space, concealing and idealizing the apparatus "working toward his will."

Since the New Chancellery's destruction, scholarship has exposed its mythology as an ideological fiction, turning away from propaganda to unearth its plans and internal documentation. Yet the image (broadly speaking) of its symbolic-spatial order and amplification of Hitler's power persists. The key to this phenomenon lies in asymmetries of the historical record. The architecture's deployment in propaganda to produce a durable (if temporary) symbol of Hitler's power was its most important function. The building evinced the NS state's irrationality, but its symbolic surfaces and photographic reproductions beautified and obscured the visibility of that irrationality. Although such a built image of power may be reinscribed, appropriated, or dismantled by a subsequent regime, its mediated memory persists. Architectural photographs are more accessible than plans and technical documents; they are easily assembled into an ideological narrative, positing equivalence between visual presentation and physical construction. Dismantling a building's representational identity requires something else: a more metaphorical destruction of its image and the construction of a new architectural proposition in its place. The dual process of the New Reich Chancellery's physical and symbolic demolition remained, however, radically incomplete.

In the four years following Hitler's defeat, the occupying Soviet forces and East German government transformed the New Chancellery from monumental ruin to quarry to empty space. The structure sustained damage in early 1945 but ultimately survived the war intact.[56] Its ruin initially served as a site of investigation involving the search for Hitler's destroyed body and evidence of Nazi crimes. It was also a site of symbolic reinscription, as Allies flocked to the building, gawked at its spaces, scrawled their names on the walls, looted souvenirs, and documented their visits in photographs and newsreels. Churchill notably toured the ruin during the Potsdam Conference in 1945, a victor's rite repeated through 1947.[57] The Allies turned the ruin inside out, exposing its subterranean bunkers and occupying its interior with their own sovereign bodies, gazes, and cameras.

Although the New Chancellery was adjacent to the Russian sector's western border, the structure (unlike other NS buildings) was not recommissioned for use by the occupying Soviet authorities due to the constant stream of visitors and, presumably, its unfunctional design.[58] It initially seemed that the local powers planned to allow the site's continued profanation and eventual disintegration. Newspapers mention its use as a garden, black market, and filming location for Roberto Rossellini and Wolfgang Staudte.[59] Soon, however, the ruin became entangled in the architectural politics of reconstruction, which, in its earliest phases, largely took the form of demolition.[60] The New Chancellery's staggered deconstruction began in 1947, with the salvaging of marble and nonstructural materials.[61] In early 1949, it progressed to demolition, periodically interrupted as crews were deployed to dispatch the ruined City Palace.[62] By early 1950, a pile of rubble was all that remained; by 1951, a parking lot covered the site.

In a sense, the New Chancellery's demolition was *anti*-representational. Where it appeared in the media, largely without accompanying images, it was briefly mentioned, misrepresented in significant detail, and vague regarding the fate of materials—and this was likely precisely the point, to assert the architecture's *lack* of symbolic value through its physical substance's anonymized redistribution.[63] Its destruction, however, was simultaneously linked to representational *construction*: the Soviets' reclamation of Berlin, in part through the renovation of Wilhelmplatz as Thälmannplatz.[64] This project, which would have maintained and once again renovated Berlin's historic governmental center, was slated to be completed as part of the celebrations for Stalin's seventieth birthday on November 30, 1949, just following East Germany's founding. Its abrupt abandonment was likely influenced by the site's uncomfortable proximity to the border with West Berlin as the Cold War heated up and by the desperate need for housing.[65] In general, the documentation of Thälmannplatz's ill-fated planning is notably silent regarding the previous occupying structure.[66] There is virtually no bureaucratic archival documentation of the New Chancellery's demolition.

If the actors appear somewhat nebulous in what follows, this is largely owing to gaps and omissions in the historical record. Nonetheless, from what we can glean of this event, a closer look at the New Chancellery's demolition reveals striking parallels with its construction. Both were improvisational, conditioned by shifting demands of representational, architectural politics, and, therefore, concealed from public view, poorly documented and/or revised in the archival record.[67] Like its appearance, its *disappearance* is most comprehensively, albeit problematically, documented in photographs.

The New Chancellery's demolition images, which never appeared in circulation, suggest an undeniably symbolic event. Demolition photographs primarily record technical information but may also be used to legitimize the construction of a new urban image.[68] In this case, images show the reinscription of Berlin's symbolic-spatial topography mediated through the process of the New Chancellery's erasure. They also establish a new perspective—modifying the building's legibility through the fragmentation of its physical structure and previous ideological image. This strategy is apparent in nonstructural demolition photographs, which emphasize the architecture's naked materiality and demystification through the unmounting of its marble surfaces. One photograph of the hearth in Hitler's office, for example, brings the viewer closer to the structure (eschewing a wide-angle lens), which is stripped of its pretension to power along with its marble cladding, exposed in its concrete reality, notably bunker-like. Such images further replace NS propaganda's lush, visual richness with a tactile roughness, foregrounding the disjuncture between surface and structure. A photograph of the Marble Gallery, which shares the same date, performs a similar act of inversion and critique, mimicking

Figure 2.4. Marble Gallery viewed from the west, with the door to Hitler's office at left edge. Dated September 15, 1947. Ullstein Bild Foto Archiv / Granger Historical Picture Archive.

previous images of the space, highlighting its telescopic length and (unmounted) polished surfaces while indicating the presence of a new architectural order outside the frame. Orderly stacks of marble metonymically suggest the work of reconstruction orchestrated by Soviet authorities and workers, efforts implicitly localized decidedly elsewhere.

Whereas such images invert strategies of NS architectural photography, structural demolition images foreground the bodies visibly occupying and dismantling Hitler's space of power. Photographs of workers handling oversized materials displace his invisible presence and aggressively employ the body's scale to "cut his architecture down to size." Despite showing only fragmented views of the space, the angled perspectives, offsetting orthogonal lines, and tightly framed tableaus all give a sense of the building's monumental proportions while refuting the impression of its disciplinary effects. Further, the photographs inscribe demolition as an act of state building: constructing a new architectural image of sovereignty, embodied by the workers. These photographs mediate the production of East Berlin's new urban image—without, however, revealing its final form.

In a sense, the photographs lay the foundation for a narrative of disassembly and resurrection before the trajectory of that narrative was firmly established. For, between

Figure 2.5. Workers carry part of a capital from the portico outside Hitler's office through a portal on Voßstraße. Dated February 1949. Bundesarchiv-Bildarchiv, Koblenz.

Berlin's occupation and the establishment of the two German states, provisional designs for the city's reconstruction had to accommodate the shifting political context of their implementation.[69] The New Chancellery's demolition made way for a reconstructed governmental center on Thälmannplatz. But despite the announcement of these plans, concomitant with the marginalized celebration of the Chancellery's demolition in extremely brief newspaper reports, they never materialized. Instead, the regime opted to relocate the capital's center to its most Prussian heritage site, incorporating fragments of the City Palace ruin into the new silhouette of Marx-Engels-Platz. In doing so, the East German state (again) appropriated more space for the sovereign people (and leaders) to "show their face to the world," establishing distance from the erstwhile center of NS power and the border with the Federal Republic, which (they claimed) was its "continuation" in the postwar period.[70]

Whether these photographs were intended for publication is unclear. Like the building whose erasure they documented and preserved, the images remained buried. Today they are primarily to be found in Germany's Federal Archives, with many lacking attribution or bearing incomplete and/or incorrect accompanying information. If the New Chancellery was an expendable part of East Berlin's topography, its destruction was justifiably omitted from official representation of the city's architectural resurrection. Because the archival record of these events is marked by significant omissions, we can only speculate as to why the New Chancellery's demolition failed to appear in the Soviet reconstruction narrative of Berlin. Perhaps the reuse of materials drew uncomfortable attention to resonances between supposedly fascist and antifascist styles of building. Ascribing significance to the New Chancellery's demolition presumed a highly charged symbolic object; its public representation potentially re-mystifying the very trappings of NS power that the occupying Soviet and East German authorities sought to dismantle. If there was nothing spectacular about the building, there was no need to make a spectacle of its unbuilding. In any event, hardening East–West relations precluded further renovations of the New Chancellery's image, as its site was subsumed by the nonspace of the Wall's "Death-Strip" separating the two German states.[71]

Yet due to the obfuscation of the New Chancellery's disappearance, there was hardly a public confrontation with or demystification of its image. Indeed, it seems to have never reappeared in East Germany at all. As for West Germany, the Chancellery's images briefly returned to prominence in the 1970s as a wave of postmodern appropriations of NS iconography swept the western public sphere—e.g., in Hans-Jürgen Syberberg's *Hitler—ein Film aus Deutschland* (1977). Still, the site continued to draw visitors curious to see the void left by the Third Reich's implosion. And the suppression of its destruction generated its own mythology: rumors about its marble's reuse in new construction as well as the misapprehensions that it was destroyed in 1945 or that its subterranean tunnels allowed Hitler's escape. The New Chancellery's disappearance, paired with its preservation in NS photographs, have merely reified its ideological image and shaped the reception of the building and its fragments ever since. Its destruction negated the necessity for further public engagement; the architecture was consigned to the archive, its image frozen in time.

When the exposure of the New Chancellery's remains in 1989, following the fall of the Wall, brought flocks of tourists, the site was closed for archeological inspection and then refused historic protection by the city government.[72] Current visitors, of which there are still quite a few, are thus faced with a disjuncture between expectations shaped by historical representations and the contemporary site's anonymity. Two isolated signs from the Topography of Terror and a private historical society note the New Chancellery's and Führerbunker's locations, nestled between a kindergarten, the Singapore embassy, and offices of German states. But this relative invisibility has done little to diminish fascination with the architecture and its fragments. Furthermore, the overlapping mediation of Nazi and Soviet architecture, for instance, in nearby exhibitions of the Wall's photographs and fragments, obfuscates the former by privileging the destructive history of the latter. Here and at sites purportedly employing its materials, Berlin's Soviet architectural heritage acquires a heightened affective charge through the additional "toxic" presence of Nazi materials.

Yet, as this essay has argued, the New Chancellery's mythical power did not originate in its architecture but, rather, through its reproduction in images—some of which, notably, are employed on the very signs meant to demystify its spectral presence. Without recourse to the building itself, these representational artifacts continue to circulate, unchecked by reality, left to fill in the gaps and reconstruct its memory. However problematic the counternarrative of Berlin's Soviet reconstruction may be, considering the violence wrought by their own architectural ideology on the city, that narrative's inclusion in the New Chancellery's mediation might assist in efforts to confront visitors with the historical materiality of NS architecture rather than merely perpetuating its mythology. At the very least, I contend, a more comprehensive account of the New Chancellery's construction and destruction has the potential to deepen our critical understanding of Berlin's contemporary and historical landscape and alert us to the necessity of attending to both the physical and photographic layers of its palimpsest-like topography.

Notes

This essay expands on the first and second chapters of my dissertation, "Framing the Führer: The Construction, Demolition, Mediation, and Memory of the New Reich Chancellery," completed in 2020 at the University of Michigan.

1. Jennifer Jordan, *Structures of Memory: Understanding Urban Change in Berlin and Beyond* (Stanford: Stanford University Press, 2006), 184–93.

2. Andreas Huyssen, *Present Pasts: Urban Palimpsests and the Politics of Memory* (Stanford: Stanford University Press, 2003), 55–58.
3. The site lies just south of the Holocaust Memorial and Brandenburg Gate. For Berlin's memorial district, see Karen Till, *The New Berlin: Memory, Politics, Place* (Minneapolis: University of Minnesota Press, 2005), 20–22.
4. Robert R. Taylor, *The Word in Stone: The Role of Architecture in the National Socialist Ideology* (Berkeley: University of California Press, 1974).
5. For example, Anselm Kiefer's painting *Innenraum* (1981) and Oliver Hirschbiegel's film *Der Untergang* (2004).
6. For Wilhelmstraße's development as a center of governance, see Laurenz Demps, *Berlin-Wilhelmstraße: Eine Topographie preußisch-deutscher Macht* (Berlin: Ch. Links Verlag, 2010), 199–200.
7. Nicknamed the "Service Building," its modest, modern style evinced the democratic priorities of the state in crisis. Dietmar Arnold and Reiner Janick, *Neue Reichskanzlei und "Führerbunker": Legenden und Wirklichkeit* (Berlin: Links, 2005), 33–35; Angela Schönberger, *Die neue Reichskanzlei von Albert Speer: Zum Zusammenhang von nationalsozialistischer Ideologie und Architektur* (Berlin: Mann, 1981), 17–21.
8. Despina Stratigakos, *Hitler at Home* (New Haven: Yale University Press, 2015), 30–43. Speer simultaneously remodeled the Siedler building's "Red Room" as Hitler's ceremonial office. Schönberger, *Die neue Reichskanzlei von Albert Speer*, 22–26.
9. Arnold and Janick, *Neue Reichskanzlei und "Führerbunker,"* 55–56; Schönberger, *Die neue Reichskanzlei von Albert Speer*, 22–27.
10. Stratigakos, *Hitler at Home*, 28.
11. For the artistic stylization of the Führer-mythos, see Eric Michaud, *The Cult of Art in Nazi Germany* (Stanford: Stanford University Press, 2004).
12. Arnold and Janick, *Neue Reichskanzlei und "Führerbunker,"* 56–58; Schönberger, *Die neue Reichskanzlei von Albert Speer*, 27–30.
13. Arnold and Janick, *Neue Reichskanzlei und "Führerbunker,"* 59–60; Schönberger, *Die neue Reichskanzlei von Albert Speer*, 30–36. Plans for the Berghof's expansion in 1935 likewise included bunkers. Stratigakos, *Hitler at Home*, 69–78.
14. Schönberger, *Die neue Reichskanzlei von Albert Speer*, 37–44.
15. For Berlin's redevelopment, see Hans Joachim Reichhardt and Wolfgang Schäche, *Von Berlin nach Germania: Über die Zerstörungen der "Reichshauptstadt" durch Albert Speers Neugestaltungsplanungen* (Berlin: Transit, 2008); Dagmar Thorau and Gernot Schaulinski, *Mythos Germania: Vision und Verbrechen* (Berlin: Berliner Unterwelten, 2014).
16. Jost Dülffer, "NS-Herrschaftssystem und Stadtgestaltung: Das Gesetz zur Neugestaltung deutscher Städte vom 4. Oktober 1937," *German Studies Review* 12, no. 1 (1989): 69–89.
17. Arnold and Janick, *Neue Reichskanzlei und "Führerbunker,"* 74–76; Schönberger, *Die neue Reichskanzlei von Albert Speer*, 60–63. For NS building's incoherent ideology and counterproductive initiatives, see Barbara Miller Lane, *Architecture and Politics in Germany, 1918–1945* (Cambridge, Mass.: Harvard University Press, 1968). For Speer's collaboration with the SS, see Paul Jaskot, *The Architecture of Oppression: The SS, Forced Labor and the Nazi Monumental Building Economy* (New York: Routledge, 2000).

18. Ian Kershaw identifies 1938 as the turning point in the regime's transformation into a "modernising dictatorship." The "key development was unquestionably the growth in autonomy of the authority of the Führer to a position where it was unrestrained in practice as well as theory." "'Working Towards the Führer.' Reflections on the Nature of the Hitler Dictatorship," *Contemporary European History* 2, no. 2 (1993): 112–13.
19. Ian Kershaw, "Hitler and the Uniqueness of Nazism," *Journal of Contemporary History* 39, no. 2 (2004): 243.
20. Kershaw, "'Working Towards the Führer,'" 113–14.
21. Kershaw, "'Working Towards the Führer,'" 111–12.
22. Kershaw, "'Working Towards the Führer,'" 107.
23. Kershaw, "'Working Towards the Führer,'" 117.
24. Kershaw, "Hitler and the Uniqueness of Nazism," 244.
25. Its total cost was around 90 million Reichsmarks, about $1.2 billion today. Arnold and Janick, *Neue Reichskanzlei und "Führerbunker,"* 104.
26. Punishing conditions resulted in the death of at least one Czech builder. Schönberger, "Die neue Reichskanzlei in Berlin von Albert Speer," in *Die Dekoration der Gewalt: Kunst und Medien im Faschismus*, ed. Berthold Hinz (Giessen: Anabas-Verlag Kämpf, 1979). Demolition along Voßstraße also sacrificed the NSDAP headquarters, renovated by Speer in 1932.
27. Speer received the official order for construction in January 1938. Schönberger, *Die neue Reichskanzlei*, 51.
28. "I believe we have established a new political tempo: if it's possible to incorporate a nation into our empire in three or four days, it must also be possible to erect a building in one or two years." Hitler quoted in Schönberger, *Die neue Reichskanzlei*, 179–80. Translations throughout are my own.
29. Hitler in Schönberger, *Die neue Reichskanzlei*, 179.
30. Hitler in Schönberger, *Die neue Reichskanzlei*, 182.
31. "This building will someday fulfill another purpose . . . It will serve its current function for only ten or twelve years," Hitler in Schönberger, *Die neue Reichskanzlei*, 179. This expiration date is also noted in Hitler's introduction to Rudolf Wolters and Heinrich Wolff, *Die neue Reichskanzlei: Architekt Albert Speer* (München: Zentralverlag der NSDAP, 1940), 8.
32. Renovations and repairs continued through 1943. Arnold and Janick, *Neue Reichskanzlei und "Führerbunker,"* 104.
33. Hitler in Schönberger, *Die neue Reichskanzlei*, 183.
34. The stark emphasis on the latter suggested the building's ever-so-slightly altered function, as Hitler's private residence and office (which he predominantly employed) stayed put in the adjacent Schulenburg Palace. Arnold and Janick, *Neue Reichskanzlei und "Führerbunker,"* 100.
35. The garden was also the location of the Führerbunker, a reinforced extension built from 1943 to 1945 on the bunker beneath the Salon. Arnold and Janick, *Neue Reichskanzlei und "Führerbunker,"* 126–30.
36. The comparison, an implicit rebuke of the Treaty of Versailles, was continuously trumpeted in propaganda. Schönberger, *Die neue Reichskanzlei*, 94. Hitler found the Reception Hall

too small and immediately demanded its enlargement. Arnold and Janick, *Neue Reichskanzlei und "Führerbunker,"* 105–6. To the east was a Cabinet Meeting room that neighbored Hitler's office; it was never used, as the body was dissolved in 1937. Arnold and Janick, *Neue Reichskanzlei und "Führerbunker,"* 101.

37. Alex Scobie, *Hitler's State Architecture: The Impact of Classical Antiquity* (University Park: Pennsylvania State University Press, 1990), 98–108.
38. This section draws from Schönberger's careful analysis of plans reproduced in her appendix. *Die neue Reichskanzlei*, 157–62.
39. Arnold and Janick, *Neue Reichskanzlei und "Führerbunker,"* 100.
40. Arnold and Janick, *Neue Reichskanzlei und "Führerbunker,"* 100. Speer was forced to add an artificial solarium in 1941. Arnold and Janick, *Neue Reichskanzlei und "Führerbunker,"* 106n84. Arguably, these conditions reinforced the sense of Hitler's primacy, making other users constantly aware of their unimportance. I thank Claire Zimmerman for this suggestion, which is further supported by the lavish offices for higher-ups located in the older buildings. Wolters and Wolff, *Die neue Reichskanzlei*, 110.
41. Arnold and Janick, *Neue Reichskanzlei und "Führerbunker,"* 106.
42. Carl Schmitt writes, "the appeal to an order from the Führer . . . for all intents and purposes, could not be monitored or examined by anyone." A gap arose between the "apex of political power" and the apparatus of its implementation. Occupying this vacuum, the Reich Chancellery acted as a "great transformer to and from this pinnacle." "Stellungnahme III: Stellung des Reichsministers und Chefs der Reichskanzlei," in *Antworten in Nürnberg*, ed. Helmut Quaritsch (Berlin: Duncker & Humblot, 2000), 94–98.
43. Schönberger, *Die neue Reichskanzlei*, 171.
44. Claire Zimmerman, *Photographic Architecture in the Twentieth Century* (Minneapolis: University of Minnesota Press, 2014).
45. Wolters and Wolff, *Die neue Reichskanzlei*. A number of NS newsreels released around the time of the diplomatic welcome and the Kulturfilm *Das Wort aus Stein* (1939) consistently reproduce the spatial narrative of the building interior by way of its enfilade.
46. Schönberger, "Die Neue Reichskanzlei in Berlin," 172n14. Schönberger speculates that the hues of marble were selected as specifically suitable for reproduction in color photography. Rudolf de Sandalo, photographer of Mies van der Rohe's Tugendhat House, contributed a famed image of the Reich Chancellery portal to the volume. Max Baur is credited for seventeen images. See also Rolf Sachsse, "Architektur und Fotografie im NS-Staat," in *Die Erziehung zum Wegsehen* (Dresden: Philo Fine Arts, 2003), 75–89.
47. Photographs of the portals and Honor Court are often employed this way on the covers or in relevant sections of architectural monographs on Nazi architecture, e.g., Albert Speer and Karl Arndt, *Albert Speer: Architektur, Arbeiten 1933–1942* (Frankfurt: Propyläen Verlag, 1978); León Krier, *Albert Speer: Architecture 1932–1942* (Monacelli Press, 2013). For a critique of these volumes' stylistic resonance with NS propaganda, see Reichhardt and Schäche, 16–17. Krier's monograph, first released in 1985, was the polemical introduction of the New Reich Chancellery and many of the planned buildings for Berlin's NS reconstruction to a younger generation of architects. The section on the New Chancellery largely reproduces a truncated version of the original monograph from Wolters and Wolff with the

new addition of sectioned detail drawings supplied by Speer. Unsurprisingly, it contains no information regarding the building's administrative spaces.

48. Thereby intertwining classical and modern references. "The walls of the peristyle of the *Domus Augustana* were lined with reflecting stone so that the emperor might see whatever was happening behind him." Scobie, *Hitler's State Architecture,* 107.
49. For a discussion of modernist architects' use of reflective materials and photographic/cinematically oriented layouts to produce moments of "visual reckoning" and optical abundance, in reference to Mies's destroyed Barcelona Pavilion, see Zimmerman, 58.
50. For signifiers of sovereign, masculine domesticity employed in the Berghof's interior, see Stratigakos, *Hitler at Home,* 79–89.
51. Further support for this claim comes from the oversized globe (famously mocked by Chaplin) and the desk's mosaic inlay of Mars, Medusa, and Athena, who all stare unblinkingly at the presumed visitor. Such elements are not on view in this image, however.
52. Arnold and Janick, *Neue Reichskanzlei und "Führerbunker,"* 109–10.
53. The Berghof and Hitler's Munich apartment were also used to impress and intimidate foreign visitors. Stratigakos, *Hitler at Home,* 194–220.
54. Arnold and Janick, *Neue Reichskanzlei und "Führerbunker,"* 120–21.
55. Arnold and Janick, *Neue Reichskanzlei und "Führerbunker,"* 117–24. "As soon as Hitler departed . . . the building offered a ghostly sight." Its chief technician recalls, "The whole structure was practically empty, when you walked through the huge halls, the steps echoed from the marble floor." Arnold and Janick, 106, 76n83.
56. Bombs struck the Party Chancellery and Siedler building but destroyed the Schulenburg Palace entirely. The New Chancellery's reinforced steel and concrete structure was helpful in this regard, as older brick architecture in the area was most prone to collapse. Demps, *Berlin-Wilhelmstraße,* 199.
57. See AP Archive, "The Big Three in Berlin," in *British Movietone News* (BM 45952); Bundesarchiv-Filmarchiv, "Frau Roosevelt besucht Deutschland," in *Welt im Film* (1946); "Kanadas Ministerpräsident in Berlin," in *Welt im Film* (1946); "Staatsmänner auf Reisen," in *Welt im Film* (1946); "Bevin und Bildaut in Berlin," *Neue Zeit,* April 29, 1947. See also: Hugh Trevor-Roper, *The Last Days of Hitler* (New York: Macmillan, 1947).
58. The Aviation Ministry was occupied by the East German Economic Commission; the Reichsbank was employed as SED Headquarters. Demps, *Berlin-Wilhelmstraße,* 199.
59. Reported in the *Berliner Zeitung, Neue Zeit,* and *Neues Deutschland* from 1947 to 1948.
60. See Wolfgang Kil, "Mondlandschaften, Baugrundstücke," in *So weit kein Auge reicht: Berliner Panoramafotografien aus den Jahren 1949–1952; Aufgenommen von Fritz Tiedemann* (Berlin: Berlinische Galerie, 2009).
61. Alongside the Führerbunker's attempted demolition. The bunker's destruction order was given in October 1947, but crews encountered difficulties owing to the reinforced structure's durability, insufficient explosive material, and concerns over damaging nearby building foundations. They ultimately blew off the roof, reburying the remains. Demps, *Berlin-Wilhelmstraße,* 199–200.
62. Demps, *Berlin-Wilhelmstraße,* 207–12.
63. Allegedly, its limestone and red marble were used in the Soviet monument in Treptower

Park and the Thälmannplatz U-Bahn station (now Mohrenplatz); structural materials incorporated into the Volksbühne, Kulturbundklub, Weidendammer Bridge, and the main building of the Humboldt University. Demps, *Berlin-Wilhelmstraße*, 213–14.
64. Ernst Thälmann, former leader of the Communist Party in Germany, was imprisoned and executed in Buchenwald.
65. Demps, *Berlin-Wilhelmstraße*, 202–11.
66. For a comprehensive history (with, likewise, almost no mention of the New Chancellery), see Maoz Azaryahu and Kerstin Amrani, *Von Wilhelmplatz zu Thälmannplatz: Politische Symbole im öffentlichen Leben der DDR* (Gerlingen: Bleicher, 1991).
67. For example, regarding the Führerbunker's "successful" demolition, an archeological investigation commissioned by the city government in the early 1990s revealed that while its inner walls were destroyed and filled in with debris, the structure and the New Chancellery's nearby foundation were left largely intact. Demps, *Berlin-Wilhelmstraße*, 199–200; Alfred Kernd'l and Landesamt Archäologisches Berlin, *Zeugnisse der historischen Topographie auf dem Gelände der ehemaligen Reichskanzlei Berlin-Mitte* (Berlin, 1993).
68. See the chapter on rubble photography in Miriam Paeslack, *Constructing Imperial Berlin: Photography and the Metropolis* (Minneapolis: University of Minnesota Press, 2019).
69. In the war's immediate aftermath, the establishment of new state architecture was conditioned by physical limitations (structurally sound sites available for use in various occupation zones) and other building priorities. There was no consensus within the emergent Soviet state regarding the direction for reconstruction. The "16 Fundamentals of Urban Planning" from July 1950 reveal a shifted emphasis toward construction of plazas, boulevards, and monuments. But even these evince conflicting opinions regarding, for example, demolishing the City Palace. Through its complete absence from these discussions and records, the New Chancellery's removal offers a singular point of implicit agreement. Demps, *Berlin-Wilhelmstraße*, 207–11.
70. See Klaus von Beyme, *Der Wiederaufbau: Architektur und Städtebaupolitik in beiden Deutschen Staaten* (München: Piper, 1987); Michael Z. Wise, *Capital Dilemma: Germany's Search for a New Architecture of Democracy* (New York: Princeton Architectural Press, 1998).
71. A report from 1953 in a West German newspaper notes the questioning and seizure of film from American presidential candidate Adlai Stevenson by police after he visited the site. "Stevenson vor der ehemaligen Reichskanzlei von Volkspolizisten vorübergehend festgenommen," *Frankfurter Allgemeine: Zeitung für Deutschland,* July 13, 1953.
72. The contradictory reasoning voiced anxiety over the site's potential attraction and rejected preservation on the grounds that it was devoid of historical value. See Jordan, *Structures of Memory*; Kernd'l, *Zeugnisse der historischen Topographie*.

Chapter 3

DIY Fascism
Architecture and the Autarchic Exhibition of Italian Minerals

Ruth W. Lo

Autarchy, the Italian fascist state's economic policy of self-sufficiency, had impacts on architecture that are by now well known.[1] Scholars have written extensively on innovations in material and building technologies, as well as a turn to the use of autochthonous minerals, traditional construction methods, and new interpretations of classical and regional stylistic expressions.[2] Among the most extensively studied is the architecture of the *Esposizione Universale Roma* (EUR), a master-planned neighborhood on the outskirts of the capital that exemplified many fascist autarchic policies, from its copious use of Italian stones to the monumental neoclassical style that underscored the regime's links to ancient Rome. Autarchy's impact on postwar architecture is also well documented through the works of Pier Luigi Nervi, especially the thin-shell concrete constructions that developed out of the exigencies of material scarcity.[3] Long overlooked as part of this history, however, is the Autarchic Exhibition of Italian Minerals (*Mostra autarchica del minerale italiano*—MAMI) of 1938. The exhibition significantly impacted architectural design and construction in the final years of fascism and ultimately shaped Italian postwar developments that are familiar today.

While MAMI was ostensibly focused on mineral display, its relationship to architecture appeared in multiple ways. The exhibition's bombastic celebration of Italian minerals validated the use of certain building materials as an act of ethnonationalism while condemning imported materials and styles as unpatriotic. Economic realities left little choice but for the fascist regime to take this position. Some architects acted as loyal agents of the state, supporting it by using domestic materials in their designs as well as by being directly involved with MAMI. Recognizing the political function of architecture, the regime invited leading architects to design MAMI's pavilions and displays. A total of forty architects were involved, and this overabundance of designers signaled the importance

of architecture to an exhibition that showcased Italian building materials.[4] Many of the participating architects would later adapt and transform their ephemeral work for MAMI into designs for permanent structures, such as those at EUR. MAMI thus provided a fitting opportunity for architects to experiment with ethnonationalist materials and designs before their application in more enduring contexts in the regime's final years.

This essay examines the conception and organization of MAMI with a focus on the role that architects played as they served the autarchic goals of fascist Italy. MAMI aimed to demonstrate that global politics pushed Italy to be ever more creative with its domestic resources, turning economic limitations into opportunities to develop new construction techniques and aesthetic expressions. As such, the exhibition reframed architecture as a main area for the practice of fascism's new "do-it-yourself" national ethos. Architects working under fascism were accustomed to generating designs that expressed the regime's ideologies, but during the autarchic period they needed to further contribute to the fascist political economy by responding to national economic interests. As architects became technocrats, the bidirectional influence of politics and

Figure 3.1. Nocturnal view of the Autarchic Exhibition of Italian Minerals at the Circus Maximus in Rome. On the left is the Pavilion of Arms designed by Mario De Renzi. Copyright Roma, Accademia Nazionale di San Luca, Fondo Mario De Renzi, www.fondoderenzi.org.

architectural production impacted their work. In other words, architects responding to autarchy developed architecture's functional relationship to politics quite apart from its propagandistic purpose and symbolic meaning. Ultimately, the fascist regime charged MAMI's architects with the same ethnonationalist task that it set the mineralogists: to draw parallels between the mineral makeup of Italian architecture and the genetic material of the Italian race—both products of Italian land.

MAMI among Fascist Exhibitions

The Autarchic Exhibition of Italian Minerals took place at the Circus Maximus, the oblong field on which chariots once raced in ancient Rome, from November 18, 1938, to May 9, 1939. Organized by the National Fascist Party (*Partito Nazionale Fascista*—PNF), MAMI focused specifically on the regime's achievements in extracting minerals and fossil fuel resources and their contributions to the national goal of attaining economic self-sufficiency. Leading architects designed pavilions that flaunted the aesthetic possibilities of using autarchic materials as well as structural innovations developed in response to economic limitations. The exhibition's buildings were thus intended to provide physical evidence of Italy's ability to be autarchic without compromising fascism's stylistic and formal expressions. This, the exhibition made clear, was the result of the successful collaboration of architects and mineralogists, both experts in their respective industries, that served the regime as technocrats.

To understand the architectural and ideological importance of MAMI, it is necessary to consider the event within the sequence of major fascist exhibits in Rome. Fascism's embrace of exhibitions was a rejection of the historicism of museums. As Jeffrey Schnapp has written, exhibitions for the fascist regime were the "impermanent sites of volatile memory" that manipulated historical narratives, generated origin myths, mobilized the collective, and forged a new national identity.[5] This began with the Exhibition of the Fascist Revolution (*Mostra della Rivoluzione fascista*—MRF) in 1932, an event in the *Palazzo delle Esposizioni* that celebrated the tenth anniversary of Mussolini's March on Rome. Historians have thoroughly analyzed the planning and design of the MRF, which the regime assigned to Adalberto Libera and Mario De Renzi, two proponents of Italian Rationalism.[6] Journals, newsreels, posters, and postcards featured this exhibition widely, especially its imposing temporary façade with four twenty-five-meter fasci in oxidized copper that covered the original neoclassical entrance. The regime inaugurated a second large-scale exhibit, the Augustan Exhibition of Romanità (*Mostra Augustea della Romanità*, variably translated as "Roman-ness," "Romanity," or "spirit of Rome"—MAR), at the same location on September 23, 1937. This extravagant celebration of the *Bimillenario Augusteo* actually served to underscore fascism's new version of a Roman empire following Mussolini's conquest of Ethiopia.[7]

Concurrent with MAR, the PNF began a quartet of exhibitions at the Circus Maximus immediately after Mussolini declared the founding of a fascist Italian empire: (1) National Exhibition of Summer Camps and Assistance to Children (*Mostra nazionale delle colonie estive e dell'assistenza all'infanzia*), June–September 1937; (2) Exhibition of National Textiles (*Mostra nazionale del tessile*), November 1937–March 1938; (3) Dopolavoro Exhibition (*Mostra del Dopolavoro*), May–August 1938; and (4) MAMI.[8] All of these exhibitions supported specific fascist policies, beginning with the first on children's welfare that showed the PNF's unambiguous commitment to Mussolini's pronatalist directives issued in the 1927 Ascension Day speech.[9] The second exhibition on textiles featured advances in state-sponsored production, such as the cultivation of cotton in the new Italian colony of Ethiopia, as well as the research and development of synthetic materials such as rayon and lanital, an "autarchic fiber" derived from casein.[10] The third exhibition focused on fascist after-work activities, including educational and regime-approved leisure programs such as film, sports, concerts, and tourism. MAMI, the final exhibition, capped off the series with some parallels to the Exhibition of National Textiles in addressing Italy's economic situation, but the overall tenor of the displays delivered a more imperialist and militaristic vision of fascism than the previous three exhibitions. MAMI's architecture included a pavilion specifically devoted to the regime's extractive undertakings in Africa, another dedicated to the defense of race, and a hall of Italian arms. These signaled that the regime saw colonialism, race, and military prowess as important factors to Italy's attainment of autarchy. The culmination of the fascist exhibitions in Rome was, of course, EUR, the world exposition of an ex novo satellite city outside of Rome populated with government and residential buildings that provides the most familiar image of fascist architecture known today.

Minerals, Autarchy, Patrimony, and Race

Among the series of fascist exhibits in Rome, the Autarchic Exhibition of Italian Minerals directly addressed the regime's efforts at economic independence, as its name suggests. The PNF inaugurated MAMI on November 18, 1938, just as the Exhibition on National Textiles had opened at the Circus Maximus exactly one year earlier on the same date—the anniversary of the League of Nations' imposed sanctions on Italy.[11] Fascist autarchic policies affected many aspects of Italian everyday life, and one of the biggest impacts was on architecture.[12] Reinforced concrete, which was commonplace in Italy in the 1920s and 1930s, had become a preferred method of construction for Italian Rationalism, an influential style of architecture during the interwar period.[13] Trade sanctions, however, prevented the importation of metal, making it difficult to secure the steel rebars needed to construct in reinforced concrete. Additionally, Italy was poor in marl, a common mineral in Portland cement and a basic ingredient in concrete. At MAMI, the small Pavilion of Marl designed by Ugo Luccichenti called attention to the importance of mining this carbonate mineral. The pavilion's narrative simultaneously advocated for an increase in marl production and the judicious use of concrete in construction, since Italy produced the least amount of cement in Europe.[14]

The steel and marl shortage led the regime to institute additional autarchic measures to regulate architecture and construction. In 1937, one year before the PNF mounted MAMI, Mussolini's government legislated reinforced concrete for use in structures more than five stories tall.[15] In 1938, the regime banned the use of reinforced concrete for all building types except those for military purposes.[16] Scholars have also noted other obstacles to reinforced concrete construction during the autarchic period, including Italy's inability to afford foreign timber for the formwork and the difficulty of altering Italy's artisanal production practices to accommodate large-scale metal manufacturing.[17] As a result, architects during the *ventennio*, many of whom had achieved fame through their designs in reinforced concrete, needed to adapt to new regulations by using alternative materials.

To cope with the import sanctions, the regime pinned its hopes of attaining self-sufficiency on the exploitation of resources available in Italy's territorial holdings. Italy had already laid claim to parts of the Istrian peninsula, the territory partitioned after World War I. On May 9, 1936, Mussolini proclaimed Italy an empire with sovereignty over Ethiopia. In a speech to the National Guild Assembly on May 15, 1937, he stated:

> The actual and potential resources of the Empire are exceptional. I should not say so if I had not proofs. In our struggle for self-sufficiency the Empire will make a decisive contribution to our supplies of cotton, coffee, meat, hides and skins, wool, timber, and precious metals beginning with gold.[18]

The Italian government thus shrewdly turned international punishment for its act of aggression into a means of legitimizing the seizure of territories and their resources for its own use.

To emphasize the utility of the empire to Italian autarchy, the PNF dedicated large sections of MAMI to activities in the colonies and occupied areas. In the Pavilion of Solid Combustibles (designed by the architects Eugenio Montuori and Giovanni Guerrini), the mineralogists of the Italian Coal Company (*Azienda Carboni Italiani*—ACaI), a governmental entity created by Mussolini, designed exhibits that focused on the firm's achievements on the Istrian peninsula.[19] Scale models and photographs illustrated the successes in Arsia (Raša in Croatian), featuring new mining towns built on reclaimed land designed by the Triestino architect Gustavo Pulitzer-Finali.[20]

An entire pavilion was dedicated to various types of mining in the newly established Italian East Africa (*Africa Orientale Italiana*—AOI) to stress the importance of expanding territorial possessions to help Italy achieve self-sufficiency. In this pavilion designed by Franco Petrucci and Carlo Enrico Rava, the exhibits showcased the activities carried out by the Ethiopian Mining Company (*Compagnia Mineraria Etiopica*—COMINA), a subsidiary of Montecatini, the leading mining and chemical company under the fascist regime and the main sponsor of MAMI. Like the exhibits throughout MAMI, COMINA's geologists mixed photographs of mining—in this case, for precious metals in Ethiopia and Eritrea—with mineral samples, as well as life-size models of tents and prospecting tools.[21] In the exhibition catalogue, a full-page spread featured Mussolini's profile casting a large shadow over a map of Italian East Africa accompanied by the quote, "To the battle of autarchy, the empire will make a decisive contribution."[22]

The regime's relentless drive to obtain resources for empire building served another purpose as well: fascism's demographic project. Minerals and autarchy were connected to fascism's population campaign, and the regime believed that mineral extractions and their subsequent transformation into industrial materials and energy sources would be especially helpful to the building of a stronger, larger, and racialized Italian stock. MAMI's broader purpose, I would argue, was to support the fascist metanarrative on the inalienable character of the Italian land from which minerals and people come. The architects and mineralogists thus shared the ideology and language of racial theorists and eugenicists. Mineral and material autarchy paralleled racial autarchy, further underscoring what Aaron Gillette has identified as the conception of genetic purity under Italian fascism.[23] The contributions of MAMI's experts also emphasize what Elizabeth Emma Ferry, anthropologist of mining, terms "the importance of place and locality in the idiom of patrimony."[24] In other words, the fascist affiliation of minerals and race was similarly based on a shared history and the materials—both mineral and genetic—that defined *italianità,* or "Italianness."

Through the lens of mining, MAMI stretched fascism's definition of patrimony. No longer was the regime's assertion of legitimacy upheld by defining the *patria* through the cultural and historical. This definition now also included the natural environment and its resources. In addition to Roman archaeology, a field that Mussolini fervently promoted in order to link his regime to ancient Rome, patrimony expanded to a different kind of "archaeology," one that mined Italy's geological past of earth, veins, and rocks for the fascist present. Minerals, the natural deposits of the land, turned out to provide the regime with an indisputable claim to authority even more legitimate than ancient ruins. An advertisement for MAMI ordered Italians to visit the exhibition with the reminder that "Every Italian must know the mineral patrimony of the fatherland."[25]

MAMI thus underscored the important roles of mineralogists and geologists during fascism, whereby the regime marshaled their scientific expertise into contributing to political ideology.[26] The exhibition attested to their ascribed function as technocrats: they were the specialists with deep knowledge of natural resources in Italy and its territories who could guide the regime to achieving economic autarchy and, eventually, racial superiority. The leading mineralogists and geologists were no longer anonymous and out of the public view; they were named experts as the PNF tasked presidents of mineral organizations with writing exhibition texts and essays for the catalogue. Drawing on ancient and fascist history, citing production and export statistics, and projecting positively on the future of the minerals, these scientists demonstrated their commitment to maximizing extraction of the Italian land for fascism's autarchic goals. To facilitate an understanding of mining as patrimony and to draw a connection to race, MAMI's mineralogists worked in concert with the architects to make visible to the public that which generally remained invisible. Because mining typically took place underground and in quarries, one of the exhibition's main responsibilities was to put labor and minerals on view above ground to let Italians see a different form of patrimony in literal terms.

MAMI's connection to racial theories emerged through its depiction of Italian rock and sedimentary resources and the process of their transformation. The exhibition's representation of the productive underground supplemented fascist propaganda on fertility, both of the land and the people.[27] As an effective strategy of display, MAMI used overabundance (mineral samples piled high and excessive varieties of Italian stones), by then a familiar fascist visual trope.[28] Italians were accustomed to seeing images that exaggerated Italy's fecundity, from photographs of prolific families to collages of fruit harvest celebrations. MAMI's theme was furthermore well suited to portray positive transformation, a narrative linked to the popular fascist concept of *bonifica*. Reclamation, as the word loosely translates to in English, was an ideology applied to widely different parts of life under fascism, including the reclaiming of swamps to turn them into arable land and the redemption of the Italian people through a comprehensive demographic project.[29] Minerals became another way of connecting the transformative process to the *bonifica*, as the regime's scientists, engineers, architects, and laborers turned extracted ores and stones into productive energy, military equipment, and building materials.

Technology was an important part in all of these processes of transmutation, and it therefore played an outsized role at MAMI. The exhibition used technology to validate Italian progress achieved through scientific rationality under fascist leadership. Machinery of different scales was on display everywhere throughout MAMI, including life-size derricks, mechanical devices operated by workers, and technology at sites of extraction shown in photographs and newsreels.[30] These multimedia displays and simulations illuminated how technology contributed to fascist autarchy, but they also served another crucial purpose. The rationality of technology was necessary to counteract the antirationality of nationalism. The regime essentially used the former to justify the latter. This is similar to what Jeffrey Herf has termed "reactionary modernism," the reconciliation of antimodern nationalist sentiments and modern technology, in his study of Weimar and Nazi Germany.[31] In both cases, Italian and German technocrats took on the important role of incorporating modern technology into modern nationalism. They gave literal form—including architecture and infrastructure (streets, bridges, pipelines, and pumping stations)—to rationalize both nations, otherwise built on antirational patriotism, with technological objectivity.

MAMI's depiction of the process of transforming minerals into Italian products underscored technology's transcendence of space and especially of time. This treatment recalls Herf's analysis of technology and politics in Weimar and Nazi Germany through the theories of Heinrich Hardensett, a German engineer who divided capitalist man from technical man.[32] Hardensett contends that the former held ephemeral and abstract values while the latter produced enduring order through permanent and concrete objects—the technocratic forms.[33] The same opposition was present in fascist Italy, where the regime assigned technology the function of creating a lasting empire. This idea permeated MAMI and contemporary architectural writings, where engineers and architects emphasized the timelessness of autarchic architecture and materials. Architects and architectural theorists used words such as "perennial" and "eternal" to describe autarchic architecture, recalling ancient Roman architecture and evoking buildings constructed with Italian stones and marbles that have been continuously used for millennia.[34]

The Architecture of Mineral Autarchy

To ensure that the public understood interconnections among the regime's various goals, the PNF entrusted the architects with designing MAMI's pavilions and the mineralogists and geologists with exhibition content. The organizers appointed four leading architects of the day—Mario De Renzi, Giovanni Guerrini, Mario Paniconi, and Giulio Pediconi—to take charge of MAMI's Technical-Artistic Office (*Ufficio tecnico-artistico*). The regime deemed their work to be representative of new imperial fascist values, striking a good balance in the persistent architectural debate between traditionalism and Rationalism during the *ventennio*. De Renzi, Guerrini, Paniconi, and Pediconi adapted existing pavilions from previous PNF exhibitions at the Circus Maximus, but they also added new ones.[35] While the architecture of MAMI was not radically dissimilar to the original pavilions by De Renzi, Guerrini, and Adalberto Libera, there was a subtle shift in style from pure Rationalism to the *stile littorio*. This stripped-down, abstracted classicism infused international modernism with regionalist traditions and would become fascism's official monumental style by the end of the 1930s. Many of the architects commissioned by the PNF for MAMI were also designing buildings for the new fascist city of EUR, where the *stile littorio* would be applied on a large scale.

With the help of structural engineers, architects experimented with autarchic materials within the spatial and temporal confines of MAMI. Some of the defining formal elements and use of materials at the exhibition would later appear in the more permanent setting at EUR. Photographs of the exhibition show that MAMI's architects added double-height colonnades in front of the original pavilions raised on pilotis, creating a visual dialogue with the rounded arches of the Palatine ruins on the northern edge of the Circus Maximus. With the addition of this modern, abstracted classical feature, MAMI's architects underscored the connection between fascist and ancient Rome by uniting the exhibition with its chosen backdrop. Similar colonnaded porticoes would recur in EUR structures, including at the *Museo della Civiltà Romana*, the *Palazzo degli Uffici*, as well as the *Palazzo dei Congressi* and the buildings along the avenue leading up to it. These historicizing columns and porticoes were born precisely out of the conditions of autarchy.

Because the sanctions greatly impacted Italy's importation of steel, architects reverted to building with stone and traditional construction methods out of necessity—but also as an act of patriotism.[36] Guerrini's placement of statues within the colonnaded bays in MAMI's Pavilion of Art also preceded a similar design in his *Palazzo della Civiltà Romana* (also known as the Square Colosseum) at EUR. Mario De Renzi's Pavilion of Arms with a barrel-vaulted roof could be seen as a precursor to Libera's *Palazzo dei Congressi* with a cubic volume topped by a cross vault. While the latter structure is much larger and more complex in design, the two vaulting systems with glazed lunettes share obvious visual similarities. MAMI was thus a meta device as well as a testing ground for fascist architecture in the late 1930s. It was an exhibition on material autarchy housed in pavilions that demonstrated the regime's architectural response to the imposed economic sanctions.

Although some of MAMI's pavilions were modified from previous PNF shows at the Circus Maximus, the architects made a point to use autarchic materials in the construction of new ones. An article in *Architettura*, a fascist industry journal, cited the use of 6,000 cubic meters of timber, 200 tons of iron, 15,000 square meters of fiber-cement slabs, 8,000 square meters of marbles and stones, 5,000 square meters of linoleum, 3,000 cubic meters of gravel, 25,000 square meters of Populit, Eraclit, and similar composite slabs, and 10,000 square meters of terracotta and cement tile flooring.[37] The entire exhibition (including the pavilions, displays, and simulations of mines and quarries) was completed in seventy days with 142,000 builders working in shifts to ensure that MAMI would open on November 18, 1938, the third anniversary of the sanctions.[38] In the twenty-eight displays divided among thirteen sections, the exhibition showcased Italy's underground resources and featured the processes of rendering raw materials into valuable industrial elements from their extraction to production and then usage. The exhibits were organized into displays of Solid Combustibles; Liquid Combustibles; Ferrous Minerals; Lead and Zinc; Aluminum and Magnesium; Mercury; Various Minerals; Marble, Granite, and Stones; Sulfur; Pyrite; Siliceous Soils and Kaolinite; Asbestos; Cement Marl; Talc and Graphite; Fumaroles; Sea Salt and Rock Salt; and Mineral Waters. Other exhibits addressed the intersections of minerals with culture, imperialism, trade, research, defense, race, and education. These included exhibits titled Art; Italian Africa; Autarchy; Research and Invention; Defense of Race in Mining; Commerce; Arms; and Technical Education of Mining.

The most symbolic use of an autarchic material was at MAMI's central building, the Pavilion of Autarchy, Research, and Invention by Ernesto Puppo and Annibale Vitellozzi. Placed at the western end of Circus Maximus, the structure formed an axis with the Obelisk of Axum, a spoil of war that was erected in front of the Ministry of Italian Africa in 1937, on the eastern end. From the entrance to the exhibition, visitors were immediately confronted with the Pavilion of Autarchy in the distance framed by the lateral porticoes in a perspectival view. The symbolic importance of this pavilion was signaled not only by its central placement at MAMI but also its imposing façade featuring a giant eagle relief alluding unequivocally to the ancient Roman legionary standard, the bronze *aquila*. However, the fascist eagle by the sculptor Romeo Gregori was made entirely out of aluminum, the autarchic metal par excellence and one of the few metals produced in abundance in Italy.[39] Mounted on a wooden frame, the aluminum eagle clasped the fascist symbol of power, the fasces, firmly in its claws. The materiality of the eagle took on heightened significance as it was linked to many aspects of the exhibition, ranging from an extensive display on bauxite mining to MAMI's aluminum commemorative pin with three fasces. The eagle, placed under the bold lettering of "AVTARCHIA" and above the dictum "Mussolini is always right," became a glyph of MAMI and appeared ubiquitously in propaganda materials for the exhibition.

Although the aluminum eagle dominated the Pavilion of Autarchy, Puppo and

Figure 3.2. Aluminum eagle by the sculptor Romeo Gregori on the façade of the Pavilion of Autarchy, Research, and Invention designed by Ernesto Puppo and Annibale Vitellozzi. Fondo Fotografico Montecatini, Centro per la Cultura d'Impresa.

Vitellozzi's structure featured many other autarchic material and construction innovations. The large pavilion of seven hundred square meters with a height of twenty-seven meters was made of concrete *(calcestruzzo)*, but the wall above the entrance to which the aluminum eagle clung was clad with the more autarchic material of stone blocks.[40] Below this, the portico featured red porphyry cladding that, according to the president of the Autarchy Council Ernesto Santoro, Italy had to import up until a few years ago but was now producing in quantities that greatly surpassed national needs.[41] On the pavilion's lateral façades, Puppo and Vitellozzi used glass blocks *(vetrocemento)*, another autarchic material, to provide filtered light to illuminate the structure's interior. For the roof, the architects used Eternit, a corrugated fiber cement, one of the many new agglomerations popularized during the period of Italy's sanctions.[42]

The Pavilion of Arms, a new structure designed by De Renzi for MAMI, experimented with an autarchic method of construction using plywood to create an expansive parabolic roof. With the calculations of the engineer Ottorino Gorgonio, De Renzi employed a system patented by Legnami Pasotti of Brescia, a firm that monopolized this type of construction in Italy and Ethiopia.[43] Three-hinged arches made of latticed wooden ribs created a structure that spanned thirty-five meters atop a rectangular base of stone blocks.[44] While wood was not exceedingly plentiful in Italy, architects and engineers considered timber construction to be more autarchic than reinforced concrete, which had been popular prior to the trade embargoes. De Renzi's choice to showcase the formal and aesthetic possibilities of wooden structures at MAMI made sense, especially because the pavilion was a temporary structure and the regime had restricted the use of steel primarily for military purposes. In fact, Legnami Pasotti underscored the autarchic qualities of its wooden structures in its advertisements of the late 1930s and early 1940s: the material provided an economical and expeditious method of construction to cover a large area, which the firm deemed perfect for Italy's wartime needs.[45] Considering the significance of De Renzi's Pavilion of Arms to the regime's autarchic economic efforts, the PNF carefully documented the construction process and copiously featured the wooden ribs in MAMI's promotional materials.[46]

The inclusion of a Pavilion of Arms at MAMI underscored the importance of minerals to the military, a key element in Italy's battle in achieving a self-sufficient empire. Upon entering the MAMI complex, visitors were immediately confronted on the left with machine guns that protruded from De Renzi's pavilion. The extraordinary size of the pavilion also enabled the presentation of large and numerous Italian arms on the inside, and De Renzi's parabolic roof allowed for planes to suspend above tanks and missiles. Against the glass lunettes, the aircrafts appeared midflight and conveyed a sense of motion that reminded visitors of an Italy actively at war. The pavilion made clear that for the nation to emerge victorious, the battle for autarchy had to be fought on multiple fronts. To emphasize this point, the pavilion's prescribed path ended at a personified statue of Italia as the goddess of agriculture and war by the sculptor Romeo Gregori, the

Figure 3.3. Collage from MAMI's exhibition catalogue that features the wooden ribs of the Pavilion of Arms designed by Mario De Renzi. Wolfsonian Museum.

same artist who crafted the giant aluminum eagle.[47] MAMI thus portrayed the fight for minerals and food as entwined.

Another pavilion that addressed one of the regime's most important causes was the Pavilion of Land Reclamation, where the exhibition and architecture drew connections between mineral autarchy and agriculture. A team of architects designed the pavilion with wood and brick masonry, two autarchic materials, to feature the regime's progress in building new towns. In the central court called the "Hall of Autarchy," a statue of a brawny man emerged from a circular black void, representing the regime's process of transforming barren land into fertile agricultural landscape. Other parts of the pavilion focused on the role of technology in the redemption process. However, unlike other exhibitions on land reclamation that relied on abundant images, collages, and scale models of weirs that "disciplined water,"[48] MAMI's pavilion included a functional water pump in its courtyard. Removed from the context of a pumping station, this single pump became a sculpture in the center of a fountain within the Pavilion of Land Reclamation.

What distinguished MAMI and the PNF exhibitions at the Circus Maximus from other fascist exhibitions was the way in which both created a simulacrum through the imbrication of the real and the hyperreal. In the pavilions, photographs and photocollages of extraction sites were placed next to raw materials. These were then juxtaposed with charts, data, maps, and explanatory texts by experts, oftentimes the presidents and specialists of mineral unions, as well as quotes and maxims by the Duce and his functionaries. In addition to the abovementioned water pump at the Pavilion of Land Reclamation, a life-size oil derrick was erected by the General Italian Oil Company (*Azienda Generale Italiana Petroli*—AGIP) in the center of Paniconi and Pediconi's Pavilion of Liquid and Gas Combustibles. AGIP's geologists and members of the Italian Geological Society installed the functional rig at MAMI to conduct actual borehole drilling at the Circus Maximus.[49] The derrick soared far above MAMI's buildings, serving as a vertical visual anchor, and its latticed structure was replicated by a series of four fasces that lined the southern side of the exhibition's entrance. The largest and most impressive simulacrum was a "functional" marble quarry staffed with workers operating saws, pulleys, and carts that transported blocks of cut rock to the ground at the Circus Maximus. A representation of a generic, traditional quarry in the Carrara area of Tuscany, the simulacrum at MAMI included the "most rational system for pulling large stones from the mountains" and a central piazza to cut the marble into blocks.[50] By populating many exhibits with people operating machinery, chiseling stones, and casting metal, the PNF effectively transformed MAMI into a theme park for fascist edutainment. The spectacle of the simulacra made construction materials intrinsic to defining the fascist state and its Italianness.

MAMI was especially adept at blending the real and hyperreal in its mining pavilions as a way to emphasize the growing importance of carbon and metalliferous resources for an increasingly bellicose Italy. Photographs of actual mining shafts through-

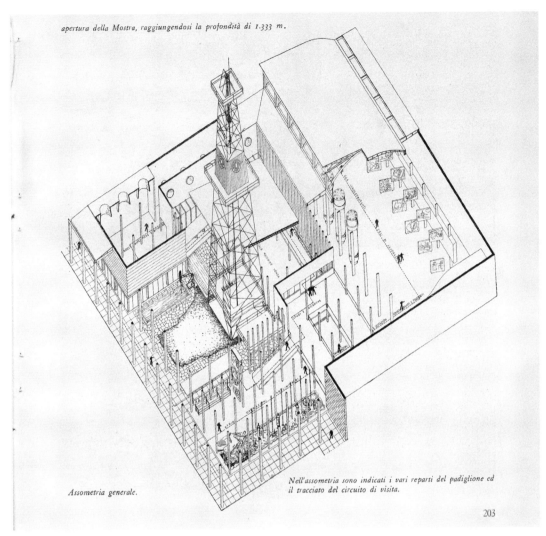

Figure 3.4. Axonometric drawing of the Pavilion of Liquid and Gas Combustibles designed by Mario Paniconi and Giulio Pediconi with a functional oil derrick. *Architettura: rivista del Sindacato nazionale fascista architetti*, April 1939.

out the Italian peninsula and extrapeninsular territories were placed next to one-to-one mockups of generic tunnels, and mineral samples were exhibited together with scale models of mining sites and new towns. In several pavilions, trabeated wooden structures and tracks for carts were built above ground to imitate subterranean mining tunnels. Adding to this physical experience, visitors encountered photographs and statues of Mussolini wearing a miner's coverall throughout the exhibition. One of the most popular images of the *Duce minatore* (Mussolini the miner) at MAMI was based on the manipulation of a photograph originally by the Istituto Luce, the regime's official

Figure 3.5. A "functional" marble quarry simulates stonecutting at the exhibition. Luce Historical Archive, Rome.

photo agency, taken during Mussolini's visit to the sulfur mines at Grottacalda, Sicily, in August 1937. Like other representations of Mussolini as ideal fascist—such as the *Duce aviatore* (aviator), *Duce sciatore* (skier), and *Duce trebbiatore* (wheat thresher)—the *Duce minatore,* so ubiquitously featured at MAMI, had become an emblem that symbolized Italy's efforts at mineral autarchy.[51] The same image was constantly reproduced in different types of media, from journals to Luce newsreels, but it also showed up at exhibits outside Rome that related to MAMI's theme of mineral autarchy. For example, the same manipulated photograph from Mussolini's visit to Grottacalda had already been displayed at large scale in the Exhibition of Sardinian Extractive Industries *(Mostra delle industrie estrattive della Sardegna)* in October 1937.[52]

While the replica tunnels in the various pavilions at MAMI had no precise referent, the scale models were linked to exact mining sites primarily in the Italian islands and colonies. Models and photographs represented the topography and industrial practices of extracting, processing, and transporting fossil fuel resources, but there was heavy emphasis on the development of coal-mining new towns with modern, Rationalist architecture. Carbonia in Sardinia, the seventh fascist new town, featured prominently at MAMI as the crowning jewel of Italy's autarchic drive.[53] Inaugurated on December 18, 1938, by Mussolini, Carbonia was founded by the fascist regime to provide housing for the workers in the nearby coalfields of the Sulcis region. Standing on the *arengario,* the balcony, of the *Torre Littoria* in Carbonia's central piazza, the Duce called his "engineer, technician, and worker comrades" to action in mining Sulcis coal and contributing to the national autarchic goals.[54] A year prior, the regime had already undertaken experiments in building a coal-mining town in Arsia on the Istrian peninsula. MAMI's scale models and photographs illustrated the successes of both mining new towns, and they reminded exhibition visitors that the regime's land holdings beyond the Italian peninsula needed to be further exploited for the new fascist empire.

Even though MAMI appeared to have concentrated principally on the extraction of primary materials in Italy and its territories, the exhibition had a significant impact on the architecture and construction industries in the late 1930s. Building materials became the tools of representation as they moved from the earth to the construction site, and the exhibition clarified how boosting Italy's underground extractions would affect architecture in several ways. As MAMI's architects had used the exhibition's ephemeral setting to experiment with material, structure, and style while observing fascist autarchic rules, they later adapted similar forms and materials to buildings in more permanent settings, as at EUR. At MAMI, scale models represented the regime's many architectural projects tied to mining, and included new towns in the Rationalist style as well as new hospitals and schools for the "defense of race in the mining sector."[55] Less conspicuous at the exhibition was the growth in architectural material research that developed from the constraints of the trade sanctions and gave rise to novel uses for domestic materials such as stone and glass as well as the popularization of a plethora of new composite materials. The exhibition inspired Italian architects to explore new construction methods, the results of which would only become obvious after the fall of fascism, when postwar challenges demanded their inventive skills once again.

Notes

1. I use the spelling "autarchy" throughout this essay because I believe it best reflects the fascist Italian concept of *autarchia,* which encompasses both autarky (a national policy of economic self-sufficiency) and autarchy (absolute sovereignty). This is also the spelling that the fascist regime used in its English-language materials.
2. Among the most prolific scholars on these subjects is Sergio Poretti. See, for example, *Italian Modernisms: Architecture and Construction in the Twentieth Century* (Rome: Gangemi, 2013); "Modernismi e autarchia negli anni trenta," in *Storia dell'architettura italiana: il primo Novecento* (Milan: Electa, 2004), 442–75; and "Tecniche di costruzione fra modernismo e autarchia," *Roma moderna e contemporanea,* no. 2 (1995): 775–96.
3. Scholarship on the architecture of Pier Luigi Nervi is abundant. Notable publications on Nervi's oeuvre include Thomas Leslie, *Beauty's Rigor: Patterns of Production in the Work of Pier Luigi Nervi* (Urbana and Chicago: University of Illinois Press, 2017); Claudia Greco, *Pier Luigi Nervi: Dai primi brevetti al Palazzo delle Esposizioni di Torino, 1917–1948* (Lausanne: Heinz Wirz, 2014); Tullia Iori and Sergio Poretti, eds., *Pier Luigi Nervi: Architettura come sfida* (Milan: Electa, 2010); Tullia Iori, *Pier Luigi Nervi* (Milan: Motta Architettura, 2009); and Ada Louise Huxtable, *Pier Luigi Nervi* (New York: G. Braziller, 1960).
4. The most comprehensive review of MAMI's architecture is "Mostra autarchica del minerale italiano," *Architettura* 18, no. 4 (April 1939): 197–235.
5. Jeffrey T. Schnapp, "Mostre," in *Kunst und Propaganda im Streit der Nationen 1930–1945,* ed. Hans-Jorg Czech and Nikola Doll, Deutsches Historisches Museum, Berlin (Dresden: Sandstein Verlag, 2007), 60.
6. See, for example, Jeffrey T. Schnapp, *Anno X. La Mostra della Rivoluzione fascista del 1932: genesi—sviluppo–contesto culturale-storico—ricezione* (Rome and Pisa: Istituti Editoriali e Poligrafici Internazionali, 2003); Marla Stone, "The Anatomy of a Propaganda Event: the Mostra della rivoluzione fascista, 1932," *Carte Italiane* 1, no. 12 (1992): 30–40; Marla Stone, "Staging Fascism: The Exhibition of the Fascist Revolution," *Journal of Contemporary History* 28, no. 2 (April 1993): 215–43; Aristotle Kallis, "Exhibiting Fascism in Rome: The 1932 Exhibition of the Fascist Revolution (MdRF)," in *The Third Rome, 1922–1943: The Making of the Fascist Capital* (Basingstoke: Palgrave Macmillan, 2014), 201–10; and Terry Kirk, "Marcello Piacentini, the Mostra della Rivoluzione Fascista, and the University of Rome," in *The Architecture of Modern Italy, Volume II: Visions of Utopia, 1900–Present* (New York: Princeton Architectural Press, 2005), 84–94.
7. On the Mostra Augustea della Romanità, see, for example, Kallis, "The 1937 Mostra Augustea della Romanità," in *The Third Rome, 1922–1943,* 211–16; Joshua Arthurs, "The Totalitarian Museum: The Mostra Augustea della Romanità, 1937–1938," in *Excavating Moder-*

nity: The Roman Past in Fascist Italy (Ithaca and London: Cornell University Press, 2012), 91–124; and Flavia Marcello, "Mussolini and the Idealisation of Empire: The Augustan Exhibition of Romanità," *Modern Italy* 16, no. 3 (July 2011): 223–47.

8. Scholarship on the four PNF exhibitions at the Circus Maximus include Schnapp, "Mostre"; Kallis, "The PNF Exhibitions at the Circo Massimo (1937–39)," in *The Third Rome*; Aristotle Kallis, "The Factory of Illusions in the 'Third Rome': Circus Maximus as a Space of Fascist Simulation," *Fascism* 3 (2014): 20–45; and Flavia Matitti, "Note sulla presenza degli artisti alle mostre del Circo Massimo, 1937–1938," in *La capitale a Roma: Città e arredo urbano; 1870–1945*, ed. Luisa Cardilli and Anna Cambedda Napolitano (Rome: Carte Segrete, 1991), 132–39.

9. Mussolini made his Ascension Day speech on May 26, 1927. In it, he called for Italian women to be more productive to increase the Italian population from forty to sixty million in twenty-five years in order for Italy to occupy a position of authority. An English translation of Mussolini's full speech was published in the *New York Times* on May 29, 1927, p. 12. For more on the fascist Italian demographic campaign, see Carl Ipsen, *Dictating Demography: The Problem of Population in Fascist Italy* (Cambridge: Cambridge University Press, 1996).

10. For more information on the Mostra nazionale del tessile, see Eugenia Paulicelli, "The Intelligent Fibres: Between Innovation and Autarchy," in *Fashion under Fascism: Beyond the Black Shirt* (Oxford and New York: Berg, 2004), 99–120; and Mario Lupano and Alessandra Vaccari, eds., *Fashion at the Time of Fascism: Italian Modernist Lifestyle, 1922–1943* (Bologna: Damiani, 2009), 268–77.

11. The genesis of fascist Italian autarchy can be traced to a succession of events that began with Mussolini's invasion of Ethiopia on October 3, 1935, which turned into a protracted conflict that lasted until February 1937. To condemn Italy, the League of Nations imposed sanctions on November 18, 1935, a date that would become highly symbolic and a fascist rhetorical device. These trade restrictions prompted the regime's inevitable move toward autarchy.

12. Architects vigorously debated the impact of autarchy on Italian architecture in newspapers and journals. A series of articles was published in *Il Giornale d'Italia* in the column "Per l'Autarchia" in July of 1938. Some of these included: Marcello Piacentini, "Politica dell'architettura, I. Bilancio del razionalismo," July 13; Marcello Piacentini, "Politica dell'architettura, II. Nuova rinascita," July 15; Marcello Piacentini, "Politica dell'architettura, III. Riforme concrete," July 17; Gio Ponti, "Idee di Gio Ponti sulla politica dell'architettura," July 19–21; and Pierluigi Nervi, "I problemi economici delle costruzioni e la politica dell'architettura," July 23.

13. Michelangelo Sabatino, "The Politics of *Mediterraneità* in Italian Modernist Architecture," in *Modern Architecture and the Mediterranean: Vernacular Dialogues and Contested Identities*, ed. Jean-François Lejeune and Michelangelo Sabatino (London and New York: Routledge, 2010), 60; and Michelangelo Sabatino, *Pride in Modesty: Modernist Architecture and the Vernacular Tradition in Italy* (Toronto: University of Toronto Press, 2010), 92–127; and for a concise summary of the history of reinforced concrete in Italy, see Tullia Iori, "Engineers in Italian Architecture. The Role of Reinforced Concrete in the First Half of the Twentieth Century," *Proceedings of the Second International Congress on Construction History, Queen's*

College, Cambridge University, 29 March to 2 April 2006, vol. 2 (Exeter, UK: Short Run Press, 2006), 1981–95; and Maria Giulia Marziliano, "Cultura tecnologica e autarchia," in *"L'Italia che si rinnova": Contributo al Quadro interpretative delle dinamiche di trasformazione nella cultura tecnologica del Progetto, 1922–1945* (Santarcangelo di Romagna: Maggioli Editore, 2010), 93–158.

14. Partito Nazionale Fascista (PNF), *Guida della mostra: L'autarchia del minerale italiano* (1938), 107–9; and Partito Nazionale Fascista (PNF), *Mostra autarchica del minerale italiano* (Milan: Officine Grafiche Esperia, 1938), 180.

15. Regio Decreto Legge n. 1326, *Nuove disposizioni che vietano l'impiego del cemento armato e del ferro nelle costruzioni ed in alcuni altri usi*, September 7, 1939.

16. Angelo Giuffrida, "Esame generale della limitazione d'impiego dei materiali d'importazione nelle costruzioni civili," *Annali dei Lavori pubblici* (August 1938): 633.

17. Tullia Iori, *Il cemento armato in Italia dalle origini alla seconda guerra mondiale* (Roma: Gangemi, 2001), 158–60 and Poretti, *Italian Modernisms*, 135–6.

18. Istituto per gli studi di politica internazionale, *Autarchy* (Milan: Industrie Grafiche A. Nicola & C., 1938), 24. This pamphlet was published in English and therefore was propaganda intended for a foreign audience.

19. PNF, *Guida della mostra*, 1–3; and PNF, *Mostra autarchica del minerale italiano*, 27–37.

20. See, for example, Francesco Krecic, "Gustavo Pulitzer Finali and the Genesis of Arsia, the White Town of Coal," in *The Presence of Italian Architects in Mediterranean Countries, Proceedings of the First International Conference: Bibliotheca Alexandrina, Chatby, Alexandria, November 15–16, 2007* (Florence: Maschietto Editore, 2008), 256–65.

21. PNF, *Mostra autarchica del minerale italiano*, 134–44.

22. PNF, *Mostra autarchica del minerale italiano*, 133.

23. Aaron Gillette, *Racial Theories in Fascist Italy* (London and New York: Routledge, 2002), 83.

24. Elizabeth Emma Ferry, *Not Ours Alone: Patrimony, Value, and Collectivity in Contemporary Mexico* (New York: Columbia University Press, 2005), 7.

25. The printed advertisement shows different photographs from the exhibition, including the visits by King Victor Emmanuel III, Mussolini, Neville Chamberlain, and Lord Halifax, as well as a perspective view of the exhibition.

26. On the role and contribution of scientists, especially those of the National Council for Research (*Consiglio Nazionale delle Ricerche*—CNR), to fascist autarchy, see Roberto Maiocchi, *Gli scienziati del duce: Il ruolo dei ricercatori e del CNR nella politica autarchica* (Rome: Carocci, 2003).

27. On fascist fertility and pronatalism, see Ipsen, *Dictating Demography*, 173–83; on women's duty to reproduce, see Victoria De Grazia, *How Fascism Ruled Women: Italy, 1922–1945* (Berkeley: University of California Press, 1992), 41–76, and Perry Willson, *Women in Twentieth-Century Italy* (New York: Palgrave Macmillan, 2010), 61–78.

28. MAMI's emphasis on mineral excess went beyond the displays of Nazi Germany's 1934 exhibition *Deutsches Volk—Deutsche Arbeit* in Berlin that focused on German work. In the Hall of Energy and Technology, Ludwig Mies van der Rohe and Lilly Reich designed the mining exhibit and Walter Gropius and Joost Schmidt designed the nonferrous metals exhibit. Mies and Reich's exhibit had freestanding walls made of rock salt and coal. While

MAMI did not use minerals to form architectural elements, it featured piles of raw materials throughout the exhibition. Michael Tymkiw, *Nazi Exhibition Design and Modernism* (Minneapolis: University of Minnesota Press, 2018), 41–51.

29. The fascist concept of *bonifica* was central to its vision of modernity. Originally referring to land reclamation, especially in the Pontine Marshes south of Rome, it soon broadened to include other aspects of life, such as humanity, culture, agriculture, and even leading to the idea of "total reclamation *[bonifica integrale]*." Ruth Ben-Ghiat explains that *bonifica* became a technocratic social planning device that reflected the scientific thinking of the regime. Ruth Ben-Ghiat, *Fascist Modernities: Italy, 1922–1945* (Berkeley: University of California Press, 2001), 4–6. Suzanne Stewart-Steinberg further elaborates on Ben-Ghiat's analysis by examining the concept of reclamation itself. Suzanne Stewart-Steinberg, "Reclamation," *Political Concepts: A Critical Lexicon*, issue 3 (November 2016), https://www.politicalconcepts.org/reclamation-suzanne-stewart-steinberg/. On the reclamation process, architecture, and planning of the Pontine Marshes, see for example Federico Caprotti, *Mussolini's Cities: Internal Colonialism in Italy, 1930–1939* (Youngstown, N.Y.: Cambria Press, 2007); Diane Ghirardo, *Building New Communities: New Deal America and Fascist Italy* (Princeton: Princeton University Press, 1989); and Helga Stave Tvinnereim, *Agro Pontino: Urbanism and Regional Development in Lazio under Benito Mussolini* (Portland, Ore.: International Specialized Book Service Inc., 2007).

30. The exhibition was copiously photographed and filmed by the Istituto Luce, the official documentary agency of the fascist regime. The newsreels included visits by Mussolini, the king, and fascist officials, "Mussolini inaugura a Circo Massimo la mostra autarchica del minerale italiano" (Giornale Luce B1415, November 23, 1938); "Il Re visita la 'Mostra autarchica del minerale italiano' accompagnato dal segretario del partito" (Giornale Luce B1419, November 30, 1938); and "Alfieri visita la mostra autarchica del minerale italiano, accompagnando i dipendenti del Ministero della cultura popolare" (Giornale Luce B1422, December 7, 1938).

31. Herf explains his concept of "reactionary modernism" in Jeffrey Herf, *Reactionary Modernism: Technology, Culture, and Politics in Weimar and the Third Reich* (Cambridge: Cambridge University Press, 1984), 1–17.

32. Herf, *Reactinoary Modernism*, 182–84; and Heinrich Hardensett, *Der kapitalistische und der technische Mensch* (Munich and Berlin: Verlag von R. Oldenbourg, 1932), 5.

33. Herf points out that Hardensett's "capitalist man" was represented by "Jews and other transient groups," so the division between capitalist and technical man was also along racial lines. Herf, *Reactionary Modernism,* 182.

34. See, for example, Marcello Piacentini, "Per l'autarchia politica dell'architettura, II. Nuova rinascita," *Il giornale d'Italia* 38, no. 167 (July 15, 1938): 3; Giuseppe Gorla, "Autarchia nelle costruzioni edili," *Rassegna di architettura* 38, no. 1 (January 1938): 34–35.

35. "Mostra autarchica del minerale italiano," *Architettura*, 197.

36. A parallel situation occurred in Nazi Germany whereby architects used stone and brick masonry instead of steel, glass, and reinforced concrete due to wartime material shortage, especially of metal. However, in Germany the use of masonry was further manipulated by Albert Speer to cater to Hitler's aesthetic preference of neoclassicism, and as such, into an ideological implication for propaganda. Paul Jaskot, *The Architecture of Oppression: The SS,*

Forced Labor, and the Nazi Monumental Building Economy (London and New York: Routledge, 2000), 57–58.

37. Claudio Longo, "Mostra autarchica del minerale italiano," *Architettura*, 199.
38. Claudio Longo, "Mostra autarchica del minerale italiano," *Architettura*, 200.
39. On aluminum and fascist Italian autarchy, see Marco Bertilorenzi, "The Italian Aluminum Industry: Cartels, Multinationals and the Autarkic Phase, 1917–1943," *Cahiers d'histoire de l'aluminium* 41 (2008): 42–71. Jeffrey Schnapp has also written on the importance of aluminum to the development of Italian coffee culture in the domestic realm in Jeffrey T. Schnapp, "The Romance of Caffeine and Aluminum," *Critical Inquiry* 28 (Autumn 2001): 244–69.
40. "Mostra autarchica del minerale italiano," *Architettura*, 214–15. Photographs and descriptions of this pavilion can be found in PNF, *Mostra autarchica del minerale italiano*, 15–18.
41. PNF, *Mostra autarchica del minerale italiano*, 16.
42. "Mostra autarchica del minerale italiano," *Architettura*, 216.
43. Gennaro Tampone, "Architettura lignea 1920–1940 in Italia e Germania," *Bollettino ingegneri*, no. 1–2 (2008): 10; and Gennaro Tampone, "Strutture e costruzioni autarchiche di legno in Italia e Colonie: Caratteri e criteri di conservazione," *Bollettino ingegneri*, no. 11 (2002).
44. "Mostra autarchica del minerale italiano," *Architettura*, 227.
45. Legnami Passotti's advertisements from this period often included the phrase "Autarchia!" Some advertisements even featured photographs of De Renzi's Pavilion of Arms at MAMI, while others mentioned that this construction method has been widely used in Italy and its colonies.
46. Images of the wooden parabolic arches appeared on several pages of the exhibition's catalog. PNF, *Mostra autarchica del minerale italiano*, 3–4, 12.
47. This sculpture of Italia was most likely made of marble as the sculptor Romeo Gregori, born in Carrara, specialized in this material.
48. For example, the 1932 National Exhibition on Land Reclamation (*Mostra nazionale delle Bonifiche*) in Rome organized by Arrigo Serpieri.
49. The records of this exploratory borehole are conserved in the Georesource Archive at the Italian Ministry of Economic Development. For the history of the Circus Maximus borehole and its drilling rig, see Alessio Argentieri, Giuseppe Capelli, and Roberto Mazza, "Il sondaggio 'Circo Massimo' (Roma 1939), un sito della memoria geologica," *Acque Sotterranee—Italian Journal of Groundwater* (2019): 79–83.
50. PNF, *Mostra autarchica del minerale italiano*, 127.
51. Angelo Pietro Desole argues that photographs of mining during the autarchic period clearly conveyed fascism's ideological agenda even though they often appeared to be documents of industrial activities. Desole examines, especially, the *Duce minatore* image and its replication. Angelo Pietro Desole, "Costruire il futuro: L'industria mineraria e il ruolo della fotografia modernista durante il fascismo," *Rivista di studi di fotografia*, no. 4 (2016): 46–67.
52. Images of the *Duce minatore* showed up repeatedly on the walls of this exhibition. Istituto Luce, "Mostra delle industrie estrattive della Sardegna" (Gornale Luce B118306, October 13, 1937).
53. PNF, *Mostra autarchica del minerale italiano*, 26–41.

54. Part of Mussolini's speech, "Il discorso di Carbonia," was reprinted in PNF, *Mostra autarchica del minerale italiano,* 26. For an analysis of this speech, see Paola Atzeni, "Il discorso di Carbonia: 'logos e polis,'" *La ricerca folklorica,* no. 58 "Linee di sangue: Metafore e pratiche tra dono, filiazione e appartenenza" (October 2008): 121–36.
55. This is the name of a pavilion at MAMI. Angelo Tarchi, president of the Council on the Defense of Race in the Mining Sector, describes the rationale of the pavilion and its exhibition components in PNF, *Mostra autarchica del minerale italiano,* 200.

Chapter 4

The Concrete Politics of Housing

Assembling Cecap Guarulhos in Authoritarian Brazil

José H. Bortoluci

When is a building complete? João Vilanova Artigas, in the public exam required for his return to the School of Architecture of the University of São Paulo (FAU–USP) as a full professor in 1984, asserts categorically that architecture "does not exist on paper." According to him, in order to exist, architecture has to acquire materiality beyond the apparatus of design. At the same time, Artigas repeatedly argued that design was a crucial practice through which architects could engage in the production of a new society. *Desenho,* one of the terms in Portuguese for "design," designates the drawing and, as its etymology suggests, an instrument to help define the *desígnio* ("intention" or "outline") of the built environment and of society.[1]

This chapter looks at a housing project designed by a team that Artigas led, but it also attempts to challenge his understanding of the centrality of design—a conception of the built environment that, among other things, offered him political justification to continue working as an architect during the military dictatorship in Brazil. The built environment is continuously produced through intersecting practices of design, construction, and habitation. This continuous process of assemblage articulates materials, spaces, and ideologies at play in any given historical conjuncture. The bid for hegemony, in the case of the built environment, is played out through the articulation of ideas, but also through plans, charts, laws, spreadsheets, bricks, and concrete. Through this articulation, the built environment works as an arena for disputes about power and hegemony.

The idea of *articulation* has been fruitful in contemporary debates in sociology and political theory. Ernesto Laclau and Chantal Mouffe, in an influential post-Marxist theory of the political, mobilize the concept of articulation to develop a theory of hegemony that deals with the problem of constituting a "people."[2] They define articulation as "any practice establishing a relation among elements such that their identity is modified as a result of the articulatory practice."[3] The dynamic of hegemony, then—and, in a certain sense, the political as such—is the pragmatic, contextual articulation of different democratic demands in a hegemonic discourse that establishes internal relations of equivalence and external relations of difference between "the people" and other members of society (namely, the elites). By the constitution and deployment of that discourse, a political collective may advance a bid for hegemony within a certain political community by articulating the image of a people with certain demands for rights and for political participation.

In a different tradition, the idea of articulation finds resonance in Bruno Latour's description of the formation of assemblages between humans and nonhuman actants.[4] My concept of articulation captures the discursive and material (or nonhuman) dimensions of both definitions. Articulation is therefore the process through which elements of political repertoires and the built environment are sewn together by means of semiotic and material practices, leading to the transformation of those constitutive elements. Architecture acquires a different dimension in this interpretation as a type of material object activated by political life as well as by populations of makers and users. Its interpretation requires the context and a view of the dynamics of construction and use to become meaningful in a historical sense.

This chapter thus looks at the articulation of Cecap Guarulhos, a housing project designed by a group of eminent architects (including Artigas) who understood it as a laboratory for the industrial development of the country, but also for the development of a sense of collective life and, possibly, an active working-class identity among the dwellers—in an absolute challenge to the directives of the authoritarian government of the time. This progressive ideology had to coexist in continuous conflict and negotiation with two other ideologies: the authoritarian national developmentalism of the military dictatorship, and the repertoires embodied in the expectations and practices of Cecap's residents.

Cecap Guarulhos (also known by other names, such as Cecap Zezinho Magalhães, Cecap Cumbica, and Parque Cecap) was planned as a city within a city. When complete, the project was to have 10,519 units.[5] The architects and planners involved in the project calculated that, when finished, the project would house fifty-five thousand people—a population larger than 94 percent of Brazilian cities at the time. It was to have the same dimensions as the mythical Conjunto Urbano Nonoalco Tlatelolco in Mexico City, the paradigmatic case of the ideology of public housing via state intervention in Latin America in the 1960s. But the project's scale was not the only reason for the general excitement that Cecap raised among progressive architects and planners, despite the authoritarian context of the time. The involvement of some of the key names in the field in São Paulo (particularly Artigas, the most prominent brutalist architect in São Paulo and a known leftist activist who had been arrested by the military regime a few years before the commission and who would be compulsorily retired from his position at FAU–USP while he worked on Cecap's design) made this project unique. The project was meant to ignite a process of rationalization of the construction industry that, in the most optimistic estimates, could transform housing design and construction in Brazil.[6]

The process would not be devoid of contradictions. During the late 1960s and early 1970s, the military regime imposed an unprecedented level of repression on militants, students, intellectuals, workers, and any individual or institution that opposed its rule. At the same time, it promoted a "conservative developmentalism," with significant public investment in the construction of all sorts of projects, from highways and dams to housing complexes and urban infrastructure. This growing investment in construction provided new work opportunities even to some of the most persecuted architects in São Paulo, such as Paulo Mendes da Rocha and Artigas.

In what follows, I develop a historical ethnography of the social life of Cecap Guarulhos, the most important housing project developed in São Paulo in the 1960s and an important experiment in terms of the practices and discourses of the brutalist program for low-income housing elaborated within the progressive, culturally dominant sector of the field of architecture in the mid-twentieth century.[7]

The Dictatorship's Standpoint: Housing as Job Creation

The creation of Banco Nacional de Habitação (National Housing Bank—BNH) in August 1964, only four months after the coup that instituted the military dictatorship in Brazil, was a preemptive act meant to address potential unrest in Brazil's largest cities. The contraction of wages across most economic sectors together with the continuous expansion of urban areas posed a double pressure on the urban poor during the regime. The population of the city of São Paulo increased by six million from 1960 to 1985, and the entire metropolitan region increased by ten million individuals—a significant indicator of the dimension of housing needs. The construction boom that BNH helped to foster was crucial to incorporating part of the growing urban population into the job market as well as creating the generalized illusion that even the poorest of urban dwellers would be able to afford a home. The bank provided credit for the construction industry through other public and private banks and for municipal or state agencies (such as Cecap, in São Paulo) that were directly responsible for commissioning and building housing projects.

The military regime understood the construction industry as a key mechanism in incorporating the growing undertrained labor force into the economy productively. This industry was to be the main governmentally subsidized channel to "absorb labor," as the First National Development Plan clearly stated.[8] This understanding of the place of housing construction in the larger political economy of the regime illustrates how the government attempted to maintain certain elements of the politics of national developmentalism, cherished by large sectors of the left, within an authoritarian political framework, at the same time adopting mechanisms that would perpetuate Brazil's economic inequality and relatively low levels of productivity.

BNH's policies were eminently oriented toward quantitative concerns. The bank financed the construction of 4.4 million housing units from 1964 until its demise in 1986; only 13 percent of the invested resources were channeled to low-income housing, while the largest share was appropriated by the real estate market for the construction of units that only the middle and upper classes could afford.[9] The newspapers and popular magazines of the late 1960s and throughout the 1970s are rife with advertisements for new apartment buildings in São Paulo, which was then in the midst of frantic horizontal (with the outwardly growing peripheries) and vertical expansion (with the new middle-class apartment buildings blossoming in the central neighborhoods). In an official BNH publication, the president of the bank provided an overview of the challenges it faced: given the population growth rate, the bank needed to fund the construction of five million new housing units in addition to 1.5 million units to replace the decaying existent housing stock.[10] In the same publication, the bank's president reiterated a reputedly federal directive: the *housing question,* from the government's perspective, was primarily a *job creation question.*

> In the construction sector, traditional means of production are preferred at this time, given the need to create jobs for the nonqualified workforce. Modern industrial methods of production, though, might be objects of study and experiment, but their use in Brazil is premature, also because they are usually more expensive than traditional methods that employ low-skilled, low-wage labor. The construction sector is the one that has more successfully fulfilled the need to create jobs, and it should continue to be for years a bastion of job creation in our country.[11]

The bank failed to deliver the initially proposed number of low-income units, and the practice of autoconstruction in peripheral areas continued to be the most important form of housing provision. Concurrently, the bank's directive to promote low-wage, labor-intensive construction jobs led to the perpetuation of traditional construction techniques and archaic methods of labor control at the construction site. BNH consciously hindered the industrialization of construction and the development of Taylorist methods of labor management, at the same time transferring resources to construction companies that profited from the construction boom the bank financed. This process was part of a larger strategy of economic growth that nonetheless maintained low wages, gradually worsening the already drastic economic inequality in Brazil.

The Architect's Plan: Cecap as a Laboratory for the Industrialization of Construction

The fact that the federal government was not directly responsible for the construction of the housing units that it funded through BNH opened space for semiautonomous action on the part of state and municipal housing agencies (although they could seldom reverse the general regulations BNH imposed). That was the case in the state of São Paulo in the late 1960s, when the directors of Cecap could use its relative autonomy to propose an ambitious program of low-income housing.

This endeavor was carried out under the initial leadership of José Maria Magalhães de Almeida Prado. Despite his conservative political trajectory, Magalhães is usually described as a pragmatic politician. Also, he had family members in the Communist Party—possibly his brother—who must have provided a first channel of communication between him and Ruy Gama, a leftist architect who worked in a state agency. Gama was hired by Magalhães to work at Cecap and coordinate the planning and execution of Cecap Guarulhos. According to later recollections of several architects involved in the project, Gama was one of the masterminds behind Cecap Guarulhos and was responsible for appointing the progressive architects who would be involved in the design and construction of Cecap Zezinho Magalhães—the largest and most important of Cecap's projects, named for the president of the agency after his sudden death in 1969.

Cecap was a feeble, unimportant state agency before Magalhães's presidency. Magalhães had the ears of São Paulo Governor Abreu Sodré and a strong connection with key figures in the state and federal governments. Two of his first acts as Cecap's president were the incorporation of the large land lot where Cecap would be built, a 1,780,000-square-meter (180-hectare) property that belonged to one of the state banks.[12] Magalhães and the state government recognized the importance of the region, strategically located in a key national corridor connecting São Paulo and Rio de Janeiro. The large piece of land was located nineteen kilometers (almost twelve miles) from the municipality of São Paulo and was part of Guarulhos, a city in the metropolitan region that was predicted to grow exponentially in the following years. This prediction proved true: its population rose from 13,439 people in 1940 to 530,000 in 1980, during the last phase of Cecap's construction. Today, Guarulhos has the second-largest population in the state of São Paulo, with 1.3 million inhabitants.[13]

Magalhães initially hired Fábio Penteado to design the project. Penteado was a respected architect trained at FAU–Mackenzie; his lack of involvement with politics was also a positive factor in his hiring. Penteado came from a wealthy family and would not raise any political "red flag," so to speak. But Gama and Penteado persuaded Magalhães to also hire Artigas and Paulo Mendes da Rocha. Artigas, together with Mendes da Rocha and Penteado, coordinated the work of a team of architects in an independent office relatively distant from the inner workings of Cecap. They also had the support of other firms that provided sociological studies on potential residents as well as technical assistance for the planning of the infrastructural systems of Cecap (urbanism, sanitation, and so on).

Industrialization was widely praised among architects in São Paulo in the 1950s and 1960s. It was commonly described as a seed of national progress to which architects could contribute. Cecap was designed under this ideology. Apartment buildings and other facilities—which were to include six schools, a stadium, several shopping areas, a social club, and a hospital—were designed to be built with prefabricated, light, concrete pieces. Beams, slabs, stairs, and other smaller components would be precast in a nearby factory and assembled at the construction site. The architects drew all the necessary pieces, which they expected would be cast in a concrete plant next to Cecap that BNH would fund. In the design team's proposal, this plant would produce building components not only for Cecap but also for several other housing projects in the region. The prefabrication would also represent savings of 37 percent on concrete when compared to more traditional methods of construction, mainly due to the possibility of fabricating thinner walls and more economical foundations, water, and sewage systems, as well as the fact that it demanded considerably fewer worker hours at the construction site.[14]

The planned community spaces were designed to accommodate the population of the surrounding areas as well, allowing for agglomerations of up to two hundred thousand people.[15] In addition to the push for industrialization, a second value oriented the planning and design of Cecap: the importance of community life and shared public spaces. In a later interview, Artigas articulated these two dimensions of that political repertoire: "I was always sure that there would be a proletarian revolution and that development would result in the creation of a national industry capable of serving our people and rendering favorable the emergence of a working class, as it was envisioned by Karl Marx."[16] At least for Artigas, the community spaces and the corridors that forced a conviviality among future dwellers, as well as the industrialization dynamics that Cecap Guarulhos would trigger, were not to be architectural antidotes against a popular uprising; they would work as limited but hopefully effective instruments for its coming into being—in stark opposition to the directives of the federal government.

The project was deemed exceptional by many important architects and publications of the time. *Veja*, a popular Brazilian weekly, celebrated the fact that "in Guarulhos, Cecap . . . will build 10,560 apartments (480 of which are already finished), writing the richest and most colorful chapter of the painful history of social housing in Brazil."[17] One of the most celebratory statements was published in the pages of *Acrópole*, the chief architectural journal in São Paulo at the time. Eduardo Corona, the editor, argued that

> [architects] created a magnificent design that will actually solve an important problem . . . All this . . . combined with intelligent design and a decent

architecture ... make the Cumbica housing project the most important human, social, economic, and political achievement of recent times in Brazil.[18]

The same *Acrópole* editorial would also emphasize that Cecap's visibility reached an international audience, something quite uncommon for a Brazilian housing project: "Due to its high sense of perfection, it is being discussed in several countries, including the Soviet Union."[19]

Architecture journals also emphasized the two most important principles that informed the project: the valorization of shared spaces and the rational design and construction methods that were to be employed in its construction, without much attention to Artigas's nascent dreams that those spaces could foster a popular revolt.[20] Ruy Gama clearly indicated in a debate at FAU–USP in 1968, on the occasion of the release of Cecap Guarulhos's design, that São Paulo offered a special opportunity for the much-desired industrialization of construction: since Cecap built and sold houses for unionized workers, and given São Paulo's position as the capital of Brazilian industry (concentrating 40 percent of national industrial production) as well as its housing deficit of more than two hundred thousand units, São Paulo had the necessary conditions for the definitive development of industrial methods of construction.[21]

In order to convert these principles into plants, blueprints, and other apparatuses of design, Artigas and his team had to rely on their mind's eye and on available data on the expected future residents.

Who Will Live at Cecap? The Imagined and Existing People

Cecap imposed a few requirements for the purchase of an apartment. Apartments were to be sold to unionized workers, and they were not to exceed sixty square meters (646 square feet)—although they granted an exception in the case of Cecap Guarulhos, where apartments would be sixty-four square meters (689 square feet). Workers with lower salaries would have preference; other criteria included time of unionization, number of children, and time living in São Paulo.

The design team also made use of sociological research to learn more about the potential residents. This research, conducted by Eugenia Paesani, debunked a few of the initial impressions of the architects. For example, Artigas and his team proposed that the units be delivered equipped with all basic appliances, such as ovens and fridges. They even sketched some of these items and started to plan for their future production. Nevertheless, Paesani's report indicated that potential buyers already had access to those items, purchased at standard retail stores. The lower middle class and the working class benefited at the time from the expansion of the Brazilian market and national industry and could have access to these basic items that were considered luxuries only a few years earlier.

This lack of knowledge about basic consumer habits of the potential buyer highlights the distance between the field of architecture and the daily experience of the working classes. This distorted view was remedied during the design and construction process, but those amendments did not radically change the architects' perspective on their connection with "the people." Marina Heck, a sociology student at the time, who worked as a secretary to the design team, remembers that the political potential of the sense of community that the project tried to instill was a central issue for the architects: "They thought they were changing the world . . . They used to interpret what people needed, what they desired. That has always been a discourse at FAU and of architects more generally."[22]

But a contrasting image emerges in the advertisements that circulated in several media vehicles at the time. Those ads show a very distinct image of "the people"—namely, of potential buyers. They appeal not to the image of a destitute working class and evidently not to any potentially disruptive population. Instead, they mobilize commonsensical images of model middle-class families who could appreciate the benefits of living in a calm neighborhood surrounded by green and with ample space for children to play. This is reflected in one of the names under which Cecap was advertised: Parque Cecap (Cecap Park). The image of Cecap as a middle-class garden city was reinforced by renderings that combined a feeling of the peacefulness of a typical suburban neighborhood with the modernity of Cecap's design.

One of the advertisements shows a young couple embracing in front of two of the planned buildings; the main line of the ad points out confidently that "seu sonho aconteceu": "your dream came true." The main aspect of this dream, of course, is the "dream of an owned house"—"a sonho da casa própria," a common epithet of respectability and attainment of dignity in Brazil that all potential buyers could easily recognize and relate to. Another advertisement directly and humorously appealed to the desire for home ownership: it proposed that "instead of envying other people's houses, buy a house that others will envy." During those same years, BNH reinforced on television and in newspaper ads the concept that the ownership of a house would be the pinnacle in terms of family security as well as a sure path to societal integration and social peace. This suburban imagery and framing clashes with the "progressive" concepts that informed the architects' urbanistic imagination for Cecap,[23] but it was seen as a more efficient way to connect with the families that could become interested in the project.

These conflicting imaginations are not merely differences in perspective. The design team had in mind a family with a monthly income of up to 1.5 minimum wages, but Cecap eventually sold units to families with a higher income: the equivalent of three minimum wages or more. Additionally, the apartments sold in the late 1970s had an

The Concrete Politics of Housing

even higher value (5.13 minimum monthly wages on average), as the land prices at Cecap increased considerably with the installation of public facilities and services, with urban improvements, and with the increasing demands for housing in Guarulhos. This population of unionized workers was part of an emergent lower middle class that could afford an apartment at Cecap Guarulhos.

Construction as an Arena of Material and Ideological Battle

The land where Cecap would be built was occupied by around thirty-eight families before construction. It was damp terrain, almost a swamp according to the narrative of several individuals involved in construction. One of the workers who participated in Cecap's construction and who later bought an apartment at the complex remembers that "there was a lot of farming here earlier, and this soil had to be replaced. So we had to replace layers of soil two, three meters deep. Everything was flooded and the houses that existed here were precarious; they belonged to the farmers who lived here."[24] Thus the construction of Cecap began with the dismantling of these farms and the removal of those families and clearing of the terrain.

The first eight apartment buildings were commissioned in 1970 and built using traditional methods and materials after BNH's decision to fund the project only partially.[25] In Penteado's view, the main reason for BNH's refusal to fund the industrial facilities required for the industrial production of construction components and other materials was precisely the bank's mission to provide new jobs in the construction industry. It is unclear, based on available information, how the decision process inside the bank and the federal government led to limiting the investment that could eventually enable the construction of this industrial park. Very likely, lack of interest in the industrialization of construction provided the reason for the final economic decision to finance only a fraction of the initially planned units—a de-escalation that rendered impossible the initial proposal of industrialization. This was the first serious blow to the plans of building Cecap using industrial methods: without the economies of scale that would have ensued from the commission of the entire project, the proposed methods of construction would be prohibitive in terms of cost.

The first stage of construction lasted from 1968 to 1972. Thirty apartment buildings were erected during this phase (1,800 units), all of them with traditional methods. These blocks form the only "freguesia" that was completely erected. During the second stage (1972–76), sixteen new blocks were built (960 units) with a few changes in construction methods and components. Stairs were prefabricated at this stage, and some of the slabs were adapted owing to defects that were found on the first built units.[26] The construction company responsible for the project began to make use of metallic frames and the new, faster method of concrete curing. The third and final stage of construction took place from 1978 to 1981, during which thirty-two blocks (1,920 units) were built, with a few changes in the fabrication of some components, such as stairs and cabinets.[27]

Before the first phase of construction, the design team had to redraw all the pieces and components, which maintained most of their design features but were adapted to construction with concrete cast at the construction site and other traditional methods of construction with concrete—using those customary "tiny wood frames," in architect Giselda Visconti's words. Only in the second phase were some of the components prefabricated, such as stairs and columns, which were produced using steel forms (not wood forms, as in the more traditional and widespread uses of concrete).[28]

Inhabiting Cecap (1970–1990)

Most of the families who initially purchased apartments at Cecap were civil servants such as bank clerks, teachers, and administrative staff in several state departments. Apartments were affordable for those families, according to most of the narratives of some of the first residents. The majority were newlywed couples; in most cases, the husband usually worked in São Paulo and the wife more commonly worked at home.

Inhabiting Cecap involved an adaptation and a negotiation with its modernist environment, with which most families were not familiar. Many of them were living in apartment blocks for the first time. The austere modern design of the housing blocks and their almost industrial-looking materiality caused confusion among most of the families, who were often not used to this type of built environment. At the same time, Cecap's modernist lines and the philosophy of community life that it proposed attracted a few of the initial families. One of the early residents mentioned that the project attracted her and her husband "because it was Artigas's, because of the model, because of the community work, because of the idea of Cecap itself. We fell in love because of what we saw ... because we were idealists, too."

For the families who moved to Cecap in the early 1970s, challenges abounded. Several of the residents had to commute to work daily. This was one of the main complaints of the first families at Cecap: not only were there few bus lines that connected the project and downtown São Paulo, but the housing blocks also were surrounded by mud most of the time.[29] The distance from the city and the lack of local businesses also made the prices at the makeshift local stores (and later, the bakery and the local grocery store) artificially high. Cecap was experienced by the first cohort of residents almost exclusively as a residential neighborhood, a modernist dormitory town. That would be partially remedied in the late 1970s and throughout the 1980s when a few facilities were built at Cecap, increasing the urban services available to the local population.

Floods were frequent, and the promised schools and other community services were built a decade after the first occupation as a result of the organized efforts of Cecap residents. Inhabiting Cecap then involved dealing with incompleteness and having to use the available political channels to demand basic infrastructure and amenities—an experience that was characteristic of most popular neighborhoods in São Paulo. The nearby airport, which would become Brazil's largest and the second most important air hub in Latin America, was also a contentious issue for the first wave of residents. Most of them manifested strong opposition to the project. Many dwellers had serious concerns that the air traffic in the region would lead to unbearable noise, that it would shake the windows unceasingly and could eventually damage the structures of the apartment building. The Community Council campaigned against it, and the local newspaper published several articles alerting the public to the problems that it would bring to the community. These concerns and fears gave way to a more harmonious relationship with the new neighbor: the new airport raised land prices and increased the attractiveness of Cecap, as many current residents suggest.

The class differences between the planned and the actual residents had spatial manifestations in the complex. One of the early residents remembers that "the first complex, São Paulo, was built so that only half would have garages; the other half would not have any spot for parking. The other 50 percent were built by the dwellers. They built it like this because they thought that only half of the people here would have cars, because they would be low-income families who wouldn't be able to afford a car. But this changed, and today you see people with three, four cars, and we need more parking spots."

In this context of struggle, negotiation, and adaptation, the Community Center was a privileged space of community exchange and socialization in the first decade of Cecap's occupation. It also was the space where residents organized the Community Council, the main organization responsible for representing the interests of the dwellers. The council was created at a time of increasing levels of organization in communities throughout the outskirts of São Paulo and was the key voice of the community in its negotiations with public agencies, including city hall.[30] Many old residents also remember the existence and the dynamism of other organizations and community activities, such as carnival parties, frequent soccer matches, and a "Mothers Club." The last worked initially as a provisional school funded partly by the community and partly by the city government, but it was also a space for women's organization and socialization, as interviews with many old residents suggest.

The intense community life that Cecap's design was intended to instill was also received with discomfort by some of the residents, who claimed that it was bothersome to have everyone's eyes turned to them when they purchased a new car or when they arrived late at night.[31] But some of the modern features pleased the residents, such as the open spaces under the buildings, which were used as parking spots and playgrounds for the children.[32]

Until the 1970s the fact that the complex was not surrounded by fences and other apparatuses of security was seen as an advantage. A 1973 news story reports that "lots of things are still missing in these open and colorful blocks, which are often visited by

Figure 4.1. Aerial view of Cecap Guarulhos, 1975. Arquivo Histórico de Guarulhos.

students and authorities, but the dwellers do not complain about three of these things: There is no gate to the complex. No doorman. And no police station."[33] This would change in the next two decades, when residents began to demand and later accomplish the construction of security fences, gates, and the hiring of private security personnel to guard Cecap Guarulhos. This was not just a local process: starting in the 1990s, gated communities multiplied in Brazil, and the language of fear and security became widespread in all sectors of Brazilian society.[34]

In 1977, Cecap had a population of ten thousand people. When some of the first buildings started to present structural problems, the Community Council brought them to the attention of Cecap authorities.[35] In 1980, Cecap, as a state level organization, was closed; BNH, which had funded most of Cecap's projects, would be terminated six years later. In the same year of Cecap's dissolution, a very significant story was published at *Folha de São Paulo*. The story, titled "It Was Supposed to Be a Model, but It Is Only a Failure," narrates the common tale of discrepancy between the project plan and its realization. "The work of famous architects, Parque Cecap Guarulhos was to be the Brazilian model of public housing. But ten years later, it is just a jumble of unfinished

Figure 4.2. View of Parque Cecap surrounded by security fences, 2007. Gabriel Fernandes, CC BY-SA 2.0.

buildings."[36] The story describes several problems of infrastructure as well as the discrepancy between the expected incomers and the actual dwellers.

Residents kept changing Cecap over the years. Also, the population at Cecap changed, especially when compared with the initially imagined profile of the families who would occupy those apartments. In one of the most recent estimates available, roughly fifteen thousand people live at Cecap and around 81 percent of the resident families are apartment owners.[37] By all accounts, the sociability of Cecap today is very similar to many middle-income closed communities that have been built in the São Paulo metropolitan region during the past three decades.[38] Today Cecap Guarulhos is seen as a middle-class apartment complex, and each of the *freguesias* is administered as a typical apartment complex, in relative autonomy from the other complexes.

Cecap as a Continuous Material and Ideological Articulation

All significant projects conducted during those years by the key progressive architects in São Paulo (and certainly in many other contexts) were described as laboratories, but usually with less fanfare than Cecap. An important dimension of the *built environment as a laboratory* is the politics of scale that it entails: the rhetoric of the housing project as a laboratory depends on the assumption that it might work as a knot of circuits of practices that could generate new concepts, techniques, habits, discourses, and materials that could later be replicated elsewhere; for the architects involved, it could potentially work as a gateway between the single and the multiple: a high-intensity knot in a dispute for hegemonic social–spatial projects.

This situated bid for hegemony—that is, in this case, about how the "people" should be constituted as a political subject inside a larger social dispute about the future of Brazilian society in a context of political authoritarianism—had at least three key dimensions that should coincide with the life of the built environment at Cecap, according to the perspective of the architects involved. First, these actors were invested in helping to put in place a new *design* template for low-income housing. Second, the project was expected to transform *construction* technology in Brazil. Finally, in their most hopeful moments, some of the architects expected to radically change people's lives (their *habitation*, broadly understood)—initially the future dwellers' lives, and later the lives of all individuals who would potentially benefit from the design and technical innovations that could spill over from there.

These dimensions were open to dispute and reconfiguration in all their moments, not least because of the radically different understanding about the place of housing in the ideologies of the state and residents. The complex, conflictual, and long-lasting process of articulating Cecap significantly tamed the radical intent of many of the architects involved, but it also generated a quite successful middle-class housing project that continues to evolve with the interventions and rearticulations promoted by its residents. So, one could argue, this complex dispute of ideas and material transformation is still being played out in the way Cecap is a living community and built environment.

Notes

This article is part of a larger dissertation project on the politics of architecture in São Paulo from the mid-1960s to the mid-1990s, funded by fellowships and grants from the Capes Foundation and the Fulbright Foundation as well as the University of Michigan.

1. João Vilanova Artigas, *Caminhos da arquitetura* (São Paulo: Lech, 1981), 39.
2. Ernesto Laclau, *On Populist Reason* (London: Verso, 2007); Ernesto Laclau and Chantal Mouffe, *Hegemony and Socialist Strategy: Towards A Radical Democratic Politics*, 2d ed. (London: Verso, 2014).
3. Laclau and Mouffe, *Hegemony and Socialist Strategy*, 15.
4. Bruno Latour, *Reassembling the Social: An Introduction to Actor-Network-Theory* (New York: Oxford University Press, 2005).
5. In comparison, the infamous Pruitt–Igoe housing project in St. Louis, Missouri, totaled 2,870 apartments, and Queensbridge Houses, the largest housing project in the United States, was composed of 3,142 units.
6. Artigas expresses this excitement very clearly: "Have you ever wondered how much innovation a project like this will foster? The national industry—from floors to finishing as well as

piping—may receive orders for more daring projects; it may test them and rest assured of a solid market—the 10,500 apartments in this project." Artigas quoted in "Uma cidade nova está nascendo em Guarulhos," *Folha de São Paulo* (May 16, 1971): 12.

7. This chapter combines different sources: archival materials (plans, blueprints, and photographs); architectural journals from the period of the design and construction of the project; life history interviews with current and old dwellers; published interviews with late architects involved in the project (João Vilanova Artigas, Ruy Gama, and Fábio Penteado), as well as interviews I conducted with other architects involved; and newspaper stories on the project published from the 1960s until the 1990s.
8. Marta Ferreira Santos Farah, *Processo de trabalho na construção habitacional: tradição e mudança* (São Paulo: Annablume, 1996), 25.
9. Céline Sachs, *São Paulo: políticas públicas e habitação popular,* trans. Cristina Muracho (São Paulo: Editora da Universidade de São Paulo, 1999), 133.
10. Paulo Júlio Valentino Bruna, *Arquitetura, industrialização e desenvolvimento* (São Paulo: Perspectiva, 1976), 108.
11. Bruna, *Arquitetura, industrialização e desenvolvimento,* 119.
12. Fabiana Cerávolo, "A pré-fabricação em concreto armado aplicada a conjuntos habitacionais no Brasil: o caso do 'Conjunto Habitacional Zezinho Magalhães Prado.'" (MA thesis, Universidade de São Paulo, 2007), 66.
13. Tiago Cavalcante Guerra, ed., *Cecap Guarulhos: histórias, identidades e memórias* (São Paulo: Scortecci, 2010), 23.
14. Sylvia Ficher, "Subsídios para um estudo do conjunto habitacional Zezinho Magalhães Prado" (undergraduate thesis, Universidade de São Paulo, 1972).
15. "Cumbica," *Desenho,* outubro, 1971.
16. Alberto Fernando Melchiades Xavier, ed., *Depoimento de uma geração: arquitetura moderna brasileira* (São Paulo: Cosac & Naify, 2003), 218.
17. "O desafio do arquiteto," *Veja* (June 20, 1973): 72.
18. Eduardo Corona, "O Conjunto Habitacional de Cumbica," *Acrópole* 348 (1968): 11–12, 12.
19. Corona, "O Conjunto Habitacional de Cumbica," 11.
20. "Cumbica," *Desenho* (student publication) (October 1970): n.p.; "Conjunto Habitacional em Cumbica," *Acrópole,* 372 (1971): 32–37.
21. "Cumbica," n.p.
22. Interview with the author, November 13, 2012.
23. "Cumbica," n.p.
24. Several quotations from and information about residents were extracted from life history interviews collected by Tiago Guerra and the team of researchers that he coordinated in a project on the oral history of Cecap. Extracts of these interviews were published in Guerra, *Cecap Guarulhos: histórias, identidades e memórias,* but Guerra also generously granted me access to all the interviews in their entirety.
25. "Casa: solução e não problema," *Folha de São Paulo* (April 8, 1972).
26. Cerávolo, "A pré-fabricação em concreto armado aplicada a conjuntos habitacionais no Brasil," 97, 102.
27. Cerávolo, "A pré-fabricação em concreto armado aplicada a conjuntos habitacionais no Brasil," 109.

28. Solimar M. Isaac, "Parque Cecap Guarulhos: transformação urbana" (MA thesis, Universidade de São Paulo, 2007), 54.
29. "Conjunto Residencial, a cidade planejada," *Folha de São Paulo* (October 2, 1973): seç. Local, 12.
30. Guerra, *Cecap Guarulhos: histórias, identidades e memórias*, 59.
31. Guerra, *Cecap Guarulhos: histórias, identidades e memórias*, 113.
32. Guerra, *Cecap Guarulhos: histórias, identidades e memórias*, 114.
33. "A primeira casa que a gente teve," *Veja* (June 20, 1973).
34. Teresa P. R. Caldeira, *City of Walls: Crime, Segregation, and Citizenship in São Paulo* (Berkeley: University of California Press, 2001).
35. "Habitação, um grave problema." *Folha de São Paulo* (March 25, 1990): Local, 19.
36. "Era para ser um modelo, mas é apenas um fracasso." *Folha de São Paulo* (November 30, 1980): 4.
37. Isaac, "Parque Cecap Guarulhos: transformação urbana," 19.
38. Raquel Rolnik, *São Paulo*, 2d ed. Folha Explica 17 (São Paulo: Publifolha, 2003).

Chapter 5

Freehold/Freedom

Exurban Existence in the
United Arab Emirates

Kishwar Rizvi

Democracy and citizenship are considered the basic privileges granted by modern nation-states. Yet at the start of the twenty-first century, they are neither easily accessible nor evenly distributed across the globe. The United Arab Emirates (UAE) stands out as a dystopic dreamland in which neoliberalism appears to have run rampant, putting emphasis on the movement of capital and people across socioeconomic divides. Thus, refugee and labor camps fill the imaginary of outsiders, even if the majority of people live in quotidian spaces made unremarkable through imitation and replication of American-style real estate speculation and design.[1] Promising investor satisfaction and commercial stability, the UAE has evolved urban strategies that serve to keep the economy solvent even as they limit political or economic decision-making.

In an age of increasingly impervious borders, citizenship and freedom (to live, to move, to work) are at the forefront of discussions about nationhood. In the UAE, an authoritarian regime imposes restrictions on all its residents regardless of whether they are nationals or expatriates. Yet for the latter, whether they are laborers in the construction industry or managers in the financial sector, restrictions also bring differing degrees of precarity, especially in residency. For noncitizens, the opportunities for permanent residency are available to only a select few, leaving others waiting to return to homes left behind, sometimes decades ago. Their children may be born in the UAE, but they cannot call it home, even if it is the only country they have ever lived in.

Urban and architectural design are called upon to provide housing that is responsive to basic needs while also providing spaces of socialization and emotional comfort. Housing—where it is located, what form it takes, and who can access which type of development—is perhaps the first consideration for those planning residency in the UAE. However, it has not been given much scholarly attention, perhaps as archival material is difficult to access in the UAE and much of the residential market is controlled by state actors or their proxy developers.[2] Nonetheless, housing remains one of the largest real estate markets, ever expanding across economic scales.

Biopolitics, as a force of raw power, is deployed by the state on individuals' bodies through surveillance and displacement. In the most extreme case—say, of the labor camp—the life of the migrant, the worker, the nonresident, is reduced to what Giorgio Agamben would call "bare life," the absolute and often violent control by sovereign power over the individual's existence. Agamben argues that this sovereign power and the life it engenders (a life less lived, perhaps) is at the core of modern democracy.[3] Certainly, urban practices in cities such as Dubai reveal stark divisions based on income and, most important, citizenship and its absence. Yet, in order to implement the project of nation-building, which in the UAE relies heavily on foreign workers, the state must find ways to provide simulacra of home, ways for the expatriates to "belong." Residential enclaves, be they labor "villages" or gated communities, provide important insights into the manners in which architecture is deployed to at once settle and segregate disparate communities, and where bare life is hidden below the surface of highly controlled spatial strategies.

The Abu Dhabi–born Indian author Deepak Unnikrishnan explores the lives of migrant workers in his novel, *Temporary People* (2017), a surreal exploration of everyday life in the interstices of racial bias and economic exploitation. According to him, the state imposes a sense of impermanence that "is so normalized that people don't think about it until they have to go . . . Privilege is being a little more permanent than others, being allowed to linger more in a place without people paying much attention to you. But when you're not of privilege, you have to be more careful."[4] Impermanence, complacency, competition, and insecurity all represent the immigrant experience, in which resources are few and the opportunities for social mobility limited, especially for those lower in the class system. In such contexts, housing is the most basic of privileges, and yet it is also where socioeconomic status is enacted, where the simulacra of normalcy are deployed, and where a sense of belonging is imagined.

This essay interrogates how citizenship denied nonetheless secures architecture that provides grounding even in the most precarious of contexts; that even in authoritarian states, local establishments, such as schools and supermarkets, help create permanence through the suspension of difference. For expatriate communities in Dubai, residential enclaves simulate lifeworlds far removed from reality, creating Truman Show–like enactments that nonetheless dig deep into the local ethnosphere. Among the insights that the residential enclaves provide is that freedom may exist even in the absence of citizenship, and that even as political freedom is seldom negotiable, economic mobility may provide varying degrees of access. Most important, perhaps, is the notion that bounded temporality may be veiled behind structures of seeming permanence.

In the case of Dubai, the largest city of the Emirates, commentators have focused on

Figure 5.1. View of communal park in Green Community Motor City, Dubai, 2019. Photograph by author.

either skyscrapers and luxury malls or their architectural inverse, low-cost labor camps. Less attention has been drawn to the large middle-income real estate developments tucked away in the desert that serve many expatriate residents.[5] These are exemplified by massive freehold projects, such as Arabian Ranches and their less prestigious counterparts, such as Green Communities.[6] On the surface, these developments appear generic, impersonal, and consumer driven. To some observers they may exemplify Marc Augé's "non-places," sites that are devoid of history yet rely on "memory" as a marketing strategy, and which can be replicated and situated without concern for context or meaning.[7] They are temporary, transient, and geared toward the individual. Yet as spaces of inhabitation, it may be argued, the residential enclaves transcend such reduction, primarily because they require a particular kind of, admittedly problematic, sociability. Here New Urbanism is soiled and reformed; it showcases community even as it continues to promote bare existence over integration.[8] Working against time (the residency permit, the freehold lease) and recreating memories of home (Kerala, Beirut, Manila), residents subvert the segregated residential enclaves into heterotopias of survival, often by the inclusion of amenities and small architectural gestures that allow for customization. In such ways, Arabian Ranches and Green Community may provide important insights into the future of nonresident and transient inhabitation across the world.

Neoliberalism without Freedom

Demographic imbalance is at the core of the UAE's complex rule; of the more than 9.5 million inhabitants of the country, only approximately 10 percent are nationals. Although multiple generations may have worked and lived in the UAE, kinship and tribal identities ensure that the citizenry of the seventh-wealthiest country in the world (ahead of Norway and the United States) remains small.[9] Special enclaves and gated residential developments thus serve as proxy communities for expatriates, who recreate heterotopias blending nostalgia and innovation, building new forms of inhabitation that seem both familiar and foreign. The cultures of consumerism that are propagated as ideals, however, mask the stringent religious and political priorities of the ruling elite.

The divisions between Emirati nationals and expatriate residents remain strictly demarcated. There are, of course, hierarchies and delineations within Emirati society, with the ruling elite enacting their status in particular ways. Their private lives are closely guarded and managed in order to adhere to traditional norms. For example, while younger, wealthy Emiratis may have apartments in luxury towers in downtown Dubai or Abu Dhabi, those with children and elderly parents often live in exurban villas, inhabiting exclusive spaces often hidden from view. They interact with the rest of the public in luxury malls, private schools, and, now increasingly, in art galleries and museums. Among the reasons given for such spatial separation is the need to preserve traditional values and keep behavior that may offend conservative sensibilities "out of sight."

Similar compartmentalization happens on the economic and urban scale. The UAE's autocratic economic system of oligarchies extolls capitalism, with its reliance on global commerce and aspirations for international investment. However, monarchical rule and extreme prosperity from large petroleum and natural gas reserves focuses wealth on select members of the Emirati ruling classes and business elite. Institutions exist for the well-being of UAE nationals, who share in the country's economic successes and for whom government initiatives such as education and health services are primarily developed. The services available to nonresidents and expatriates are dependent on their economic and visa status, both of which are intrinsically linked to race and national origin.

In the same manner, an urbanism of separation is indicative of the security state, which in Achille Mbembe's words "thrives on a state of insecurity." Indeed, as he further elaborates, "the security state—being explicitly animated by a mythology of freedom that at bottom stems from a metaphysics of force—is, in short, less concerned with the distributions of places and remuneration than by the project to control human life in general, whether it is a case of its subjects or of those designated as enemies."[10] Expatriates are the majority in the UAE, and the rulers see them not as adversaries but rather as temporary workers to be controlled and surveilled in order to be most productive. Freedom in their case is defined by socioeconomic status: the higher the worker's status, the "freer" they might be.

Freedom may exist for those able to afford certain privileges, but it does not give access to political or democratic representation. While capitalism and democracy are often linked, the implications to public life cannot be taken at face value. As the journalist Martin Wolf writes in the *Financial Times*:

> Democracy and capitalism rest on an idea of equality that everybody may share in political decision-making and do the best they can in the market. These freedoms were revolutionary not that long ago. Yet deep conflicts also exist. Democratic politics depends on solidarity; capitalists do not care about nationality. Democracy is local; capitalism is essentially global. Democratic politics is founded on the equality of citizens; capitalism cares little about the distribution of riches. Democracy says all citizens have a voice; capitalism gives the rich by far the loudest.[11]

The large income disparity in the UAE between citizens and visa-holders suggests unequal opportunities. Nonetheless, people from all over the world vie for the chance to live and work in the UAE, especially in Dubai. The economic opportunities of working and living here offset the lack of permanence owing to restrictive residency policies. Certainly, the scarcity of financial opportunities in much of Asia and Africa is one reason; another is the constantly unraveling political situation in the region, which has made the Emirates a clearing house for everything from art to ammunition.[12] Because of its role in global finance and real estate, the UAE also attracts multinational companies and their employees from across Europe and the United States. Thus, people come from diverse parts of the world, seeking opportunities big and small.

What brings people to Dubai is the freedom the city affords, not democracy. That freedom is not without limits; the city-state is highly surveilled, and the price of transgression is very high (imprisonment and deportation, among other punishments). But for many visitors, those limitations also come with benefits. Compared to the countries many leave behind, job security and better wages exist alongside safety and well-functioning public services. If their families join them, there is schooling for their children and, given the diversity of expatriates, often the possibility of creating affinity groups based on language, nationality, and even religious identity.[13] Yet deep differences remain within these diverse groups, not least between them and the Emiratis themselves. Among those most striking differences is the way these populations inhabit the city in parallel lives that intersect but do not often intertwine.

For those who choose to come to the UAE for work, the country provides an important economic opportunity to change their circumstances. In a provocative study on the UAE's need for migrant workers, Eric Posner and Glen Weyl write:

> Huge income inequalities persist: About 85 percent of the population of the UAE, for example, consists of migrant workers living on roughly $5,000

per year. Fifteen percent of the population are Emirati nationals, who live on roughly three hundred thousand dollars a year, implying greater economic inequality than existed even in Apartheid South Africa or the antebellum South. But these foreign migrant workers earn vastly more in the GCC nations than they would at home in Bangladesh or India, where they would make around $1,000 per year. By welcoming migrant workers, the UAE and its neighbor Qatar do more than any other rich country to reduce global inequality.[14]

The excerpt above glosses over the high costs of these economic opportunities, which include the loss of human dignity through strict visa restrictions, indentured servitude and confinement for those whose passports are withheld by recruiting agents. Nonetheless, the impact of this so-called openness also manifests itself on middle-class migrants for whom employment results in the social and economic mobility sometimes denied them in their home countries. They are economic mercenaries, as Syed Ali has called them, with little incentive for civic participation or political activity. The latter is, in fact, highly discouraged.[15]

Indeed, the case of the UAE demonstrates the need to uncouple democracy from the idea of freedom. Is it possible to have a liberal economic order without a liberal political order? And can one participate in building a nation without truly being a part of it?[16] A study of enclave residences sheds light on the ways in which urban and architectural decisions form the lived experience of the thousands of temporary workers who consider the UAE home. Changes in residency laws and the permitting of freehold ownership have also altered the housing market, especially for middle-income expatriates, who are willing to invest in the UAE and, in some cases, raise their families there. Nonetheless, promising investor satisfaction and commercial stability, the UAE has evolved urban and political strategies that serve to keep the economy solvent even as they limit entry into nationhood.

Urban Strategies of Zoning and Segregating

Dubai's beginnings are well recorded by visitors and locals. Once a small fishing port, the economy of the village depended on pearl diving and trade between neighboring entities along the Persian Gulf and the Indian Ocean. British cargo and passenger ships provided mobility for goods and people, making Dubai a multiethnic and polyglot collection of languages and customs.[17] Its current diversity is thus of little surprise, even if the demographic percentages may have shifted and the local population has been far outnumbered by temporary workers and tourists. The Magnum photographer Eve Arnold visited Dubai and Abu Dhabi in 1970, when they were still part of the Trucial States (before the 1971 federation that resulted in the United Arab Emirates). Her photographs of Dubai show a low-rise city emerging from a collection of fishing villages,

Figure 5.2. "Deira Dubai along the Creek," circa 1970. Eve Arnold for Magnum Photos, courtesy of Magnum Photos/Beinecke Rare Books and Manuscript Library, Yale University.

with women and men performing everyday tasks such as herding animals and working in construction.[18] Two- and three-story buildings were appearing just beyond the Dubai Creek and the shoreline, but the vast expanse of the desert beyond lay empty.

In just under fifty years, Dubai has grown from these modest beginnings to a towering megapolis, boasting the largest shopping mall, the tallest building, and the largest human-made island, among other superlatives.[19] Its signature building type has shifted from low-rise apartments and single-family bungalows to luxury apartment towers constructed in the downtown area along Sheikh Zayed Road and in the popular Dubai Marina en route to Jebel Ali and Abu Dhabi. The beachfront, in particular, became the site of retail and hospitality investments, from the seven-star Burj al-Arab and the Madinat Jumeirah resort (which covers almost half a kilometer square) to the developments known as JBR (Jumeirah Beach Residences) that occupy two square kilometers. All three of these are located on the Persian Gulf, vying for prominence alongside the largest man-made island development, the Palm Dubai.

According to a 2015 report by the Al Qasimi Foundation:

> Since the 1990s, Dubai has pursued an aggressive economic diversification agenda, at the core of which has been an immense program of urban development (Buckley, 2009). Funded heavily through international debt capi-

Figure 5.3. "Construction in Dubai, view from the Persian Gulf," circa 1970. Eve Arnold for Magnum Photos, courtesy of Magnum Photos/Beinecke Rare Books and Manuscript Library, Yale University.

tal, and driven primarily through newly liberalized and internationalized real estate markets, the array of megaprojects under way in recent years has brought construction and real estate to the fore as two of the most important non-oil sectors in the city's economy.[20]

These observations are nowhere more visible than on Sheikh Zayed Road, a crucial artery running the length of the city that connects Dubai to Sharjah on the north and Abu Dhabi on its south. The artery is flanked on either side by skyscrapers, slicing a metal and glass canyon through the desert. It also divides the city along functional and socioeconomic lines, with the beachfront villas and luxury hotels sprawled along the coast and industry and commerce located in the interior.

At the center of Dubai is the business district, which is comprised of high-rise commercial ventures such as the Dubai International Finance Centre (DIFC) and the Burj Khalifa, currently the world's tallest skyscraper.[21] Designed by the American firm Skidmore, Owings, and Merrill and completed in 2010, the Burj Khalifa sits in the center of a large development project by Emaar (Engineer Management Automation Army Reserve) and DAMAC Real Estate holdings. Surrounding the Dubai Mall and Burj Park stand residential towers emblazoned with the names of their developers. The

Figure 5.4. Entrance gate in the Dubai International Finance Centre, 2018. Photograph by author.

large-scale branding of this iconic public space is indicative of the power of land speculation in Dubai, where real estate holdings are owned by local businessmen.[22]

The DIFC, inaugurated in 2004, represents Dubai in its essence as an economic "free zone," offering a 100 percent ownership of the retail properties without the need for local Emirati partners. The institutions housed in the collection of multistoried buildings include multinational financial companies, private investors, retail outlets, art galleries, and other local and international institutions. The DIFC has its own governance, and as "an independent jurisdiction within the UAE, DIFC is empowered to create its own legal and regulatory framework for all civil and commercial matters."[23] Operating in some ways as a semiautonomous entity, the DIFC exemplifies a capitalist dream, market-driven and catering to elite consumers from across the world. Although in the heart of Dubai, it fashions itself as placeless and modern; recognizable, and yet restricted to those with the means to gain entry.

The urban imprint of Dubai reifies social difference, whether it is on the scale of the shopping mall or the gated community; everyone is meant to know their place and stay within their social limits. The city is separated into economic enclaves that help incentivize investment by nonresident and foreign entrepreneurs (through reduced taxation, for example). Yet despite being marketed exuberantly, Martin J. Murray has noted, "City builders in the United Arab Emirates have employed the zone format to distinct advantage—to dilute and control foreign influence, to elevate and protect the status of privileged nationals, and to leverage existing oil and gas resources to create diversified industries."[24] Since the opening of Jebel Ali in 1985, several free zones have come into being under the moniker of "city," such as "Media City," "Internet City," and so on.

Spatial compartmentalization and urban enclaves "have become places of permanent exception, with their own territorial sovereignty, their own laws, and their own rules of inclusion-exclusion. These enclaves are neither completely 'inside' the city or 'outside' existing governance frameworks. Instead, they constitute a kind of 'third space,' operating in a legal limbo or void where conventional regulatory regimes are suspended."[25] Ahmed Kanna writes that the new developments taking place in the desert behind Sheikh Zayed Road are "governed by an exclusionary, ethnocratic logic that in fact strongly resonates with conservative discourses."[26] The free zone thus applies to how people live in the UAE, especially Dubai, where segregation by class, race, and economic status creates ethnic ghettos.

Freehold and the Assertion of Difference

Within prescribed and separated residential enclaves, expatriates from diverse backgrounds fashion new ways of living and socialization. In the absence of citizenship and with little recourse to the apparatus of democratic representation (e.g., elections and unions), the home becomes one of the primary factors of public self-representation for expatriate residents. Many work in professional jobs as lawyers, doctors, accountants, and engineers, not just as laborers in the oil and construction industries. "One quarter of [the UAE's] GDP is derived from oil-related sectors, and the rest comes mainly from services, manufacturing and construction."[27] These professionals' children are born in the UAE, attend schools and universities there, and enter the workforce themselves. Thus, more than one generation chooses to live in the Emirates, with fewer and fewer returning to homes far away. The economic and psychological security provided by property ownership also contributes to the nationalist project of the UAE even though the contributions come from noncitizens.

The owners of properties in high-end luxury residential complexes such as those surrounding Burj Khalifa are Emiratis, Iranians, Russians, and a host of wealthy investors who can afford multimillion-dollar residences in the poshest part of Dubai. Yet the engine of the city is powered not by the elite few but by the masses of middle-income workers, from management to corporate heads, schoolteachers and small-business owners, who seek housing solutions in more affordable areas of the city. They are people who have moved to Dubai for work and often in order to escape political or financial insecurity in their home countries; they have money to invest or children to raise away from the difficult situations they have left behind. They are economic migrants seeking better livelihoods and opportunities for themselves and good schooling for their children. They don't live in luxury high-rises along the Dubai Marina; instead, they invest in new freehold property designed for upwardly mobile expatriates.

Freehold developments such as Arabian Ranches and Green Community Motor City are tucked away in the desert or in industrial areas, off Dubai's main commercial arteries. Similarly hidden from view are the residential enclaves of Emiratis, especially the ruling elite, whose private villas are often congregated within designated and sometimes gated neighborhoods.[28] Although more academic attention is paid to the labor camps with which these segregated sites share uncanny and unexpected relationships, freehold development is seldom considered in the literature on urbanism in Dubai.[29]

In 2002, Sheikh Mohammed bin Rashid Al Maktoum, vice president and prime minister of the UAE and the ruler of Dubai, passed a decree allowing freehold property ownership in the city. According to the Dubai-based property portal Bayut.com:

> This form of ownership [freehold] gives the buyer absolute ownership over both the unit and the land that it stands on. Dubai Land Department (DLD) registers the buyer's name as 'landowner' in the registry and grants a title deed for the property. Freehold property in UAE unit can be freely sold, leased or occupied at the will of the freeholder. The freehold contract is applicable in perpetuity, and when the owner passes away, an heir can inherit it. So essentially, the property stays in the same family. It is important to note, though, that foreign nationals can only purchase freehold property in UAE from the designated freehold areas. Freehold areas in Dubai for expats span over 23 neighbourhoods. Non-citizens can buy freehold property in most parts of Dubai, including Palm Jumeirah, Dubai Marina, Emirates Hills and Al Barsha. In addition, freehold property owners and their families can get renewable UAE residence visas. However, being a resident in the UAE is not a requirement to own freehold property. Foreign nationals living abroad can also own freehold property in UAE. Buyers should only buy freehold properties from government-approved real estate agents or developers.[30]

Emaar Properties and other large-scale developers (e.g., Nakheel) responded to this decree immediately, as freehold ownership would lead thousands of middle- and upper-middle-class expatriates to invest in long-term housing projects in the UAE.[31] Often, buyers of freehold properties were investors with no intention of residing in the en-

Figure 5.5. Al Reem Housing, Arabian Ranches, Dubai, 2019. Photograph by Azza Abou Alam.

claves; rather, they would "flip" the property as soon as doing so was viable, making a handsome profit along the way. In this way, freehold opened up not just residency possibilities but also economic opportunity. Nonetheless, the villas also created a sense of rootedness for residents on longer-term visas despite the uncertainties of employment or business partnership. Emaar led the way with Arabian Ranches, an exclusive gated community located about thirty kilometers south of Burj Khalifa and downtown Dubai and about twenty-five miles southeast of Sheikh Zayed Road. The development was launched in 2004, and the site became one of the most popular residential complexes in the city. Arabian Ranches would cater to the higher end of this spectrum of freehold property, recreating for its residents a sense of prosperity and safety. Located on Sheikh Mohammed bin Zayed Road, it was easily accessible and close to downtown Dubai. For residents in the first phase of construction, being on the outskirts of Dubai introduced a commute, but because roads and infrastructure were already in place, traveling to the city was easy. Indeed, escaping back into a secluded gated community became a respite from the fast pace and traffic of Dubai.[32] The opening of Arabian Ranches invited frenzied speculation by many local and foreign investors, with tales of flipped sales in the early years yielding immense profit for prescient buyers.

The first phase of Arabian Ranches occupied 1,650 acres and included 1,100 townhouses with eight different layouts.[33] The plan of the development was organic, following the model of American gated communities with their emphasis on privacy and

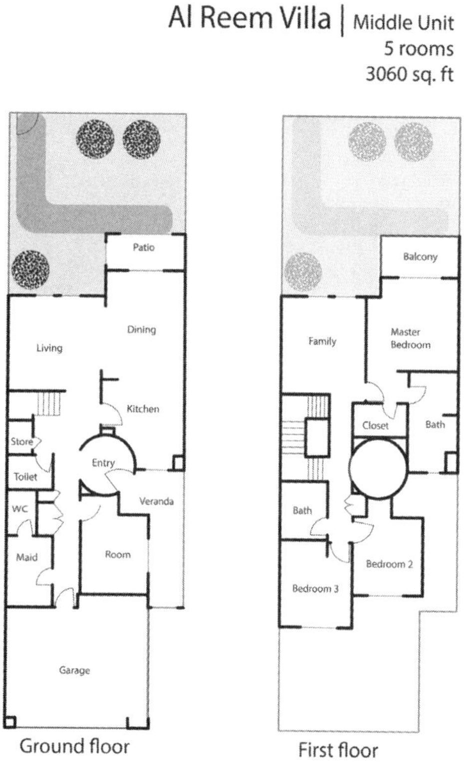

Figure 5.6. Al Reem, Arabian Ranches, Dubai. Floor plans drawn by Reze Bergemann.

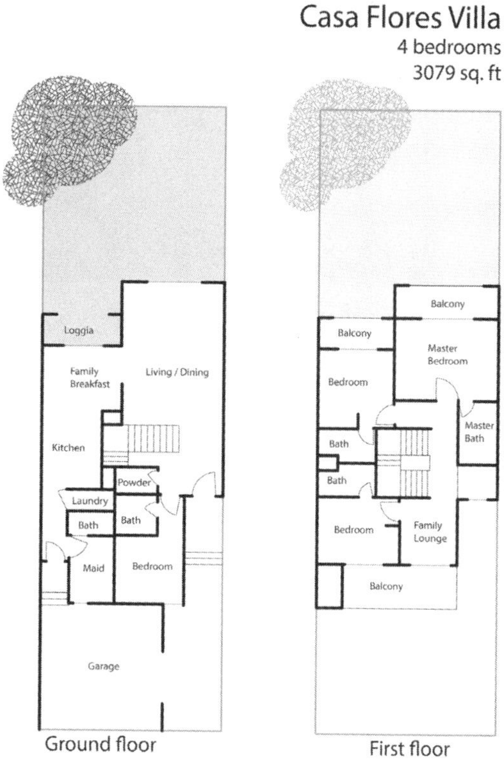

Figure 5.7. Casa Flores Villa, Green Community Motor City, Dubai. Floor plans drawn by Reza Bergemann.

exclusivity. Access to Arabian Ranches is through designated entrances monitored by guards and security cameras twenty-four hours a day. The residences themselves are detached two- and three-bedroom houses with landscaped entrances off the main avenues.[34] The villas in Al Reem (built in the first phase), for example, are designed with open floor plans and accommodations for live-in help. Even the most modest of them (with three bedrooms) has an accessible maid's room and space to park two cars. A small garden courtyard in the back allows for private outdoor space, natural light, and coolness. The villas are two-storied, modestly scaled, and compact, allowing for efficient indoor cooling during Dubai's extremely hot weather.

The design of the villas is a mix of Arabic and Spanish architecture resembling the suburban architecture of the southwestern United States. This is unsurprising, given the inspiration for the gated communities themselves. Indeed, even the foliage replicates the hacienda model of tropical gardens instead of the desert environment of Dubai. The marketing of Arabian Ranches, like its name itself, implies a romantic desert utopia of limitless possibilities, evoking the pioneering spirit of the American West with its ranches and wide vistas. Instead of heroic cowboys, there are managers and CEOs; instead of white settlers, there are Pakistani, Australian, and Lebanese migrants.

Amenities were added to the residential complex soon after the first fifty residents moved in; they included cafés, stores, and, most importantly for families with children, reputable schools such as the renowned Jumeirah English Speaking School (JESS). The latter helped define the desired demographics for Arabian Ranches, making it appeal to upper-middle-class expatriates with families intent on investing in both their children's education and also in the idea of the residential enclave as an upwardly mobile space. In fact, the gated community itself as an urban type signals an aspiration founded on exclusion and separation.

Other spatial symbols of success included tennis courts, a swimming pool, and a championship golf course, the Links Golf Club, which has a signature 18-hole and par-72 golf course designed by Ian Baker-Finch in association with Nicklaus Design. The marketing literature defines the aesthetic as "a true desert-style grass course."[35] The contradiction of having a golf course in a desert notwithstanding, the immense resources needed to recreate the verdant environment of the Arabian Ranches highlights the prosperity of those able to reside within the community.

Along with the aspirational way of life comes the stereotype of people in high-end residential enclaves, among them the "Jumeirah Janes" with their "haughty attitudes and leisure lifestyle [who] live apart from the non-upper class, often in gated communities, which they share with wealthy non-Westerners."[36] As Blakely and Snyder write, "When being in the right crowd is an important part of signaling status, gates, with exclusivity, are very appealing . . . Gated communities are elite not just because of what they include, but because of what they exclude: the public, strangers, and undesirables. The result is privacy and control."[37] While gated communities may be desirable spatial markers of socioeconomic success, they are far from ideal. In the American context from which the Dubai model derives, the gated community reveals socioeconomic and racial segregation, reifying the schisms inherent in a capitalist caste system. In the case of Arabian Ranches, segregation is reified through urban and architectural strategies of exclusion, from physical barriers and walls to aesthetic choices that displace the spatial logic of building in the desert.

Domesticity and Perceptions of Belonging

The more recent Green Community housing development in Motor City consists of villas, townhouses, bungalows, and luxurious terraced apartments. Motor City, named for the Dubai Autodrome nearby, is between Dubai and Abu Dhabi and separated from the Dubai Marina and Jumeirah beachfront by Sheikh Zayed Road.[38] Green Community Motor City, like its counterparts Green Community East and Green Community West (about fourteen miles away on Sheikh Mohamad bin Zayed Road), replicates a lush

Figure 5.8. View of artificial lake in Green Community Motor City, Dubai, 2019. Photograph by author.

theme park, with expansive gardens, fountains, and miniature lakes. Green, in this context, is not meant to signify ecological or environmental concerns; rather, it points to the abundance of vegetation on the property. Although a "green community" in a "motor city" would at first seem an anachronism, the gesture toward environmentalism is a clever marketing move. In architectural terms it images a pastoral ideal of artificial, well-manicured panoramas in contrast to the suburban villas of Arabian Ranches.

Green Community is a prime example of how real estate development in Dubai creates new communities based not on linguistic or cultural likeness but on socioeconomic status. Unlike the more upscale Arabian Ranches, Green Communities cater to a more diverse population, given its range of housing options, from independent townhouses to one- and two-bedroom apartments. The demographics consist of middle-class workers in Dubai and Abu Dhabi who are often employees of multinational corporations or small business owners and service providers. They are Lebanese, Pakistani, Polish, and Egyptian, all united by a desire to create a home among the multiplicity of histories, traditions, and languages.

The development consists of an organic plan centered on gazebos and rivulets that provide peaceful vistas across the properties. Despite generic postmodern architecture, pockets of specificity make the enclave habitable. Take, for example, the Lebanese restaurant Al Arrab Motor City, which overlooks one of the "lakes" in the development. The restaurant, with indoor and outdoor spaces, caters to a variety of residents. Shisha pipes are served, and Arabic music plays to the delight of those who recognize the lyrics and popular songs. In Ramadan, the restaurant is open late into the night, catering to Muslim residents breaking their fast. Tastes, sounds, and the sociability they create locate the restaurant within the community of expatriates for whom they are familiar. Such spaces invite others to participate in the creating of new allegiances, perhaps through other forms—be they educational (for their children in the nearby nursery school), cultural (other Arabic speakers, other Muslims, and so on), or otherwise. The landscaping around the development consists of large expanses of well-pruned grass but also includes plantings that are equally unusual in the Arabian Gulf. Flame-of-the-forest and banyan trees point to tropical spaces to the east such as Karachi and Bangkok. It is unclear who the gardeners and designers are or what the intentions were, yet the effect is simultaneously one of displacement and rootedness. They are reminders, too, of how small gestures, such as a tree, can provide the possibilities of new homecomings. For expatriates working in Dubai, it is these markers—familiar foods or foliage—that make the experience of inhabiting what is otherwise a transient and unstable space possible.

Fragmentary disjunctions, when multiplied to the extent that they are in the UAE, become the norm in a country that is grappling with what citizenship and statehood mean. On the one hand, there is the discourse of cosmopolitanism that adheres closely to the vision of the founder of the UAE, Sheikh Zayed Al Nahyan, in which the country is a "complex social experiment, hosting people from all over the world. This vision also serves to give the rigid hierarchical economic and political structure a positive perspective, despite the discrepancies faced by the less-privileged residents of the United Arab Emirates."[39] The celebratory amalgamation, however, masks the deep inequality at the core of the country, spatialized in the stark contrasts between seven-star luxury hotels and austere labor camps, both of which are symbolically key to Dubai's success and growth.

Those who occupy the middle ground, living in the gated communities discussed here, enjoy much greater freedom and privilege than those at the lower ends of the economic bracket. The stability afforded by freehold property ownership goes hand in hand with economic prosperity and is further motivated by recent expansions in visa categories that implement a new system for long-term residence visas, enabling "foreigners to live, work and study in the UAE without the need of a national sponsor and with 100 per cent ownership of their business on the UAE's mainland."[40]

The long-term visa categories further incentivize ownership of freehold property, which allows titleholders and their immediate families the ability to renew their UAE residency. While citizenship remains almost unattainable for non-Emiratis, property ownership does allow for some form of rootedness.[41] Land, the most primal form of possession, provides a sense of belonging even if permanence is not guaranteed. In the case of freehold property, economic prosperity leads to participation in the nation-building project of the UAE, for which the opening of real estate markets and provision of long-term visas are meant to boost investment and move the country away from oil dependence toward other forms of capital generation (e.g., medical tourism and education).

In the real estate market of Dubai, middle-income housing enclaves and gated communities provide opportunities for real estate speculation, income generation, and participation in the processes of growth envisioned by the government of the UAE. They also fit well into the strategy of zones and segregation that typify urban planning in the country. While on the one hand these separate environments create a superficial simulacrum of suburban living (the "good life") as dreamed by American popular television and film industries, they also demonstrate how disparate communities adapt and create shared forms of communal living.

At first glance, the residential enclaves may appear to prove the success of neoliberalism, with its focus on economic and global mobility. Yet in the context of the UAE, they also highlight how the state controls and isolates people, be they citizens, residents, or visitors. Scholars have argued that demarcated zones most effectively serve the state, which uses geographic spaces to create a consumption infrastructure that most efficiently results in labor mobilized toward productivity. That is to say, "Absent democracy, high levels of consumption yield a specific substitute form of political and social stability among the beneficiaries."[42] That the beneficiaries are not just the Emirati elite is an important addendum to this observation.

For expatriate workers who commit to long-term residency options in the UAE, often because of economic or political necessity, the forgoing of democratic self-representation appears to be a small price to pay for the security of living and working in a system that rewards productivity (admittedly, of a particular, consumerist type). Punishment is meted out quickly for any indiscretion, whether incurred through the consumption of alcohol in the dry emirates to leering at women or trying to bribe a policeman. Transgressions may result in severe punishment, the most extreme of which is death (for taking or selling drugs) or deportation back to the home country. The UAE has the most stringent security apparatus, including CCTV monitors in public spaces and censorship of social media platforms such as WhatsApp, thus making free speech a near impossibility. Such restrictions are not imposed on outsiders alone, but rather the Emiratis are themselves well aware of the limitations imposed on their movement, employment, and self-expression.

Giving up the freedoms seen as basic rights encoded in most democratic nations appears at first glance to be a high price to pay. Yet as the millions of people competing for work visas and employment opportunities in the UAE attest, it is far from a deterrent to immigration. Indeed, the capitalist monarchy of the UAE manages to sustain institutions often associated with democracy, such as education and the arts, within regulated limits. Segregation is an effective manner of controlling the varied demographics that outnumber Emirati citizens tenfold. Urban strategies that divide the spatial and social are thus called upon to assimilate varied demographics and to secure inhabitation, even against the backdrop of an authoritarian surveillance state as exemplified in the ominous Aldar Headquarters Building in Abu Dhabi.

Residential enclaves such as Arabian Ranches and Green Community in Motor City are important examples of how middle-class aspirations are tamed and inscribed into the national narrative of tolerance and heterodoxy. American gated communities with their attendant racial and economic discrimination are useful models for the newly established freehold properties, which attract middle- to upper-middle-class expatriate investors and residents. Yet a closer look at the secondary resources allotted to the housing options in the UAE, such as schools and restaurants, indicate that specificity and customization are the true keys to the communities' success. Freedom is assessed in more quotidian ways, with economic stability and personal safety given precedence over what many may construe as an idealized and unrealized concept of democracy. Disentangling freedom from democracy reveals instead an urbanism of accommodation, one that allows new communities to form and to create discrete utopias in one of the most dystopic parts of the world.

Notes

1. On the fascination with neoliberalism and the urban spectacle of Dubai and the United Arab Emirates, see Mike Davis, "Sand, Fear, and Money in Dubai," in *Evil Paradises: Dreamworlds of Neoliberalism*, ed. Mike Davis and Daniel Bertrand Monk (New York: New Press, 2007), 48–68; Christopher M. Davidson, *Dubai: The Vulnerability of Success* (New York: Columbia University Press, 2008); Michael Sorkin, "Connect the Dots: Dubai, Labor, Urbanism, Sustainability, and the Education of Architects," *Architectural Record* (August 2009): 33–34; Yasser Elsheshtawy, *Dubai: Behind an Urban Spectacle* (New York: Routledge, 2010).
2. More recent works include Kishwar Rizvi, "Dubai, Anyplace: Histories of Architecture in the Contemporary Middle East," *A Companion to Islamic Art*, ed. Gülru Necipoğlu and Finbarr B. Flood, (Malden, Mass.: Blackwell), 2017; Todd Reisz, *Showpiece City: How Architecture Made Dubai* (Stanford: Stanford University Press, 2020); Roberto Fabbri and Sultan Sooud Al-Qassemi, eds., *Urban Modernity in the Contemporary Gulf: Obsolescence and Opportunities* (New York: Routledge, 2022).
3. As explored in Giorgio Agamben, *Homo Sacer: Sovereign Power and Bare Life* (Stanford: Stanford University Press, 1995).
4. Deepak Unnikrishnan interview, *Guernica*, 2017. https://www.guernicamag.com/deepak-unnikrishnan-didnt-talk-pain/. Accessed June 12, 2020.

5. To avoid the dangers of essentialism or voyeurism, this essay will focus on sites and demographics that the author has had direct access to.
6. The difference between leasehold (begun in 2001) and freehold (begun in 2002) is explained on Buyut.com's site: https://www.bayut.com/mybayut/buying-leasehold-freehold-property-uae/.
7. Marc Augé, *Non-Places: An Introduction to Supermodernity* (New York: Verso, 1995; reprint, 2006), 63.
8. On New Urbanism, see Andrés Duany and Elizabeth Plater-Zyberk, "Neighborhoods and Suburbs," *Design Quarterly* no. 164 (1995): 10–23; the seminal examples are Seaside and Celebration in Florida. Discussion and critique are provided in a special issue of *Built Environment (1978–)* 29, no. 3 (2003).
9. Grant Suneson, "These are the 25 richest countries in the world," *USA Today,* July 7, 2019. https://www.usatoday.com/story/money/2019/07/07/richest-countries-in-the-world/39630693/. Obesity, diabetes, cardiovascular, and mental health issues are on the increase. Indeed, as recent scholarship has shown, the UAE presents the same health profile as countries such as the United States despite having a much higher average GPD. Some of that scholarship has been conducted at the NYUAD Public Health Research center in Abu Dhabi. https://nyuad.nyu.edu/en/research/centers-labs-and-projects/public-health-research-center.html.
10. Achille Mbembe and Steven Corcoran, "The Society of Enmity," in *Necropolitics* (Durham: Duke University Press, 2019), 54.
11. Martin Wolf, "Democracy and Capitalism: The Odd Couple," *Financial Times,* September 19, 2017. https://www.ft.com/content/cec2664c-9a2e-11e7-b83c-9588e51488a0.
12. On arms trading and culture, see Alexandre Kazerouni, *Le miroir des cheikhs: Musée et politique dans les principautés du golfe Persique* (Paris: Presses Universitaires de France, 2017).
13. The UAE has taken great pains to show itself as a tolerant and multiethnic society. Thus, according to official policies, there is freedom to practice diverse religions. However, there are strict rules against proselytizing and other forms of conversion from the official version of Islam. There has been a crackdown on movements such as the Muslim Brotherhood, which was instrumental in churning politics in Egypt during the Tahrir Square protests of 2011 that overthrew the government of Hosni Mubarak.
14. Eric A. Posner and Glen Weyl, "A Radical Solution to Global Income Inequality: Make the U.S. More Like Qatar," *The New Republic,* November 6, 2014. https://newrepublic.com/article/120179/how-reduce-global-income inequality-open-immigration-policies.
15. Syed Ali, "Living in 'Fly-by' Dubai," in *Dubai: Gilded Cage* (New Haven: Yale University Press, 2010), 134.
16. An important historical example is given in Mabel O. Wilson, "Notes on the Virginia Capitol: Nation, Race, and Slavery in Jefferson's America," in Irene Cheng, Charles L. Davis II, and Mabel O. Wilson, eds., *Race and Modern Architecture* (Pittsburgh: University of Pittsburgh Press, 2020), 23–42. Another nuance is provided in the relationship between representative democracy, industrialization, and resource extraction. See Timothy Mitchell, *Carbon Democracy: Political Power in the Age of Oil* (New York: Verso, 2013). See also Laura Lindelang, *Iridescent Kuwait: Petro-Modernity and Urban Visual Culture since the Mid-Twentieth Century* (Berlin: de Gruyter, 2021).

17. Fatma Al-Sayegh, "Merchants' Role in a Changing Society: The Case of Dubai, 1900–90," *Middle Eastern Studies* (1998): 87–102.
18. Kishwar Rizvi, "Eve Arnold in the Trucial States: The United Arab Emirates before Federation," *Platform: A digital forum for conversations about buildings, spaces, and landscapes* (December 6, 2021). https://www.platformspace.net/home/eve-arnold-in-the-trucial-states-the-united-arab-emirates-before-federation?rq=Rizvi.
19. The real estate market is more diverse than it would first appear, with Sharjah and Abu Dhabi playing vital roles in the distribution of institutions, workforce, and even social norms. For example, unlike Dubai, these Emirates do not allow the sale or consumption of alcohol. Until recently, Sharjah served as a labor feeder into Dubai, providing more affordable housing options in which lower-middle-class men and women from across Asia could live and commute into Dubai. Now, however, Sharjah is vying to compete with the retail market in Dubai by transforming its downtown area from middle-class low-rise apartment buildings on the stretch well known as Bank Street to high-end hospitality and entertainment, building off the heritage sites occupied currently by the Sharjah Art Foundation. https://www.heartofsharjah.ae/. Accessed September 22, 2019.
20. "Fact Sheet: Urban Planning in the United Arab Emirates and Ras al Khaimah," August 31, 2015. https://publications.alqasimifoundation.com/en/fact-sheet-urban-planning-in-the-united-arab-emirates-and-ras-al-khaimah.
21. For a discussion of the building within the context of Dubai's architecture, see Rizvi, "Dubai, Anyplace."
22. The CEO and founder of DAMAC is Hussain Sajwani; that of EMAAR is Muhammad Alabbar. Both men trace their lineage to the city, where their fathers were local tradesmen.
23. "Laws and Regulations," Dubai International Finance Centre, https://www.difc.ae/business/laws-regulations/. Accessed October 1, 2019.
24. Martin J. Murray, *The Urbanism of Exception: The Dynamics of Global City Building in the Twenty-first Century* (Cambridge: Cambridge University Press, 2017), 271.
25. Murray, *The Urbanism of Exception,* 309. Murray also cites in this context Alessandro Petti, "Dubai Offshore Urbanism," in Michiel Dehaene and Lieven De Cauter, eds., *Heterotopia and the City: Public Space in a Postcivil Society* (New York: Routledge, 2008), 287–96.
26. Ahmed Kanna, *Dubai, the City as Corporation* (Minneapolis: University of Minnesota Press, 2011), 38. He goes on to add: "The irony is that urbanists such as starchitects see themselves as global actors, generally unencumbered by local baggage. However, New Dubai projects, for example the gated communities of EMAAR and Nakheel and the shopping malls of the giant holding corporations, but also, I suggest, the more recent examples of starchitectural whimsy, resonate with and reinforce local hegemonies and structures of ethnic and class exclusion. In short, local systems of hierarchy are a strong influence on starchitectural and other urbanist spaces, shaping both their conceptualization and social effects."
27. And to further nuance it: "Only 1 percent of the Emirati labor force is employed in the private sector and 60 percent in the public sector." Riaz Hassan, "The UAE's Unsustainable Nation-building," *YaleGlobal Online,* Tuesday, April 24, 2018. https://yaleglobal.yale.edu/content/uaes-unsustainable-nation-building.
28. For example, in Abu Dhabi they are in the Khalifa neighborhood, which is not gated but is semiprivate.

29. Even on the labor camps the scholarship tends to skim the surface, owing to their inaccessibility to outsiders. An attempt at correcting that is given in Todd Reisz, "Drawing up Dubai's Labor Camps from 1950 to 2008," *Jadaliyya* (November 16, 2017). https://www.jadaliyya.com/Details/34704.
30. "Leasehold or Freehold: which one is right for you?" Bayut.com. https://www.bayut.com/mybayut/buying-leasehold-freehold-property-uae/. Accessed September 15, 2019.
31. Dubai Holdings, a large conglomerate, was founded by Sheikh Muhamad bin Rashid Al Maktoum in Dubai in 2004. One of its largest portfolios is real estate. On Nakheel and the real estate bubble of 2003–8 see Bertrand Renaud, "Real Estate Bubble and Financial Crisis in Dubai: Dynamics and Policy Responses," *Journal of Real Estate Literature* 20, no. 1 (2012): 51–78.
32. I have visited and conducted interviews with residents of Arabian Ranches since 2009. Given the dependency of expatriates on visa and other permits, my sources have chosen to remain anonymous. Emirati sources, too, preferred not to have their identities revealed.
33. The subcommunities that make up Arabian Ranches 1 are Al Mahra, Al Reem, Alma, Alvorada, Aseel, Hattan, La Avenida, Mirador, Mirador La Coleccion, Palmera, Saheel, Savannah, Terra Nova, and Golf Homes. Al Reem, one of the most affordable Ranches properties, was also available for the rental market.
34. The houses range in size from 1,690 square feet to 3,060 square feet, typical of villas of the higher end of the market.
35. As reviewed in the international golf reservation website Golfscape. https://golfscape.com/dubai-golf-courses/arabian-ranches-golf-club. Accessed October 15, 2019.
36. Ali, "Living in 'Fly-by' Dubai," 128. Ali gives an interesting breakdown of the demographics in such high-end housing before and after the economic crash.
37. Edward J. Blakely and Mary Gail Snyder, "Forting Up: Gated Communities in the United States," *Journal of Architectural and Planning Research* 15, no. 1 (1998): 61–72.
38. Developed by Union Properties in collaboration with National Properties.
39. I discuss Sheikh Zayed's vision in the context of his eponymous mosque in Abu Dhabi in my book *The Transnational Mosque: Architecture and Historical Memory in the Contemporary Middle East* (Chapel Hill: University of North Carolina Press, 2015).
40. Begun in 2019, these visas would be issued for five or ten years and renewed automatically. "Long Term Residence Visa in the UAE," https://government.ae/en/information-and-services/visa-and-emirates-id/residence-visa/long-term-residence-visas-in-the-uae. Accessed December 10, 2019.
41. In exceptional cases, UAE citizenship may be granted to non-Emiratis through the discretion of the ruling emir. The India billionaire Yousuf Ali became the first recipient of the Gold Card permanent residency, one of 6,800 granted in 2019 "for investors, entrepreneurs, specialised talents, researchers, and outstanding students residing in the UAE." *Gulf News*, June 3, 2019. https://gulfnews.com/uae/indian-businessman-yousuf-ali-gets-first-gold-card-in-uae-1.1559564794643.
42. Harvey Molotch and Davide Ponzini, "The New Arab Urban: Test Beds, Work-arounds, and the Limits of Enacted Cities," *AlMuntaqa* 2, no. 1 (2019): 9–23, 18.

Part II

Technocracy

Ideologies of Expertise

Affinities between technological instrumentality, administrative rationality, exclusion, and fascist politics are brought out variously in the essays in this section. Several of the authors show how technocratic and bureaucratic procedures enacted in the built environment offered cover to authoritarian programs, concealing policies of antidemocratic enforcement by state and private actors. Other authors explore the affinity of technologically enabled spectacle and fascist myth.

Paul B. Jaskot and Eve Duffy's essay, "Germanizing Krakow: The Political Complexity of Architecture under Nazi Occupation," reports on an ongoing digital humanities project that uses spatial visualization to facilitate forensic analysis of sites of National Socialist genocide. Specific to this effort are a series of urban plans for the Germanization of Krakow, showing gradual developments of social control, from ghetto enclosure preliminary to the evacuation of the Jewish population to incarceration. The essay traces the iconography of this incremental process as envisioned by National Socialist architects and regional administrators alongside planning ideologies, through specific urban design proposals that manufactured a "Germanized" history of Krakow. The result is the visualization of political relationships in social space, a result heretofore inaccessible to critical scholarship.

Half a century prior, waves of immigrants began arriving on Ellis Island, seeking entry into the United States. In "Afro-Caribbean Migration and Detention at Ellis Island," Itohan Osayimwese starkly recasts the island's archipelago of inspection stations, detention cells, and quarantine zones as sites of bureaucratic passage for some and a concentration camp for others. Rarely straightforward, the terms of exclusion have often been elusive, latent in the architecture and the procedures it hosted, and its uses subject to arbitrary interpretation, as when C. L. R. James found himself detained for both his race and his politics. Osayimwese leaves us with the image of James and others like him stranded on this haunted island, perhaps as representatives of democracy's unfulfilled promise, or perhaps of the island-like character of the *demos* itself.

María González Pendás, in "Curtain Wall Inside-Out: Technocracy, Theocracy, and Technoaesthetic Formations of Cold War Fascism," draws a complex line between technocracy and state fascism by connecting both to the Catholic theocracy of the Franco regime. In her probing analysis of curtain-wall modernity in post–World War II Spain, via a series of design competitions for government architecture, González Pendás links prewar fascist regimes to the postwar survival of fascism as a state system under Franco. That Spanish technocrats and politically adroit ideologues joined modernist, International Style aesthetics to an entire administrative mechanism for ensuring nonhereditary sovereignty and "democratic authoritarianism" meant that a model for fascist organization survived in Europe into the 1970s, a direct genealogical link back to Nazi Germany and Fascist Italy.

Despite gaining political independence from the Portuguese and Spanish empires more than a century earlier, Latin American countries like Brazil, Peru, and Colombia remained economically bound to, if not entirely dependent on, European and North American powers. Ana María León's "Sert Goes South: Planning South America" explores the long reach of Euro-American technocratic planning through the professional partnership of CIAM's president José Luis Sert and Paul Lester Wiener as they sought and designed commissions for a series of Latin American cities undergoing what was by then called "development" under variously antidemocratic political regimes. In León's account, Sert and Wiener were no mere opportunists. Rather, their work reflects structural contradictions within the modernist project, in which an emancipatory urbanism runs together with the disinterested autonomy of the professional "expert."

Finally, Nader Vossoughian, in "Albert Speer, Ernst Neufert, and the Modularization of the World," traces the postwar career of Speer and his former employee (and Bauhaus student) Ernst Neufert. The chapter narrates a dark, absurdist echo of the banality of evil, as Speer turned his attention from the efficient engineering of wartime munitions and Nazification projects to the efficient design of a brewery during the late 1960s following his release from prison. The thread running from wartime to postwar was the modularization characteristic of both Speer's and Neufert's work in the service of totalitarian control. That Speer's authorship remained concealed provides critical insight into postwar German attitudes to its fascist past, particularly when coupled with Speer's ongoing desire to participate in professional practice.

Chapter 6

Germanizing Krakow

The Political Complexity of Architecture under Nazi Occupation

Paul B. Jaskot and Eve Duffy

The historical complexity of architecture's relationship to politics in the modern era is perhaps nowhere better exemplified than in the prominent role that building played in National Socialist Germany. Decades of scholars have attempted to parse the variable ideological associations ascribed to monumental state and Party building, while others have plumbed the depths of its administrative alignment with (and within) the highest levels of government authority.[1] For the latter, Hitler's own aesthetic preferences impacted specific building in Berlin and elsewhere more than any other political leader of the period. Simultaneously, his drive to meld his architectural agenda to his political one meant that architectural interests as well as building more generally became integrated into every significant corner of the state.[2] This included the destruction that manifested itself in the great conflagration of World War II as well as the devastating genocide of European Jewry. If there was to be an extreme case where nationalism and other ideological interests melded effectively with aesthetic interests under profound political pressure, Nazi Germany was it.

Surprisingly though, relatively little attention has been paid to how this matrix of interests, goals, and directed events proved most deadly and effective during the war and the German occupation of Eastern Europe.[3] The dynamic between construction, as a practical and ideological weapon, and destruction, in its broadest sense including genocide, needs to be understood more critically and precisely.[4] Our turn to Krakow under the Nazi occupation is an attempt to lay out what such a political history of architecture under occupation might look like.

As is well known, Krakow became a key location within the National Socialist plan for military expansion and the implementation of genocide in Eastern Europe during World War II. Here Hans Frank and the General Government he led developed their policies of oppression and occupation by establishing a formidable German presence as well as claiming Krakow as "Germanized" again. Yet, while these policies and ideologies have been analyzed by scholars, little attention has been spent on how they were related to the built form of Krakow. Architecture participated in the technocratic process of occupation and warfare, and the competing and conflicting policies of ideology and political economy, genocide and productivity help to clarify architectural decisions. This essay addresses key urban planning and architectural initiatives meant to "Germanize" Krakow, establish military rule, and rid the city of its Jewish population. In particular, it will look at the dynamics between conflicting notions of what building could do or claim to do for different factions within the Nazi occupiers in the first few "optimistic" years of planning. A crucial question here is how they incorporated plans for important victim spaces, above all the Jewish ghetto, which existed from March 1941 until March 1943. The imbrication of both grand and practical plans for building with racism, exploitation, and murder makes this particular political history a challenge to the generally affirmative tone of much architectural history today.[5]

The initial plans for rebuilding Krakow, led by architect Hubert Ritter, were ambitious and followed the goals of rebuilding cities established by Hitler for Nuremberg, Berlin, and elsewhere. So, too, of course, were the goals of concentrating and ultimately murdering the Jewish population of Krakow and the surrounding areas as part of the radicalization of the Holocaust. Visualizations from the Nazi past as well as in the present help us to conceptualize these disparate histories together, seeing how the ambitions for establishing Nazi presence complemented and contradicted spatial planning for the Jewish community. This work builds on the important scholarship of historians and art historians who have analyzed Krakow such as Monika Bednarek, Niels Gutschow, Richard Němec, and, especially, Jacek Purchla.[6] It also analyzes archival holdings on Ritter and extends to the broader project of positioning the ghetto within Distrikt Krakau, the administrative geographic unit of which it was a part. Further, the ultimate goal is a study at multiple scales of both the ghetto and its district within the historical geography of ghettoization under German occupation.[7] Hence, our argument foregrounds what historical and digital visualizations may help us do to raise and interrogate the material culture of the built environment under German occupation in Eastern Europe. Indeed, the broader project of which this work is a part questions the common case-study model of scholarship on ghettos to ask whether there is anything *systemic* to be said about the spatial formation and significance of ghettos as a whole.[8] The problem thus arises of whether the particularity of an analysis of the built and spatial strategies of Krakow can help us think through (or not) other visualizations of ghettos within and beyond Nazi-occupied Europe.

The chapter will begin with the role of General Governor Frank in the spatial planning and imagined future for Nazi occupation in Krakow and contrast that with complementary but different visions of spatial planning by Ritter. The analysis of plans, photographs, and models from Ritter and his staff emphasizes the importance of visual material culture as a means to help clarify goals within the Nazi occupation, as do the administrative, organizational, and political priorities articulated in documents by Frank. Overlaps and incongruities between these quite different Nazi officials will then be further clarified through contemporary visualizations of these sources using digital methods. In both the historical and digital visualizations, the analytic focus concerns what questions are raised by the spatial relationship (if any) between perpetrators' plans and victims' spaces.

The use of a diverse range of visual evidence helps us to interrogate the planned and actual built environment under German occupation in Eastern Europe at different spatial and temporal scales and in an integrated way. Drawing on Saul Friedländer's call for an "integrated history" of the Holocaust, our larger project here tries to see the European Jews and Germans, the individual and the systemic, the social and the political economic, as relational terms.[9] Indeed, a core claim is that the visual evidence of the Nazi built environment has long demanded such an integrated analysis given that it is precisely through the control and experience of space that policies of occupation could actualize the ideological goals of the perpetrator at the same time that they influenced the daily choices (or lack thereof) in the lives of Jewish victims. It is exactly in space that the brutal aspirations and the struggle for existence played out.[10] But before such an integrated history can be managed for the built environment, this essay also argues for a foundational political history of the larger cultural project that forms the dark shadow behind the violent glare of the Nazi political economy that enabled and enacted genocide. Visualizing space as a historical practice in conjunction with other visual evidence reveals previously obscured potential relationships between political economic structures and policies, ideological beliefs, and social or individual experience.[11] The spaces of occupied Krakow help us to see what such a critical project might look like.

The historical city of Krakow is one of the great urban monuments of medieval and early modern Europe. From the Wawel Castle to the market square of the Old Town, this Polish city has many important examples of significant local architectural innovation. Its spaces and buildings also mark the cultural impact of historical developments in Southern, Western, and Eastern Europe that came to the city through its extensive trade routes as a political and economic crossroads of the region. By the nineteenth century, the city also included the substantial contribution of Jewish citizens who made up approximately one-quarter of the population. While overshadowed by the capital Warsaw, Krakow maintained its cultural, economic, and political importance through the troubled Polish Republic of the interwar period.[12]

A radical disruption to this history occurred with the beginning of World War II and the occupation of Poland by the National Socialist military authorities in September 1939. With Hitler's proclamation of the Generalgouvernement on October 12, 1939, much of what had been central Poland including Warsaw and Krakow became the designated territory of Hans Frank. This space existed as an area to be "Germanized"; at the same time, Hitler had been unwilling to allow its annexation (at least immediately) into the Reich, given that it was insufficiently Aryanized for Nazi racial ideology. Social, political, and economic changes would have to be made as the Germans set about making both long-term plans for a postwar greater Germany as well as the short-term needs of extending the military infrastructure. One major example of these changes would be shifting the center of government from Warsaw to Krakow. For the former, the Nazi leaders had nothing but disdain based on concepts of the racial and political inferiority of the Poles; for the latter, they had hopes, as in Prague, of reviving a supposed German historical core.[13]

That Frank saw the built environment as important for his political goals was clear almost from the beginning of this regime. For him, building served an ideological, political, and practical role. Ideologically, the "return" to Krakow corresponded to Frank's decision to locate his government in the Wawel, which was consistently renamed the "Burg" (castle) in Generalgouvernement documents to remove any association with its Polish past. The site dominated the city, and Frank, as the new absolute ruler, was to be the new king. This was no mere rhetoric, although the multiple photographs of Frank and other Nazi leaders (who, according to the NS publication the *Krakauer Zeitung*, appeared every three days for ceremonial visits) at the Wawel certainly played that role of propagandistically asserting their dominance.[14] Rather, the takeover of the castle corresponded to the special status of the Generalgouvernement within Nazi policy, where here the use of premodern, particularly imperial, models were explicit.[15] Because the Generalgouvernement was deemed racially and economically ideologically inferior, it was to be an older form of colony ruthlessly exploited for its resources and for its labor, with local Poles kept at best at subsistence rations. As with using the name of the "Burg," so too was "colony" a specific designation in memoranda. Both cemented the racial hierarchy that enabled the Nazi ruling class.[16]

Politically and practically, building also served Frank's interests. Politically, building was part of the vast bureaucracy set up by Frank not only to fulfill the economic and military agenda but also to establish his singular rule in the face of competing Nazi forces. The polycratic nature of the Nazi hierarchy spilled over easily into the control over the vast territory of the East, and, especially in the euphoria of the early war years, the competing interests of Himmler, Göring, and others vied for power over the administration, resources and assets, labor, and other spoils of war.[17] Competition over the control of building and construction was no less intense, especially given the importance Hitler assigned to building both for the war effort as well as his main peacetime agenda. Frank marked this particularly by making "Abteilung Bauwesen" (Construction Office) a major free-standing division within his administration, which had twelve divisions overall. This included an office for "Hochbau" (Building) that dealt with all matters of building construction as well as the "Baudirektion" (Construction Division) that focused especially on construction on the Wawel and other significant Frank priorities. Building also included creating a transportation network that would support the military and agricultural goals of the Germans, but it extended to locally adapted practices around administrative needs, industrial sites, and housing for resettled Germans and German administrators. In 1940, Frank called on Richard Rattinger, a Munich architect, as his main advisor to work for him as the "Sonderbeauftragter und Chefreferent für alle Hochbaufragen im Generalgouvernement" (Special Appointee and Chief Consultant for All Building Questions in the Generalgouvernement), further centralizing direct control over architecture in Frank's office till the architect's death in July 1942.[18]

Such power politics complemented as well the practical needs particularly of vernacular construction that would enable the occupation and the war effort. This included, for example, the completion of multiple garage complexes for the Ordnungspolizei (booked under Hochbau in 1940) throughout the Generalgouvernement as well as securing sufficient numbers of workers by highlighting "construction and maintenance of public buildings" as a major priority in the law from October 26, 1939, which introduced conscripted Polish (non-Jewish) labor.[19] For building, the law would eventually lead to the formation of the "Baudienst," a German organization to mobilize thousands of Polish young adults through the war for building efforts.

This impressive administrative infrastructure concentrated in Frank's authority would seemingly have its complement in the larger plans for the Nazi transformation of the entire "German" built environment emanating from Berlin. As with areas of particular concern for future German settlement within the occupied territory, these grandiose but very real plans involved the implementation of architectural and spatial planning as well as a developing genocidal policy of ridding "German" territories of first Jews and then Slavs.[20] But the different scales of spatial planning did not always coincide, as more localized politics came into contact with approaches to the continent-wide reach of the early Nazi military successes.[21] The varied conceptions could work at different temporal scales as well, with Frank emphasizing short-term interests while Berlin architectural initiatives had the view of longer-term wartime and postwar priorities. In this sense, it is easy to dismiss the longer-term plans as mere propaganda and paper architecture; but, given that the Nazi authorities actively worked on both long-term and immediate architectural goals at least through the crises sparked by the defeats surrounding the Battle of Stalingrad (1942–43), looking at both helps us clarify the ways in which building functioned to conceptualize a developing racist and imperial project.

These complementary but also conflicting political functions of architecture were embodied in the "General Reconstruction Plan for the Building of Krakow" ("Der Generalbebauungsplan von Krakau"), finalized in 1941 separate from Frank's administration. Hubert Ritter, the main city architect for Leipzig during the Weimar Republic, developed this plan for the spatial Germanization of Krakow under occupation. In many ways, Ritter was a surprising, indeed somewhat shocking choice to plan a major new Nazi capital. As a young architect, he cut his teeth in conjunction with architects associated with the moderate reformist agendas of the Werkbund among others. As a city architect in Leipzig, however, he promoted radical innovations in architecture with forms that would become associated with pure degeneracy in the *völkisch* architectural thought of Nazi critics such as Paul Schultze-Naumburg. For example, his flat-roofed mass housing used industrial production techniques, embodied in his famous "Rundling" housing estate (1930) in Leipzig. At the same time, Ritter was part of the embrace in technological solutions to architectural problems that would become deeply romanticized in examples like the German Autobahn in National Socialist–sponsored publications.[22] His design of the Großmarkthalle in Leipzig (1928) would be an illustration of this trend. All in all, Ritter was a complicated choice for Krakow, closer to Albert Speer's somewhat low-profile staff of architects chosen to rebuild destroyed German cities than he was to Hermann Giesler or Roderick Fick, architects of the high-status "Hitler Cities" of Munich and Linz, respectively.[23] Given this pedigree and the close connection of major urban planners during the Nazi period to Speer's influence, it is likely that Speer was instrumental in getting Ritter the Krakow offer, much as Speer had with other architects like Wilhelm Kreis (who worked with Speer in his efforts to transform Berlin).[24]

Ritter's plan clearly makes use of his technocratic and rationalist modernist skills at the same time that it marks how well he was able to serve the ideological goals of the state. The published plan is an extraordinary document that gives great insight into how the city's role in the new German east was to be visualized. Through text, plans, and photographs of an accompanying three-dimensional model, the Leipzig architect took up the functional principles of planning espoused by Gottfried Feder and others as he laid out the guidelines for building the new German capital. Its connection to architectural and planning principles emanating from Berlin seems explicit. Notably, while the plan appears to be self-published (Ritter's office in Krakow is the only listed publishing source), in the use of a clean serif font of capitalized letters of different point sizes and centered text it clearly mimics the title page of the main organ of Speer's Berlin office, *Die Baukunst,* an architectural supplement to *Kunst im Dritten Reich.*[25] In the plans, the photographs, and the text, the fate of the now-dominant German occupiers was directly tied to the Polish Christian population as well as the Polish Jewish one. That is to say, the visualization and the textual description include all three populations. Ritter's plan hammers home the obvious Nazi racial hierarchy among the three and integrates this racist conception within a structure of political economic control as well as architectural expression. Both the large-format published plans as well as the presentation version of the photographed model indicate the importance of the project through its highly aesthetic treatment of the book and folio.[26] While we do not know the circulation of these materials, the labor and expense that went into a presentation volume as well as the care taken in publishing the plan in an accessible and familiar format seems to indicate to us the interest in both convincing officials like Frank in Krakow and Speer back in Berlin of the prestige of the ideas as well as providing a means for a wider distribution to justify the plan's recommendations to a broader audience.

A few key areas of the texts help make the point about the combination of political, economic, and ideological goals at the heart of Ritter's plan. In historical terms, the textual argument emphasized the importance of the medieval roots of Krakow in German architecture and German trade, culminating in the construction of the Wawel, the medieval castle that also included the sophisticated panache of contributions from Italian sixteenth-century designers. After 1500, however, such a supposed cultural and racial highpoint had been systematically undermined by first the Poles and then the increased presence of Jews, a decline that had not stopped until the Nazi occupation.[27] As the named author, Ritter notes the contemporary importance of the building economy (and the attendant iron industry) as the main economic drive of the region along with historical trades like candy-making that Germans can take advantage of, while at the same time he despairs of the agricultural capacity of the Polish small farmers. With the new German presence, however, the goal of building will be to give rational form to the city, connect it especially to the economy of raw materials coming from the east in order to prepare for German "colonial" rule from the west, and to build a German space more suitable to the new order. For this, the Polish Christian presence must be controlled and limited, the German population increased, and Polish Jews "with few exceptions must leave the city." Quite clearly articulated in this opening text is the need for German space, the intersection with the greater German eastern (military) economy, and the ethnic cleansing of the area along with the "revival" of German architecture.[28] These are unified goals, not separate initiatives, openly acknowledged in this ostensibly public document and, in their general form, compatible with the position of Frank articulated above.

Speer's design for the rebuilding of Berlin and other so-called Hitler Cities also involved the antisemitic policy of clearing Jews from the area as well as sensitivity to historically "German" monuments and styles—that is to say, these plans, too, linked the politics of genocide to the importance of building as an ideological goal of the Nazi state, further connecting Ritter's conception to the planning strategies coming out of Speer's office in Berlin.[29] In Krakow, the preserved late-medieval "German" city and the equally historical Jewish community centered in the Kazimierz neighborhood were prominent parts of the city. Only here did Ritter and his official Nazi rebuilding plan include such explicit reference to and analysis of the goals of the Nazi colonizing of the East and the concomitant need to rid the city of its Jews. Put bluntly, only in the general plan for Krakow was the politically integrated history of perpetrator and victim made explicit.[30]

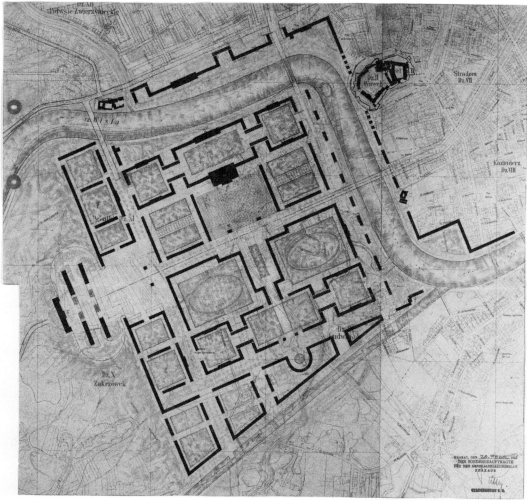

Figure 6.1. Hubert Ritter, General Reconstruction Plan for Krakow (second version), unpublished drawing, 1941. Wawel is at upper right. Architektur Museum der TUM.

Such broad textual claims are also made visually explicit in the plans and photographs of the model. For example, in the most developed drawing of the city plan, the second version, Ritter shows his reliance on typical Nazi representational city planning preferences. Note the emphasis on the axial layouts, a focus on a large central square that then would serve as a public meeting space but also frame the large structure of the *Festhalle*, and the massive scale of buildings. In addition, the rupture of the regularity of the plan at its northeast corner with the irregular form of the Wawel emphasizes the latter's importance and the orientation of the quarter from west to east. In this way, the prominence of the Wawel marks the spatial interests of Frank and the Generalgouvernement administration situated here. But it also emphasizes the impor-

Figure 6.2. Hubert Ritter, model of the General Reconstruction Plan for Krakow, 1941. The Wawel is highlighted in the center. Architektur Museum der TUM.

tant weight given to Germanic Krakow by the occupation ideology, as this monument is a synecdoche for the actual recovery of the East that was damaged by Slavs and polluted by Jews. The emphasis on the Wawel is equally prominent in the photographs of the model, taken from a low angle and from specific perspectives that show its dominant role as the focal point of the plan. The importance of "the Burg" as the mediating point between the Nazi center and the preserved historical core is emphasized as well in the text, combining its current political centrality with the legitimacy of claims to historical power.[31]

The Jewish ghetto seems to have been forgotten in the developed 1941 drawing and the model. It was not forgotten in the images included as part of the published text. (Note that the text was published in mid-1941, after the forced movement of Jews into the ghetto on March 3, 1941.) Indeed, here too the visual imagery makes clear that this is a politically and ideologically unified spatial complex: administrative center to the west, historical core to the northeast, and ghetto to the south are not only visible but clearly identified for the viewer. In this sense, the text and images, as with Frank's policies on the ground, operate at two distinct spatial and temporal scales: on the one hand, they address the immediate needs of the moment, which included local German administrative expansion as well as Polish Christian and Jewish populations; on the other, they were integrated into the broader goal of the war that presumed a military victory and spatial and racial dominance over the entire eastern territory in the near future, with a cleansing of Jewish and then Slavic populations.

The spatial proximity of different populations shown in the published plan visually complements the ideological discussion of German expansion and Jewish contraction that mark a leitmotif in Ritter's text. For example, the integration of space and racist policy is made explicit with Ritter's discussion of the expansion of housing for Nazi migrants to the area. In referencing the Jewish ghetto, he states, "Since with the Nazi plans we can count on a total disappearance of the Jews, we can remain calm about their present position in the city. Later the ghetto will be torn down and a new city quarter for housing will be built."[32] While it is important to remember that Ritter's plan was formulated in 1940–41 before the systematic genocidal policy against the Jews had been implemented, the genocidal logic of spatial elimination in the victorious future is nevertheless explicit.[33] Notably, Ritter's plans seem to coordinate well with General Governor Frank's own ideas laid out in meetings in 1940 in which he emphasized the urgent need for housing for German administrators pouring into the area, the unacceptability of Germans coming into (spatial) contact with Jews, the current need for the ghetto, and, ultimately, the future necessity of clearing Krakow of its Jews except for a few thousand handworkers.[34] Housing policy as a crucial component of Germanification formed, like the Wawel, a point of consensus between the conceptualizations of the architect and the Nazi administrator.

Whether the plan and the model help us to explain this moment in the visualization of Krakow and the Nazi east, the political economic reality on the ground and with the war naturally stymied such ideal planning here just as it eventually did in Berlin and other privileged cities. Ritter was ultimately undermined by competition from local building officials (above all, apparently, Frank's "Baudirektion"). Such typical internecine Nazi government rivalries frequently crippled one administrative group in favor of another, even when they shared similar goals. Most likely these architects and planners suggested to Frank an alternative plan to move the center of his administrative district to the north, symbolically occupying the Polish nationalist site of the Kościuszki hill.[35] In addition, the general course of the war especially after 1942 offered little room for the longer-term broad perspective of Ritter's plan and favored instead Frank's short-term practical, political, and ideological goals at the more regional level such as enacting genocidal policy along with some privileged architectural projects.[36]

Most notably, the building division completed the most important addition of a major administrative facility added to the Wawel, corresponding to Frank's administrative needs and ideological assertion of dominance. The addition had been planned by

Figure 6.3. Administrative extension of the Wawel by Frank's Baudirektion, 1941–44. Author photograph.

1941 and completed by 1944 with a façade of white plaster and limestone trim. Such simplified "modern" building forms combined with traditional stone material aligned this structure clearly with many examples of Nazi-sponsored bureaucratic construction in Berlin, Nuremberg, and elsewhere, while claiming to be a complement to the traditional forms of the Wawel.[37] On the whole, though, the course of the war mostly limited building activity in Krakow to repurposing existing administrative and housing structures while reserving much new building for military industrial purposes. In the end, Frank's priorities led to material plans and constructions, whereas Ritter's ideal plan remained a paper fantasy. Still, it would be too easy to dismiss the plan as mere propaganda. Instead, we would argue that, while weighted toward different interests, Ritter's plan and Frank's goals were both grounded in the well-established simultaneity of short-term actions and long-term planning that characterized architecture under Nazi occupation. Put in its most destructive terms, the building interests of Ritter and Frank reveal the political economic practicality and ideological commitment necessary to respond to *both* the flexible needs of military occupation and the pursuit of genocide. In this toxic equation, architecture was at no point mere propaganda to the state.[38]

And yet there are other ways of conceiving of building and the occupation of Krakow, especially of Ritter's plan. The visual material evidence—plans, photographs, and physical building sites—allows for a digital analysis that expands on a standard close reading in order to raise new spatial problems and historical questions. While it is not our main topic here, we have taken up digital methods in the broader project of which this is a part in order to explore both the individual scale of buildings and sites within Krakow but also the connection of Krakow to the extensive system of ghettos throughout occupied Eastern Europe, as well as the forced-labor construction activity involved in maintaining the German military economy. On both the micro and macro levels, our political history of building in Krakow is meant to lay the foundation for the complementary project of a broad and rigorous spatial analysis of Jewish ghettos under Nazi occupation.[39]

Our visualization of Ritter's ideal plan pushes well beyond the textual description to show other National Socialist political and ideological issues, above all the conceptual and spatial relationship between the German and Jewish communities. Our colleague Davide Contiero's reconstructions in AutoCad are derived from the material evidence of the models and photographs analyzed above. The visualization in this case raised new questions, especially as we moved the 3D model renderings into an animation. With this rendering process that complements more traditional close looking, the reconstructions led us to an analysis of the urban and architectural forms different from what we had expected. Working from the most developed stand-alone plan as well as the published report by Ritter and the photographic models, it became much clearer how the spatial conception changed from 1940 through 1941 through three distinct phases of the plan, something not previously noted by any scholar who has looked at the drawings. Paying attention especially to the western edge of the plan as well as the symbolic plaza at the heart of the design, we can see how the monumental buildings originally conceived as a residence and headquarters for General Governor Frank (here, at the bottom of the images) receded quickly to become relatively minor structures in favor of the Wawel. In addition, as that residential complex diminished in scale, the symbolic and public center of the plan as a parade ground or meeting place to stage Nazi authority increased in importance and elaboration. Thus, while the plan emphasized specific state architectural preferences emanating from Speer and Berlin such as the importance of a central plaza, it also adapted to highlight the key role of the Wawel as Frank's symbolic center and a building that mediated between the historic core and the new Nazi city. The visual analysis prompted a more careful investigation of the sources and helped us see the apparent administrative negotiation involved in developing the site.

But also surprisingly, the spatial orientation to the Jewish ghetto, which abutted (however temporarily) the southeast corner of the Nazi district, also became more emphatic. In Figure 6.5, we can see that the changes to where the plan adjoined the ghetto were dramatic (the ghetto is in the upper right of the image, just beyond the canal). In

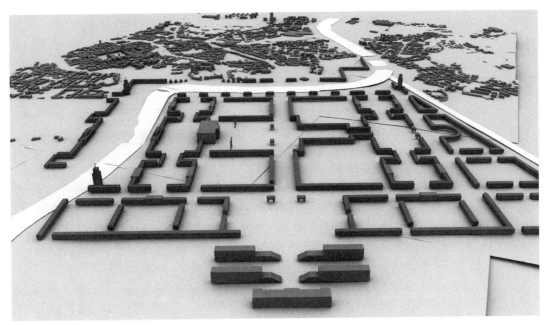

Figure 6.4. Reconstruction of the Ritter Plan (second version), Krakow, 1941. Visualization courtesy of Davide Contiero.

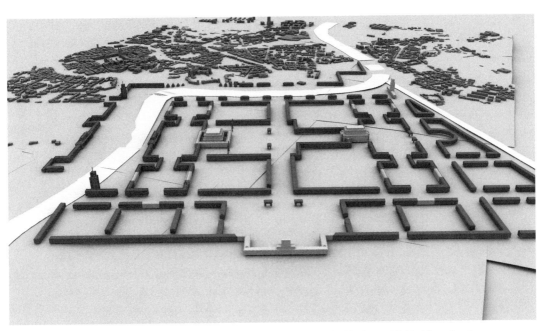

Figure 6.5. Reconstruction of the Ritter Plan (third version), Krakow, 1941. Visualization courtesy of Davide Contiero.

the initial plan, there were buildings of no striking feature; this altered in the second (February 1941) plan with the position of the tower, a form that was simplified in the third (May 1941) iteration, to form one of three towers on the key corners of the Nazi district—perhaps mimicking in a modern variation the medieval presence and focus on the Burg with its own tower forms. But such changes made to the architectural plan also *emphasized* the visual and spatial proximity of the ghetto rather than masking or obscuring it. This is shown in particular by the development of the modest skyscraper tower exactly in the southeast corner of the plan. This building established not only a profile for the Nazi ideal city; it also provided clear viewsheds both directly into the spaces of the ghetto (overseeing in particular the large plaza where the Judenrat building was located) but also *from* the ghetto to the spatial authority of the new Nazi capital. While this observation may have been made by further close looking to the original models (and does not replace that analog art historical method), the digital reconstruction makes the spatial changes and relationships within the complex city-scale of the plan more evident. These changes make clearer spatial demarcations between German and non-German spaces, something evident in Ritter's own final text cited above. They seem to be changes that correspond better to the architect's own idea for the political and ideological domination of the space. In this regard, one might ask whether they were mere symbolic forms on the model or also meant to function as monuments of practical surveillance of the surrounding (Christian and Jewish) Polish population. Visualizations then and now point in both directions. For example, the oblique view of the photos and our visualization emphasize the edges of the plan that had short-term significance—the Wawel and the ghetto—while the formal site plan of Figure 6.2 is much more in line with the long-term architectural and ideological values of a supposedly successful Nazi state. This analysis reveals no synthesis of the two; rather, the conflicts, contradictions, and complexities of Nazi spatial planning in Krakow help us to clarify the material evidence that remains, as well as pointing to more precise political questions especially concerning short-term actions and long-term (racist) goals.

Such questions at the building, neighborhood, or city scale can extend out to a broader systemic analysis of the ghetto system as a whole in occupied Europe. Our preliminary work allows us to begin to visualize important political decisions such as opening and closing dates of ghettos within the Distrikt Krakau controlled by Frank's administration. Our preliminary visualizations of two datasets related to the ghettos in Distrikt Krakau and Jewish forced labor camps in the same area, for example, seem to show no immediate correlation between distinct labor points and the spatial presence of most ghettos. Still, there is a decided clustering of activity especially evident in forced-labor construction sites around Krakow. This suggests a question of whether forced-labor construction activity related either to political decisions regarding the availability of Jewish labor or economic ones determined by existing industrial sites.

The broader role of building at the level of all construction is clearly much more central to the intersection of the military economic drive with the oppression of the Jews than has previously been suggested by scholars. Conversely, the role of civilian or conscripted building and construction personnel in perpetrating the horrors of the Holocaust is clearly under-investigated.[40] The micro- and macro-matrix of spatial relationships suggested by the political history of Frank and Ritter needs to be extended to account for a more complex and integrated history of the Holocaust, the German occupation, and the role of architecture.

We have used the material evidence of the German planning during the Nazi occupation as well as digital methods to extend and interrogate that evidence. Visualization is not a passive end goal but rather an active part of the research and scholarly process. It makes visible the historical relationship between the Jewish ghetto and the perpetrator appropriations and claims on the environment that have become invisible in the current cityscape. In this sense, the historical evidence as well as visual analysis help us to think in complex social and spatial terms about the political control over the site. Making these relationships visible has been a main goal of this work. Needless to say, the role of the construction industry—from the high design of the Wawel to the most banal vernacular industrial structure—runs like a thread through these questions. Our work here suggests a deeper connection to political, economic, and ideological goals that broaden out from an investigation of the built environment.

A political history of architecture in occupied Krakow highlights the need for more subtle differentiation of sources in relation to policies, ideological goals, and social conditions. The tension and convergence of Ritter's and Frank's ideas for the built environment help to highlight the uneven relationship between long-term and short-term agendas as well as different scales of spatial thinking. At the same time, the visualization of Ritter's plan in particular shows the radical convergence in a racist conception of social hierarchy and political domination. As a result, this analysis shows how the political and ideological mechanisms of fascism can be highlighted by a specific focus on architecture and construction. It puts the lie to any easy tendency to collapse cultural production into affirmative humanist categories. Instead, it challenges us to put human atrocities and the propensity toward violence at the center of our architectural histories.

Notes

1. As argued by many scholars since the foundational text of Barbara Miller Lane, *Architecture and Politics in Germany 1918–1945* (Cambridge, Mass.: Harvard University Press, 1968). See further Wolfram Pyta, *Hitler: Der Künstler als Politiker und Feldherr; Eine Herrschaftsanalyse* (Munich: Siedler, 2015). For advanced recent research on this topic, see Naomi Vaughan in this volume on Albert Speer's Neue Reichskanzlei in Berlin.

2. Jochen Thies, *Architekt der Weltherrschaft: Die "Endziele" Hitlers* (Düsseldorf: Droste Verlag, 1976).

3. See, for exceptions, Niels Gutschow, *Ordnungswahn: Architekten planen im "eingedeutschten" Osten 1939–1945* (Basel: Birkhäuser, 2001) and Jean-Louis Cohen, *Architecture in Uniform: Designing and Building for the Second World War* (Montreal: Canadian Centre for Architecture, 2011).

4. Compare, for example, Baron von Haussmann's combination of aesthetics and politics, construction and creation. Joan DeJean, *How Paris Became Paris: The Invention of the Modern City* (New York: Bloomsbury, 2014). In a parallel vein, see José H. Bortoluci's contribution to this volume on housing in São Paulo in which he argues for a broader understanding of architectural meaning as process beyond design.

5. For a comparative dynamic of the racialized "sorting" of society through urban and architectural planning, see Mabel O. Wilson's contribution to this volume on the Smithsonian Institute and Washington, D.C.

6. Examples of their work include Monika Bednarek, ed., *Kraków under Nazi Occupation 1939–1945* (Krakow: Muzeum Historyczne Miasta Krakowa, 2011); Gutschow, *Ordnungswahn*; Richard Němec, "Raum: Theorie und Realität um 1941," in *Kunst und Revolution*, ed. Milena Bartlová and Vybíral Jindřich (Prague: 2018), 416–49; Jacek Purchla and Paulina Roszak-Niemirska, *Niechciana stołeczność: architektura i urbanistyka Krakowa w czasie okupacji niemieckiej 1939–1945* (Krakow: International Cultural Centre, 2022). The latter museum catalog is an excellent encyclopedic overview of key building sites in Krakow during the German occupation.

7. Such are the long-term goals of our broader collaborative's analysis of the spatial significance of the Nazi ghetto system throughout occupied Europe in the "Holocaust Ghettos Project" led by Anne Kelly Knowles. For this project, Justus Hillebrand is the architect of our ghettos database. We are indebted to our colleagues for their many contributions to the conceptualization of this study of Krakow.

8. Admirable examples of this case-study model are the excellent contributions to Wendy Z. Goldman and Joe William Trotter, Jr., eds., *The Ghetto in Global History: 1500 to the Present* (London: Routledge, 2018). We do not wish to critique this work as much as to ask whether there are other options, especially with digital methods.

9. Alexandra Garbarini and Paul B. Jaskot, "Introduction: Integrated Histories of the Holocaust," *New Approaches to an Integrated History of the Holocaust: Social History, Representation, Theory*, vol. 13, *Lessons and Legacies* (Evanston: Northwestern University Press, 2018), 3–10.

10. Notably, the vast literature on the architectural history of Nazi Germany has focused almost exclusively on the perspective of the perpetrator; this is understandable given the nature of the sources. Digital visualization is one method to try to get to at least some of the ways that a built environment may have had meaning for other constituencies than the patron. For examples of two different but complementary analyses of this digital potential, see Kim Gallon, "Making a Case for the Black Digital Humanities," in *Debates in the Digital Humanities 2016,* ed. Matthew K. Gold and Lauren F. Klein (Minneapolis: University of Minnesota Press, 2016), 42–49; and Willard McCarty, "Modeling the Actual, Simulating

the Possible," in *The Shape of Data in Digital Humanities: Modeling Texts and Text-Based Resources*, ed. Julia Flanders and Fotis Jannidis (London: Routledge, 2018), 264–84.

11. Here we follow the groundbreaking example of Diane Favro and Christopher Johanson, "Death in Motion: Funeral Processions in the Roman Forum," *Journal of the Society of Architectural Historians* 69, no. 1 (March 2010): 12–37. See also Paul B. Jaskot, "Digital Art History as the Social History of Art: Towards the Disciplinary Relevance of Digital Methods," *Visual Resources* 35, nos. 1–2 (2019): 21–33.
12. Jacek Purchla, *Cracow in the European Core* (Krakow: International Cultural Centre, 2000).
13. For Krakow, see Monika Bednarek, "Kraków as the 'Capital' of the General Government," in Bednarek, ed. (2011), 116. See also Martin Winstone, *The Dark Heart of Hitler's Europe: Nazi Rule in Poland under the General Government* (London: I. B. Taurus, 2015).
14. Dieter Schenk, *Krakauer Burg: Die Machtzentrale des Generalgouveneurs Hans Frank 1939–1945* (Berlin: Ch. Links, 2010), 75.
15. See, also, where this was made explicit in the introduction to Max Freiherr Du Prel, *Das Generalgouvernement, Im Auftrage und mit einem Vorwort von Dr. Frank* (Würzburg: Konrad Triltsch Verlag, 1942).
16. See, for example, "Bericht über den Aufbau im Generalgouvernement bis 1. Juli 1940," Bundesarchiv (BA) R52II, file 247, accessed at the U.S. Holocaust Memorial Museum (USHMM), RG 14.025M, in which the importance of the "Burg" among other building projects (181) and the explicit colonial project (3, 23) are addressed.
17. Such internecine competition was perhaps most grotesquely emphasized in the policies toward Polish Jews and the development of ghettos. See Christopher Browning, "Nazi Ghettoization Policy in Poland: 1939–41," *Central European History* 19, no. 4 (December 1986): 343–68. This competition continued throughout the war, as indicated for example on May 25, 1943, in a seven-page letter Frank sent to Hitler asserting his authority in the face of encroachment by Himmler's office of the Reichskommissar für die Festigung des deutschen Volkstum (copy accessed in International Tracing Service, 1.2.7.7.001, available at the USHMM).
18. Jacek Purchla, *Miasto i polityka: Przypadki Krakowa* (Krakow: Universitas, 2018), 106–9.
19. "Verordnung über die Einführung des Arbeitspflicht für die polnische Bevölkerung des Generalgouvernements," as cited and translated in Witold W. Mędykowski, *Macht Arbeit Frei? German Economic Policy and Forced Labor of Jews in the General Government, 1939–1943* (Boston: Academic Studies Press, 2018), 41. For a list of buildings worked on in 1940 for the Ordnungspolizei, see BA R52II, file 247 (accessed at the USHMM, RG 14.025M), 169–71.
20. See Gutschow, *Ordnungswahn*.
21. See the analysis of planning conflicts, especially in occupied Czechoslovakia, in Richard Němec, "National Socialist Architectural Policy in the Occupied Countries of Central and Eastern Europe," *Acta Poloniae Historica* 114 (2016): 123–58.
22. See Thomas Zeller, *Driving Germany: The Landscape of the German Autobahn, 1930–1970* (New York: Berghahn, 2007).
23. For Ritter's biographical information, see Rit_Hu 302–201 in the Technische Universität (TU) archive, Munich. In this file, he notes that he left his job in Leipzig in 1930 due to

"political reasons," although what this means is not clear. See also the overview of his plan in Purchla, *Miasto i polityka,* 110.

24. In an excellent overview of current research on the city, Żanna Komar states that Ritter was, at least officially, sent by the Ministry of the Interior. Żanna Komar, "Architecture in German-Occupied Kraków: Selected Research Problems," *kunsttexte.de* 3 (2019), accessed February 28, 2020, https://edoc.hu-berlin.de/bitstream/handle/18452/21477/Komar.pdf. See, also, Speer's practice of combining architectural collaboration with politics in Nader Vossoughian's contribution to this volume.
25. See the mention to Feder's *Die neue Stadt* (Berlin: Springer, 1939) in the short bibliography at the end of Ritter's text. Ritter, *Der Generalbebauungsplan von Krakau* (Berlin [?]: Der Sonderbeauftragte für den Generalbebauungsplan von Krakau, 1941), 28. Komar notes that he apparently finished his design back in Berlin (Komar, "Architecture in German-Occupied Kraków").
26. For the photographs, see TU Munich, Rit_Hu 167.
27. Such logic parallels that in the Frank-sponsored text by Du Prel, *Das Generalgouvernement.*
28. Ritter, *Der Generalbebauungsplan von Krakau,* 11–12.
29. Paul B. Jaskot, "Anti-Semitic Policy in Albert Speer's Plans for the Rebuilding of Berlin," *The Art Bulletin* 78, no. 4 (1996): 622–32.
30. See, also, the foundational work on the "Hitler Cities" by Jost Dülffer, Jochen Thies, and Josef Henke, eds., *Hitlers Städte: Baupolitik im Dritten Reich* (Cologne: Böhlau Verlag, 1978). Note that the enabling law that Ritter suggests at the end of his published plan that aligned his authority to Speer and then Hitler was typical of the structure claimed by the Inspector Generals of Building in other "Hitler Cities."
31. The centrality of the Burg for the whole plan is indicated in multiple places in Ritter's text, e.g., Ritter, *Der Generalbebauungsplan von Krakau,* 18.
32. Ritter, *Der Generalbebauungsplan von Krakau,* 20.
33. See the careful chronological changes to conditions for Jews in the Generalgouvernement laid out in Mędykowski, *Macht Arbeit Frei?.*
34. See in particular the meeting notes from April 12, 1940, reproduced in Werner Präg and Wolfgang Jacobmeyer, eds., *Das Diensttagebuch des Generalgouverneurs in Polen, 1939–1945, Quellen und Darstellungen zur Zeitgeschichte,* vol. 20 (Stuttgart: Deutsche Verlags-Anstalt, 1975), 165.
35. Gutschow, *Ordnungswahn,* 54–57. See also the evident frustration of Ritter with the change in location of Frank's administrative center in the published plan, where he indicates that the change came after much of the ideas presented here were already made and designed (Ritter, *Der Generalbebauungsplan von Krakau,* 19).
36. Bednarek, "Kraków as the 'Capital' of the General Government," 138, 145.
37. Purchla, *Miasto i polityka,* 135–36. For a contemporary view of the plans, see H. Urban, "Krakaus gegenwärtige und Zukünftige Neubauten," *Das Generalgouvernement,* nos. 7–8 (1941), 27–33.
38. Notably, in 1944 and in spite of the disastrous course of the war for Germany, the architectural journal *Moderne Bauformen* was still publishing articles that discussed how architecture *currently* under construction or recently completed served the needs of the military goals as well as long-term interests of a victorious Nazi state. See, e.g., Hermann

Mäckler, "Wohnsiedlung eines deutschen Industriewerks," *Moderne Bauformen* 43, nos. 1/3 (January/March 1944): 1–11.

39. We have begun our collaborative exploration of the ghetto system by building a large database extracting evidence from the U.S. Holocaust Memorial Museum's work on ghettos in German-occupied Europe. We are grateful for the input of the collaborative team led by Anne Kelly Knowles.

40. See, in particular, the role of the Baudienst in the Holocaust in Jan Grabowski, *Hunt for the Jews: Betrayal and Murder in German-Occupied Poland* (Bloomington: Indiana University Press, 2013), 121–29.

Chapter 7

Afro-Caribbean Migration and Detention at Ellis Island

Itohan Osayimwese

Contrary to popular narratives that figure it as largely white and European, the Ellis Island immigration station policed the racial and ethnic composition of the United States from very early in its history. This chapter approaches Ellis Island from the unsung perspectives of African-descended Caribbean immigrants who passed with difficulty through its gates. I draw on literary analysis, formal architectural analysis, and new materialist methods to analyze the immigration station's distinctive spatiality and materiality. This essay therefore contributes to a history of U.S. immigration that reveals the role of the built environment in practices of discrimination and struggles for rights, freedoms, and recognition among its diverse populations.

A Caribbean Ellis Island

Ellis Island holds an almost mythological place in the national psyche of the United States. Where the word "Mayflower" connotes a benign story of brave English men and women sailing across the Atlantic to found a new country, "Ellis Island" conjures a whitewashed history of the peopling of the country from the end of the nineteenth century.[1] As historian David Roediger explains, through a complex sequence of transformations, Ellis Island and the U.S. immigration experience came to be equated with whiteness—understood as the dominant order whereby U.S. society is organized to defend and uphold the privilege and power of its lightest-skinned population.[2] However, the work of academic and lay historians is making visible the racial, ethnic, and cultural diversity of immigration that was fully recognized and feared in the nineteenth century. The dehumanizing experiences of Chinese, Filipino, and Japanese immigrants at Ellis Island, Angel Island, and other immigration stations in the country thus challenges the progressive narrative that has long dominated academic and popular histories.[3]

Meanwhile, the experiences of immigrants of African ancestry, an estimated

Figure 7.1. Three Somali immigrants at Ellis Island, circa 1914. National Park Service.

100,000 of whom entered the United States through Ellis Island, still remain largely unacknowledged.[4] This is in part because of the peculiar social structure of the United States which, for a long time, only had room for two categories: "voluntary immigrants of European descent and involuntarily incorporated racial minorities."[5] For this reason,

Figure 7.2. Women from Guadeloupe in front of Kitchen and Laundry Building, Ellis Island, circa 1911. National Park Service.

the voluntary migration of African-descended people was subsumed into the larger narrative of U.S.-born people of African ancestry.

Until recently, most African-descended immigrants in the United States emigrated from the Caribbean. Free Afro-Caribbean people migrated in significant numbers to South Carolina and Louisiana during the 1791 Haitian Revolution. Caribbean-born African-descended people also dominated the population of free people of color in the North. Sociologist Philip Kasinitz has identified three subsequent waves of Caribbean migration. The first migration started around 1880 and peaked in the 1920s. This wave came to an almost complete halt after the Johnson–Reed Act of 1924, which established quotas based on the number of people from each country already residing in the United States. A second and much smaller wave of Caribbean immigrants arrived between the 1930s and 1965. The third wave of Caribbean migration spans 1965 to the present. The 1960s marked a new phase in part due to restrictive immigration policies implemented in England, which redirected the flow of former colonial subjects toward the United States. At the same time, immigration reform in the United States eliminated national quotas in lieu of hemispheric limits.[6]

There are a few well-known life stories of Caribbean immigrants. Winston James and Tammy Brown explain that Caribbean immigrants in the 1920s developed a keen political consciousness that manifested as radical activism in African American political organizations and culture.[7] As a result, some lives are well-documented and offer insight into the Afro-Caribbean immigrant experience. Perhaps best known is the story of Marcus Mosiah Garvey. Born in Jamaica in 1887, Garvey left school at fourteen to train as a printer's apprentice, then traveled to South and Central America and London. Upon returning to Jamaica in 1914, he founded the Universal Negro Improvement Association (UNIA). UNIA nurtured racial pride, promoted self-reliance, economic independence, and the creation of a Black-led nation in Africa. When UNIA did not gain much ground in Jamaica, Garvey relocated to the United States. After working as a crew member on the SS *Tallac* to pay his way to the United States, Garvey was processed at Ellis Island on March 23, 1916.[8] From there he seems to have quickly made his way to Harlem, where he settled among a growing number of Caribbean émigrés and African Americans who had fled Jim Crow laws in the South. He lodged with an immigrant Jamaican family in "a little hall-bedroom, hardly heated or well ventilated."[9] From this base, Garvey promoted UNIA's goals until his politically motivated imprisonment and deportation in 1927.[10] Curiously, his immigration story goes unremarked in most scholarship.

Garvey's arrival as a crew member on a ship reminds us that Afro-Caribbean immigrants came to the United States via various routes that may not be visible in conventional archives. Merchant marine work was an important occupation for British West Indian men when economic opportunities remained limited on the islands after Emancipation. Though the communal experience of hardship on board sometimes led to what Marcus Rediker describes as an "alternative social order" of egalitarianism, Afro-Caribbean men often found themselves restricted to lower-ranking positions such as cooks, stewards, and simple seamen.[11] Nevertheless, because ship work came with room and board, sailors were sometimes able to accumulate enough capital to purchase property or open a business. These men circulated between port towns on the west bank of the Atlantic where they formed enclaves that remain at the core of many Caribbean communities today.[12]

This phenomenon extended beyond the British West Indies. Rose Mary Allen shows that for Afro-Caribbean men in the Dutch Antilles, maritime work was linked to permanent emigration and increased wealth and social status at home. Of the fifty-two crew members on board the *Prins der Nederlanden,* which arrived at Ellis Island in October 1919, twenty-six were "African blacks" from the Dutch West Indies. There were also British West Indians among the crew. By the time the ship left New York in November, ten people had formally severed ties with the crew and three had deserted. Allen hypothesizes that some of these were African-descended men who settled in the United States.[13] Thus, European merchant ships were transformed from historical vehicles of enslavement to modern instruments of opportunity for Afro-Caribbean men.[14] Indeed, scholars have argued that free and enslaved African-descended sailors contributed to the creation of a Black Atlantic community and consciousness. It was this very network of seafarers who, in the 1920s, were responsible for popularizing Marcus Garvey's ideas about Black self-determination.[15]

Nevertheless, the stories of Garvey and other Caribbean immigrant political leaders and intellectuals are not representative. More common was the experience of Vera Clark Ifill, born in Barbados in 1914 to parents who had emigrated to the United States around 1904. Like many West Indians, the Ifills took their children back home to be raised by extended family members. After Vera Ifill's grandparents died, Ifill's mother returned to the island to collect her children. The family journeyed to the United States on the *Vestris* in January 1921. Because the Ifills were poor, they traveled in the third class and were accommodated in the hold of the ship. The experience in the hold was unpleasant: they were in a large, congested area where they slept on bunk beds. The space was cold, and one of Vera Ifill's sisters suffered from frostbite.[16]

Though Ifill does not make the analogy, one wonders if the experience of migration characterized by overcrowding, cold, and hunger in the hold of a ship meant something different to Afro-Caribbean people. Art historian Cheryl Finley has shown how African diasporic expressive practices have sustained a collective memory of slavery through the use of the slave ship icon.[17] Trinidadian-born Marxist writer C. L. R. James's essay on Herman Melville's *Moby-Dick*, written during his 1952 incarceration on Ellis Island, also hints at this connection. James presents Melville's fateful whaling voyage as an augur of World War II.[18] But the figure of the whale was a popular symbol of enslavement, and, as a literary work, *Moby-Dick* was embedded in the "discursive field" of transatlantic slavery.[19] Similarly, in his autobiography *A Long Way from Home*, the Jamaican-born revolutionary socialist and Harlem Renaissance poet Claude McKay wrote of the contrast between the dirty depths of steerage accommodations and the soaring brightness of the New York City skyline experienced by immigrants. He points out that this perception of the city was misplaced. In reality, to live there was to "descend into precipitous gorges, where visions are broken."[20] Here, the analogy to enslavement transcends the immigrant ship to encompass the oppression of African-descended people in the city.

On arrival at Ellis Island, the Ifills were herded "like cattle" with countless other immigrants into "cages" in the Registry Room.[21] These cages feature in the stories of the many ethnic groups who arrived at Ellis Island and signal the dominant detention function of the island proposed in this chapter.[22] Though Vera Ifill's mother had left the United States only a few months earlier, the Ifill family was detained. After a period of detention, the family was allowed to go home to the Bronx.[23] Unfortunately, Vera Ifill's father was murdered a few months later. Her life changed dramatically thereafter, and the family was expelled from their apartment and forced to move from place to place. She dropped out of school in ninth grade in order to work, got married and had children, and moved to California where she and her husband established a successful business.[24] These facts were recorded as one of only a handful of interviews of Caribbean immigrants conducted as part of the Ellis Island Oral History Project. They do little to convey the complexity of Ifill's experience in the United States. Here I seek to counteract the invisibility of individuals like Vera Ifill by speaking their names and building the visual and textual archive of their immigration. Writing these histories is crucial for fulfilling the promise of liberty and equality for all that has haunted the United States since its founding.

The Design of Ellis Island

Like the dominant narrative of Ellis Island, the spatial and material character of the island is more complex than it appears. Accompanying the standard story of brave Europeans entering the gates is the iconic image of a magisterial building, its polychrome walls and domed towers visible for miles above a flat island landscape.[25] For many, this building—currently a museum run by the National Park Service—*is* Ellis Island. But, at its peak, Ellis Island consisted of a vast complex of structures dispersed across three islands.

Perhaps the archaeological term *stratification* best captures the materiality of the island, which is the outcome of multiple phases in which the material record of human activity was deliberately reused in the construction of the next phase.[26] Before it was occupied by European settlers, the island was a fishing and oyster trapping ground for the Lenape nation who inhabited what would become New York City and the state of New Jersey. An archaeological survey and excavation conducted during the conversion of the site into a museum in 1984–85 revealed intact evidence of prehistoric Native American inhabitation.[27] A failed attempt in 1970 by a coalition of Indigenous people to occupy the island and return it to Native American use hints at ownership claims that remain unresolved today.[28] Indeed, since the 1980s, repatriations of Lenape ancestors for reburial on Ellis Island illustrate the ways in which descendant communities maintain ongoing connections to this space.[29]

Renamed "Ellis" after a colonial settler who purchased it, ownership was transferred in 1808 to the federal government, which constructed a military fortification. This defensive use made sense because of the geographical location of the island off the southern tip of the colony's commercial capital, Manhattan, which enabled preemptive attacks against incoming enemy ships. In the eighteenth century there were already discussions about using the island as a quarantine site, which foreshadowed the island's subsequent history.[30]

The Lenape island was only three acres in area, so it was immediately expanded by the federal government to eleven acres through innovative land reclamation techniques. Rubble from military fortifications, channel dredging, ships' ballast, and New York City subway soil were poured into a cribwork seawall.[31] This human-designed landscape became the site of the first federal immigration station in 1892. The station included an enormous Main Building of wood; five extant structures from the old military battery

Figure 7.3. Women from Guadeloupe in front of Main Building, Ellis Island, circa 1911. National Park Service.

were also reused as part of the scheme.[32] Notably, descriptions of the Main Building indicate that detention was one of its primary functions: it included an "outdoor pen," three detention rooms, and a third floor consisting only of a catwalk that allowed officials to surveil the throng of immigrants awaiting processing below.[33] A fire destroyed most of the structures on the island in the summer of 1897.

As a consequence, the immigration station was rebuilt with close attention to fireproofing in 1898–1900. Based on the parti of the old structure, a new Main Building resulted from a competition won by the Beaux-Arts–trained architects William Boring and Edward Tilton. Their award-winning design was built of red brick over a steel frame. The Renaissance-inspired three-story structure was buttressed on four corners by high towers that culminated in copper repoussé domes and soaring spires.[34] The façade was ornate. Heavy limestone surrounds framed each arch, door, and window and defined each register of the tripartite façade. Rusticated quoins emphasized each corner. A corbel table supported a deeply cut cornice and ornate parapet, all built in gleaming limestone. Eagles, escutcheons, and sculpted heads capped key termini. Against the background of red brick, these limestone decorative elements created a vibrant, polychromatic effect.

A cavernous central space formed the core of the building and held baggage and a Railroad Ticket Office on the first floor and a large immigrant interrogation space (the Registry Room) on the second floor. Massive arched windows articulated the central processing area on the main façades in the spirit of the great French railway stations of the nineteenth century.[35] According to a 1902 article, railway stations were the closest analogues to the new immigrant station—"a problem quite without precedent."[36] Cutting-edge Guastavino vaults were added to the ceiling of the Registry Room in 1918 to improve its ability to resist fire.[37] Like its forebear, the third floor retained a panoptical catwalk with a view of the processing area below on one side and dormitories for detained immigrants on the other. Wings containing smaller rooms for specialized questioning and medical examination, offices for staff, and dormitories for detained immigrants flanked the central section to the east and west. In fact, turn-of-the-century critics noted that the otherwise well-designed immigrant station suffered from the "dangerous tendency of the Beaux-Arts idea" to produce buildings of incongruous scale in which monumental central masses dwarf diminutive wings.[38]

The building, captured in many period photographs, was highly recognizable. Its metal mesh cages, darkened cavernous corners, and massive arched windows were favored backdrops in Lewis Hines's important 1904–9 series of social reform photographs of immigrants.[39] More recently, visual culture scholar Erica Rand has commented on the dominant presence of images of this building in the iconography of contemporary Ellis Island heritage tourism—usually as an abstract backdrop for depictions of generic light-skinned nineteenth-century immigrants on kitschy tourist souvenirs.[40]

In addition to the Main Building, the chief structures on the island included the Kitchen and Laundry Building, Power House, Incinerator, and covered walkways. Like the first Main Building, its successor reused construction material from previous buildings: the 1985 dig uncovered intact parts of the stucco-covered western wall of the original military barracks.

At the same time as these new buildings were constructed on the enlarged Lenape island (Island 1), the federal government constructed an entirely new island (Island 2) immediately to the south. Earth, stone, and rubble from the first immigration station were used as fill for Island 2.[41] The goal was to alleviate poor conditions by erecting dedicated hospital structures and staff housing not available on Island 1. Still another island (Island 3) was created to the south of Island 2 in 1905 using cellar dirt, stone, clay, old masonry, earth, and sand. This fill was deposited on top of submerged land and retained using wood and stone cribwork. Additional hospital structures including contagious disease wards and mortuary and autopsy facilities were placed here. A narrow wood bridge connected Islands 2 and 3. Finally, in 1923, the inlet between them was filled in order to create a single landmass.[42] A ferry dock linked this new landmass to Island 1.

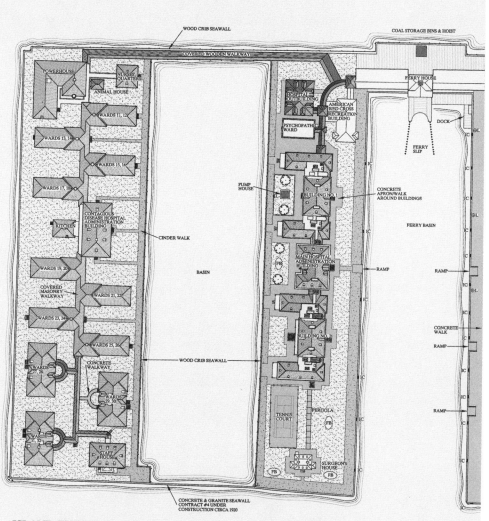

ISLAND THREE   ISLAND TWO

CIRCA 1920 - ELLIS ISLAND
1"=60'-0"   1:720

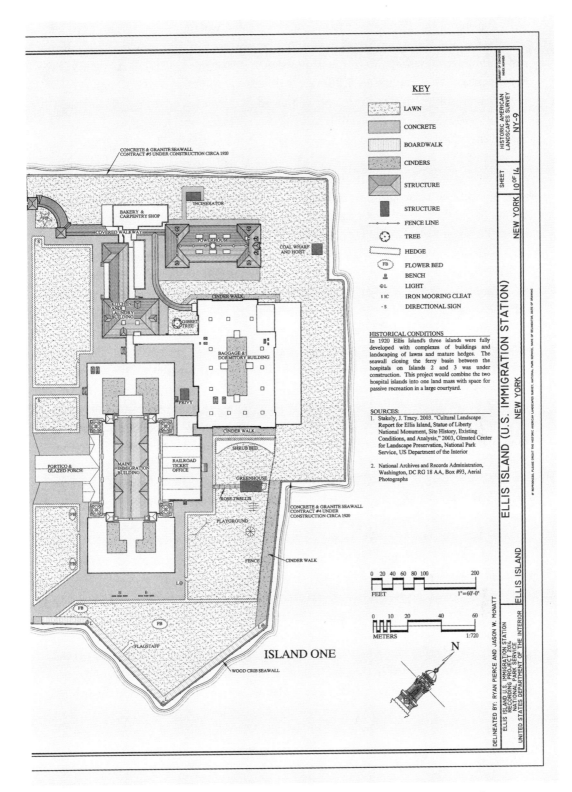

Figure 7.4. Ellis Island site plan, circa 1920, during construction of the seawall merging Islands 1, 2, and 3. Historic American Landscapes Survey, National Park Service.

By the end of this process of expansion, the area on which the second immigration station stood was almost ten times the original size of the Lenape's island. The majority of this land was human-engineered. I want to suggest that this apparent artificiality had consequences. Land made from infill reacts differently to external forces than organically formed soil. In 1898, the new fill deposited to create Island 2 caused the underwater supports for Island 1 to fail. In response, contractor Warren Roosevelt left out some of the planned fill and altered the geometry of the new installation. In 2003, landscape architect J. Tracy Stakely noted the presence of sinkholes on Ellis Island, which he attributed to a lack of continued maintenance. But New York's infilled shorelines were subject to flooding and sinkage throughout the nineteenth century. And they were difficult to build on and did not easily accommodate requirements for human life such as potable water.[43] Rather than assuming that the built environment starts and ends with the designer's intention, a "passive, mute, stable and unchangeable" structure, and human inhabitation, we need to reposition architectural materiality in relation to the self-organization and self-adaptation of various artifact-organisms in complex, multiscalar environments.[44] Was the material instability of Ellis Island apparent to observers? What might it have felt like for newly arrived immigrants to step on this shifting ground?

Even as structural instability and erosion compromised the new fill for humans, a novel ecosystem of fish, birds, and other wildlife was likely emerging on the marshy edges of the human-made landscape. On one hand, the introduction of contaminated soil contributed to the century-long deterioration of shellfish and reef habitat around Manhattan.[45] On the other hand, the increased acreage of the islands offered alternative habitats for animals pushed out of the mainland.[46] The appearance of two new landmasses would also have altered the experiences of people and animals who frequented it. Not only does any island afloat in an endless sea create a different relationship between human life and time, but with its human-engineered enlargement, Ellis Island, like other nearby islands and Manhattan itself, leapfrogged geologic time.[47]

I suggest that the islands' exceptionality supported their successful use by the Immigration Service to shape and enforce an exclusionary vision of the nation.[48] In his essay on how immigration officials rhetorically and relationally constructed disability and race at Ellis Island, Jay Dolmage draws an analogy between the "garbage" used as fill and the careful construction of the "normalcy" of the white mainstream population against the immigrant as the "waste" of other nations.[49] In a related argument, Ayasha Guerin makes the case that in the nineteenth century, New York City's flood zone was a landfilled space where enslaved and low-wage laborers historically navigated unsustainable, exploitative, but sometimes empowering relationships between race, nature, and capital. It was the particular confluence of the liminal spatiality and unstable materiality of reclaimed soil between land and sea that supported these relationships.[50]

Overall, we can identify a dominant logic in the architecture, design, and spatial organization of the immigration station. This logic was recognized by the architects Boring and Tilton in an 1898 article: "The difficult problem to be solved in the establishment of the greatest immigrant station in the world. . . . immigrants to be kept free from all outside interference until discharged; to be treated as *semi-prisoners,* with all consideration due to *future* citizens of the United States."[51] Dolmage aptly explains this vision as it was translated into floor plans and building sections: the "choreographic and architectural brainchild of Jeremy Bentham and Henry Ford—a panopticon and an assembly line."[52] Within the Main Building and between the original island and engineered islands there was a centrifugal, horizontal, and vertical organization of social disorder. Spaces for detention and disease were placed on the periphery of the Main Building, on its upper floors, and arranged according to risk on the two adjacent islands. Island 2 hosted the General Hospital Building as well as the Psychopathic Ward; Island 3 was dedicated to contagious diseases and spaces for death. Furthermore, Ellis Islands' exceptional temporality and materiality might have destabilized the immigrant arriving after a lengthy ocean voyage. Time passed in a unique way for immigrants processed within view but still removed from the liberty they sought on New York's shores. Walking on the unstable ground of the immigration station may have aggravated some immigrants' sense of loss and uncertainty. My analysis suggests that detention, exclusion, and precariousness were the dominant features of Ellis Island's design from the outset.

There were, however, moments of resistance within this dominant logic. First, the contingencies of the experiment that was Ellis Island meant that actual room use shifted regularly and did not match up with floor plans and design intentions.[53] Second, as entities outside time and space with unstable topographies, the islands offered a psychological petri dish for the invention of new identities. Some people attempted to transform their stations in life by adopting new life stories.[54] Third, more than four hundred square feet of graffiti found in the Main Building illustrate the ability of immigrants to speak back to institutional power.[55] The graffiti also attests to the possibility of immigrants anchoring themselves despite the slow/fast time and space of the islands. Finally, this graffiti marks the transgression of the original design intention by other agentive forces.[56] Perhaps, we can say, following Manuel DeLanda, that it is on the (graffiti-clad) surface where "exotic material behavior" occurs, that the building itself resisted the singularity and causality presumed by its designers.[57]

From Detention to More Detention

Drawing on written records, scholars have argued that Ellis Island was transformed from a more benevolent immigration station to a sinister site of detention and, later, a concentration camp. But detention was built into the design of the site from as early as 1890. Rather than a seismic shift, the turn in the 1920s toward more detention at Ellis Island represented an expansion of its original mission.

The restrictive immigration acts of 1921 and 1924 were at the root of this alleged metamorphosis. Immigration scholars have often argued that the Acts pitted immigrants from northern and western Europe against seemingly less-desirable eastern and southern Europeans. Mae Ngai reveals, however, that this view of national origin may "obscure from view other ideas about race, citizenship, and the nation that the new law both encoded and generated."[58] The Acts restricted immigration based on quotas, themselves determined by a seemingly scientific snapshot of the country's inhabitants in 1920. However, "inhabitants" was defined to exclude all "aliens" living in the country who were ineligible for citizenship (including almost all Asians and their descendants, all African-descended people, and all Native Americans and their descendants). The result was a demographic picture of the nation that was skewed in favor of white and European populations. This biased picture of the American population reproduced its foundational prejudices. As a result of the erasure of African-descended peoples from the population count, independent African nations received very small quotas. While colonized, African-descended people were subsumed into quotas set aside for their colonizers. In practice, this meant that fewer Afro-Caribbean people were allowed to enter the United States after 1924.[59] Ultimately, the 1924 Act was a race-based legislation that was written to appear as though it were not racist.[60]

Building on Ngai's argument, I suggest that the transformation in 1920s immigration policy disproportionately affected Afro-Caribbean peoples.[61] Situated at the confluence of colonial identity and blackness, Afro-Caribbean populations were located in an ambivalent place in U.S. immigration law. Formerly enslaved African-descended people within the United States were given citizenship in 1870 in what Ngai describes as a gratuitous gesture.[62] The subsequent exclusion of "the descendants of slave immigrants" from population counts for immigration quotas illustrates this insincerity. How would the law deal with "descendants of slave immigrants" from outside the United States and their continental African cousins?

African-descended migrants were an unexpected problem. As one federal judge opined in 1880, no one seriously believed that "the [N]egroes of Africa [would] emigrate."[63] In 1914, a bill to exclude all members of the "African race" from entering the United States was passed by the Senate. The bill caused great consternation among foreign- and native-born African-descended people and was defeated in the House of Representatives in part through the activism of Booker T. Washington and W. E. B. Du Bois.[64] But officials found other ways to exclude African-descended populations. Statistical evidence supports this claim: after peaking in 1924, immigration from the Caribbean did not again reach pre-1924 levels until the 1940s. Furthermore, an annual report of the Commissioner General for Immigration discloses that a disproportionate number of African-descended immigrants were refused admission in the late 1920s. Indeed, prospective Jamaican immigrants of the period complained about the arbitrary hurdles they faced when attempting to obtain visas from the American consulate in

Figure 7.5. Algerian man awaits deportation at Ellis Island, circa 1910. Manuscripts and Archives Division, The New York Public Library. "Algerian man" New York Public Library Digital Collections.

Kingston.[65] As a result, the United States saw negative net Afro-Caribbean admission throughout the 1930s as more immigrants left than arrived in the country.

Effects of the change in immigration policy that started in the 1920s include an exponential increase in illegal immigration, the production of the category of the "illegal alien," and an attendant new emphasis on deportation as an instrument of immigration policy.[66] Illegal aliens or those who entered or remained in the country unlawfully constituted a new class of persons "whose inclusion in the nation was at once a social reality and a legal impossibility."[67] This upsurge in unlawful entry into the country stimulated increased control of both land borders and the interior of the nation. Deportation had existed since colonial times, but it now took on a new form. Whereas the statute of limitations on deportation in 1917 was five years, after 1924 a person could be deported at any time after illegal entry regardless of how long they had lived in the country. Even more problematically, they could be deported from almost anywhere in the nation's interior.[68]

Specific numbers are not available for Afro-Caribbean deportations but, overall, the Immigration Service formally removed 466,767 people of all ethnicities between 1921 and 1940. This was a significant increase over the twenty-year period before 1921.[69] The fact that "black alien immigrants" departed the country in 1921 and 1922 in higher numbers than ever before supports the hypothesis that they were targeted.[70]

Ellis Island as Camp

New immigration policies in the 1920s resulted in changes to Ellis Island. Once conceptualized as an immigration station, it was now publicly acknowledged as a space for the interrogation and detention of illegal aliens.[71] Deportees were brought in groups from across the country to New York City. A barge took them to Ellis Island where they were processed and separated: those suffering from mental illness were sent to the hospital, and men, women, criminals, and prostitutes were held in separate quarters. Deportees were also segregated by race and separated from voluntary deportees and incoming migrants.[72]

Thus, a dual system that utilized design to advance social control was in place. An October 1933 *New York Times* article went as far as to describe the jail-like atmosphere that the erstwhile immigration station had developed: "Some of the guards are armed, doors are locked and windows barred."[73] Ranged along the corridors of large buildings, these elements produced a space of confinement much like the modern penitentiary. Unlike the penitentiary, though, this space relied (in the final analysis) on the older paradigm of expelling physical bodies rather than on Foucauldian discipline.[74]

An increasingly orchestrated temporal regime also governed life for deportees. A 1921 letter of complaint from a white South African man, Mark Glanvill, described the experience. According to his account, deportees moved from day cells to corridors to mess hall to caged-in porch to night cells in an unending cycle.[75] Implicit in his description is a proliferation of spatial containment to heighten the detention function of the immigration station. Notably, Glanvill complained about the presence of "negroes" in the swarming "dregs of humanity" he encountered at Ellis Island. Newspaper reports also drew attention to the appalling conditions for detainees, who were often left in limbo for four months or longer.[76]

The detention function of Ellis Island expanded further during World War II when the FBI interned thousands of "alien enemies" including Germans, Italians, Japanese, Romanians, Hungarians, Latin Americans, North Africans, Afro-Caribbean people, and others at Ellis Island.[77] As immigration scholar Anna Pegler-Gordon notes, earlier histories of immigrant exclusion and detention prefigured alien enemy internment, while some tactics developed in response to the "alien enemy problem" were later applied to immigration control.[78] The multiple layers of spatial containment already in place at Ellis Island enabled internment: Japanese, German, and Italian alien enemies were segregated in reprogrammed or newly added spaces. For instance, a 1944 magazine article noted that Ellis Island's Registry Room had been converted into a dormitory stuffed with military bunkbeds for married German alien enemies.[79] Over time, the room had been partitioned, its staircase relocated, toilets added, and new playing fields provided outside specifically for the latest detainees.[80]

Upsetting this new spatial order could destabilize the sense of control that internment provided. This was the case when four Japanese nationalists joined a meeting of Nazi supporters in the German dormitory in August 1942.[81] Their actions challenged the long-standing segregation of Europeans and Asians and illustrated the continuity of geopolitics within the rarified atmosphere of the immigration station. Similarly, internment could overturn established spatial practices on Ellis Island. In one case, Nazi supporters refused to be served by "American negroes," causing immigration authorities to remove "colored men" from the staff.[82]

World War II ended with the Cold War and a shift in global geopolitical alignments. Existing immigration laws had banned anarchists since 1903. Taking advantage of the postwar political climate, the McCarran–Walter Act of 1952 expanded the exclusion of anarchists to embrace all those advocating totalitarianism. Thousands accused of being communists would be detained at Ellis Island over the course of the Cold War.[83]

Two of the few documented stories of Afro-Caribbean confinement and deportation took place in this context. Born in Trinidad in 1901, C. L. R. James had moved to England in 1932 to become a novelist and political activist. He arrived at Ellis Island on the *Laconia* on January 1, 1938, for a six-week lecture tour.[84] By 1940, he had overstayed his visa and gone underground. In the summer of 1952, James was arrested for immigration violations. Though he had married an American woman, fathered a son, and applied for citizenship, his application was denied because of his Marxist views, and he was interred at Ellis Island and deported after six months.[85]

Written during his internment, James's *Mariners, Renegades, and Castaways: The Story of Herman Melville and the World We Live In* (1953) was part of his campaign to avoid deportation by promoting American civilization as the key to humanity's future. But the book was also a record of his experience at Ellis Island. Among other themes, he discusses the effects of spatial segregation: being placed with communists made him fear for his life because he had spoken out against the Soviet Union. James revealed how mobility and spatial dislocation were weaponized. For instance, it was a controlled privilege for political prisoners to be allowed in the same room as general prisoners in order to use the telephone or buy food.[86] As James points out, being on Ellis Island was not a simple case of detention. Despite immigration officials' representation of incarcerated people as "detainees," James insisted that he and others were "prisoners."[87] Importantly, for James it was the "islandness" of the place that made this possible. Like the men on Melville's vessel, James found himself "suddenly projected onto an island isolated from the rest of society, where American administrators and officials, and American security officers controlled the destinies of a thousand men."[88] James compared Ellis Island to Nazi concentration camps, "Russian slave labor camps," and a South Korean prisoner of war camp.[89] Ellis Island was trying to replace the legal system that developed in the United States as an expression of a "deep faith in civil liberties . . . intended to help the alien" with a structure designed for the "extermination of the alien as a malignant pest."[90] In Ellis Island, James saw the promises of the experiment that was American civilization gone awry.

Similarly, Claudia Jones's deportation story speaks to a Black history of Ellis Island deportation and spatial violence. Born in Trinidad, Jones emigrated on the *Voltaire* to the United States in 1924 at the age of six.[91] Like many before them, the family settled in Harlem. Her mother soon died, and her father struggled to provide for his four daughters. The family had to make do with a basement apartment next to a leaking sewer, and Jones contracted tuberculosis. Unable to attend college due to poverty, she joined the Communist Party where she received a rich political education and practical training. Rising through the party's ranks, she became an experienced speaker, writer, and leader. Jones was arrested multiple times for her political activities and was detained in 1948 and 1951 at Ellis Island. She was charged under the McCarran Act with conspiracy to overthrow the government and sentenced to imprisonment and deportation.[92]

Jones published a public letter from Ellis Island in November 1950 in which she described conditions of "imprisonment": it was an environment of sweltering gender-segregated rooms, barred windows, barbed wire fences, bright outdoor lights, constant surveillance, and solitary confinement. She labeled it a concentration camp.[93] Her inability to see the Statue of Liberty from the "McCarran Wing" became a metaphor for the unconstitutionality of her imprisonment. Like C. L. R. James, Jones used Ellis Island as a foil against which to define an idealized American past characterized by democratic and revolutionary traditions. She explicitly identified her solidarity with African

Americans and her diasporic West Indian identity as factors in her expulsion. In her letter, Jones mentions a fellow West Indian immigrant also incarcerated in the McCarran Wing.[94] Deportation was a tool of state violence, especially for racialized others.

It is notable that several commentators described Ellis Island as a concentration camp. A 1942 article in the *New York Times* is illustrative: "New York has a concentration camp of its own. . . . It lies out in the harbor, in the upper bay, beneath the green pepper-pot domes of the big Kremlin on Ellis Island."[95] "Concentration camp" originated in nineteenth-century U.S. military parlance to denote temporary accommodation for a large number of troops awaiting active service. By 1895 it had acquired its current meaning as a place in which a large number of persecuted minorities are imprisoned in inhuman conditions.[96] The application of the term to Ellis Island in the 1940s and 1950s was fraught because it was considered antithetical to the democratic values espoused by the United States.[97] Recent scholarship in "camp studies" theorizes the historical and contemporary political and existential condition of the immigrant, refugee, and prisoner in relation to the spatial and temporal exceptionality of the camp. Such scholarship argues that the camp has played a crucial role in the modern production of citizenship and its fundamental logics of exclusion.[98] Similarly, I have shown that exclusion was a foundational function of the Ellis Island Immigration Station. This function expanded in the 1920s, when immigration laws directed the authority of design against not only those produced as unassimilable into the nation-state but also those who existed at the margins of citizenship and those constructed as enemies of the state. African-descended people emigrating to the United States were caught up in this tangled web.

Notes

1. Approximately twelve million immigrants were processed at Ellis Island between 1892 and 1954. Barry Moreno, *Encyclopedia of Ellis Island* (Westport, Conn.: Greenwood Press, 2004), xi.
2. David Roediger, *Working Toward Whiteness: How America's Immigrants Became White: The Strange Journey From Ellis Island to the Suburbs* (New York: Basic Books, 2006), 9.
3. Roediger, *Working*, 9. Also see Mae M. Ngai, *Impossible Subjects: Illegal Aliens and the Making of Modern America* (Princeton: Princeton University Press, 2004); and Erika Lee, *At America's Gates: Chinese Immigration during the Exclusion Era 1882–1943* (Chapel Hill: University of North Carolina Press, 2003).
4. Moreno, *Encyclopedia*, 14; Joseph Keith, *Unbecoming Americans: Writing Race and Nation from the Shadows of Citizenship, 1945–1960* (New Brunswick: Rutgers University Press, 2013).
5. Philip Kasinitz, *Caribbean New York: Black Immigrants and the Politics of Race* (Ithaca: Cornell University Press, 1992), 6.
6. Afro-Caribbean migration increased from 412 immigrants admitted in 1899 to 12,243 admitted in 1924. By 1930, there were 177,981 foreign-born African-descended adults and

their children—mostly from the English-speaking Caribbean—in the United States. A government-sponsored guest worker scheme during World War II channeled thousands of Afro-Caribbean people to work in farms and factories on the East Coast, and some of these guest workers remained in the country. With immigration reform, the number of arrivals grew exponentially from 123,000 in the 1950s to 470,000 in the 1960s. Between 1981 and 1990, 872,000 Caribbean immigrants entered the country. See Winston James, "The History of Afro-Caribbean Migration to the United States," In Motion: The African-American Migration Experience: Caribbean Migration, New York Public Library, accessed July 2, 2019, http://www.inmotionaame.org/texts/viewer.cfm?id=10_000T; Tammy L. Brown, *City of Islands: Caribbean Intellectuals in New York* (Jackson, Miss.: University Press of Mississippi, 2015), 25; Kasinitz, *Caribbean*, 23–32.

7. Winston James, *Holding Aloft the Banner of Ethiopia: Caribbean Radicalism in Early Twentieth-Century America* (New York: Verso, 1998); Brown, *City of Islands*.
8. Colin Grant, *Negro with a Hat: The Rise and Fall of Marcus Garvey* (New York: Oxford University Press, 2008), 72–73; "Extract from the Crew List of the S. S. *Tallac*," in Robert Hill, *The Marcus Garvey and Universal Negro Improvement Association Papers*, v. I: 1826–August 1919 (University of California Press, 1983), 186.
9. Grant, *Negro with a Hat*, 75.
10. "This Month in History- March," National Park Service, Ellis Island, accessed July 2, 2019, https://www.nps.gov/elis/learn/historyculture/this-month-in-history-march.htm.
11. Alan Cobley, "That Turbulent Soil: Seafarers, the 'Black Atlantic,' and Afro-Caribbean Identity," in *Seascapes: Maritime Histories, Littoral Cultures, and Transoceanic Exchanges*, ed. Jerry H. Bentley, Renate Bridenthal, and Kären Wigen (Honolulu: University of Hawai'i Press, 2007), 156.
12. Risa Faussette, "Race, Migration, and Port-City Radicalism: West Indian Longshoremen and the Politics of Empire, 1880–1920," in *Seascapes*, 169–185.
13. Rose Mary Allen, "'Learning to be a Man': Afro-Caribbean Seamen and Maritime Workers from Curaçao in the Beginning of the Twentieth Century," *Caribbean Studies* 39, no. 1/2 (2011): 43–64.
14. Alan Cobley, "Black West Indian Seamen in the British Merchant Marine in the Mid Nineteenth Century," *History Workshop Journal* 58, no. 1 (Autumn 2004): 259–274.
15. W. Jeffrey Bolster, *Black Jacks: African American Seamen in the Age of Sail* (Cambridge, Mass.: Harvard University Press, 1998), 232; Cobley, "Black," 260.
16. Andrew Phillips, oral history with Vera Clark Ifill, May 23, 1989, Oral History Library, The Statue of Liberty—Ellis Island Foundation Inc., https://www.libertyellisfoundation.org/oral-histories.
17. Cheryl Finley, *Committed to Memory: The Art of the Slave Ship Icon* (Princeton: Princeton University Press, 2018), 11.
18. Justin Slaughter, "C. L. R. James in the Age of Climate Change," *Jacobin*, June 7, 2017, https://jacobinmag.com/2017/06/moby-dick-clr-james-mariners-renegades-castaways.
19. Michael Berthold, "*Moby-Dick* and American Slave Narrative," *The Massachusetts Review* 35, no. 1 (Spring 1994): 135–148, quoting Hortense Spillers.
20. Claude McKay, *A Long Way from Home* (London: Rutgers University Press, 2007), 79.
21. Phillips, oral history.

22. Moreno, *Encyclopedia,* 209.
23. In her oral history, Ifill speculates that her lack of U.S. citizenship or concerns about her immunization status may have been the reason for their detention. She also states that she has no idea how long her family was detained for (Phillips, oral history).
24. Phillips, oral history 9.
25. On celebratory narratives of Ellis Island in relation to the myth of the American dream, see Mario Varricchio, "Golden Door Voices: Towards a Critique of the Ellis Island Oral History Project," *Oral History Forum d'histoire oral* 31 (2011): 1–28. Roughly 80 percent of immigrants passing through Ellis Island did not experience any hassles, and this group generally came from old immigrant nationalities such as the British, Germans, Irish, and Swedes. Vincent Cannato, *American Passage: The History of Ellis Island* (New York: Harper, 2009), 5.
26. For similar perspectives, see Cynthia Owen Philip, "Celebrating an Island Artifact," *Archaeology* 43, no. 5 (1990): 44–51; Charlie Hailey, *Spoil Island: Reading the Makeshift Archipelago* (New York: Lexington Books, 2013), 20, 28.
27. Philip, "Celebrating," 49.
28. Paul Chaat Smith and Robert Allen Warrior, *Like a Hurricane: The Indian Movement from Alcatraz to Wounded Knee* (New York: The New Press, 1996), 92–93; Carmen Nigro, "Occupying Ellis Island: Protests in the Years between Immigration Station and National Park," New York Public Library, 2015, accessed October 29, 2019, https://www.nypl.org/blog/2015/07/13/occupying-ellis-island.
29. Fawn Wilson Pooacha, "Ancestral Delaware Remains Finally Laid to Rest," Delaware Indian News Special Report, July 2003, accessed February 20, 2020, http://nathpo.org/News/NAGPRA/News-NAGPRA31.htm and https://apnews.com/def42b717582dc8667f43da8b445e16d. Thank you to Ally LaForge for bringing this material to my attention.
30. Moreno, *Encyclopedia,* xxi.
31. Hailey, *Spoil Island,* 20, 28; Philip, "Celebrating," 47. On cribwork, see Kevin Bone, "Horizontal City: Architecture and Construction in the Port of New York," in *The New York Waterfront: Evolution and Building Culture of the Port and Harbor,* ed. Kevin Bone (New York: The Monacelli Press, 2004), 84–151 (96).
32. Philip, "Celebrating," 48.
33. Moreno, *Encyclopedia,* 87.
34. Philip, "Celebrating," 47.
35. Moreno, *Encyclopedia,* 148.
36. "Architectural Appreciations: The New York Immigrant Station," *Architectural Record* 12 (1902): 727–733 (729).
37. Moreno, *Encyclopedia,* 101.
38. "Architectural Appreciations," 732; A. D. F. Hamlin and F. S. Lamb, "The New York Architectural League Exhibition," *The Architectural Review* 6 (1899): 40–41.
39. Michael Sundell, "Golden Immigrants at the Gold Door: Lewis Hine's Photographs of Ellis Island," *Social Text* no. 16 (1986–1987): 168–175; Louis Takács, "Let Me Get There: Visualizing Immigrants, Transnational Migrants & U.S. Citizens Abroad, 1904–1925," accessed September 30, 2022, https://scalar.usc.edu/works/let-me-get-there.
40. Erica Rand, *The Ellis Island Snow Globe* (Durham: Duke University Press, 2005).

41. Moreno, *Encyclopedia*, 137; J. Tracy Stakely, "Cultural Landscape Report for Ellis Island," National Park Service Olmsted Center for Landscape Preservation Brookline, Massachusetts, May 2003, 42.
42. Moreno, *Encyclopedia*, 137; Stakely, "Cultural," 47.
43. Stakely, "Cultural," 42, 113; Ayasha Guerin, "Underground and at Sea: Oysters and Black Marine Entanglements in New York's Zone-A," *Shima* 13, no. 2 (2019): 30–55 (32), www.shimajournal.org; David Squires and Kevin Bone, "The Beautiful Lake: The Promise of the Natural Systems," in *The New York Waterfront*, 31, 116; "Reclaiming Riker's Island," *New York Times*, November 25, 1900, 15; "An Enormous Building," *New York Times*, July 28, 1891, 8; "Bad Work at Ellis Island New Buildings," *New York Times*, June 30, 1892, 9.
44. Maria Voyatzaki, ed., *Architectural Materialisms: Nonhuman Creativity* (Edinburgh: Edinburgh University Press, 2018), 13.
45. Guerin, "Underground," 34.
46. Cf. Oostvaardersplassen in the Netherlands; see Jamie Lorimer, *Wildlife in the Anthropocene: Conservation after Nature* (Minneapolis: University of Minnesota Press, 2015), 97–117; D. H. Frieling, "A Garden in Europe: The Case of the Ijsselmeer District of the Netherlands," *The Town Planning Review* 57, no. 1 (1986): 35–50.
47. On the exceptionality of islands, see Hailey, *Spoil Island*, 21–22, 58–60.
48. Ellis Island poses an interesting contrast to the link between national renewal and land reclamation in the Netherlands. See Peter Stephenson, "Does New Land Mean New Lives? Symbolic Contradiction and the Unfinished Reclamation of the Markerwaard," *Etnofoor* 3, no. 2 (1990): 17–31.
49. Dolmage, "Disabled," 49. Also see the definition of "spoil islands" in Hailey, *Spoil Island*, 19, 24–25, 36.
50. Guerin, "Underground," 30.
51. "Ellis Island Emigrant Building," *Inland Architect and News Record* 31, no. 4 (1898): 26–27. Italics are mine.
52. Dolmage, "Disabled," 25–26, 32. Dolmage offers a Foucauldian analysis of Ellis Island as a "rhetorical space" of heterotopic deviation. I offer a complementary reading that explores the spatial and architectural *design* of the islands and their material lives.
53. Katherine Reed, "'The Prison, By God, Where I Have Found Myself': Graffiti at Ellis Island Immigration Station, New York, c. 1900–1923," *Journal of American Ethnic History* 38, no. 3 (Spring 2019): 5–35 (8).
54. Moreno, *Encyclopedia*, 61; Rand, *Snowglobe*, 80; Philip Sutton, "Why Your Family Name Was Not Changed at Ellis Island (and One That Was)," July 2, 2013, https://www.nypl.org/blog/beta/2013/07/02/name-changes-ellis-island.
55. Reed, "'The Prison,'" 19.
56. James Brooke, "Old New York Is Being Unearthed on Ellis Island," *New York Times*, June 16, 1986.
57. Manuel DeLanda, "One Dimension Lower," *Domus*, no. 886 (November 2005): 136–37.
58. Mae Ngai, "The Architecture of Race in American Immigration Law: A Reexamination of the Immigration Act of 1924," *The Journal of American History* 86, no. 1 (June 1999): 67–92 (69).

59. Irma Watkins-Owens, *Blood Relations: Caribbean Immigrants and the Harlem Community, 1900–1930* (Bloomington: Indiana University Press, 1996), 3.
60. Ngai, "The Architecture," 68.
61. Mae Ngai, "The Strange Career of the Illegal Alien: Immigration Restriction and Deportation Policy in the United States, 1921–1965," *Law and History Review* 21, no. 1 (Spring 2003): 69–107 (103).
62. Ngai, "The Architecture," 81.
63. Ngai, "The Architecture," 81.
64. James, "The History."
65. James, "The History." Also see Ngai, "The Strange," 103.
66. Ngai, "The Strange," 70.
67. Ngai, "The Strange," 71.
68. Ngai, "The Strange," 76, 77, 97, 103.
69. "Formal removal" included deportations, exclusions, and removals. See Mae Ngai, *Impossible Subjects: Illegal Aliens and the Making of Modern America* (Princeton: Princeton University Press, 2004), 274.
70. James, "The History."
71. Moreno, *Encyclopedia*, xviii.
72. Anna Pegler-Gordon, "'New York Has a Concentration Camp of Its Own': Japanese Confinement on Ellis Island during World War II," *Journal of Asian American Studies* 20, no. 3 (October 2017): 373–404 (377); Moreno, *Encyclopedia*, 53–54.
73. Moreno, *Encyclopedia*, 54.
74. Also see Dolmage, "Disabled," 36.
75. Moreno, *Encyclopedia*, 55.
76. Moreno, *Encyclopedia*, 53.
77. Moreno, *Encyclopedia*, xviii.
78. Pegler-Gordon, "New York," 387. Also see Tetsuden Kashima, *Judgment without Trial: Japanese American Imprisonment during World War II* (Seattle: University of Washington Press), 107.
79. Kashima, *Judgment*, 379, 380, 387, 396; Moreno, *Encyclopedia*, 179.
80. Moreno, *Encyclopedia*, 76, 203.
81. Pegler-Gordon, "New York," 389.
82. Moreno, *Encyclopedia*, 180.
83. Moreno, *Encyclopedia*, xviii, 204; Cannato, *American Passage*, 360.
84. "This Month in History- January," National Park Service, Ellis Island, https://www.nps.gov/elis/learn/historyculture/this-month-in-history-january.htm.
85. Anna Grimshaw, ed., *The C. L. R. James Reader* (Oxford, UK: Blackwell, 1992), 1–22; Maxwell Uphaus, "Herman Melville and C. L. R. James: Oceanic Fears, Maritime Hopes," *Soundings: An Interdisciplinary Journal* 101, no. 1 (2018): 18–29.
86. C. L. R. James, *Mariners, Renegades, and Castaways: The Story of Herman Melville and the World We Live In* (New York: C. L. R. James, 1953), 150, 153, 154.
87. James, *Mariners*, 168, 173.
88. James, *Mariners*, 150.

89. James, *Mariners,* 151, 164.
90. James, *Mariners,* 172–173.
91. New York, Passenger and Crew Lists (including Castle Garden and Ellis Island), 1820–1957; Year: 1924; Arrival: New York, New York; Microfilm Serial: T715, 1897–1957; Microfilm Roll: Roll 3449; Line: 6; Page Number: 21; accessed October 27, 2019, Ancestry.com
92. Clarissa Atkinson, "A Strange and Terrible Sight in Our Country," *Women's Review of Books* (September/October 2006), https://oldestvocation.com/strange-and-terrible-sight-in-our-country/; Clarissa Atkinson, "'A Pride in Being West Indian': Claudia Jones and The West Indian Gazette," accessed October 26, 2019, https://oldestvocation.com/a-pride-in-being-west-indian-claudia-jones-and-the-west-indian-gazette/; Marika Sherwood, *Claudia Jones: A Life in Exile* (London: Lawrence & Wishart, 1999), 22–23.
93. "Letter from Claudia Jones to John Gates, Editor of *The Daily Worker,* Nov. 8, 1950," https://oldestvocation.com/claudia-jones-letter-ellis-island/.
94. Denise Lynn, "The Deportation of Claudia Jones," accessed October 27, 2019, https://www.aaihs.org/the-deportation-of-claudia-jones/; Carole Boyce Davies, ed., *Claudia Jones: Beyond Containment* (Ayebia Clarke Publishing, 2011); Carole Boyce Davies, *Left of Karl Marx: The Political Life of Black Communist Claudia Jones* (Durham: Duke University Press, 2008), 121; "Freed Red Leader to 'Deport' Self," *The Stars and Stripes,* November 24, 1955, 3, Ancestry.com.
95. Pegler-Gordon, "New York," 374–375.
96. *Oxford English Dictionary,* s.v. "concentration camp, n.", March 2020, https://www.oed.com/dictionary/concentration-camp_n?tab=factsheet#8637436.
97. Somini Sengupta, "Accord on Term 'Concentration Camp,'" *New York Times,* March 10, 1998, Section B, 4.
98. Giorgio Agamben, *Homo Sacer: Sovereign Power and Bare Life* (Stanford: Stanford University Press, 1998); Giorgio Agamben, *State of Exception* (Chicago: University of Chicago Press, 2005); Michel Agier, *Managing the Undesirables: Refugee Camps and Humanitarian Government* (Malden, Mass.: Polity Press, 2011); Simon Turner, "What Is a Refugee Camp? Explorations of the Limits and Effects of the Camp," *Journal of Refugee Studies* 29, no. 2 (2016): 139–48.

Chapter 8

Curtain Wall Inside-Out

Technocracy, Theocracy, and Technoaesthetic Formations of Cold War Fascism

María González Pendás

Gridded and indisputable in its "mechanical perfection," the glass and aluminum façade going up in New York City seemed to precisely bear the sociopolitical order of which it was part. And that was, for critics, the problem. "This façade seems perfect for an electronic brain, which works as follows: you push buttons marked as *freedom, democracy,* and *free elections,* connect to a network of *goodness,* and put it to work," one declared. "The merit is that everything is automatic and fatal." With architecture as evidence, democracy appeared to be mechanical and deadly. Amid such contempt for a politics of freedom, the building that was seen to give it form fared no better: a "demoralizing example," another continued, "of what should not be done if we want to resolve the real problems of architecture."[1]

Time would soon prove the critics, American writer Lewis Mumford and Spanish architect Luis Moya, glaringly off the mark in their prediction. The façade they mocked was none other than that of the United Nations Secretariat in New York, its curtain wall recently completed when Moya lectured on the building and translated Mumford's damning review of it across the Atlantic in Madrid in October 1950. Eventually, the technoaesthetic system that the UN modeled—in which a grid of aluminum or steel mullions hangs from a concrete slab free of loads to brace plate glass—would resolve quite a few problems, architectural and otherwise. It seemed, across time and place, good for everything from "exporting democracy" and variously evoking Americanism, capitalism, and corporatism to providing "spectacles of modernization" for dictatorships the world over.[2]

Though ill conceived, Moya's critique is nonetheless telling of some of the ways in which architecture encountered democracy, or the lack thereof, in the mid-twentieth century. In mapping "freedom" onto the UN façade, Moya adopted an ideological formalism that likened modular geometry to computation and individual sovereignty, material efficiency to social efficacy, and the glassy logic of the curtain wall to an organizational logic that he tied to democracy. Of course, neither the curtain wall nor the mechanization and efficiency with which he entwined it were necessarily wedded to any one political ideal or form of governance, values as radically contingent on time and place as any other technological system or style. Yet Moya was not alone in his analysis. Although the curtain wall was insufficiently democratic for Mumford, he still linked technological and political systems. More trustingly, *Architectural Forum* reviewed the hanging façade of the Secretariat as a construction feat well fit for the institution it clad, in that it proclaimed "the dignity, security, and power of states organized into a community."[3] As the architecture of choice for the transatlantic transfer of the League of Nations, the curtain wall was perceived by many as capturing the "scientific technocracy" and democratic register that the United States would imprint on global governance at the United Nations—an institution devoted to the "freedom of thought, conscience and religion" born out of the ashes of hard-fought fascism.[4]

The issue for Moya was that fascism was alive and well, at least in Spain. Ever since the civil war that led to the dictatorship of Francisco Franco in 1939, Moya had been an avid supporter of the fascist state and a champion of crafting it architecturally. In 1938, his *Sueño arquitectónico para una exaltación nacional* (Architectonic dream for national elation) offered a potent proposition to the necropolitics that would give rise to the regime: an ideal city of death capped—Boullée-like—with a colossal pyramidal cenotaph. By 1940, Moya was urging his peers to "learn from" El Escorial, the pinnacle of the Spanish Renaissance, in the pressing task to conceive not only a genuinely national and dictatorial style but a "truly imperial architecture."[5]

Claiming El Escorial was no mere disdain for modernism in favor of a classical language. In fact, Moya's architectural formulations attended to fascism's ideological contours well, including its modernizing disposition. For one, Moya fed the utopian desires and "palingenetic myth" that Roger Griffin has shown to sit at the modernist core of all fascisms, the kind of regenerative will that makes modernity entirely compatible with nativism. Across fascisms, Griffin writes, "efforts were directed towards bringing into being a new *future*, even if the utopian vision was formulated in the apparently 'pastist' discourse of 'reconnecting forward.'"[6] As the palace-monastery that Philip II built in local granite as headquarters of the Habsburg Empire, El Escorial offered a solid archive for such a historical maneuver, helping many imagine a continuum between a fascistic future and the bygone empire. For fascism emerged also as a violent afterimage of empire, what Aimé Césaire already noted in 1955 for the German context as the "terrific boomerang effect" of the logic of Western Christian colonization marching onward but turning inward into its own territories and peoples.[7] The imperial mourning that produced fascism in Spain, as in Latin America, pertained less to the capture of physical space or claims of scientific racism than to the capture of souls through spiritual rac-

Figure 8.1. "Perspective sketch from the northeast of El Escorial Monastery, as one would encounter it arriving from Madrid." Fondos Documentales de la Biblioteca de la ETS de Madrid.

ism, recalling evangelization as a technique of Spanish colonial rule.[8] As the Falangist Ernesto Giménez Caballero put it in 1935, El Escorial ought to be a repository in which to construct a "static, trans-temporal, and totalitarian ideal of the future fascist State," the stone "engine" of a Catholic empire still in progress.[9]

Moya's allegiance to the monument relied on a similar historical and morphological argument, a deep-seated belief that architectural forms follow from and produce specific sociopolitical orders. Wed to static ideas of fascism, stone-built classicism, and the relation between the two, Moya had little reason not to distrust the glassy grid of the UN—an institution that had shunned Franquismo in 1945—and to denounce it as testament to the "immoral" bedrock of secular democracy going global.[10] Yet the architect's reading of the building was exhaustive, eventually taking more than twenty-two pages of plans, text, and construction details in *Revista Nacional de Arquitectura (RNA)*. Soon enough, Spanish architects began to experiment widely with the curtain wall— precisely for the purpose of designing the regime's governing infrastructure. In 1955, Alejandro de la Sota cited "the revolutionary UN building" as referent for a Finance Delegation; by 1956, when the Ministries of Industry and Commerce held a joint design competition, all entries worth official mention featured gridded skins.[11]

Curtain Wall Inside-Out

Figure 8.2. Perspective view for the New Headquarters for the Ministries of Industry and Commerce Competition, Madrid, by Antonio Perpiña, 1956. First Prize. Fundación Biblioteca COAM.

Contrary to Moya's worst fears, such transatlantic translations advanced neither democratic freedom nor a "softened" Franquismo, as some have claimed, but rather helped to transform and strengthen a version of fascism—one that would sustain one of the longest dictatorships in modern Europe.[12] This essay follows Spanish architects as they redeployed the technoaesthetic system of the curtain wall not simply as modernizers navigating Franquismo but also for the purposes of reinventing and reinforcing the regime *in its own fascistic terms*. Understanding the resilience of fascism beyond classic interwar formulations has proven challenging to historians—as it was indeed to Moya—and as fascistic values, governance, and rhetoric changed across space and over time. Scholars have long pointed out how Franquista Spain fostered a unique version of National Catholicism.[13] Critically, however, many within the regime also understood that endurance required a revolution of the imagination. The challenge was to transform a militant regime born out of war and in tune with Nazism and Italian Fascism into a new institutional fascism, one that would suit both the Cold War West and Spain's own religious neoimperialism. This task was met in the shaping of a technocracy that made the rule of technology compatible with both the rule of the leader and with a Christian evangelical mission. And the curtain wall proved, as I will argue, fitting to conceive of such a transformation.

Figure 8.3. SEAT Auto-Industry Warehouse by architects Cesar Ortiz-Echagüe, Rafael Echaide, Manuel Barbero, and Rafael de la Joya, Barcelona, 1959. Colección Plasencia/IEFC.

By looking at a series of design competitions for government architecture leading up to 1956, this chapter follows Spanish architects as they explored the curtain wall as both a technoaesthetic system and an instrument of political imagination, that is, as a tool that allowed them to think differently about Franquismo and its performance. Through the 1950s, the curtain wall remained a compelling desire more than a material technology, its construction unfeasible for some time. The first curtain wall built in Spain dates from 1959 and clad not a civic building but an industrial one, albeit one closely associated with the regime: a warehouse for the state-owned car manufacturing company SEAT (Sociedad Española de Automóviles de Turismo). In all of its expensive materiality (the project drained state coffers) the building still operated chiefly as media, an image in the lyrical reflection of U.S. modernism to capture and help project the regime's embrace of western modernization.[14] Indeed, by then, Franquismo had signed military-economic agreements with the United States (1953), was a UN member (1955), and had a developmentalist plan in motion.

Curtain Wall Inside-Out

But before that—before pristine images of glassy grids served a westernizing propaganda and before their materiality embodied a developmentalist economy—the curtain wall worked in different, arguably more powerful ways for the purposes of Franquismo. As a technology of pen and tracing paper rather than steel and glass, the curtain wall system helped architects and officials discern how an efficiently managed, technically invested yet still dictatorial and theocratic state would function and what it might look like in the aftermath of World War II. It first served them, in other words, as a source of ideas about how fascism could continue to operate both functionally and aesthetically. A new imagination of fascistic possibility took shape on drawing boards just as a distinct form of pious technocracy was taking shape institutionally—architects advancing two steps ahead of the regime. Much like Moya, Spanish architects likened the logic of the grid to North American technical expertise and organizational efficiency. But they also understood, unlike him, how well these ideals could align with a holy mission and, in so doing, with fascism redesigned.

Franquista Pious Modernization

In March 1956, the Franquista Ministry of Governance launched a design competition for a joint Headquarters of the Ministries of Industry and Commerce in Madrid. The competition guidelines were succinct, asking architects to provide for a "functioning scheme" and sufficient square footage.[15] This was detailed in a breakdown of every delegation, section, and subsection of the bureaucratic maze. For the Ministry of Industry alone, ten pages outlined office sizes for every assistant, section chief, vice secretary, and general technical secretary, including more than sixteen thousand square feet to expand the National Productivity Commission funded by the North American Technical Aid Program that had resulted from the U.S. 1953 agreements. The General Technical Secretary to the Minister, one of the largest offices, required space for four service chiefs, four subservice chiefs, four section chiefs, eight secretaries, eight engineers, seven technicians, four administrative technicians, and fourteen assistants.[16]

However well the swelling administration was defined numerically, little was prescribed in terms of the organizational or visual system with which to tackle the task—hence the competition. Not intended to settle on a final design, the competition had been launched "in the interest of gathering as many ideas as possible in order to determine the final norms" for the institution.[17] In other words, architects' expertise was summoned to speculate on the forms and the norms of the regime's governing infrastructure, a creative process meant to be somewhat collective: through the summer, entries were exhibited in Madrid's National Library and were later published in *Gran Madrid* for designers, cadres, and an interested public to assess the directions that architecture was offering the state.[18]

By then, it was clear that such a route was one of modernization. This was patent not

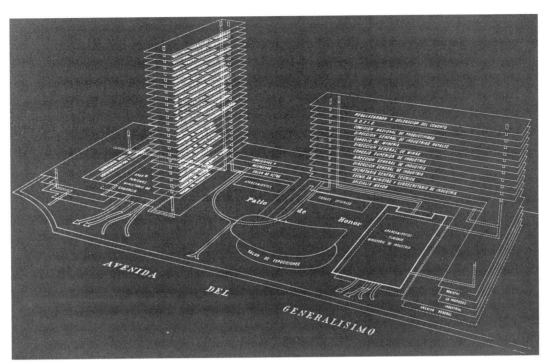

Figure 8.4. Organizational axonometric for the New Headquarters for the Ministries of Industry and Commerce Competition, Madrid, by Antonio Perpiña, 1956. First Prize. Courtesy of Fundación Biblioteca COAM.

only in the breakdown of the competition brief but also in the designs that answered it. All of the showcased entries deployed a modular rationale, with the grid as chief design technique both in plan and elevation; claimed glass, steel, and aluminum as their material repertoire; and cast architecture as a means of efficient organization. The winning entry, for instance, opened with diagrams detailing and spatializing the functional distribution of the new ministries, a strategy that resulted in a direct quote of the UN: two towers, one for each ministry, with curtain walls on the broad façades and a series of free-form volumes across the site. One of the second-prize winners featured a one-story horizontal volume raised on *pilotti* spanning the site and pierced by two towers. The whole rendered in a homogeneous grid, and as conveyed in a collage, the project reflected both cloudy skies and postwar Miesian modernism. Such ideas, of course, did not become normative or even plausible overnight. The winning entry would evolve during the following decade in ways that retained the modular system but shed steel for concrete. But in the summer of 1956, the curtain wall seemed to fulfill many techno-aesthetic longings.

A visitor to the halls of the National Library encountering these drawings would have remarked on their novelty. After all, the one prominent ministry then under

Figure 8.5. Collage of the North façade for the New Headquarters for the Ministries of Industry and Commerce Competition, Madrid, by Alejandro de la Sota, José Antonio Corrales, José Romany, Francisco Saénz de Oiza, and Ramón Vázquez Molezún, 1956. Second Prize. Courtesy of Fundación Biblioteca COAM.

construction in Madrid, the Air Force Ministry, distinctly mimicked El Escorial. But while the official embrace of such iconic modernism was somewhat new, the embrace of modernization was not. The ways in which fascist regimes relied on technological, bureaucratic, and scientific modernization has long been the subject of scholarly attention. This body of work has dismantled the once-held assumption that, in their sustained attack on the values of the Enlightenment, fascist movements disavowed modernization. Much to the contrary, fascists not only "considered themselves an avant-garde" as George Mosse has put it, but also made modernization's emphasis on rationality entirely compatible with the irrationality of racial, national, and religious essentialism that underscored fascist violence. As Griffin explains it, the fascist grip on modernization was never merely opportunistic or simply paradoxical in the form of what Jeffrey Herf has called "reactionary modernism" but utterly in line with nativist–imperialist renewal. Notably, this synthesis sustained fascism's praxis and ideology of terror and was, as scholars such as Paul Jaskot, Ruth Ben-Ghiat, Tiago Saraiva, Andreas Malm, and others show, particularly well carried on through architecture, media, science, and technology.[19]

Spain was no exception, as Franquismo called forth the collision of modernization and evangelization, of reason and faith. Lino Camprubí and Ana Fernández-Cebrián have explained how, from territorial reorganization through dams and energy plants to the promotion of grain genetics and irrigation infrastructures, architects and engineers "filled with content the historical redeeming mission that Francoism had invented for itself." These efforts were first factual and infrastructural, but they became propagandistic in the 1950s and 1960s when media technologies cast modernization both in a more advanced state that conditions on the ground allowed and, critically, under a providential and supernatural light.[20] To be sure, architecture contributed to this media and material history of fascism in very concrete ways. The progression of the curtain wall from image to building—or from the 1951 reception of the UN to the 1959 SEAT warehouse—would belong to such history. But as is apparent in the figure of the competition, architectural work was geared to not only physically building Franquismo or crafting its message but also, and more uniquely, to imagining its governmental and social performance. In other words, architects were as much called to make the pious modernization of the state functional and visible so as to render it feasible.

Before returning to the specific ways in which architects approached such questions, it is necessary to understand the institution that most successfully reconciled modernization, religion, and the ghosts of imperialism: the Catholic organization Opus Dei. Founded in Madrid in the 1930s and the first secular institute of the Roman Catholic Church, Opus Dei would become a powerful cosmopolitical institution but was first key to Franquismo. At its inception, priest José María Escrivá de Balaguer led a small group of university students building careers in the natural sciences, the law, and technical professions (including architecture) while remaining fully dedicated to their faith. Escrivá's main proposition—as captured in the name, Work of God, and is well known—cast professional excellence as a pathway to sanctity. Members thus followed orthodox Catholic practices of asceticism and atonement to reach holiness and support the nation's development in the very same breath. Though essentially devoted to a religious ethic, Opus Dei folded in a wholistic social ethic, as José Casanova has argued: "a world-view that inspired all worldly activities, private or corporate, closer to what is usually called an ideology with certain utopian transformative elements different from the typical conservative mentality."[21]

This worldview ripened in the *Centro Superior de Investigaciones Científicas* (CSIC, National Research Council), a stronghold of the regime's efforts of industrial and scientific modernization where Opus Dei's orthodox biopolitics was aligned with, and in fact was made structural to, a progressive material mentality. As historian of capitalism Bethany Moreton has shown, through a "vigorous modern fusion of piety with efficiency," Opus Dei members found ways to not simply think of themselves as pious yet modern but as materially liberal *because of* their pious sacrifice.[22] That men of technology, economy, and the sciences would hope to imbue modernization with spiritual value was not especially new, particularly in the context of fascism.[23] But Escrivá and his acolytes advanced a specific version of holy modernity, one that conceived of modernization as serving a new mission of evangelization. In doing so, and less well recognized in the literature, Opus Dei participated in the imperialist ambitions of the regime, as well. For Escrivá, technical and scientific work was a means to sanctity and to development but also, and importantly, to what he called "an apostolate of a professional character."[24] Fully devoted to their careers and their faith, well trained in techniques of modernization, and embedded in its institutions, Opus Dei members were asked to "win over the masses," Escrivá wrote, to "turn the flock into a legion, the drove into an army, and from the herd of swine draw, purified, those who no longer wish to be unclean."[25] Defined by Opus Dei's clandestine origins amid the anticlericalism of the Second Republic, Escrivá's evangelical tactics were secular and tacit in form but still universal in scale.

The missionary zeal of Spanish imperialism was thus cast under a twentieth-century guise, with evangelization no longer in the hands of the sword-bearing crusader but of the suit-wearing expert. Chief among these was a lawyer, Laureano López Rodó, the director of Legal, Administrative, and Management Services at the CSIC and a professor of administrative law at the University of Santiago de Compostela, in the northwestern region of Galicia. In his early writings and teaching, López Rodó advocated the legalization of the Franquista administration in the form of an *Estado de Derecho,* or German *Reichtsstaat,* as he considered jurisprudence to be the most effective means by which to govern society. In keeping with Opus Dei logic, however, his claim to law as the means for the state to "most profoundly penetrate social life" was both modernizing and evangelical, an attempt to fold the Opus Dei ethos into a new governmental model.[26]

Ideas for a law-bound state were somewhat unique in the context of a regime first governed militarily. The institutional form of Franquismo had been debated since 1939 as some were concerned with the normalization and survival of a fascist state implemented through war—the ultimate state of exception. Franco had signed off on a few laws in this regard, but they all deferred to a central sovereignty, centered more precisely on Franco. This dictatorial rule relied on censorship and violence but also on the staunch policing exerted at the local level by two institutions: the Church and the local branches of the state administration. One moral, the other legal, both were critical to exercising control over everyday life.[27] By 1956, the means and the forms of governance took on new relevance after student protests revealed democratic ideals brewing in the university and amongst the Falangist youth. The turmoil was swiftly suppressed by force, and Franco dismissed both the Minister of Education and the leader of Falange. But he also reckoned with the need to tighten the administrative structure of the state. To this end, he asked the new leader of Falange—architect-turned-politician José Luis Arrese—to rework the functions of the party, resulting in the *New Organic Law of the Movement,* a proposal that empowered the party's role in the state apparatus. During the fall of 1956, Arrese's draft circulated among the political elites as Franco debated its implementation.[28]

Meanwhile, others in the civil margins were concocting alternatives. In early September 1956, Madrid hosted the Tenth Congress of the International Institute of Administrative Sciences (IIAS), a Brussels-based organization dedicated to the transnational and scientific study of public administration, and whose meeting that year centered on reform.[29] López Rodó, an IIAS member, attended the event just as he was finalizing a lecture for the International Summer Program of the University of Santiago, which he delivered a week after. In it, he outlined a deep reorganization for a "modern world" Franquismo. "The best administration," he said, "is one that meets the highest grade of efficiency."[30]

With efficiency as mantra, the lawyer laid out a three-tier governmental reform. First, at an institutional level, he proposed a more "simple and modern organization" of ministries and official organs for a state "formed by efficient pieces that would push aside antique mechanisms." López Rodó merged ideas from the French state with corporate America to craft a state-as-machine-as-business model in which the state is "the greatest business and only through the modernization of its offices can it be up to the task."[31] A second level of reform pertained to "bureaucratic modernization" and called forth "the mechanization of administrative work" and of communication systems among state organs. To this end, López Rodó spoke of adopting "the latest advances in cybernetics, the rationalization of work, and industrial psychology to secure maximum performance" for a state that could "offer the least resistance to its environment and accomplish the most acceleration in its action."[32] The final level of reform pertained to the actors charged with such proficient performance. In keeping with the IIAS discussions, López Rodó called for an expansion of, and better training for, a new class of civil servants. Such servants would be functionaries selected by merit, not by party or military affiliation. They would be lawyers like himself and also economists, engineers, and other professionals akin to rationalization and efficiency—the men, in other words, called to occupy the offices and walk the corridors of the buildings recently displayed at the Biblioteca Nacional.

The key to López Rodó's reform, however, relied on a single expert overseeing the state's machinations via a new General Technical Secretary for the "central coordination of the government."[33] Similar offices already existed at ministerial levels, but this one would advise the Head of State directly—Franco's technician, so to speak—to modernize the entire administration, manage a new functionaries system, and devise a new political economy. López Rodó's lecture was published in the Opus Dei journal *Nuestro Tiempo*, a document that ostensibly helped Franco's second-in-command convince the dictator to think along similar lines. Soon after, Franco dismissed Arrese's proposal for a stronger Falange and issued a decree to create the General Technical Secretary to the Presidency of the Government. By December 1956, Franco had appointed López Rodó to the task.[34]

What followed were an array of laws and appointments that, as announced in the press, reorganized and expanded the "complexity and greater number of technical and administrative activities assumed by the State, which assigns them to functionaries whose specialization is precise."[35] Increasingly, the rule of the leader became shared with and administered by nonparty and nonmilitary professionals, men who would morph Franco's authority into a legally structured and technically sanctioned form of sovereignty. These men were also (for the most part) affiliated with the CSIC or fellow Opus Dei members. They included economist Alberto Ullastres and lawyer Mariano Navarro Rubio, appointed as Ministers of Commerce and Finance in the 1957 cabinet change that both brought Falange its final strike and led to the neoliberal political economy behind Spain's developmentalism—the kind of economic and industrial policies later announced by the SEAT with a curtain wall designed, as it turns out, by architect and Opus Dei member César Ortiz-Echagüe.[36]

López Rodó, Ullastres, and Navarro Rubio were only the most prominent of a new cadre entering the government in the name of technical expertise, efficiency, and reason. These claims afforded them a safe distance from both party politics and traditional fascism. Their common ends seemed, at face value, both secular and apolitical: a rational and efficient state administration, a well-planned industrial development, and a liberal economy. But their faith was also an important source of authority, not least in the eyes of Franco, a devotion to both modernization and God, to the material and the evangelical progression of the nation–empire. Such pious experts thus posed little threat to either the regenerative imperial will of fascism or to the dictatorship itself: Franco remained the nominal center of power, and political decisions were driven by technicians in the name of efficiency and sanctity. In this new distribution of power, the *demos* was never in play.

The relationship between Opus Dei sacramental logic, its evangelical zeal, and the political inclinations of its members has long been negated by insiders, who cast their lay and professional disposition under the secular assumption that modern religion is a private, nonpolitical matter.[37] Indeed, the writings by which López Rodó envisioned and implemented his reform remained squarely secular. It is important to understand, however, that for Escrivá it was always crucial that this distance be performed *as such*. For the success of Opus Dei relied not only on the equivalence between professional and apostolic work but also on the mapping of the latter onto the former. As architect and Opus Dei defector Miguel Fisac once explained it, "our apostolate implied our introduction in civil institutions (. . .) that we work through the means and the buildings of the state."[38] As Escrivá would also command it, however, this work's holiness as proselytism ought to be a "quiet and effective mission," exerted discreetly through silence and atonement. "You must wear an invisible cloak," he wrote, "that will cover every single one of your senses and faculties."[39]

The political religiosity of López Rodó's legal theories is thus indiscernible in the rhetoric. But when read along the grain of Opus Dei's mentality, such abstraction in fact speaks of an affinity between visions for an efficient and growing administration and for a global evangelical mission—an affinity between bureaucracy, God, and empire not unlike that drawn by the colonial Spanish Church in the sixteenth century and administered from El Escorial. This abstraction also speaks of the performative or representational dimension of technocracy, which was reduplicated in the face of secular proselytism. "Opus Dei members became the carriers of modernization not because they were good experts," as Casanova writes, "but because they were good technocrats. They had a mystique of professionalism, a visionary view of the future as manifest in their ideology of development, and a technocratic view of social change."[40]

The unholy success of the Franquista technocrat thus hinged on his ability to act efficiently and expertly but also on the aura he conveyed around such values; not only on his devotion to reason and God but also on his ability to perform a distancing between the two. The technocrat's mystique required, in other words, an aesthetic register. As we have seen, López Rodó spoke of furnishing Franquismo with efficiency and with the latest advances in computation, communication, and organization—a modernization whose ulterior motive was evangelical. The lawyer was never explicit about the kinds of visuals and spaces that could accommodate these ideals, but by the time his proposal hit Franco's desk, the technoaesthetics of the curtain wall had for some time helped architects imagine as much.

Architectural Imaginings of Technocracy

If dictatorial governance needed a stronger legal organization, it also required an architectural one. Since at least 1943, the state had managed an expansive building program aimed at consolidating its governing infrastructure, particularly in a network of regional headquarters for the Ministries of Government and of Finance, the so-called

Civil Governments (CG) and Finance Delegations (FD) that were crucial, as noted earlier, to the kinds of local administrative policing required by the Franquista central sovereignty. As would be the case with new buildings for the Industry and Commerce Ministries, competitions were held to elicit both ideas and an expert conversation of sorts; entries were often exhibited following the jury decisions and the top designs published in *RNA*. The process was to some extent inclusive, although it called forth not public opinion but experts—architects—to think collectively about the building type.[41]

Competition briefs, which carried the same language and were published in the Official State Bulletin (BOE), asked designers to "clearly indicate" the civic "character" of the building while also facilitating "efficient execution" of administrative functions and clarifying its "circulation and functional modes."[42] Tensions between these two performative requirements—the representational and the operational—became a running concern for designers looking to bring an efficient administration together with a stately presence. In 1943, the architect of the winning entry for the CG building in Murcia claimed to facilitate "maximum easiness for public access, maximum visibility, and minimized circulation" within a limestone-clad neoclassic palazzo.[43] Entries for other locales similarly bridged this duality with versions of the courtyard typology that would ostensibly improve organization of and communication between offices while according to styles that, from neo-Escurialense to German Neoclassicism and Italian Rationalism, spanned the repertoire of fascistic officialdom.

In this way, architects intended to improve not just civil functioning but also, and perhaps most importantly, the social experience and perception of the state. Designers for the 1951 winning entry for the FD in Logroño, for instance, spelled out the challenge as both programmatic and emotional: "We must remember the feeling—what could be defined as psychosis—that people suffer by the aversion they experience when visiting our public offices."[44] To ease citizens into the state, they proposed a rather traditional distribution of offices around a central hall for "great organizational clarity and open distribution" that they clad in a stripped brick colonnade suggestive of Italian Rationalism. In 1954, the runner-up for the FD in Gerona rendered a similarly empathetic government, at least as suggested in a sketch in which a public appears to interact easily with well-disposed officials by virtue of a double-height space of dynamic lines and open counters, which was closed off with a neoclassic stone and brick composition. In submissions over the years, façades thus signified the state in masonry-clad classicism, whereas bright and neutral interiors helped it function both effectively and affectively. The fascist state, architects seemed to understand, was as much about the administration of power as about the public state of mind.

Alejandro de la Sota, an active participant of the competition series, was an acute interpreter of these tensions. The designs he presented through the years and the scores of preparatory sketches kept in his archives show him intently working through the relationship between effective bureaucracy and fascistic representation. Moreover, they

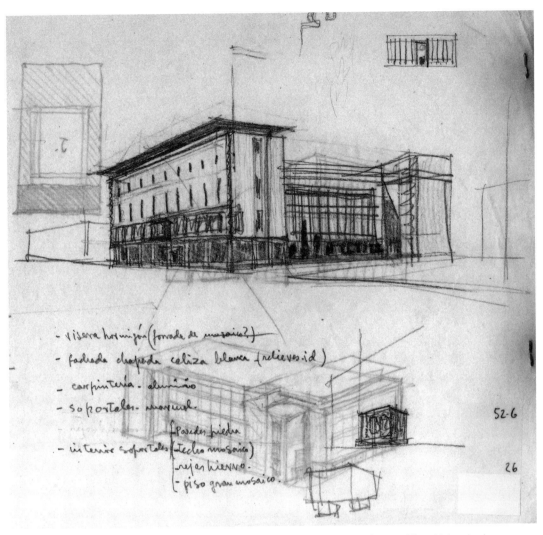

Figure 8.6. Exploratory sketch for the New Finance Headquarters Competition, Valencia, by Alejandro de la Sota, 1952. Fundación Alejandro de la Sota.

show Sota looking to resolve the duality through gridded compositions of glass and aluminum. In thinking of his proposal for the FD in Valencia in 1952, for instance, Sota first sketched variants of neoclassical façades, the symmetry and ornamentation of which he gradually broke off by penciling them over with grids. The intervention was formal and material, and he indicated the windows in the traditional load-bearing limestone façade as being aluminum-framed. Behind this front, he proposed a four-story-high hall closed off by a glass wall.[45] Sota thus solved the dual performative charge through a double dichotomy: stone spoke of the state upfront, and gridded glass afforded it open and efficient functioning in the back.

Curtain Wall Inside-Out

This design did not get Sota far, but it laid the ground for his proposal a year later for a new FD in Tarragona. As explored in multiple sketches, Sota broke with symmetry in a composition in which two overlapping volumes acquire different materiality and function: the bureaucratic workings of the administration in glass and aluminum, and the official image in stone or masonry. At one point, Sota gridded the taller volume with full-height windows and clad the front lower one in stone. The final design inverted the system, offering a more restrained solution to the administrative offices in front with brick and stripped windows. Not willing to give up on a full-glass façade (but not quite ready to put it up front), Sota opened the back with a four-story-high glass wall and an interior with cubicles for crossed views and clarity of communication and circulation.[46]

Speaking to shifting sensibilities at the Ministry of Finance, Sota received first prize *ex aequo,* with his corecipient proposing a sober neoclassic design. The recognition encouraged Sota to more fully embrace aluminum and glass for his 1954 design for a Provincial Government in La Coruña. By then, he was explicit about his ambition to "conjugate the parts" of state representation and the "technical administration" of governance. Once more resorting to grids and interlocking volumes, Sota clad a lower front volume in stone as a marker of the state and deployed glass in the taller volume behind. As per the stripped windows he rendered as reflective in a montage of the model, Sota also began to espouse, if not yet fully the curtain wall, a slab typology.[47]

Images of and ideas about the curtain wall had continue to circulate after Moya's moralistic critique and thorough formal unpacking of the UN buildings. Notably, the October 1952 issue of *RNA* was dedicated to "Glass." Edited by architect Javier Sáenz de Oiza after a year of North American travels, the issue now celebrated the Secretariat and its neighboring offspring, the Lever House, as "crystalized" instances of the promises of modernity. Pointing also to Mies van der Rohe, whose work in Chicago the Spaniard had visited, Oiza noted how "a new architecture finds in new materials—glass, steel, and aluminum—the substance for a new aesthetic adventure." As he dramatically concluded: "Blind, fatally blind are those who look for a great new order through plaster and mortar, pinnacle and capital."[48] While Oiza's praises of Mies's postwar modernism remained secular, he might have been attuned to its Catholic undercurrents and the ways in which, as Fritz Neumeyer has shown, the German architect thought of building technologies as a means for the "spiritual conquest of the future."[49] In his explorations with gridded techniques, Sota thought of ways to incorporate similar promises, alongside related forms of corporate management, into the state.

This vision came into clearer focus once Sota partnered with architects Antonio Tenreiro and Ramón Vázquez Molezún to enter the competition for the FD in La Coruña during the summer of 1955. In keeping with Sota's volumetric schemes and Molezún's explorations with modular structures, grids now directed both the structure and the façade. With a steel portico system on a 5.9 × 5.9-meter module, the plan allowed for a range of spatial distribution for the offices on the larger first two floors and half-module cubicles above, whereas a gridded façade now wrapped the two interlocking volumes homogeneously.[50] At the end of August, Sota gave a public lecture in which he evoked the "revolutionary UN building" and Mies's "reason (and) classicism" as references for his latest design. In their design for La Coruña, Sota explained, rigorous modularity afforded "flexibility" of program and "open and light" space for effective administration, the technique by which the problem of "public buildings of this type" could be solved in "simple and clear" terms.[51]

Notably, Sota spoke at the University of Santiago, where Laureano López Rodó was teaching and in the same series in which the lawyer would debut his governmental reform alongside similar values of efficiency a full year later.[52] Also, only after Sota's lecture, in late September 1955, did the exhibition *Modern Art in the United States* by the Museum of Modern Art open with images of Mies's Lake Shore Drive Apartments. As scholars have noted, this exhibition, which was traveling the country under the joint auspices of the Ministry of Culture and the U.S. State Department, was a cultural instrument of Cold War diplomacy, a means to "articulate the benefits of American style democracy" globally and through modernism.[53] Yet Christian values also determined the democratic, industrial, and capitalist efforts of U.S. expansionism, a pressing relationship amid the religious rifts of Cold War foreign politics as President Truman launched the nation into a "crusade of prayer."[54] The ways in which the American curtain wall might have captured this Christian logic is the subject of a different analysis.[55] But when looked at from the perspective of Spanish fascism and of the pious motivations shaping its shift towards technocracy, this exhibition and the curtain walls it carried speak less of democratic exchanges than of shared sentiments to bring technology and efficiency *together with* an evangelical imperialist mission.

In La Coruña, Sota, Tenreiro, and Molezún at least embraced the "mathematical logic" of the American curtain wall, as one critic described it, but they did not fully give in to its material logic.[56] In their design, the aluminum T-profiles that wrapped the building braced both glass and light prefabricated concrete panels, thus combining reflective and opaque surfaces. Their intention then was not to relinquish masonry or the imagery of stone and of the fascist state. Rather, the aim was to incorporate something like the material aesthetics of stone into the curtain wall system. As Sota later put it, his concern in these design competitions was not necessarily to articulate an entirely new image of the state but reform it by "profoundly lightening the concept of the building."[57]

In doing so, Sota and those who sanctioned his designs gradually shed a classicist language. But they never let go of a morphological stance—the one Moya manifested—that trust in architecture to shape the state through image, form, and materials. Only now they imagined how steely grids and associated values of efficiency, organization, and technological expertise could meet the mark. For the architects, the technoaesthetics of the curtain wall afforded this while accommodating an efficient administration.

The Delegación de Hacienda for La Coruña won first prize, and the architects went back to the drawing board to specify the steel structure, aluminum façade, and copper wiring. In the meantime, the competition for the joint Ministries of Industry and Commence was announced. Sota's team then expanded to include Oiza (among others) and devise the second-prize project described above. By the spring of 1956, our architects left little doubt of the willingness to not only modernize the organs and functions of the fascist state but also to render such will visible. From the preparatory sketches to the painstakingly itemized final designs, architects now appeared fully committed to gridded techniques, glass, and steel for an efficiently organized and rationally managed if still dictatorial civic administration—committed to shaping the state through the rule of technology that, by López Rodó's hand and as seen before, would indeed take over the apparatus of government by year's end.

None of these projects would be built as proposed. And, to be sure, the endurance of Franquismo encompassed broader political, military, and media apparatuses. But when looked at from the microhistory of these competitions, the history of Spanish fascism appears steadily reliant on architects and their imagination. Through their explorations of the curtain wall, architects joined in the formation of a unique mode of technocratic fascism—one where religious-imperialist ideals thrived not merely alongside but *through* modernization, however secular that collision was made to seem. Like the figure of the technocrat, the curtain wall put the rule of technology to the service of the rule of the leader, refashioning the regime away from the messages and images of traditional fascism. More fundamentally, while still bound to paper, the curtain wall afforded such technological imperatives a much-needed mystique; an aura that invested the dictatorship with faith in the power of efficiency, organization, and mechanization while still dictated by God. Not everyone involved in designing the civic architecture of Franquismo, whether through buildings or laws, were members of Opus Dei. But they all shared a belief in modernization as redemptive of the powers of fascism.

"Ideologies are never invested in the miracle of being," Hannah Arendt noted with an eye on fascism. "[T]hey are historical, concerned with becoming."[58] As our story of fascistic survival tells it, the Cold War becoming of fascism hinged on the silencing of religious and fascistic markers through technological tropes—a process of abstraction imagined architecturally and that in and of itself pursued religious imperialist ends. As was the case for Luis Moya, such abstraction foreclosed candid understandings of how and where fascism continued to operate after 1945; of how its "ghosts [might be] stalking Europe (not to speak of other parts of the world)?" as Umberto Eco eventually asked. "We must keep alert," he warned in 1995. "Ur-Fascism is still around us, sometimes in plainclothes."[59] Indeed, in exposing some of the ways in which fascism lived through the very technoaesthetic registers that promised freedom from it, this chapter is but one attempt to keep architects and their historians on the alert.

Notes

1. L.M., untitled, and Luis Moya, "Edificio de la Naciones Unidas en Nueva York," *Revista Nacional de Arquitectura, RNA* 109 (1951): 21–22. All translations by the author unless otherwise noted.

2. Beginning with the Ministry of Education that Lúcio Costa and Le Corbusier designed in 1943 for the regime of Fulgencio Batista in Brazil, curtain wall systems—or the illusion of such technology—were far from a North American phenomenon or in any way tied to democracy. For classic interpretations of the curtain wall in the context of U.S. politics, see Manfredo Tafuri, "The Ashes of Jefferson" in *The Sphere and the Labyrinth* (Cambridge, Mass.: MIT Press, 1987); Jane C. Loeffler, *The Architecture of Diplomacy: Building America's Embassies* (Princeton: Princeton Architectural Press, 1998); and Reinhold Martin, *The Organizational Complex: Architecture, Media, and Corporate Space* (Cambridge, Mass.: MIT Press, 2003). For studies of the curtain wall in an expanded geopolitical context, see Lisa Blackmore, *Spectacular Modernity* (Pittsburgh: University of Pittsburgh Press, 2017) and Alexandra Quantrill, "The Aesthetics of Precision" (PhD diss., Columbia University, 2017).

3. "United Nations Builds a Vast Marble Frame for Two Enormous Windows," *Architectural Forum* 90, no. 6 (June 1949): 81. For Lewis Mumford on the antidemocratic drive of a technologically driven society, see "Authoritarian and Democratic Technics," *Technology and Culture* 5, no. 1 (Winter 1964): 1–8.

4. Eleanor Roosevelt, "On the Adoption of the Universal Declaration of Human Rights," in *Great Speeches by American Women*, ed. James Daley (Mineola, N.Y.: Dover, 2008), 128–29; and Mark Mazower, *Governing the World: The History of an Idea* (New York: Penguin Press, 2012). For ways in which democratic and antifascist sentiments were explored through media in the immediate postwar years, see Fred Turner, *The Democratic Surround* (Chicago: University of Chicago Press, 2013).

5. Luis Moya, "Orientaciones de arquitectura en Madrid," *Reconstrucción* (December 1940): 15. A thorough analysis of architecture's role in the early shaping of Franquismo is Zira Box, *España, año cero: la construcción simbólica del franquismo* (Madrid: Alianza Editorial, 2010).

6. Roger Griffin, *Modernism and Fascism: The Sense of a Beginning under Mussolini and Hitler* (Palgrave Macmillan, 2007), 352.

7. Aimé Césaire, *Discourse on Colonialism* (New York: Monthly Review Press, 1997), 36. See also Partha Chatterjee, *Nationalist Thought and the Colonial World: A Derivative Discourse* (Minneapolis: University of Minnesota Press, 1997).

8. See especially Stanley Payne, *Fascism in Spain, 1923–1977* (Madison: University of Wisconsin Press, 2000), 31; Federico Finchelstein, *Transatlantic Fascism: Ideology, Violence, and the Sacred in Argentina and Italy* (Durham: Duke University Press, 2009); and Carl Fischer, "Fascism on Ice: Miguel Serrano in Chilean Antarctica," *Revista de Estudios Hipánicos* 54, no. 2 (2020): 505–32. Payne's early categorization of Franquismo as fascist was not without contention, but historians are fast addressing the need to better understand fascism as both a global phenomenon and one sustained visually, as in Julia Adeney Thomas and Geoff Eley, eds., *Visualizing Fascism: The Twentieth-Century Rise of the Global Right* (Durham: Duke University Press, 2020).

9. Ernesto Giménez Caballero, *Arte y Estado* (Madrid: Biblioteca Nueva, 2009). For the ways in which El Escorial shaped a fascist spatial imagination, see Nil Santianez, *Topographies of Fascism* (Toronto: University of Toronto Press, 2013).
10. Moya, "Naciones Unidas," 22.
11. *El Ideal de Galicia*, September 13, 1955, 7; *Gran Madrid* 31 (1956): 13–16.
12. The idea that Franco's *dictadura*—hard dictum—became a *dictablanda,* or a softer form of dictatorial rule, pervades sectors of Spanish politics and culture that whitewash the regime of its violent nature. Some scholars have tied *dictablanda* to the modernization of art and architecture in the 1950s, as in José Manuel Pozo, *Los brillantes 50* (Pamplona: T6 Ediciones, 2004), 19, and "Edificios contra el franquismo" *El Pais*, May 2, 2012. For scholarship fostering a critical revision of the politics of Franquista art and architecture, see María Dolores Jiménez-Blanco, ed., *Campo cerrado: Arte y poder en la posguerra Española, 1939–1953* (Madrid: Museo de Arte Reina Sofia, 2016).
13. See note 8 above. A seminal argument on the implications of Italian Fascism with the religious is Emilio Gentile, *Politics as Religion,* trans. George Staunton (Princeton: Princeton University Press, 2006).
14. Albert Crispi, "Filial Seat en Barcelona, 1957–1965," *Blanco y Negro*, AF34 (2019): 36–44.
15. *Boletín Oficial del Estado* (hereafter *B.O.E.*), March 5, 1956.
16. Legado Ramón Vázquez-Molezún, Archivo Histórico Colegio de Arquitectos de Madrid, COAM, Madrid, RMV A001767: F0090.
17. *B.O.E*, March 5, 1956.
18. *Gran Madrid* 31 (1956): 13–16.
19. George Mosse, *The Fascist Revolution: Toward a General Theory of Fascism* (New York: Howard Fertig, 1999), 137; Jeffrey Herf, *Reactionary Modernism: Technology, Culture, and Politics in Weimar and the Third Reich* (Cambridge: Cambridge University Press, 1984); Paul Jaskot, *The Architecture of Oppression* (New York: Routledge, 1999); Tiago Saraiva, *Fascist Pigs: Technoscientific Organisms and the History of Fascism* (Cambridge, Mass.: MIT Press, 2016); Ruth Ben-Ghiat, *Fascist Modernities: Italy, 1922–1945* (Oakland: University of California Press, 2004); and Andreas Malm, *White Skin, Black Fuel: On the Danger of Fossil Fascism* (New York: Verso Books, 2021). For the seminal articulation of fascism as an ideology of terror, see Hannah Arendt, *The Origins of Totalitarianism* (New York: Harvest Books, 1968), 468–471.
20. Lino Camprubí, *Engineers and the Making of the Francoist Regime* (Cambridge, Mass.: MIT Press, 2014), 3; and Ana Fernández-Cebrián, *Fables of Development: Capitalism and Social Imaginaries in Spain (1950–1967)* (Liverpool: Liverpool University Press, 2023).
21. José Casanova, "The Opus Dei Ethic and the Modernization of Spain" (PhD diss., New School for Social Research, 1982), 95. Casanova's research was the rare independent scholarly study of an organization steeped in controversy since its inception. Weighty but uneven literature about Opus Dei spans insiders' promotions, defectors' critiques, and journalistic reporting. See, for instance, Robert Hutchison, *Their Kingdom Come: Inside the Secret World of Opus Dei* (New York: St. Martin's, 2006). For a recent account of Opus Dei's ubiquity in U.S. right-wing media and politics, see Betty Clermont, "Opus Dei's Influence Is Felt in All of Washington's Corridors of Power," *Church and State: Challenging Religious Privilege in Public Life*, January 22, 2019, http://churchandstate.org.uk/2019/06/opus-deis

-influence-is-felt-in-all-of-washingtons-corridors-of-power/. Casanova's efforts only have been recently expanded into historical studies of modernization and neoliberalism by Camprubí, *Engineers*, 41–65, and Bethany Moreton, "Our Lady of Mont Pelerin: The 'Navarra School' of Catholic Neoliberalism," *Capitalism: A Journal of History and Economics* 2, no. 1 (2021): 88–153.

22. Moreton, "Our Lady," 124.
23. For recent scholarship calling attention to this relationship, see "Pious Technologies and Secular Designs," ed. María González Pendás and Whitney Laemmli, special issue, *Grey Room* 88 (Summer 2022).
24. José María Escrivá, *The Way* (New York: Scepter Publishers, 1979), #347.
25. Escrivá, *The Way*, #822.
26. Laureano López Rodó, *Política y Desarrollo* (Madrid: Aguilar, 1971), 125; and Casanova, "Opus Dei Ethic," 281.
27. Raymond Carr, *Modern Spain, 1875–1980* (Oxford: Oxford University Press, 1980), 46.
28. Stanley Payne, *The Franco Regime, 1936–1975* (Madison: University of Wisconsin Press, 2011), 440–444.
29. "News and Notes," *The Journal of Politics* 18, no. 30 (1956): 608.
30. López Rodó, *Política y Desarrollo*, 125. See also Antonio Cañellas, *Laureano López Rodo* (Madrid: Biblioteca Nueva, 2011), 2187.
31. Rodó, *Política y Desarrollo*, 130.
32. Rodó, *Política y Desarrollo*, 125–126.
33. Rodó, *Política y Desarrollo*, 129.
34. Luis Crespo Montes, *Las reformas de la Administración Española* (Madrid: Centro de Estudios Políticos y Constitucionales, 2000), 33–36; Payne, *The Franco Regime*, 470.
35. *ABC*, October 11, 1958, 39.
36. An overview of this new political economy is in Payne, *The Franco Regime*, 467–475 and, more directly tied to Opus Dei if not yet to Opus Dei architects, in Moreton, "Our Lady."
37. Hutchison, *Their Kingdom Come*, 117.
38. Alberto Moncada, *Historia oral del Opus Dei* (Madrid: Plaza y Janes, 1987), 78
39. Escrivá, *The Way*, #946.
40. Casanova, "Opus Dei Ethic," 63.
41. While some of the buildings that resulted from this program have been remarked upon in the scholarship, no study exists of this vast initiative, the records of which are in *Archivo General de la Administración*, Alcalá de Henares, signature: (04)078.000_ EBA41/0_26/15915.
42. "Delegacion de Hacienda en Tarragona," *B.O.E*, June 30 (1953): 3939.
43. *RNA* VIII-75 (1948): 91–94.
44. *RNA* VIII (1952): 6.
45. *RNA* 142 (1953): 6–10 and Archivo Fundación Alejandro de la Sota, Madrid (hereafter Archivo Sota), signature 52G.
46. *RNA* 149 (1954): 19–22 and Archivo Sota, signature 55X.
47. Alejandro de la Sota, "Palacio Provincial para La Coruña," May 1955, Archivo Sota, signature 54A.
48. Francisco Javier Sáenz de Oiza, "Vidrio," *RNA* 130 (1952).
49. Fritz Neumeyer, *The Artless Word* (Cambridge: MIT Press, 1991), 457.

50. *RNA* 172 (1956) and Archivo Sota, signature 54A.
51. *El Ideal Gallego,* September 1, 7; *RNA* 172 (1956): 7.
52. While not an Opus Dei member, Sota had frequented Escrivá and even sketched some designs for Opus Dei's early homes. Although absent from Sota's biographies and archives, evidence of this affiliation appears in John Coverdale, *Uncommon Faith: The Early Years of Opus Dei* (New York: Scepter, 2002), 275. Sota's lecture was delivered at the Opus Dei–run auditorium of La Estila.
53. Peter Minosh and Hunter Palmer, "Built in USA: Midcentury Architecture as a Vehicle of American Foreign Policy," in *Mass Media and the International Spread of Postwar Architecture* 4 (2019), 173. MoMA's earlier show *Built in USA* did not show in Spain, but *Modern Art* expanded its agenda in time and space.
54. "Truman Says Faith Is Best US Weapon," *New York Times,* December 25, 1950, 1. See also William Inboden, *Religion and American Foreign Policy, 1945–1960: The Soul of Containment* (Cambridge: Cambridge University Press, 2008); and Jonathan Herzog, *The Spiritual-Industrial Complex: America's Religious Battle against Communism in the Early Cold War* (Oxford: Oxford University Press, 2011). I have elaborated on some of these relations in "Enchanted Transfers: MoMA's Japanese Exhibition House and the Secular Occlusion of Modernism" in Vikramaditya Prakash, Maristella Casciato, and Daniel E. Coslett, eds., *Rethinking Global Modernism: Architectural Historiography and the Postcolonial* (New York: Routledge, 2022), 47–69.
55. As suggested by Annabel Wharton, *Building the Cold War: Hilton International Hotels and Modern Architecture* (Chicago: University of Chicago Press, 2004), 8–9; and Kathryn Lofton, "The Spirit in the Cubicle: A Religious History of the American Office," in *Sensational Religion: Sensory Cultures in Material Practice,* ed. Sally Promey (New Haven: Yale University Press, 2014), 135–59. This history might also help explain how religious and glassy landscapes together redefined fascism in the United States and amid democracy, paving the way toward the presidency of Donald Trump.
56. José Camón Aznar, "Arquitectura norteamericana," *ABC,* October 18, 1955, 17.
57. Alejandro de la Sota, *RNA* 172 (1956): 7.
58. Arendt, *The Age of Totalitarianism,* 469.
59. Umberto Eco, "Ur-Fascism," *The New York Review of Books,* June 22, 1995, 3, 8.

Chapter 9

Sert Goes South

Planning South America

Ana María León

> Strictly speaking, the unity of a Plan would be the unity of a unique thought. A bureaucratic and technocratic myth, the Plan is the modern dress of the idea of Providence.
>
> —Georges Canguilhem, *The Normal and the Pathological*

Although there is no record of the event, our protagonists José Luis Sert and Paul Lester Wiener might have first met at the Paris International Exhibition of 1937. Sert had escaped the Spanish Civil War, leaving behind a successful architecture career in Barcelona, and had arrived in Paris to design the celebrated pavilion for the Spanish Republic.[1] German architect Paul Lester Wiener had helped with the interiors of the U.S. Pavilion, one of several projects he did related to the U.S. government as the son-in-law of U.S. Secretary of the Treasury Henry Morgenthau.[2] The architects met three years later, in New York City. By then, Sert had left Europe for the United States, published an unsuccessful book, and failed to get a teaching offer from the Harvard Graduate School of Design (GSD).[3] He had exhausted his connections with Sigfried Giedion and Walter Gropius, and he needed a job. After Paris, Wiener assisted Lúcio Costa and Oscar Niemeyer in their design for the Brazilian pavilion at the New York's World Fair and briefly taught in Rio de Janeiro.[4] When they met in New York, Sert and Wiener were at a standstill in their careers, but their partnership became paradigmatic of the postwar transformation of the modern architect from heroic individual to technocratic expert. It also points to the construction of this expertise through images and drawings, and to the complicity it required with increasingly totalitarian states.

Wiener's contacts and Sert's credentials were joined in the 1941 founding of their firm, Town Planning and Associates (TPA), a union blessed by the seemingly divergent interests of the International Congress for Modern Architecture (CIAM) and the U.S. Department of State.[5] In 1940, Le Corbusier wrote to Sert to encourage him to speak with Wiener and connect "our friends in Rio" to the CIAM.[6] Sert was in a good position to assist Le Corbusier in his ambition to expand the CIAM to the Americas: his Spanish would be easily understandable to Portuguese-speaking Brazilians, and he needed an occupation, as he was unable to practice independently as an architect in the United States.[7] But Sert's connection to Le Corbusier was only one of the reasons Sert and Wiener started looking south. The other was Wiener's connection to Morgenthau, who would become a key participant in the Bretton Woods conference of 1944. This conference established the Bretton Woods system, the International Monetary Fund (IMF), and the International Bank for Reconstruction and Development (the World Bank). These institutions would provide substantial loans to several countries in South America. Toward the end of 1940, Morgenthau introduced Wiener to the U.S. Secretary of State, Cordell Hull, as a possible advisor in either Architectural Planning or Art and Design in Latin America.[8] Wiener and Hull began a correspondence that shaped the role Wiener and Sert would play in South America.

These personal connections produced some unexpected advantages after the attack on Pearl Harbor. In January 1942, the United States convened the third Pan-American States Conference in Rio de Janeiro with the express objective of persuading member states to sever diplomatic relations with the Axis powers with promises for increased economic assistance.[9] Brazil had an additional advantage for the United States, as its geographic location facilitated crossing the Atlantic. In contrast, Chile and Argentina had strong economic and military ties to Germany, feared getting involved in a war of rival imperialisms, and distrusted loyalty declarations from the United States.[10] The final, less forceful agreement was mediated by Brazil and strongly displeased Hull, who was supervising from Washington.[11] In this context, we can read Hull's influence in Wiener's comments of 1941 on the necessity for the United States to keep close to the southern continent and the convenience of influencing "small but powerful intellectual groups."[12] To this end, Wiener and Sert prepared a series of lectures given in South America in 1942, 1945, and 1955, financed by the Department of State with the specific stipulation that this sponsorship was not to be mentioned.[13] Upon his return, Wiener wrote and delivered confidential reports on their activities.[14] Brazil, Perú, and Colombia, all located in the northern half of South America, were promising economies that might help counter the influence Chile and Argentina held in the region. They were also the site of specific conferences or conflicts that coincided with the Department of State's use of Wiener as envoy.

Considering these narratives together—TPA's work in the region, the military governments and upheavals that took place throughout the period, and the regular interval of the CIAM congresses—reveals these unbuilt projects as architectural and political

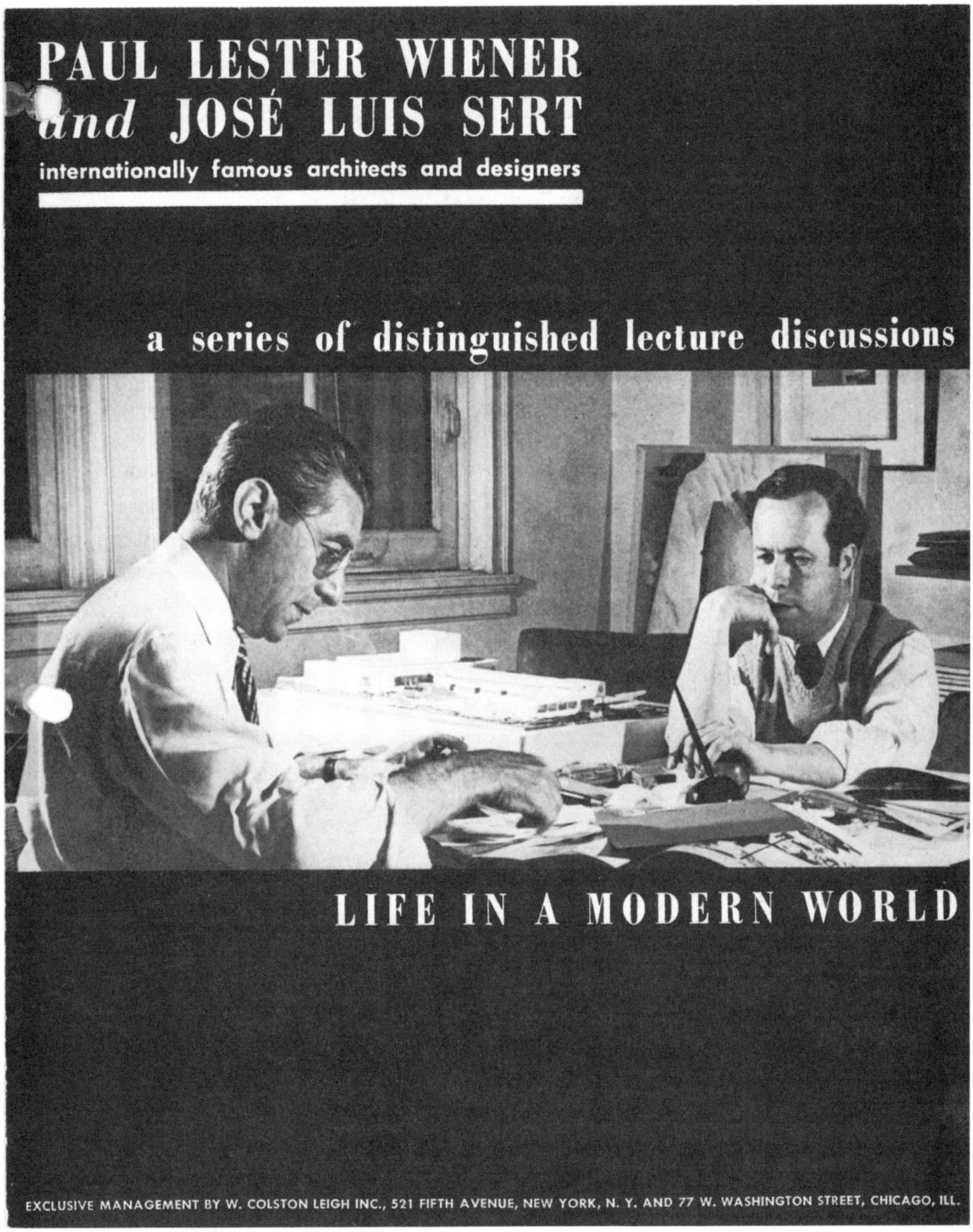

Figure 9.1. Paul Lester Wiener and José Luis Sert, undated (early 1940s). Frances Loeb Library, Harvard University Graduate School of Design.

currency. They served these different purposes for different audiences, but they ultimately benefitted their authors and sponsors rather than any specific public. As architectural currency, they provided material for architecture journals that enriched the portfolio of the architects who participated, and they participated in the promotion of modern urban planning. The commissions were instrumental to Sert's credibility as president of the CIAM and his eventual placement as dean of the Harvard GSD. As political currency, they rendered visible a modern utopia that appealed to the technocratic state the governments that financed them wished to represent. Here we might point to Néstor García Canclini's reflection on the fraught role of modernization in the formation of modernism. Comparing Latin American modernisms to their counterparts in Europe, García Canclini argues for a less teleological view of modernization, one in which we understand modernism as the result of aspirational needs and desires instead of a byproduct of technological progress.[15] Developmentalism in Latin America participated in these needs and desires, with many states more eager to represent modernization than to enact it. TPA's plans, sanctioned by the international renown of its creators, were an ideal vessel for this message. While the role of these architects, journals, and institutions in the formation of architectural modernism is well established, on a broader level I am interested in how South American architects, states, and their populations had an active role in shaping North Atlantic modernism *from below*.

Brazil

When Sert and Wiener traveled to Brazil in 1942, the country was under the government of Getúlio Vargas, who had been installed by the Brazilian military after a coup d'état in 1930 and assumed dictatorial powers in 1937.[16] Vargas had established an *Estado Novo* (new state) regime, a hybrid of contemporaneous fascist governments in Italy and Portugal. Before World War II, Germany had been one of Brazil's most important markets, and during the war Vargas had to deal with the shift of markets across the Atlantic. He reacted by playing enemies against each other in a pragmatic strategy that benefited Brazil's interests but was seen in the United States as political wavering. The difficulty of trading with the Axis powers during the war, coupled with the diplomatic and economic efforts of the United States, eventually brought Brazil to side with the Allies. At the Rio Conference of January 28, 1942, Brazil severed relations with the Axis powers; this allowed the United States to establish air bases in return for helping Brazil set up an iron industry. Sert and Wiener gave their first series of lectures in Brazil throughout winter 1942, possibly at the same time as the key Rio Conference. Their timing was excellent: Vargas had a predilection for industrial plants to promote a discourse of early developmentalism, and the United States had invested large sums of money as part of its efforts to bring the country over to the Allies. These combined interests resulted in the decision to create a new city, attached to the National Factory of Motors and meant to become a regional center to help modernize agriculture in the area. This was the City of Motors, TPA's first commission in South America.[17]

The commission was originally given to Brazilian architect–engineer Fernando Saturnino de Brito, who contacted Oscar Niemeyer to do the design.[18] Wiener was in Brazil at the time, and Niemeyer suggested he join them as a partner. Wiener agreed, but instead he returned to New York and replaced the Brazilian architects with Sert. They got the commission in May 1943.[19] At the same time, a team of Brazilian architects led by Lúcio Costa and including Niemeyer was working on another big government commission, the Ministry of Education and Health Building.[20] Vargas had declined hiring Le Corbusier for this job back in 1936 due to the strong nationalist mood prevalent in the country at the time. The choice of TPA over Brito and Niemeyer highlights the shift in Vargas's government: from nationalist politics before the start of the war to increased reliance on U.S. capital and expertise toward the end of the conflict, as the United States increased its control over the region. The rest of Brazil did not always approve of this sharp turn toward foreign expertise.

The drawings for the City of Motors show a series of large-scale highways and buildings in the midst of green space, in which the naive airplane-shaped plan of the bachelor apartments give the city the appearance of an airport runway. The proposal distanced itself from a textbook modernist vision in the enclosed city center, hinting at an understanding of public space that would evolve in later projects. The architects drew detailed building plans and sections, more interested in the "human scale" per Sert's writings of the time, while the urban plan remained at a schematic level.[21] The design was exceedingly generous in the amenities it provided for the workers, probably too generous for Brazil's urgent conditions. Still, the figurative references, good social intentions, and schematic nature of the urban scale served the political role of the plan. In Vargas's government, modernity and rationality were put to the service of the regime. For instance, state-built social amenities were intended as ways to control the behavior of the working population and "negate Communist promiscuity."[22] These moves were meant to counter Vargas's liberal decisions and his acceptance of U.S. influence and money, considering the nationalist mood that predominated in the country. In a way, Vargas was trying to play both sides, just as he did at the beginning of the war: modernism was presented as a U.S. product, but one that served a fascist regime. As a consequence of his pragmatic move to the Allied side, Vargas liberalized his regime to the point of legalizing opposition parties, including the Communist Party, in 1945.[23] These moves may have contributed to a coup d'état that same year led by General Eurico Gaspar Dutra.[24] Dutra, intent on reducing the role of the state, turned the Motor Factory into a private enterprise in 1948. With the government officials TPA had dealt with no longer in charge, the commission disappeared.

With dwindling hopes for Brazil, TPA faced a difficult prospect in 1946. Family problems forced Sert to travel to Spain, and his travel documents highlighted his precarious immigration status.²⁵ He was also busy with preparations, started in the final months of the war, for the first postwar CIAM.²⁶ In the meantime, Wiener worked as Le Corbusier's assistant in New York.²⁷ In March 1947, the relationship between the two partners was strained, and Wiener sent Sert a letter accusing him of being more interested in "academic" goals than Wiener's more "practical" aims, encouraging an equivocal impression of their roles:

> Reports from various colleagues indicate clearly their estimate of our joint relationship. You have silently encouraged, by our passive consent this estimate which more or less places me in the position of being your "promoter" and "capitalist."²⁸

Sert's partner relationship in his prior architecture firm sheds some light into this division of labor. In Barcelona, Sert had worked in close partnership with architect Josep Torres Clavé, a committed socialist who had provided the political credentials and secured the position of the firm by editing a journal promoting modern architecture. Antonio Bonet, an employee and later associate, described Torres Clavé as "a laborer of architecture" while Sert was "the person that was there to provide ideas."²⁹ Turning to capitalism, Sert might have envisioned an even clearer division of labor for TPA. Wiener's powerful political connections linked him to a growing roster of client-states, making him a capitalist in a geopolitical sense. Working in Barcelona, Sert had benefited from his family connections and his prestigious friendship with Le Corbusier. Those links were now distant, making Sert dependent on his better-connected partner. There is no record of Sert's response to Wiener's letter, but in August 1947 a new commission in Perú, which had been in the air since 1945, became a certainty. With Brazil fading in the horizon and Perú as a brand-new prospect, the architects packed their bags for England to attend the first postwar CIAM.³⁰

CIAM 6

CIAM 6 was held in Bridgwater, England, in September 1947, and Sert was named president, a charge he occupied until the dissolution of the Congress. Sert's standing had changed substantially from his position before and during the war, and much of the credit was due to the City of Motors project.³¹ The project was presented with Le Corbusier's project for the reconstruction of the French town of Saint-Dié of 1945 as the conceptual basis of the postwar work of the CIAM, intending to demonstrate the group's involvement with postwar reconstruction and new city building. The circumstances that surrounded the Brazilian plan were not part of Sert's narrative and were left unstated; the military coup was irrelevant. It was the future that mattered: TPA was working on the plans for the Peruvian city of Chimbote. The high profile of these city plans in the congress underlines the importance of Wiener's role in the partnership. Wiener was also engaged to recruit Latin American participants to the congress, including a rushed two-day trip to Buenos Aires to persuade former Le Corbusier employee Jorge Ferrari-Hardoy to attend.[32] Sert's presidency increased the stakes for more planning commissions, cementing his continued partnership with Wiener.

Perú

In Perú, Manuel Prado's presidency in 1939 had fostered good relations with the United States and started the development of the city of Chimbote, which was surrounded by rich mining deposits to be extracted through U.S. capital. The government created the Peruvian Corporation of Santa (CPS)[33] to develop the area. In 1945, Wiener and Sert visited Perú as part of their second lecture series for the U.S. Department of State. Wiener had kept in touch with U.S.-trained architect Fernando Belaúnde Terry, who at the time was deputy of Lima and soon to become a legendary figure in Peruvian politics.[34] In their 1945 visit, Wiener offered the CPS the opportunity to design a Master Plan for the city of Chimbote. At CPS's suggestion, a local team was established to gather information. Another Peruvian U.S.-trained architect, Luis Dorich,[35] was put in charge of this team. The presence of a local team, coupled with the fact that the job was for an existing population, distanced the Chimbote experience from the City of Motors and would strongly influence TPA's work.

José Luis Bustamante y Rivero, a prominent jurist and moderate leftist close to Belaúnde, was elected president of Perú in 1945.[36] His election initially meant continuity for the project, and Dorich's team gathered information on the area through 1946. That year, Bustamante's government created the National Housing Corporation (CNV)[37] to improve housing conditions. With Belaúnde as part of the board and Dorich as one of the designers, the CNV promoted the construction of residential neighborhoods units.[38] It was a time of important developments in the country's architectural discourse.[39] Dorich was named director of the newly established General Office of Planning and Urbanism, which worked with TPA on the Chimbote plan. This office and the CNV were developments under the Bustamante presidency that incorporated the discipline of architecture within the state. TPA received their contract in August 1947, but the political situation took a sudden turn. The murder of a conservative newspaper editor was blamed on Bustamante's party, the American Popular Revolutionary Alliance (APRA). Seeking to distance himself from the crime, Bustamante appointed Manuel Odría Amoretti to be Minister of Government and Police.[40] Odría, a military hero with additional training in the United States, advised Bustamante to suspend civil liberties, but the gesture aggravated hostilities between conservatives and Apristas. APRA called for a strike, and the political tension escalated into a series of riots. Thus, TPA began the design in an atmosphere of social chaos, political uncertainty, and antidemocratic tendencies, but the firm continued its work in close contact with the local team and made frequent trips to Perú.

Despite the chaotic background, the design for Chimbote would be a turning point for TPA, with changes in the scale, typology, and density of the proposal in comparison to previous projects. The influence of local culture was also favored by some of the ideas discussed at CIAM 6. Sert biographer Josep Rovira suggests that the architect not only used CIAM 6 to test his ideas for Chimbote but also used ideas introduced at the CIAM in Chimbote—particularly English architect James Richards's call against the monotony of standardization and for more attention to local forms. These ideas were echoed in Sert's report on the Chimbote plan, but this turn to local traditions can also be explained by the fact that TPA was working with a strong local team, which combined an understanding and appreciation of local culture with enthusiastic interest in the modern ideas coming from Europe. Instead of large towers in a park, the project featured low-rise high-density buildings more in keeping with local tradition and economics. The architects looked closely at local typologies, and while Sert asserted that he was incorporating the courtyard inherited from Spain, the design emulates a double patio with no lateral setbacks found in Colonial Lima as well as in Indigenous structures that precede Spanish conquest.[41] Regardless of the design's origins, TPA enthusiastically applied it to different scales and typologies.[42]

Despite the changes in scale and new appreciation for local traditions, the architects did not understand how land property was managed and proposed that families should be persuaded to exchange their present dwellings for future buildings. The resulting plan was hard to implement but well suited for political purposes, now with the added nationalist advantage of referencing vernacular typologies. Although in Perú a liberal democratic government had promoted the Chimbote plan, it would be undone by a new dictatorship, much as had happened to TPA's plans in Brazil.

Odría led a coup d'état and took over the presidency in October 1948, the climax of a series of rapid shifts in the political situation that were reflected in the urgency of the architects' design process. Compared to the City of Motors plan, the Chimbote plan was designed at a much faster pace. The Master Plan was delivered a couple of days before deadline in December 1948.[43] Still, this accelerated pace was surpassed by the rapid changes Chimbote itself was undergoing. In their calculations, TPA grossly underestimated the population growth, unaware of the unprecedented growth of the region due to massive migration from the countryside.[44] It was a process that the CIAM brand of urban planning was not ready to deal with, with the increased difficulty of presenting a plan before a regime change might overturn prior commitments.

The unstable political situation worsened, and Odría instituted a harshly authoritarian regime and banned APRA and the Communist Party. He resumed the service of the foreign debt (in default since the 1930s), improving the country's credit rating and enabling substantial loans from the World Bank and the IMF. But the nationalist mood of the country viewed these measures as excessive ties to the United States, forcing Odría to distance himself from that nation. In 1949, the managers of the CPS were removed from their posts and replaced by new personnel that had no ties to the project, and the Ministry of Public Works found the Master Plan was "impracticable."[45] By 1950, TPA had hired a lawyer to defend its interests in Perú, but to no avail. The government argued that the project did not comply with their needs and that new decrees had changed the administration of the land to different local governments. The nationalist mood of the country, exacerbated by the weakness of the Peruvian sol to the U.S. dollar, made the Chimbote plans economically excessive and politically undesirable.[46] As the prospects of the Chimbote plan disappeared from Perú, they became desirable in the next CIAM meeting in Italy, a conference that featured several Latin American projects, including works commissioned by the municipalities of Rio de Janeiro and Buenos Aires. In contrast, Sert and Wiener traveled to Italy well aware that their Peruvian adventure was over.

CIAM 7

CIAM 7 was held in 1949 in Bergamo, Italy. Sigfried Giedion was especially interested in increasing South American participation and particularly pursued Brazilian architects, whose reputation had been promoted by MoMA's 1942 *Brazil Builds* exhibition. The Brazilians sent their projects for display, but few attended.[47] In the end, it was an Argentinian plan that took the stage: Bajo Belgrano. This was a modern neighborhood designed by the Study for the Buenos Aires Plan (EPBA), an organization funded by the city hall of Buenos Aires and led by the Argentinian Jorge Ferrari-Hardoy. It was presented at the congress by his close associate, the Catalan Antonio Bonet. Both had worked for Le Corbusier in Paris, and Bonet had been Sert's employee in Barcelona. Relocated to Argentina, Ferrari and Bonet became close collaborators and had negotiated a lucrative commission for Bajo Belgrano, which they envisioned as the first step toward a modern plan for the city, one first envisioned by Le Corbusier when he visited Buenos Aires in 1929. In the context of president Juan Perón's nationalist rhetoric, the architects were persuaded to leave Le Corbusier out, to his great chagrin.[48]

Fresh from his presidential election at the prior CIAM meeting, Sert had an impressive display of three city projects: Lima, Chimbote, and Tumaco (in Colombia). The projects were presented as didactic examples of CIAM urbanism, and Sert highlighted how the Chimbote housing closely followed local typologies. The congress highlighted the difficult relationship between European and South American architects: while the latter often welcomed their colleagues' interest and expertise, they were not always willing to give up potential projects to their European counterparts. While the congress was supposed to be a friendly encounter, these architects were now in direct competition for the same client—the state. Sert and Bonet were also in competition for Le Corbusier's partnership and the prestige his endorsement attached to their work. While Ferrari and Bonet negotiated between Le Corbusier and the nationalist politics of Peronist Argentina, a different relationship was being put in place for Colombia. Responding to the excitement generated by Le Corbusier's 1947 visit, several Colombian architects attended CIAM 7, including Herbert Ritter Echeverry. One month after the congress, Ritter met with Sert, Wiener, and Le Corbusier in Roquebrune-Cap-Martin, France, to formulate the basic scheme of the architect's new commission, the Regulating Plan of Bogotá, Colombia, a commission that would have significant differences from TPA's previous ventures.

Colombia

Le Corbusier's 1947 visit to Colombia took place shortly after the conservative party returned to power after a long rule by the opposition.[49] The new government disputed previous pacts made with labor unions, and those discussions turned into confrontation and escalating violence. This was also the year of TPA's first visit to Colombia, where Sert and Wiener were overshadowed by the Swiss architect and the campaign toward modern planning waged by *Proa*, a Colombian architecture journal.

Proa had been founded in 1946 by Paris-trained architect Carlos Martínez Jiménez and presented itself as the voice of the Colombian architectural avant-garde.[50] The journal launched a campaign to "modernize" Bogotá, working as a collective that involved the Colombian Society of Architects and the School of Architecture of the National University of Colombia. This was the first architecture school in the country, founded in Bogotá in 1936, and although it had Beaux-Arts traces, the main curriculum was modernist. In Colombia the sympathies for modern architecture were strong, but they were also institutionalized and soon became part of the language of the state.[51] As in Brazil and Perú, the appeal of modernism to both the avant-garde and the state was the illusion that planning would bring order and rationality to a society in crisis, but in the case of Colombia the crisis was exacerbated, prompting *Proa* to idealize modernist planning as a solution. In its inaugural issue, the journal claimed: "Urbanism is economy, is happiness, is living with hope, is light and is hygiene."[52] Modernism was enthusiastically proposed by the local avant-garde as an image of efficiency and promptly adopted by local governments.

Proa's agenda was to involve Colombian modern architects in the process of planning, and bringing in Le Corbusier to sanction their work became almost an obsession. Their campaign backfired: Le Corbusier was eager to get a commission, and instead of endorsing a local architect he associated himself with TPA to pursue the job. His first visit to Bogotá in June 1947 was both dramatic and legendary, and it ended with the mayor's request to elaborate a Master Plan for Bogotá, a petition that had been agreed upon before his arrival. (Following his difficulties securing a commission in Argentina

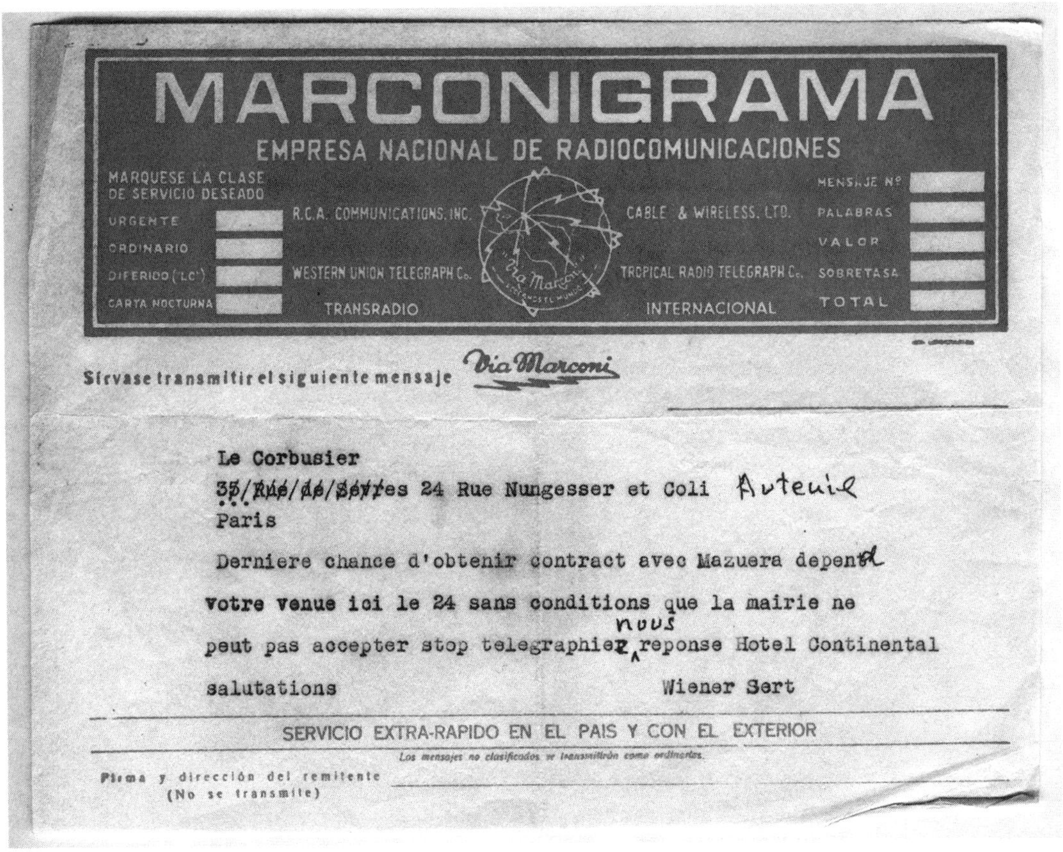

MARCONIGRAMA

EMPRESA NACIONAL DE RADIOCOMUNICACIONES

MARQUESE LA CLASE DE SERVICIO DESEADO

URGENTE

ORDINARIO

DIFERIDO ("LC")

CARTA NOCTURNA

R.C.A. COMMUNICATIONS, INC.

WESTERN UNION TELEGRAPH Co.

TRANSRADIO

CABLE & WIRELESS, LTD.

TROPICAL RADIO TELEGRAPH Co.

INTERNACIONAL

MENSAJE Nº

PALABRAS

VALOR

SOBRETASA

TOTAL

Sírvase transmitir el siguiente mensaje *Via Marconi*

Le Corbusier

~~35/Rue/de/Sevres~~ 24 Rue Nungesser et Coli Auteuil

Paris

Derniere chance d'obtenir contract avec Mazuera depend

votre venue ici le 24 sans conditions que la mairie ne

peut pas accepter stop telegraphiez nous reponse Hotel Continental

salutations Wiener Sert

SERVICIO EXTRA-RAPIDO EN EL PAIS Y CON EL EXTERIOR

Los mensajes no clasificados se transmitirán como ordinarios.

Firma y dirección del remitente (No se transmite)

Figure 9.2. Undated cable to Le Corbusier. Frances Loeb Library, Harvard University Graduate School of Design.

and Brazil after his extensive lectures there, Le Corbusier was adamant that he would travel only in exchange for a commission.) Increasingly urgent cables from Wiener and Sert negotiated the Colombian demand for Le Corbusier's presence. In the meantime, TPA got a commission to design the plan for the city of Tumaco, which had been razed by a fire in 1947. The firm started working in 1948 but soon had to cancel a trip planned for April because of an unexpected and extremely violent turn of events.

In March and April 1948, the Ninth International Conference of American States took place in Bogotá. This was the last of a series of meetings that defined postwar relations between the United States and Latin America.[53] In this context, on April 9 the liberal Colombian leader Jorge Eliécer Gaitán was assassinated. The reaction of the crowd was unprecedented, and this day of extreme destruction became known as "el Bogotazo." Violent riots attacked symbolic power structures (including the seat of the conference and the Presidential Palace) and burned down large parts of the city. Colombian cities were declared under a state of siege, and the violence shifted to the countryside, causing massive migrations to the cities, and creating an uncontrolled urban expansion.[54]

When the Bogotazo took place, Sert, in Lima, wrote to Wiener, who was in Chile:

> What a shock the news from Bogota I hope all the boys there are O.K. The next days will tell if it is going to be a short revolt or a long civil war in this last case we can eliminate Colombia from our agenda—another experience.[55]

This was effectively the start of a long civil war, but TPA saw it as an opportunity to reconstruct the city. So did local architects: in June 1948, *Proa* published a local project for the reconstruction of Bogotá by Colombian architects Jorge Arango, Herbert Ritter, and Gabriel Serrano. They included a plan showing the areas burned by the April riots, commented that with these fires "the urban problem of Bogotá has been frankly cleared and practically resolved," and claimed that demolition jobs would be unnecessary in realizing the proposals.[56] Arango and Ritter would attend CIAM 7, and Ritter, as Chief of the Municipal Department of Urbanism, would become the Colombian lead of the Le Corbusier–TPA team.[57] The commission was officially awarded to Le Corbusier in partnership with TPA in 1949, and the schematics were drawn up in August of that year during the post-CIAM meeting in Roquebrune-Cap-Martin with Sert, Wiener, and Ritter.[58] Ritter's involvement with the project is the link between the map of the destruction of downtown Bogotá and the Le Corbusier–TPA project for that area of the city. A comparison of the plans reveals how the modern plan follows the path of the destruction that resulted from the riots. In a later publication of the plan, Wiener and Sert argued that the voids were meant to constitute a series of "staggered pedestrian squares" linking the southern political center to the northern cultural and tourist center.[59] There is no mention of the destruction the city experienced, an omission that masks how the Bogotazo imbricated architecture and revolution.

By the start of 1950, Ritter was no longer working on the project, and Wiener and Sert complained to Le Corbusier that they would have to train new personnel.[60] The team continued working on the plan in their respective offices in Colombia, New York, and Paris, with TPA often acting as mediator between local requirements and Le Corbusier's more distant brand of urbanism. Although Le Corbusier's name was key to his Colombian fans, TPA's substantially larger share of the honoraria points to their involvement in the project.[61] The sums were reported by *Proa* in March 1949 as the country prepared to commemorate the one-year anniversary of the Bogotazo, which might have contributed to mounting local opposition to the plan.

In 1947, a new law was approved which required city halls to elaborate regulatory plans. The law became the legal basis of urban planning in Colombia and resulted in two more TPA commissions, for Medellín (1948–51) and Cali (1949–50).[62] Thus, in

Figure 9.3. El Bogotazo, Bogotá, 1948. Photograph by Sady González. Archivo fotográfico 1938–1949. Colección de Archivos Especiales. Sala de Libros Raros y Manuscritos. Biblioteca Luis Ángel Arango.

the period after the Bogotazo, TPA was working simultaneously on the plans for the three major Colombian cities.[63] However, these legal measures could do little against the huge scale and shifting nature of the changes the country was going through. The architects were in an almost impossible situation. They were charged with planning cities in the midst of rapid growth—cities whose form and scale were changing radically, with migrants escaping from the violence in the country and establishing themselves at the periphery. But if the plans were useless in the long term, in the short term they created a semblance of government action and order in a period of chaos.

The final plan, presented to a new government sympathetic to Spanish fascism, was promptly accepted and made into law in 1951.[64] By then, however, the plan was obsolete: rural migrations to the city exceeded all growth statistics and surpassed the limits the plan had fixed for the city's urban growth. These problems required fast, flexible solutions that conflicted with the rigidity of modern planning and the bureaucratic institutions that tried to enforce it. The project lost local support, and *Proa* published a critique

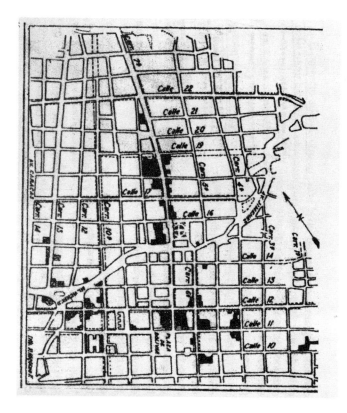

Figure 9.4. Plan of downtown Bogotá, sectors destroyed by the Bogotazo. *Revista PROA* 13, June 1948.

Figure 9.5. Bogotá Plan, Bogotá, Colombia, undated (approximately 1953), detail. Frances Loeb Library, Harvard University Graduate School of Design. Copyright F.L.C. / ADAGP, Paris / Artists Rights Society (ARS), New York 2022.

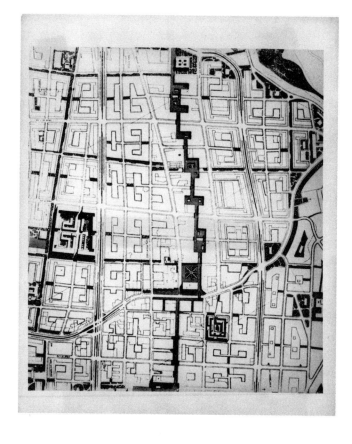

stating that the plan should have been made locally where it would have been "better executed and at an infinitely lesser cost."[65] At the same time, local governments started making decisions that contradicted the plan. The need to resolve immediate problems led to opening roads that breached the urban perimeter and occupied reserve zones established by the architects. So, while Sert was describing his plan as "a realistic, finished proposal," reality kept moving farther from the image the plan had been based on.[66]

The fragile political situation caused liberals and conservatives to support a new coup, installing General Gustavo Rojas Pinilla. The military dictatorship soon took measures to stop the violence that further eliminated any prospects for the plan's realization.[67] By Wiener's last tour of Latin America in 1955, the local sentiment was that the plan had been archived and that both Bogotá's growth and Colombia's political situation were drifting out of control. In his final report, Wiener declared himself "rather disturbed by the political situation," finding that governmental oppression had resulted in fear and a lack of interest in the promotion of urban planning.[68] The plan was unable to address urgent urban problems and was put aside in favor of measures that did.

CIAM 8 and Beyond

At the start of 1951, *L'Architecture d'Aujourd'hui* published a special edition on urbanism in Latin America featuring TPA's plans in Medellín, Tumaco, Chimbote, and Lima, stating they were "based on general principles formulated by the International Congress of Modern Architecture (C.I.A.M.) in the Athens Charter of 1933." While the issue also included other architects' projects in Brazil, Venezuela, and Argentina, most of it was dedicated to TPA's work, which the journal presented as "urbanism in Latin America."[69] Additional publications in *Architectural Forum* and *Architectural Design* further publicized TPA's work in the early 1950s.

In 1951, CIAM 8 was held in Hoddesdon, England, with the theme "The Heart of the City." TPA presented some of the Perú and Colombia projects shown previously at CIAM 7 and introduced their work in Bogotá and Medellín, which faced direct criticism. Jorge Gaitán Cortés, chief delegate of the Colombian chapter of the CIAM, presented the Bogotá pilot plan.[70] Colombian architects Hernán Vieco and Germán Samper criticized it, arguing that the plan did not adapt to the social and cultural framework of the city.[71] This so-called heart of the city—the downtown of Bogotá—was the site that had been so violently destroyed by the Bogotazo and later reconfigured by TPA's proposal. Sert's argument for a civilizing civic core—quoting the work of José Ortega y Gasset's *Revolt of the Masses*—takes on disciplinary undertones when used to frame Plaza Bolívar, the main square in Bogotá and the center of the violence.[72] The further replication of staggered pedestrian plazas along the path of the destruction of the city further suggests the architects meant to mobilize the plaza as a civilizing and ultimately disciplinary agent to control the revolting masses.

The last two countries in TPA's Latin American tour were Venezuela and Cuba during the dictatorships of Marcos Pérez Jiménez and Fulgencio Batista. TPA's work in these countries exceeds the limits of this essay, but it is important to highlight the familiar pattern of modern planning amid compromised political situations. In 1953, after delivering the final version of the Bogotá plan, Sert headed to Cambridge where he took over as dean of the Harvard GSD. After his appointment, TPA wound up their work in Latin America, and the partnership ended almost simultaneously with the CIAM's dissolution in 1960.

Lost in the Clouds

> In short, this is the story. We know from experience, how long and complex it is to arrange formal contracts in no matter which country in Latin America; it is necessary never to put too much confidence in their beautiful words, because they forget them as soon as your airplane is lost in the clouds...[73]

U.S. relations with Latin America deteriorated in the 1950s. In 1955, Henry-Russell Hitchcock organized the exhibition *Latin American Architecture since 1945* at the Museum of Modern Art, but MoMA's return to the region was not enough to compensate for the Eisenhower administration's support for military dictatorships in Perú, Paraguay, and Venezuela, and Vice-President Nixon's praise of Fulgencio Batista in Cuba. TPA's work with these regimes ran parallel with U.S. support. Their retreat from the area coincided with growing skepticism and resentment in the region toward U.S. policies and impositions. At the end of 1958, the Cuban revolution ousted Batista, and in doing so called out the role of the United States in the politics of the region.

Through its support of TPA, the U.S. Department of State indirectly contributed to the promotion of modern planning. In the extensive press coverage that TPA received in the Latin American press, Sert's and Wiener's European origins were rarely mentioned. They were consistently presented as "very distinguished foreign technicians," and "renowned architects and urbanists established in New York."[74] They were portrayed as representatives of a U.S. brand of urbanism that they actually knew little about. Conversely, their work came to represent the CIAM "brand" in the postwar conferences or a distorted version of "Latin America" in journals in the United States and Europe. The most tangible result of the projects was their images. To the regimes that sponsored them, these modern images provided the appearance of action and represented a modernism to come without the expense and conflict of the actual logistics of modernization. These regimes' desire for efficiency and control aligned with the discourse of modern architecture and contributed to the shape of these projects.

The projects promoted the work of TPA and the CIAM in Europe and gave Sert the credentials to become president of the congress and eventually dean at the GSD.[75] But while these projects impressed publics in Europe and the United States, South American architects were skeptical, noting the conflicts between the plans and their local context. In his analysis of *Proa*'s role in the architectural discourse of Colombia, Hugo Mondragón argues that the international urban modernism that TPA and Le Corbusier imported was already distanced from a local variant that had been developed based not just on international ideas but also by taking local problems into account.[76] This localized modernism included an awareness of historical presence and local context that was missing from TPA's more distant engagement. Local architects built several plans throughout the region. These plans included Sergio Larraín and Emilio Duhart's Villa Presidente Ríos in Chile (1947–51),[77] Lúcio Costa and Oscar Niemeyer's Brasilia (1956–60), Fernando Belaúnde Terry's support for the PREVI housing project in his first term as president of Perú (1963–68),[78] and Jorge Gaitán Cortés's implementation of planning efforts similar to those originally intended in the regulating plan during his tenure as Mayor of Bogotá (1961–66). These built plans attest to the ability of South American architects to navigate the complications of their political moments, although in some cases the most effective way to implement a plan was to become part of the state.

The presence of the Latin American context, culture, and typologies in TPA's work and the CIAM at large increased as the architects became more familiar with the region. In Perú, the increased collaboration with local architects in connection to changing discourses at the CIAM referenced local typologies and resulted in a plan with higher population density for Chimbote. In Colombia, *Proa*'s discourse furthered the cause of modernist planning, and the destruction of downtown Bogotá left a void that shaped the modern project. It was these sites and their architects, governments, and populations that increasingly informed the rushed pace, formal layout, and ultimate demise of these projects. In other words, they were shaped by their context, by the aspirational needs and desires of southern agents. If Sert and Wiener presented themselves as experts, the results of their efforts revealed the fragility of their claim—a fragility that was understood by audiences in the South but elided when the work was presented in the North.

Both local and foreign architects navigated the rise of increasingly authoritarian regimes with varying degrees of complicity. But TPA's inability to understand the conditions that led to the inapplicability of its plans, along with the firm's lack of acknowledgement of the changes taking place and the political roles its plans played, distanced TPA from local architects. When Sert returned to Colombia in 1977, he refused to engage in the critique of his plans, and his idealist vision of the city remained unchanged.[79] All architects were caught between their desire for the ordered, planned world that the modern plan was increasingly conflated with and the limitations caused by economic and political crises. But local architects, left watching Sert's plane, had to keep their feet on the ground while the expert consultants got lost in the clouds.

Notes

My thanks to Ijlal Muzaffar, in whose MIT seminar I began my research. Thanks also to Inés Zalduendo at Harvard University's Loeb Library Special Collections, Lauren Goss at Special Collections at the University of Oregon, Miguel Alvarez for access to the *Proa* journal archive, and the editors and participants of this volume for their insightful comments in the workshop.

1. Sert's only urban planning experience in Europe, the Macià plan (never officially commissioned), gave him a first opportunity to demonstrate his pragmatic approach in dealing with tense political circumstances and continuous changes in administration. He would soon confront a similar environment in the New World. While working on the plan, Sert maintained his campaign for modern urbanism (and possible projects) from the pages of *A.C.: Documentos de actividad contemporánea* (Contemporary Architecture: Documents of contemporary activity), the journal of the G.A.T.E.P.A.C. (Group of Spanish Artists and Technicians for the Progress of Contemporary Architecture, the self-denominated Spanish branch of the CIAM). *A.C.* was edited by Sert's partner, Josep Torres Clavé, with the outspoken purpose of promoting the tenets of modern architecture and art.
2. In 1936, in association with Levi and Higgins, Wiener designed the U.S. government building and its interiors for the International Exhibition in Paris of 1937. Eric Mumford, *The CIAM Discourse on Urbanism, 1928–1960* (Cambridge, Mass.: MIT Press, 2000), 304; and Paul Lester Wiener Papers 1913–1968, http://nwda-db.wsulibs.wsu.edu/findaid/ark:/80444/xv66707#seinfoID.
3. Giedion and Gropius pressured Joseph Hudnut, dean of the GSD, to issue Sert a vague invitation to teach. This job did not materialize.
4. Wiener handled the structure and contracts, and he designed the interior decorations and exhibition display. Afterward, he was visiting professor at the Federal University in Rio de Janeiro. Zilah Quezado Deckker, *Brazil Built: The Architecture of the Modern Movement in Brazil* (London: Spon Press, 2001), 112.
5. In 1942, Wiener and Sert founded Ratio Structures, Inc., a company dedicated to developing prefabricated and demountable housing, but it doesn't seem to have done much business. In January 1941, Sert received a letter from Le Corbusier suggesting he come work with him in Paris, an invitation later repeated but never accepted, although they collaborated later on the Bogotá plan. Sert also partnered briefly with Ernest Weissmann, also a CIAM member, to work on a New York apartment project in 1939–40.
6. Le Corbusier to Sert, May 20, 1940, in Mumford, *The CIAM Discourse*, 144.
7. Sert left his Spanish architectural degree in Barcelona. Without it, he could not register with the National Council of Architectural Registration Boards (NCARB), which controls U.S. architecture registration requirements. Sert eventually got proof of his architectural degree released by Francisco Franco in 1947 and passed his NCARB examination in 1949. Josep M. Rovira i Gimeno, *José Luis Sert: 1901–1983* (Milan: Electa Architecture, Phaidon, 2003), 157.
8. Hull was U.S. Secretary of State from 1933 to 1944 and played a key role in establishing the United Nations.
9. Eric Helleiner, "Building Foundations: U.S. Postwar Planning," in *Forgotten Foundations of Bretton Woods: International Development and the Making of the Postwar Order* (Ithaca: Cor-

nell University Press, 2014), 99–132, especially 107. The Dominican Republic, Haiti, Cuba, Panama, Costa Rica, Nicaragua, Honduras, El Salvador, and Guatemala had already declared war on the Axis powers; Mexico, Colombia, and Venezuela had severed diplomatic relations. Brazil, Ecuador, Peru, Paraguay, and Uruguay severed diplomatic relations as a result of the conference.

10. Elite members of the Brazilian and Argentinean militaries had been trained there. Buenos Aires served as the main base of Nazi efforts to "seduce the countries of Latin America." Arthur P. Whitaker, *The United States and the Southern Cone: Argentina, Chile, and Uruguay* (Cambridge, Mass.: Harvard University Press, 1976), 377–81. See chapter 16, "Relations through World War II." The officer corps of the Argentine army were trained in Germany and convinced that Germany would win the war.

11. The final agreement was to merely recommend the severance of relations, a modification of the U.S. proposal. Chile did not break relations until 1943; Argentina waited until 1945. The United States was represented by Undersecretary of State Sumner Welles, who gave in to the agreement but then had a violent clash by telephone with Hull in Washington for having violated his instructions. See Whitaker, *The United States and the Southern Cone,* 380.

12. Wiener, letter to Edward G. Trueblood of April 28, 1941, in Rovira, *José Luis Sert,* 113.

13. The lectures were done with Sert although the contract was only in Wiener's name. The partners agreed to "share the benefits and obligations under this contract equally." P. L. W. letter to Sert on May 7, 1941. From the Paul Lester Wiener Correspondence (PLWC) and in Rovira, *José Luis Sert,* 155. Wiener was not "to represent in any manner whatsoever that the Coordinator or the U.S.A. or any Department or Agency thereof is sponsoring or in any way connected with or responsible for such tour without first obtaining the written consent of the Coordinator." Lawrence H. Levy, General Counsel to the Coordinator of Inter-American Affairs to Wiener, confirming his three-month lecture tour to Colombia, Peru, and Brazil; Letter of Agreement LA-87 DAC1–5265, March 21, 1945, in Mumford, *The CIAM Discourse,* 326.

14. The Paul Lester Wiener Archive at the University of Oregon has these papers. See "1945 South American Tour. Confidential Report" in PLW SC UO Box 11 for a description of the activities realized in Colombia, Brazil, and Peru. In Patricia Schnitter Castellanos, "José Luis Sert y Colombia" (Tesis Doctoral Universidad Politécnica de Catalunya, June 2002), 36.

15. Néstor García Canclini, *Hybrid Cultures: Strategies for Entering and Leaving Modernity,* trans. Christopher L. Chiappari and Silvia L. López (Minneapolis: University of Minnesota Press, 2005). García Canclini describes how modernist groups in Italy and Russia developed without technological modernization, while in England technological innovation did not produce strong cultural modernisms.

16. Nelson Werneck Sodré, *Formação Histórica do Brasil* (Rio de Janeiro: Editora Civilização Brasileira S. A., 1976), 328–338.

17. The Motor factory used U.S. production-line methods and received supplies from the United States through a credit of USD 1,220,200 granted by the Export–Import Bank, an institution that gave similar loans to other countries in South America. Rovira, *José Luis Sert,* 115–116 and Whitaker, *The United States and the Southern Cone,* 385. Wiener was also involved in the 1943 MoMA exhibition *Brazil Builds,* which was part of the museum's

18. Preliminary sketches were made by Brazilian architect Attilio Corrêa Lima, who died in 1943.
19. Niemeyer was furious. See Mumford, *The CIAM Discourse*, 144.
20. Under Vargas's rule, modern architecture was welcome as a matter of national policy. He authorized an invitation to Le Corbusier in 1936, who had to be tempted with the possibility of two commissions in order to accept: the Cidade Universitária and the Ministry of Education and Health Building. In reality, both projects were already assigned to Brazilian architects in accordance with the nationalist mood of the country. The Ministry Building, designed by Lució Costa and a team of architects that included (among others) Affonso Eduardo Reidy and Oscar Niemeyer was started in 1936 and completed in 1945. The building became an immediate success. See Quezado, *Brazil Built*, chapter 2.
21. At the time, Sert was writing his essay "The Human Scale in City Planning" in Paul Zucker, *New Architecture and City Planning: A Symposium* (New York: Philosophical Library, 1944), emphasizing the need for a more human scale. In his analysis of the plan, Sert biographer Rovira finds "an astonishing naivety coupled with an unconditional faith in the advantages of a functional city that can no longer be perceived as schematic." Rovira, *José Luis Sert*, 127.
22. Brigadier Guedes Muñiz, quoted in Rovira, *José Luis Sert*, 116.
23. Niemeyer joined the Communist Party the same year despite his previous collaborations with the Vargas government.
24. After a brief intermediate government, Dutra was named president in 1946 and remained in power until 1951, when Vargas was reelected.
25. Just before the coup, Sert had refused new overtures from Le Corbusier to go work in his office in Paris. In 1946, Sert traveled to Barcelona because of his mother's failing health, a visit that caused him great fear of not being allowed to leave Spain or enter the United States again. He was in Spain from August to October. He also used this time to procure a certificate of his architectural degree, although the final authorization was released later. His mother recovered. Rovira, *José Luis Sert*, 157.
26. On May 20, 1944 (a couple of weeks before D-Day), the new CIAM Chapter for Relief and Postwar Planning met in New York. The meeting included Sert, Wiener, Gropius, Giedion, Richard Neutra, and others. At this time, the group was more focused on getting commissions than in building a movement, and the image of a devastated Europe meant large urban sites cleared for reconstruction. The group continued to meet for several years, but never generated a strong CIAM movement in the United States. Mumford, *The CIAM Discourse*, 145.
27. As Le Corbusier's assistant, Wiener handled the possible publication of his books in the United States and sent reports in his name regarding the UN's permanent headquarters building. Sert Archive, Folder 028, letters from October 7, 1946, to November 23, 1946. The Swiss architect visited the city that year as a member of the UN site selection committee. That committee was chaired by Dr. Eduardo Zuleta Ángel of Colombia, who would be key in Le Corbusier's involvement in this country.
28. Memorandum from Wiener to Sert, PLW SC OU and in Schnitter, "José Luis Sert y Colombia," 29–30.

29. Architect Antonio Bonet worked closely with Torres Clavé and Sert in Barcelona and described the partnership thus. "Entrevista Arq. Antonio Bonet," Folder c1305/168/1.2, 1, Bonet Archive, Col legi d'Arquitectes de Catalunya (COAC).
30. Incidentally, around the same time in 1947, Getúlio Vargas's daughter-in-law, Ingeborg ten Haeff, divorced his son, Lutero Vargas, and moved to New York, marrying Wiener in 1948. She traveled to South America with Wiener from 1948 to 1956. Wiener continued his connection to the Department of State despite having lost his family connection to Morgenthau.
31. Sert was no longer the Spanish exile looking to work on editing CIAM reports into a book or striving to get a teaching invitation from Harvard. He was now a partner in a firm with New York offices and a project for a new city.
32. Wiener visited the city on August 2, 1947, to meet with Ferrari, who in turn wrote to his associate Bonet: "I think this congress is important, and we should send a good amount of realized works." Jorge Ferrari-Hardoy letter to Antonio Bonet, August 24, 1947, Folder c1306.168.5007, Bonet Archive, COAC.
33. *Corporación Peruana del Santa,* a government organization modeled after the Tennessee Valley Authority, was created in 1943 to develop the potential of the Santa River with U.S. capital. Mumford, *The CIAM Discourse,* 188, and Josep Maria Rovira Gimeno, ed., *Sert 1928–1979: Medio siglo de arquitectura: Obra completa* (Barcelona: Fundació Joan Miró, 2004), 130.
34. Belaúnde studied architecture at the University of Miami and the University of Texas–Austin. He was elected president for the terms 1963–68 and 1980–85. He was Odría's rival in the 1956 elections, when military attempts to block his candidacy resulted in a dramatic confrontation that made him an instant local hero. He founded *Acción Popular,* a populist party that was presented as an alternative between the more radical left-wing APRA and the extreme right of Odría. In 1937, Belaúnde had founded an architecture journal, *El arquitecto peruano* (*The Peruvian Architect,* now online at www.elarquitectoperuano.com) and used it to promote alternatives for social housing, a distant echo of Sert's own campaigning for modern urbanism in Barcelona through *A.C.* In 1947, the journal's covers change abruptly from colonial buildings to modern architecture. For more on Belaúnde Terry's role in Peruvian politics and architecture, see Helen Gyger, *Improvised Cities: Architecture, Urbanization, and Innovation in Peru* (Pittsburgh: University of Pittsburgh Press, 2019).
35. Dorich graduated from MIT with a master's degree in city planning in 1944. His thesis was "Basis for a City Planning Procedure in Peru," directed by Frederick J. Adams.
36. Bustamante was aligned with the Alianza Popular Revolucionaria Americana (APRA), or American Popular Revolutionary Alliance, a center-left Peruvian political party, and the Peruvian Socialist Party.
37. Also known as the Corporación Nacional de la Vivienda.
38. The most important example is the Unidad Vecinal No. 3, or UV3. This unit included denser, four-story apartment buildings, equipment to satisfy local needs, and a focus on pedestrian movement and equipment. It had no work areas. Luis Cabello Ortega, "Urbanismo estatal en Lima metropolitana: Las urbanizaciones populares 1955–1990," *ur[b]es* 3 (January–December 2006). Dorich wrote to TPA and told them the units were being

designed according to their programs. Rovira, *José Luis Sert,* 131. In fact, Dorich was getting more of his designs built than TPA.

39. In 1947, Agrupación Espacio was formed under the leadership of architect Luis Miró Quesada. The group published a manifesto, organized a series of lectures on modern architecture, and eventually expressed their desire to join the CIAM. Dorich was one of the manifesto signers. See Sharif S. Kahatt, "Agrupación Espacio and the CIAM Peru Group: Architecture and the City in the Peruvian Modern Project," in *Third World Modernism: Architecture, Development and Identity,* ed. Duanfang Lu (London: Routledge, 2011), 85–110, and Rovira, *José Luis Sert,* 158.

40. In early 1946, President Bustamante signed a controversial agreement with the International Petroleum Company (IPC), a subsidiary of Standard Oil. The deal was viewed in Perú as "a giveaway." Daniel M. Masterson, *Militarism and Politics in Latin America: Peru from Sánchez Cerro to Sendero Luminoso* (New York: Greenwood Press, 1991), 98. Internal tensions escalated in January 1947 with the murder of Francisco Graña Garland, the editor of a conservative newspaper. Seeking to distance himself from APRA (the principal suspects of the murder), President Bustamante replaced the APRA members of his cabinet with military personnel, named General Manuel Odría as Minister of Government and Police, and placed Odría in charge of the investigation into Garland's death. Odría's influence grew in the months following the murder, a situation the United States followed closely. See Masterson, "Prelude to Rebellion: 1945–1948," in *Militarism and Politics in Latin America,* 89–110; see also Fredrick B. Pike, "The APRA Declines and New Forces for Change Emerge, 1945–65," in *The Modern History of Peru* (New York: Frederick A. Praeger Publishers, 1967), 282–290.

41. This specific layout, a double patio with no lateral setbacks, can be found in colonial houses in downtown Lima as well as in the Tawantinsuyu city of Ollantaytambo. Photographs in the Sert Archive suggest he probably visited the Urubamba valley, a region with several important Tawantinsuyu structures including this town and Machu Picchu. Tawantinsuyu is the name of what is known in English as the Inca Empire.

42. See Wiener and Sert, "Can Patios Make Cities?" in *Architectural Forum* (August 1953): 124–131. Sert was the one obsessed with the idea, to the point of adapting the house type designed for Chimbote for his own house in Cambridge, Massachusetts, in 1958. See Jaume Freixa, *Josep Lluis Sert* (Barcelona: Gustavo Gili, 1981), 82.

43. The Pilot Plan was submitted in February 1948 and approved by the Ministry of Public Works in June 1948. TPA also worked on a more schematic plan for Lima in 1947–49 but never got the official commission.

44. See Rovira, *José Luis Sert,* 128 and Franklin Pease, *Breve historia contemporánea del Perú* (México D. F.: Fondo de Cultura Económica, 1995), 204–5. TPA estimated that the population would grow from 5,000 to 50,000 in fifty years (1944–1994), but by 1985 Chimbote had 253,000 inhabitants. TPA's terminology was also inaccurate: "In the next fifty years, the city will reach a population density of 50,000 inhabitants." Density refers to the number of inhabitants per area unit, not the total population of an area.

45. Rovira, *José Luis Sert,* 134–135. Letter to TPA from C. Morales, President of the Society of Architects.

46. After TPA, Odría's government would invest heavily in infrastructure and public housing, focusing specifically on trying to control expanding informal settlements caused by rural migrations to Lima. For more on the state's involvement in urban planning, see Ortega, "Urbanismo Estatal en Lima," 83–110.
47. The projects were Affonso Eduardo Reidy's Pedregulho housing built in 1947 in Rio de Janeiro and Flavio Regis's designs for a housing district in Rio. The Latin American delegates listed in the catalog include Eugenio Battista from Cuba, Jorge Ferrari-Hardoy from Argentina, and Antonio Bonet in representation of Uruguay. Ferrari-Hardoy did not attend. The biggest delegation was from Colombia (reflecting Le Corbusier's increased influence there) and included Jorge Arango, Alberto Iriarte, Francisco Pizano, Martinez, Herbert Ritter Echeverri, Violi Lleva, and Weisberger; see *Documents: 7 CIAM, Bergamo, 1949* (Nendeln: Kraus Reprint, 1979). The publication *Documents: 7 CIAM, Bergamo, 1949* lists architects by their last names only; I have found no first names on record for Martinez, Violi Lleva, and Weisberger. Jorge Gaitán Cortés was the official CIAM delegate for Colombia, but his name is not on record as attending.
48. See Jorge Francisco Liernur with Pablo Pschepiurca, *La red Austral: Obras y proyectos de Le Corbusier y sus discípulos en la Argentina (1924–1965)* (Bernal: Universidad Nacional de Quilmes, 2008) and Ana María León, *Modernity for the Masses: Antonio Bonet's Dreams for Buenos Aires* (Austin: University of Texas Press, 2021).
49. A thorough history of Le Corbusier's visits to Bogotá and the plan can be found in María Cecilia O'Byrne Orozco, *Le Corbusier en Bogotá, 1947–1951: Precisiones en torno al plan director* (Bogotá: Universidad de Los Andes, 2010).
50. For a history of *Proa*, see Hugo Mondragón, "Arquitectura en Colombia 1946–1951: lecturas críticas de la revista *Proa*" in *Dearq* 2 (July 1, 2008): 82–95.
51. See Hernando Vargas Caicedo, ed., *Le Corbusier en Colombia* (Bogotá: Cementos Bogotá, 1987).
52. "Urbanismo es economía, es alegría, es vivir con anhelos, es luz y es higiene . . ." in Luz Amorocho, Enrique García, José J. Angulo, Carlos Martínez, "Bogotá moderna: Reurbanización plaza central de mercado y manzanas vecinas," *Proa* 3 (October 1946): 15.
53. Among the conference attendees were U.S. Secretary of State George Marshall, the president of the Export–Import Bank, and Argentinian President Juan Perón. Also in Bogotá but protesting the conference were Fidel Castro, Che Guevara, and other Latin American communist leaders. The Communist Party was accused of inciting the riots.
54. The violence caused an estimated 200,000 deaths between 1948 and 1953. The period between 1948 and 1965 is known in Colombia as "La Violencia" (the violence). Jenny Pearce, *Colombia: Inside the Labyrinth* (London: Latin America Bureau, 1990), 48–66.
55. Letter, Sert to Wiener, April 11, 1948, PLW SC UO, and in Schnitter, "José Luis Sert y Colombia," 41. Afterward, Wiener writes from Colombia to Chilean architects Sergio Larraían and Emilio Duhart: "The destruction here is greater than we expected, but we are organizing our work with the young group." May 4, 1948, PLW SC UO.
56. "El problema urbano de Bogotá ha sido francamente aclarado y prácticamente resuelto." Jorge Arango, Herbert Ritter, and Gabriel Serrano, "Reconstrucción de Bogotá," in *PROA* 13 (June 1948): 11.

57. Technically, Le Corbusier was the architect of the Pilot Plan and Ritter, Sert, and Wiener were consultants. At a second stage, Sert and Wiener were put in charge of the development of the Regulating Plan.
58. Fernando Martínez, a young Colombian architect, also attended the meeting and was put to work in Le Corbusier's office as part of the agreement.
59. Paul Lester Wiener and José Luis Sert, "The Work of Town Planning Associates in Latin America, 1945–1956," *Architectural Design* (June 1957): 202. This publication includes a slightly more extensive version of the plan shown here, including the redesign of Plaza Bolívar.
60. Letter, Wiener and Sert to Le Corbusier, January 19, 1950, Loeb Special Collections.
61. According to the contract details reported by *Proa*: of the USD 223,000 allocated for the plan, Le Corbusier received USD 73,000 while Sert and Wiener received USD 150,000 plus USD 25,000 for every year they worked as consultants. "223.000 dólares valdrá el plano regulador de Bogotá," *Proa* 21 (March 1949): 37.
62. Law 88 required all city halls with a budget greater than $200,000 Colombian pesos to elaborate regulatory plans that indicated the manner in which the future urbanization of the city should take place. Schnitter, "José Luis Sert y Colombia," 57. The law had been promoted by a group of architects including Jorge Gaitán Cortés, who was also part of the Colombian CIAM delegation and later mayor of Bogotá. Doris Tarchópulos, "Las huellas del plan para Bogotá de Le Corbusier, Sert y Wiener," *Scripta nova: Revista electrónica de geografía y ciencias sociales* 10, no. 218: 86.
63. The Tumaco plan ended in 1949, following a pattern the architects knew well by now: changes in local authorities led to different expectations, although the architects were still bound by contract to work on an altered brief that focused more on specific buildings.
64. In 1950, conservative Laureano Gómez, an admirer of Spanish dictator Francisco Franco, ascended to power. Rovira describes the regime as "a para-Fascist dictatorship, wholly under the power of the United States." Rovira, *José Luis Sert*, 150. Gómez was anxious for U.S. support; to gain it and counteract his previous Axis sympathies he sent Colombian troops to the Korean War. The Colombian army's experience in this war is believed to have advanced their professionalization. See Pearce, *Colombia: Inside the Labyrinth*, 59.
65. Carlos Martínez, "Puro tamo el Plan Regulador de Bogotá," *Proa* 65 (November 1952): 9.
66. Sert, letter to Jacqueline Tyrwhitt, November 26, 1952, SC HU CIAM C12, in Schnitter, "José Luis Sert y Colombia," 120. In his analysis, Rovira highlights that TPA's vision of planning was based on CIAM's oversimplification of functions and then further idealized by its generous conceptions of leisure facilities and controlled urban expansion. Such planning ignored the specific conditions of Colombian cities: overexploitation of land, an underground economy, and the illegal occupation of terrains. Rovira, *José Luis Sert*, 154–55.
67. Opinions on Gustavo Rojas Pinilla's military dictatorship and the means he used to pacify the country vary. Although he declared an amnesty, he did not include the Communist Party in it, and the areas that supported the party were declared war zones. This resulted in more violence and death, but in focused areas away from the main population centers.
68. "General comments on my Central and Latin American Tour, November 15, 1955–May 7, 1956. Grant 262–6. Report on Colombia." From Wiener to the Department of State, Inter-

national Educational Exchange Service. June 15, 1956, PLW SC UO in Schnitter, "José Luis Sert y Colombia," 126.
69. See "L'Urbanisme en Amérique Latine," in *L'Architecture d'Aujourd'hui* 33 (December 1950–January 1951): 4–55.
70. Gaitán Cortés later became Mayor of Bogotá (1961–66), after the military dictatorship. Tarchópulos, "Las huellas del plan para Bogotá."
71. Vargas Caicedo, *Le Corbusier en Colombia*, 15.
72. Downtown Bogotá is labeled as "the civic core" in the Le Corbusier–TPA plan. Sert discussed public squares and quoted José Ortega y Gasset at CIAM 8. His introduction to the congress was later published as "Centres of Community Life," in *The Heart of the City: Towards the Humanisation of Urban Life,* ed. Jacqueline Tyrwhitt, José Luis Sert, and Ernesto Rogers (New York: Pellegrini and Cudahy, 1952). Bonet would make a similar choice in Buenos Aires. I develop this argument further in his work in this city in León, *Modernity for the Masses.*
73. "Voila l'histoire en bref. Nous savons par experience, comme c'est long et compliqué d'arriver a faire des contracts formels dans n'importe quel pays de l'Amerique Latine, et il ne faut jamais faire trôp de confiance a leurs beaux mots, car ils les oublient aussitôt que vôtre avion s'est perdu dans les nuages . . . ," letter from Sert to Le Corbusier, February 26, 1949, in Sert Collection Folder 0029.
74. "Invitado Le Corbusier a estudiar el contrato sobre Plano Regulador," in *El Espectador.* Undated newspaper cutting found in JLSC, Loeb Special Collections, Harvard University; "Le Corbusier y el Plano Regulador de Bogotá," *Proa* 21 (March 1949): 13.
75. TPA's commissions in South America constituted Sert's main source of work and income throughout this period, in addition to his theoretical share of Wiener's lecture fees from the Department of State and occasional university lectures. Sert's practice in Europe had been mostly architectural; before the Latin American commissions, his urban planning experience was limited to the Macià plan, which was never commissioned. His only architectural job in the United States before the GSD post was his own house and the remodeling of the neighboring Johnson House, both in Locust Valley, Long Island, in 1949. He designed the Van Leer Offices in Amsterdam (1954) and built a studio for Joan Miró in Palma de Mallorca (1955). See Rovira, *Sert 1928–1979,* and Knud Bastlund, ed., *José Luis Sert: Architecture, City Planning, Urban Design* (New York: Praeger, 1967).
76. Some of these tensions can be seen in the correspondence between the Colombia office and its international counterparts while developing the Bogotá Pilot Plan. Mondragón, "Arquitectura en Colombia 1946–1951," 73–75.
77. In Chile, where Wiener also lectured, Sergio Larraín and Emilio Duhart successfully designed and built Villa Presidente Ríos, a modern urban plan for 35,000 inhabitants and workers at a steel factory in Talcahuano funded by the Export–Import Bank of the United States. Compañía de Aceros del Pacífico (CAP) was the result of agreements between the Corporación de Fomento de Chile and its agreements and contracts with the Export–Import Bank of the United States. See Verónica Esparza Saavedra, "Villa Presidente Ríos en Talcahuano, 1947–1951. Sergio Larraín G.M. y Emilio Duhart H.," V Seminario DOCOMOMO Chile, 2014. Larraín and Duhart had been in correspondence with Sert

and Wiener over a possible collaboration with TPA, but they fared better on their own and were able to build their plan. A draft of different options for honoraria, typed in paper with Larraín and Duhart's letterhead, can be found in Wiener's archive (April 14, 1948). Wiener writes to them later from Colombia, May 4, 1948, PLW SC UO. The document laid out two options, one in which TPA's honoraria included expenses (USD 30,000 for the first stage or Pilot Plan and USD 30,000 for the regulating plan) and a second one in which expenses were covered by CAP (USD 22,500 for the first stage and USD 15,000 for the second stage). Additional honoraria for architectural plans and supervision were laid out as percentages over the cost of construction.
78. The Peruvian government would continue funding the construction of popular neighborhoods (UP) until the early 1990s. Cabello explains the plans gradually improved in neighborhood design, but the building of individual houses decreased to the point of disappearing. The last UPs only turned in lots. See Cabello, "Urbanismo estatal en Lima metropolitana," 106–8.
79. Schnitter, "José Luis Sert y Colombia," 301.

Chapter 10

Albert Speer, Ernst Neufert, and the Modularization of the World

Nader Vossoughian

> Hegel remarks somewhere that all great world-historic facts and personages appear, so to speak, twice. He forgot to add: the first time as tragedy, the second time as farce.
>
> —Karl Marx, *The Eighteenth Brumaire of Louis Bonaparte* (1852)

It is widely known today that Hitler's architect and former armaments minister Albert Speer kept abreast of developments in architecture during his twenty-year internment at Berlin's Spandau Prison. The teachings of his academic mentor, Heinrich Tessenow, were never far from his mind: "I lay down on my cot," he wrote in his published diaries. "As my last reading matter, I had obtained from the library Heinrich Tessenow's *Handwerk und Kleinstadt*. I wanted once more to read the sentences with which my teacher had concluded his book in 1920."[1] Speer also kept abreast of new developments in construction and design. "Months ago," he continued, "through the approaches of Colonel Cuthill, the Berlin Memorial Library agreed to supply us with two books on architecture every month."[2] He was well aware of the acclaim that the International Style enjoyed in the United States and around the world. "Now I see that something has evolved out of the extravagant experimental architecture of those years. If I can believe the magazine *[American Builder]*, something like a universal style is arising for the first time, a style extending from London to Tokyo, from New York to Rio."[3] While in prison, Speer designed a house for an American officer and spoke on multiple occasions of his ambition to return to practice. "I'm an architect, and I hope to find people who will let me practice my profession."[4]

Speer's dream of reestablishing himself as a practicing architect never came to full fruition. He became a best-selling author in 1969, which allowed him to rebrand himself as a full-time writer and amateur historian of the Nazi Reich. Still, archival documents and interviews reveal that Speer *did* make an earnest effort to return to architecture in 1967, just a few months after leaving prison. He collaborated with the industrial architect Ernst Neufert and Neufert's new partner Wolfgang Rösel in developing an expansion plan for the Dortmunder Union-Brauerei (DUB), one of Germany's leading producers of export beer. Neufert was the author of the *Bauentwurfslehre* (1936), the most influential standards handbook of the twentieth century, as well as the *Bauordnungslehre* (1943), which subsequently shaped the standardization of the German building industry.[5] Rösel joined Neufert's office in 1961 and assumed an instrumental role in the completion of the *Kaufhaus Quelle* in Nuremberg, among other projects. He helped establish construction management as a codified academic discipline, and, beginning in 1974, taught at the University of Kassel.[6] The DUB's director, Felix Eckhardt, had been in discussion with Neufert about the commissioning of a new brewery and bottling complex. In January 1967, he suggested that Speer be involved as well. "The Speer family has been a shareholder in our company for generations," he wrote. "It was a regular exercise for us to engage the Speer family in construction-related matters, for Speer's father belonged to our advisory committee."[7] Eckhardt urged Neufert to reach out to Speer: "I believe it important that you speak with Mr. Speer," he wrote on January 25, 1967. "We want to be helpful to him so that he can be active in his old profession. I have sent a carbon copy of this letter to Heidelberg; he will most definitely be in touch with you."[8] Neufert offered his full consent: "Based on the letter from Mr. Speer dated 2/9/1967, you should have noticed that there exist no concerns between us."[9]

Speer's postwar collaboration with Neufert is incongruous with so much of what we know about his past as an architect. As Speer biographer Joachim Fest put it, "You cannot design 'Germania' and then a beer factory somewhere in Schleswig-Holstein."[10] Speer never makes reference to Neufert in his published memoirs. Many of Speer's most intimate associates (Rolf Wolters, for example) were overtly critical of the standardized building methods that Neufert employed. Speer gained international notoriety for designing a series of monumental structures such as the New Reich Chancellery in Berlin, the Nazi Party rally grounds in Nuremberg, and *"Haupstadt Germania."*[11] He is only rarely, if ever, remembered for his work as a construction manager or industrial builder. How, then, do we explain Speer's postwar collaboration with a dogmatic functionalist and "reactionary modernist," to use Jeffrey Herf's term?[12] Under what circumstances did Neufert and Speer's relationship emerge, and how might we use their work for the DUB as an opportunity to assess Speer's career anew?

My principal thesis in this essay is that Speer's impact on the history of construction management and prefabrication surpasses any influence he had on design. Barbara Miller-Lane has argued that Hitler "permitted a number of different views of Nazi architecture to exist unchallenged," that is to say, he tolerated modernism as well as neoclassicism.[13] Paul Jaskot has demonstrated that we cannot divorce the building of Hitler's *Führerstädte* from the SS's mass exploitation of prisoner labor.[14] Similarly, my research has taught me that Speer was very much engaged with logistical questions throughout his career. He was never just an artist, as his defense attorney Hans Flächsner argued at Nuremberg, but a manager and logistics specialist as well. His so-called General Building Inspectorate of the Imperial Capital of Berlin (GBI) functioned as a laboratory for the testing of standardized building systems. Neufert coordinated the development of a number of these systems—he worked for Speer between 1938 and 1945—and documented them in a major publication. Titled *Bauordnungslehre* (1943), this book offers us valuable insight into the history and operations of Speer's GBI. Indeed, its contents are a direct response to challenges that Hitler tasked the GBI with addressing. Neufert and Speer collaborated far more intimately than has typically been assumed. They set about using modular systems to concentrate power, vertically integrate the construction industry, and normalize National Socialist ideals. Parliamentary and liberal forms of governance were anathema to them, as was organized labor. Like Henry Ford before them, they believed that the mechanization of the workplace wrested authority from the worker, undermining any threat that laborers might otherwise pose. They theorized mechanization as a language of surveillance that could facilitate the tracking of information, on the one hand, and the concentration of power, on the other. They belong to a history of the *disciplinary society,* in the sense that Foucault uses the term.[15] At the same time, they bear out the neglected fact that industrial standardization and biological normalization go hand-in-hand. Passage of the Nuremberg Race Laws in 1935 should not be divorced from the modularization of the German building industry. Neufert and Speer's postwar collaboration needs to be understood within the context of a history of power that ties the biological mapping of the body and the normalization of forced labor to the modular organization of building systems and the postwar history of logistics.

To understand Speer's relationship to Neufert, we have to remember that the practice of architecture in Germany has traditionally encompassed construction as well as design. That is to say, there were no laws to prevent architects from acting as contractors *and* as designers on one and the same project, as has been the case in the United States.[16] Speer was himself unusually well steeped in construction-related issues, and his GBI maintained an active General Construction Office *(Generalbauleitung)* in addition to a Design and Planning Division *(Planungsstelle)*. Speer was a major backer of the constructivist wing of the *Neues Bauen* during the Nazi period. Already as a student, he read Richard Neutra's *Wie baut Amerika?* (1927), which influenced him greatly. After World War II, the two became personal friends, it seems, exchanging letters and paying visits. We still know almost nothing about the scope of their relationship, and scholars have not explored it to date. I personally was astonished to come across their correspondence in the Speer archives in Koblenz. What we do know is that they shared a fascination with American know-how, Fordism, and technology—*Amerikanismus* as it was called, somewhat derisively, in interwar Germany. "Your ideas and books," Speer wrote in 1968, "impressed me very much as a student. I explain to you that your book *How Does America Build?* interested me a great deal and not only me, but all my classmates as well. I ordered all of your recently published books from the library, [I] read them and was very impressed."[17] "We still recall with pleasure the wonderful afternoon we spent with you and that you were so kind to mention that you would like us to visit you again," Neutra's wife, Dione, later wrote.[18] Richard Neutra welcomed dialogue with Speer's son Albert Jr., who was just beginning his career in architecture: "It would please me to hear from your son again," Neutra writes, "and we offer hearty greetings to you and your wife with best wishes for what you are now working on and that which you plan to report on in your next project."[19]

Beginning in 1934, Speer's Bureau "Beauty of Labor" (*Amt "Schönheit der Arbeit"*) hired members of the *Deutscher Werkbund* who were non-Jewish, technically minded, and avowedly apolitical.[20] Speer brought in Werkbund editor Wilhelm Lotz, for example, presumably because Lotz shared his goal of wanting to use art and architecture to broadcast Germany's economic interests internationally. "Beauty of Labor" maintained the Werkbund's traditional focus on strengthening ties between government, industry, and the arts for the purpose of stimulating German exports, enhancing the reputation of German-made goods, and regulating quality. It sponsored research into the prefabrication of worker barracks and the rationalization of the workplace, as well as the dimensional coordination of timber structures. This was consistent with the earlier activities of modernists such as Walter Gropius, whose work was well known to Speer.[21] Long before he assumed control of the Todt Organization, which oversaw the building of the autobahn, the Atlantic Wall, and other infrastructural projects for the Nazi Reich, Speer supervised the standardization and design of factories for the military and air force. As Susanne Willems notes, "By the beginning of the third year of the war, Speer's building brigades from the GBI were involved in the building of 1,352 structures for the Luftwaffe and the U-Boat program and 83 factory-related projects."[22]

The pages of Neufert's *Bauordnungslehre* reveal that Speer's GBI facilitated the construction of steel factories, timber-framed barracks, emergency housing units, animal stalls, brick homes, and concrete apartments. As Neufert writes, "When at the beginning of the war the then General Building Inspector for the Imperial Capital, Professor Albert Speer, was given authorization to advise on the construction plans of the entire air force, it was decided that a series of roughly five different types of halls would be built, which would in turn serve a variety of different obligations that the air force needed served."[23] Speer was bent on usurping authority from his rivals in government, such as Hitler's Housing Commissar Robert Ley; he backed Hitler's quest for *Lebensraum* and supported efforts to align the activities of national standards organizations all across occupied Europe.[24] As Günther Luxbacher has noted, the director of the German Institute of Standardization tried "to organize the complete harmonization of French standards

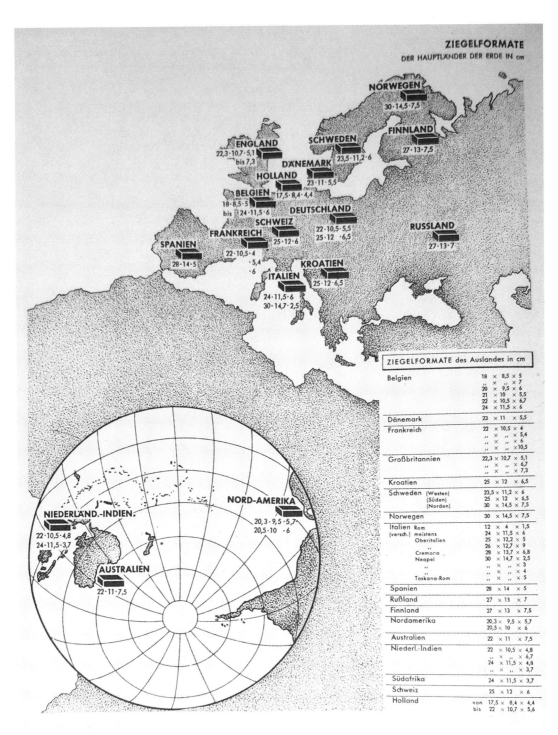

Figure 10.1. Ernst Neufert and Albert Speer dreamt of using modular systems to coordinate and regularize brick sizes around the world. Diagrams such as this one must be seen in relation to Hitler's (and Speer's) quest for Lebensraum. Neufert Stiftung.

research and French standards generally in accordance with German needs. [He] traveled to the occupied cities of Prague, Brussels and to France," where he met with senior officials. "In 1943 an intergovernmental committee was created to coordinate standardization efforts between various branches of industry."[25] Speer empowered Neufert to develop systems that could be used to coordinate the manufacturing of building supplies all across Europe. "In July 1938 I assigned Professor Neufert the task of setting up the foundations for the typification of floor plans for flats, the standardization of [building] parts, and the rationalization of building methods."[26] Modular systems and standard units of measurement tend to be tied to the exercise of power, as Witold Kula notes: "In classical Greek antiquity, no one harbored any doubt that measures, like coinage, were an attribute of the sovereign power."[27] Consistent with this view, Speer believed that Neufert's work could further the goals of National Socialism, specifically by bypassing "parliamentary deliberations." As Speer writes in his preface to the *Bauordnungslehre*:

> With this new order, one can hardly rely on arbitrary measurements of building components and on the parliamentary deliberations of participating manufacturing organizations. Rather, one must establish a building order *[Bauordnung]* in the broadest sense of the word, with a firm hand and with the collaboration of industry, in order to ease the work of the manufacturer, the planner, and the builder in equal measure, and to achieve the appropriate integration of building components.
>
> Professor Neufert, who dedicates himself to this important task as my Representative for Standardization in the Building Industry, offers here the first documentation of his collaboration with progressive and active economic groups and factories.[28]

The most significant tool that Neufert developed to further Speer's antiparliamentary and ultra-authoritarian goals was known as the octametric system of dimensional coordination. The octametric system of coordination was the German equivalent to the American four-inch system of dimensional coordination, which Alfred Farwell Bemis theorized in the middle of the 1930s.[29]

Both systems were devised to lower costs, enforce transparency in accounting, and normalize the use of interchangeable building components among designers and builders. The major differences between Neufert's system and Bemis's are three: first, Neufert's octameter promised to harmonize the dimensions of bricks, lumber, and steel in Germany and its occupied territories, while Bemis's system was conceived with the American market in mind, mostly targeting prefabricated, timber-frame homes intended for the domestic market. The octameter was based on the metric unit, on the one hand, and was compatible with the English foot, on the other. (An octameter is one-eighth of a meter and roughly four inches in length.) It represented a universal language that, Neufert believed, could unite the global building industry under a single umbrella and thereby further Nazi Germany's conquest of *Lebensraum*.

Second, Neufert used racial arguments to encourage adoption of the octameter, while Bemis focused mostly on the economic benefits of his four-inch module. As Neufert indicates in the *Bauordnungslehre*, 12.5 centimeters approximated the dimensions of the *Reichsformat*, a well-established Prussian brick size. It excluded usage of the number seven, "which appears in many Cults, most especially with the Jews."[30] Neufert argued that the octameter harmonized with the dimensions of a "male representative of our race."[31] He suggested that a unified system of dimensional coordination could help standardize Nazi Germany's race laws as well. With the octameter, officials had the tools they needed to ensure that non-Jewish prisoners of war were afforded more physical space to sleep or rest than, say, a Jewish or Soviet Russian slave laborer.

Under Neufert's system, housing could be weaponized in unprecedented ways.[32] This is because the Nazis maintained strict norms concerning the volume of space that an individual of a particular race could occupy, most especially under the conditions of total war.

Third, Neufert tied his theory of dimensional coordination to the mechanization of the construction industry. Bemis looked at dimensional coordination through the lens of Taylorism, which privileged manual labor. Neufert, by contrast, was eager to show how the octameter could be used to enforce Fordist approaches to construction, which were still in their infancy. Assembly-line production promised to amplify the power wielded by factory foremen. By allowing foremen to control the speed with which the conveyor moved, it gave managers the tools they needed to optimize production, discipline inefficient workers, and maintain quality control. In the *Bauordnungslehre*, Neufert specifically notes that the dimensional coordination of the built environment would pave the way for the creation of a House Building Machine *(Hausbaumaschine)*, a tool that expedites the rapid construction of multistory, poured-concrete *Zeilenbauten*, or linear housing blocks. Anticipating the panelized concrete assembly systems implemented in East Germany during the 1960s, and building on Walter Gropius's and Adolf Meyer's time-saving construction management proposals for the *Siedlung Törten* in Dessau, Neufert reasoned that the House Building Machine would straddle the width and cover the height of each such block, much like a shipyard gantry crane. It comprised a system of evenly spaced, prefabricated, demountable flat trusses and contained a built-in formwork and scaffolding system. Its cage-like structure functioned as a spatial grid that managers could rely on to expedite the precise installation of the building's individual components within. In general, it reflected Neufert's belief that the harmonization of all things at all scales—materials with spaces, spaces with rooms, rooms with buildings, and buildings with machines—would serve Hitler's imperial goals; it could also assist with Germany's efforts to normalize the use of slave labor, which Neufert euphemistically called *unskilled labor:* "So can an entire city be built with little, unskilled

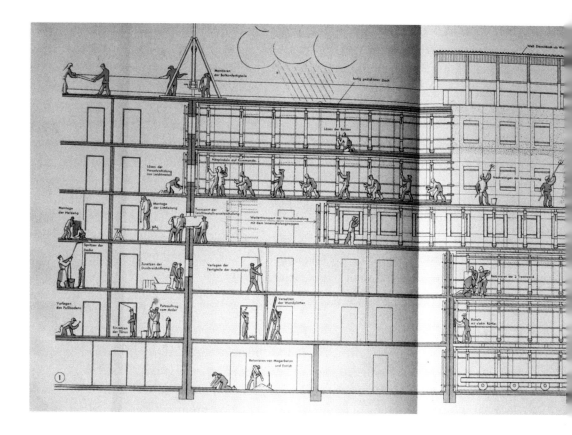

labor power in three-shifts, day and night (...) based on a mechanized, pre-set fabrication tempo, during summer as well as winter, protected from sun or eastern snow and frost."[33]

The GBI never brought the House Building Machine to fruition, nor did it manage to spread the use of the octameter all across Europe, as Neufert and Speer had hoped. Still, Neufert managed to partner with construction firms such as Jucho and trade associations such as the German Steel Construction Association (*Deutsche Stahlbauverband*) in developing and ratifying DIN 4171, a specification that standardized and harmonized the prefabrication of steel and timber. This standard remained in place until the early 1970s. Speer appointed Neufert head of a construction committee (*"Leitstelle Bau"*), which looked at how the octameter could be used to expedite Nazi Germany's postwar housing goals. The SS relied on Neufert's octametric system to mass-produce a line of Alpine-style furniture from Bavaria: "a number of very progressive industries have used these coordinate systems in their new undertakings. So, for example, the SS has based a large furniture fabrication system entirely on [the Octametric System] ..."[34] In 1944, plans were underway to utilize the octameter to expedite the expansion of Auschwitz-Birkenau.

The defeat of the Nazis in 1945 ended Neufert and Speer's project of using the oc-

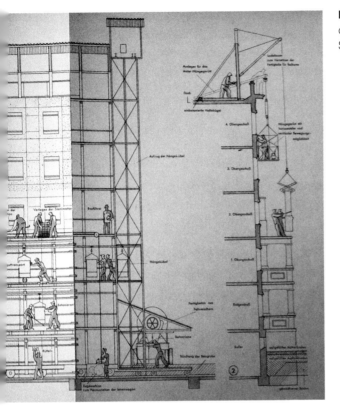

Figure 10.2. The "Hausbaumaschine" or "House Building Machine." Neufert Stiftung.

tameter to standardize and modularize the global building industry. As a Neufert critic named Graefe put it, "If we won the war, the entire planet would be octametric. We nevertheless lost the war."[35] Speer received a twenty-year prison sentence and was spared the death penalty because he convinced his captors that he was unaware of the Holocaust. (This, we know today, was patently false.) Neufert was offered a professorship in Dortmund despite his ties to Speer. He was never a member of the Nazi Party (people who worked for Speer were not required to join the party) and was able to secure letters of support from prominent artists to clear his name. Neufert used his ties to former Bauhaus faculty to cultivate the perception that he was himself a victim of Nazi aggression. The following statement of support from Johannes Itten is a case in point:

> The undersigned led his own private art school (Itten School) between the years 1926 and 1934 in Berlin and is director of the Applied Art Academy, the Applied Art Museum and the Textile Trade School in Zurich. From 1929 to 1932, I employed in my Berlin school Professor Ernst Neufert, who headed the architecture department. Professor Neufert came from the Weimar Building Trade School, and, during his tenure at my institution, fulfilled his duties in my school in a completely modern and scientific and

Speer, Neufert, and Modularization

> artistically valuable way. I came to know him as someone who brought incredible know-how, and as someone who fought for modern architecture and for modern art, which were fought against by the Nazis, with his entire being.[36]

After World War II, Neufert used his ties to Speer to win major architectural commissions. Countless alumni from Speer's office went on to become powerful figures, as Werner Durth and Niels Gutschow have observed.[37] Archival records indicate that Neufert remained loyal to Speer. He believed fervently that Speer was innocent of any wrongdoing and submitted at least one formal letter of appeal on his former employer's behalf: "Albert Speer succeeded in creating among his assistants a free and easy atmosphere of camaraderie which was free from political prying and as such perhaps unique in the major agencies of the Third Reich," he wrote in 1955.

> It is therefore no coincidence that today practically all leading modern architects were during the Third Reich in one way or another connected with Herr Speer, either directly or through their superiors, so that they were covered by Herr Speer who himself had to represent officially to the outside world the so-called national architecture.
>
> After all, those ten years have shown to all observant persons that the people, whose judgment is always right, feel that the continued imprisonment of Herr Speer is a gross injustice, so that any country which insists on a continuation of his imprisonment will make itself as unpopular as it is possible . . .[38]

The passage makes plain the fact that Neufert was unrepentant for his involvement in advancing fascism in Germany. Equally noteworthy is the sense of anger and disillusionment that the letter conveys. One senses that Neufert resented the criminal accusations that were leveled against the Nazis. One also gets the impression that Neufert never freed himself of the conspiratorial mindset that brought the National Socialists to power. Indeed, his letter contains examples of binary "us versus them" rhetoric that we often associate with populist or fascist movements today.

Whatever the case may be, it is doubtless that when Neufert and Speer reunited in 1967, both felt optimism, hope, and a degree of nostalgia. They even contemplated opening a practice together: "It would please me," Neufert wrote on June 2, 1967, "if in the process of this project a collaboration emerged between us."[39] The two understood that they needed to be discreet about their reunion, as their association may well have attracted negative press coverage. "A collaboration will always be a delicate opportunity," Speer replied. "I got the feeling through our talk, however, that a collaboration between us will proceed without any friction."[40] As part of their contractual agreement, it was decided that Speer would act as the chief manager, strategist, and client liaison on the project, while Neufert and his partner Wolfgang Rösel would assume primary responsibility for generating drawings. Neufert and Rösel promised Speer a percentage of their fee. "The honorarium for the project will be made payable by the Dortund Union-Brauerei to Professor Neufert. 50% of the fee will go toward covering office expenses. From the remaining 50%, Professor Neufert and Mr. Rösel will take half and Mr. Speer the other half, which is to say that each party will receive 25 percent of the net payment from the Dortmunder Union-Brauerei."[41] Speer's involvement was to remain anonymous. "The project will be prepared under the names of Professor Neufert and Mr. Rösel."[42]

The DUB tasked the architects with developing a schematic design proposal. In addition to designing the building's envelope, they had to offer strategies for modernizing the DUB's brewing, bottling, conveyor, and storage systems. They had to think about hygiene. A *Reinheitsgebot*—literally, a "purity commandment"—has governed the preparation of German beer in Germany for more than half a millennium, and Neufert, Speer, and Rösel had to devise new ways of protecting DUB's beverages against bacterial contaminants. They also had to consider economic issues. In the mid-1960s, Europe was undergoing a process of integration; the formation of a European common market was already well underway. Countries were making efforts to synchronize their supply chains, and the rail and beverage industries were among those leading the way. In particular, the "tall, thick, pint-sized, half-liter type [of beer bottle] with the swing-stopper made out of wire, rubber, and porcelain"[43] was in the process of being replaced by the standardized *Euroflasche,* which was "shorter, lighter, and cheaper to make (24 marks per hundred bottles rather than 34 marks). They can be transported in plastic rather than wooden crates. A crate with twenty filled Euro bottles is almost a fifth lighter and takes a fourth less storage space than a regular twenty-bottle crate."[44] The European Committee for Standardization (CEN) had tied the dimensions of the Euro bottle to that of the standard-sized pallet. Measures such as these were in turn driving the adoption of mechanized equipment (e.g., forklifts), at least partially.

For Neufert and Speer, the changes that these new European standards heralded were analogous to those brought about by the adoption of the octameter within segments of the German building industry. More important still, they viewed the project as an opportunity for management to further its surveillance reach and loosen the influence of trade unions in plant operations. In the postwar period, corporations in America had already shown that automated systems could be used to suppress wage growth and limit worker agitation, a point satirized quite powerfully in the opening scenes of Charlie Chaplin's film *Modern Times* (1936). What distinguished Neufert and Speer's proposal for the DUB was their fanatical belief that dimensional coordination could be used to reduce *engineering tolerances* as well. In engineering, tolerances refer to the allowable variation or leeway that a manufactured product or system can allow without compromising functionality or performance. Traditionally, tolerances have been kept

Figure 10.3. Standard-dimensioned crates of beer resting on standardized Euro-pallets: example of how principles of dimensional coordination were applied to the beverage industry during the 1960s. Karlheinz Graudenz, *Wege von gestern, Schritte von heute, Ziele von morgen: 100 Jahre Dortmunder Union-Brauerei AG.* Dortmunder Union-Brauerei Aktiengesellschaft, ed. (Dortmund: Fritz Busche Druckereigesellschaft, 1972), 109.

relatively high in the building industry, at least as compared to mechanical or electrical engineering. Throughout his life, Neufert was keen on bridging the divide between art and the applied sciences, between architecture and engineering, not simply because he admired the aesthetics of the machine, but because he idealized *precision* more specifically. It goes virtually without saying that technological innovation is unthinkable in the absence of precision instruments. The horizon of what is technically possible is always limited by how precisely one can measure something at any given moment in time. But precision is also a language of spatial and intellectual control, a means by which to coordinate and orchestrate how things connect. The low tolerances that govern the threading of a carriage bolt can reveal quickly if a screw we are trying to attach to it actually fits. Similarly, a factory composed of modular systems can expose lapses or mistakes in manufacturing and assembly quickly and without delay, at least in theory. Such systems of quality control held great appeal to Neufert and Speer, who feared sabotage on the part of forced laborers during World War II. They brought that concern to bear on their design for the DUB factory as well.

In their schematic design for the DUB, the architects envisioned a 400,000 cubic-meter edifice containing five "generously dimensioned filling stations for beer bottles, four filling stations for tap beer and a separate area for the filling of locomotive container wagons."[45] They wanted to take full advantage of the visibility of the DUB's existing address; it was situated in close proximity to the city's central train station, which stands at the center of the city. They also proposed burying the tracks of Dortmund's main train station, thus expanding the brewery's footprint. The architects' drawings called for an open floor plan, one which would be carried by a long-span truss system resting atop a reinforced concrete and brick infill frame. Speer and Neufert advised the client to erect an iconic "U" atop the DUB's existing structure as well, presumably to attract the attention of passengers who were entering and leaving Dortmund by train. In keeping with the client's wishes, they programmed a visiting gallery inside the new building: "The DUB calculates that 50 people at most will be able to participate in each tour. Dr. Eckhardt believes that one would only be able to give the visitor a broad overview of things."[46] Most importantly, published drawings indicate that floor dimensions were based on multiples of a standard-sized pallet. During the war, Speer's GBI had relied on modules to minimize space, control labor costs, mechanize operations, and manage information flows, as already noted. In the case of the DUB, Neufert and Speer did so again to rationalize the DUB's warehousing needs, mechanize the entire building's transport, storage, bottling, and delivery systems, and enforce discipline. Consistent with the goals of Neufert's House Building Machine, the architects dreamt of automating the DUB's operations. They conceived of their proposed building as a data-generating mechanism that provided constant operational feedback to plant managers in real time. Harmonizing people and machines, architecture and technology, the project bears out the Foucauldian argument that power—industrial power (the beer industry), in this case—stems from the control of information. Here is how Rösel describes it in the architects' meeting minutes:

> From PNR [a party consisting of Speer, Rösel, and Reutlinger; Neufert was not present at the meeting], a basic proposal for the beer loading area is presented. It minimizes reliance on labor power. The essential characteristics of this proposal are described succinctly: The delivery vehicle drives into the brewery facility . . . and presents its consignment paperwork in a waiting area. Necessary data about loading and unloading will be stamped onto a punch card or ticker tape that prompts the automatic preparation of the load in the loading area using an information and command delivery processing system. Once it is given the signal, the vehicle drives from the

storage area to the place of loading . . . Pallets will be removed by hand using rolling conveyers that are built into the floor of the truck. . . . The empty boxes are transported along a vertical conveyer . . . which moves objects from the lower level to the upper level . . . The full pallets containing 30 crates each are moved to a loading area by a machine and are automatically moved to a flow rack, where they roll to the last pallet. . . . Upon removing the flow rack, a specially designed device sorts out the beers using an information processing system and in this way prepares their loading onto trucks.[47]

Rösel is describing here what is essentially a Fordist-style system for loading, unloading, cleaning, and filling bottles of beer. Featured here is a conveyor system that promised to rationalize labor, reduce storage and production times, and synchronize production and shipping. What is not mentioned—and is of great relevance for our purposes—is the fact that the entire design was generated using a standard-sized module, a pallet that harmonized the dimensions of delivery truck storage units and rolling conveyors, the warehouse space and the bottling facility. Combined with the newly standardized *Euroflasche,* the pallet gave Neufert and Speer a uniform module that they could use to enforce the use of low-tolerance logistical systems—conveyors, forklifts, and storage rooms, for example. It was believed that such a norm could in turn be used to facilitate the measurement, comparison, and policing of worker productivity as well. Neufert and Speer's proposal rehearses the productivist dream of *Restlosigkeit,* which refers very literally to the absence of waste.[48] The design reflects Neufert and Speer's age-old hostility toward organized labor: for there are no virtually people that populate this design, only machines that regulate the tempo of production. Throughout the design, there are invisible tolerances governing every aspect of the building. Admittedly, the tolerances in question are not indicated graphically in the drawings, but they must be assumed given what we know about Neufert's life and career, as well as the way the building synthesizes design and technology.

Between August 1967 and March 1968, Neufert, Speer, and Rösel assessed the feasibility of their design. They traveled to beverage plants in Karlsruhe, Copenhagen, and Hannover, presumably to identify best practices. They commissioned a study that looked at the impact their design might have on worker productivity. "After the presentation of the project by Mr. Speer and Rösel, it is decided that by August 28, 1967, a rough estimate and calculation of labor power needs for the bottling center and the bottling distribution facility will be carried out so that the future of the project can be decided."[49] In September 1967, the architects contracted an outside firm to develop an air ventilation scheme: "The gentlemen of the Luwa Firm lay out a sketch for the ventilation," Rösel writes. "Their proposal calls for blowing air into the [brewery's] clean area through the ceiling and pushing it out through the dirty area or areas."[50] They also

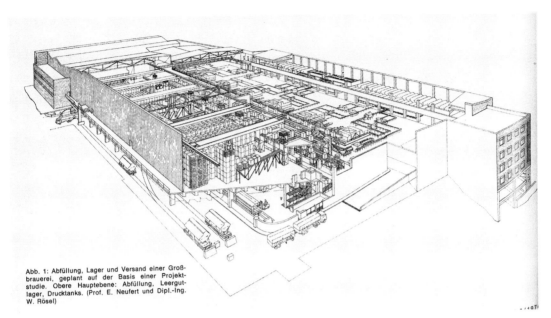

Abb. 1: Abfüllung, Lager und Versand einer Großbrauerei, geplant auf der Basis einer Projektstudie. Obere Hauptebene: Abfüllung, Leergutlager, Drucktanks. (Prof. E. Neufert und Dipl.-Ing. W. Rösel)

Figure 10.4. Albert Speer, Ernst Neufert, and Wolfgang Rösel, two-point perspective drawing of bottling, storage, and delivery proposal for DUB, upper level (unbuilt). Wolfgang Rösel.

consulted with pasteurization and cleaning specialists: "This plan," Rösel notes in the minutes, "sketched by the firm of Holstein & Kappert of Dortmund coincides with the execution plan of the DUB from August of this year. It calls for the placement of the cleaning and pasteurization machinery in separate areas, the cleaning machinery to the north [of the site], the pasteurization machine to the south."[51] The group reached out to a Swiss electronics firm: "For the implementation of the control system the working out of a program for the [factory's] computing system is required. In particular, according to the statements of the director of the company Viscosuisse of Switzerland it is necessary to utilize a control system specialist here (electronics expert), who is able to carry out both the control system and the commercial programming system."[52] They also consulted with IBM, if only to gain a third-party perspective on the feasibility of their design: "IBM will design a simulation model at the request of the DUB so that the project can be considered before the approval of the building of the storage and delivery system is made. Also, with the help of the simulation model, a number of variations will be tested in order to test the maximum efficiency and productivity of the system."[53]

The DUB's director asked Speer what he thought of the proposal: "One cannot make it any better," he replied.[54] Eckhardt then inquired about whether the building could be finished in time for the celebration of the DUB's centennial anniversary. "Mr. Eckhardt mentions the 100-year anniversary, which is going to be celebrated by the DUB in grand fashion.... He asks consideration for whether it cannot be completed in time for the centennial anniversary in two years."[55] Although Neufert assured him that it would, the DUB abandoned the proposal in the months that followed. One reason is because Eckhardt feared that consolidating all operations in one location increased the damage that striking workers could inflict on his company. It threatened to grow the power of organized labor and potentially harm productivity and revenue: "He is of the opinion that bottling should take place at a variety of locations, in order to set aside the problem of workers striking and reducing output, since it is impossible to strike against the Dortmund Union Brewery everywhere at the same time."[56] A second reason is because the design was partially obsolete by the time it was finished, as Wolfgang Rösel indicated to me in a 2015 interview.[57] The design of the new building was tied to the dimensions of a standard-sized pallet, and the pallet, moreover, was to be superseded by the ISO container in the early 1970s.[58] Containerized shipping reduced the costs associated with the global transport of goods by well over 95 percent, and while it has never replaced palletized shipping, it contributed significantly to the economic reorganization of the planet, stimulating intercontinental trade and decentralizing production and distribution. Its dimensions were never harmonized with European pallet sizes, which threw into doubt Neufert and Speer's dream of coordinating all things at all scales.

It should be emphasized that the DUB *did* decide to go forward with realizing one small piece of Neufert, Rösel, and Speer's overall proposal. It built a giant "U" atop the DUB's existing wedding cake-shaped facility. Jucho, the construction firm with which Neufert had partnered in standardizing the steel industry during the early part of World War II, carried out this task, underscoring the wide influence of the Speer network. Rösel credits Neufert with conceiving of its design, but it is equally possible that Speer first imagined it. I base this interpretation on the fact that Neufert lacked any background in lighting design or mass advertising. Speer, by contrast, excelled in this arena. His "Cathedral of Light," which was featured at the Nuremberg Nazi Party rallies, still stands as a major contribution to the history of lighting design, particularly for how it blends architecture, mass propaganda, and technology. Here again, the past repeats itself, "the first time as tragedy, the second time as farce," to quote from Marx.

Irrespective of the foregoing point, it is simply a mistake to create any divide between the architectural history of Nazi Germany, on the one hand, and that of postwar Germany, on the other. Neufert and Speer's postwar collaboration built on their wartime experiences, with a few notable shifts. They were dealing with the beverage industry rather than the construction industry. They were working in democratic West Germany rather than in authoritarian Nazi Germany. They were working against the backdrop of a peacetime consumer economy rather than a planned war economy. Still, the continuities between the two periods are striking: the architects maintained their steadfast focus on issues of spatial economy and temporal efficiency. They concerned themselves with the control of information. Importantly, some of the very strategies that they had used earlier to address fears of sabotage among forced laborers during

Figure 10.5. Albert Speer, Ernst Neufert, Wolfgang Rösel, "U" sign atop an existing DUB brewery facility.

World War II were also applied to stem the influence of trade unions in the 1960s. The octameter and the standard-sized pallet were both products of Neufert and Speer's fixation on information flows. This fixation is also the vantage point from which to think about modular systems and their ideological meanings today. For the grid, as Bernhard Siegert has noted, belongs to the infrastructure of the disciplinary society.[59] It invites us to politicize our understanding of space in ways that are of continuing relevance today. What the case of the DUB reveals is nothing if not the fact that totalitarian fantasies of control endured in architecture during the postwar period. The history of the modular organization of the built environment is inseparably tied to the history of militarism itself.

Notes

I thank Claire Zimmerman, Reinhold Martin, and the anonymous reviewers from the University of Minnesota Press for their invaluable feedback. I also thank Wolfgang Rösel for generously making himself available for an interview in 2015. I am grateful for the financial support of the Humboldt Foundation, without which research for this essay could not have been completed, as well the archivists from the Bundesarchiv in Koblenz and the Archiv der Moderne in Weimar who assisted me. Some of the arguments in this essay were first presented at the Berlage Center at the TU Delft in 2016. Thanks goes to Salomon Frausto for facilitating this visit.

1. Albert Speer, *Spandau: The Secret Diaries* (New York: MacMillan, 1976), 449.
2. Speer, *Spandau*, 273.
3. Speer, *Spandau*, 273.
4. Quote reprinted from Gitta Sereny, *Albert Speer: His Battle with Truth* (Pan MacMillan, 1996), loc. 13303–04, Kindle.
5. For a thorough analysis of the *Bauentwurfslehre*, see Gernot Weckherlin, *Zur Systematik des architektonischen Wissens am Beispiel von Ernst Neuferts Bauentwurfslehre* (Wasmuth: Tübingen and Berlin, 2017).
6. See, for example, Wolfgang Rösel, *Baumanagement: Grundlagen, Technik, Praxis* (Berlin: Springer, 1986).
7. All translations are by the author unless otherwise indicated. F. Eckhardt to Ernst Neufert, January 25, 1967, Bundesarchiv Koblenz (Hereinafter: BArch), N 1340/41.
8. Felix Eckhardt to Ernst Neufert, January 25, 1967, BArch, N 1340/41.
9. Ernst Neufert to Felix Eckhardt, February 20, 1967, BArch, N 1340/41.
10. Joachim Fest, *Albert Speer: Conversations with Hitler's Architect* (Malden, Mass.: Polity, 2007), 117.
11. See Naomi Vaughan, "The Photographic Mythology and Memory of Hitler's Destroyed New Reich Chancellery," this volume.
12. See Jeffrey Herf, *Reactionary Modernism: Technology, Culture, and Politics in Weimar and the Third Reich* (Cambridge: Cambridge University Press, 1986).

13. Barbara Miller Lane, *Architecture and Politics in Germany, 1918–1945* (Cambridge, Mass.: Harvard University Press, 1968), 190.
14. See Paul Jaskot, *The Architecture of Oppression: The SS, Forced Labor and the Nazi Monumental Building Economy* (London: Routledge, 1999).
15. See Michel Foucault, *Discipline and Punish: The Birth of the Prison* (New York: Vintage, 1995).
16. For a discussion of the history of the architectural profession in Germany, see, for example, Bernhard Gaber, *Die Entwicklung des Berufsstandes der freischaffenden Architekten: Dargestellt an der Geschichte des Bundes Deutscher Architekten BDA* (Essen: Verlag Richard Bracht, 1966).
17. Albert Speer to Richard Neutra, January 17, 1968. BArch, N 1340/40.
18. Dione Neutra to Albert Speer, June 20, 1968. BArch, N 1340/40.
19. Richard Neutra to Albert Speer, September 25, 1926. BArch, N 1340/40.
20. For an excellent discussion of the Amt "Schönheit der Arbeit," see Anson Rabinbach, "The Aesthetics of Production in the Third Reich," *Journal of Contemporary History* 11 (1976): 43–74. Speer also mentions the Deutscher Werkbund in passing in his memoirs. See Albert Speer, *Inside the Third Reich*, trans. Richard Winston and Clara Winston (New York: MacMillan Company, 1969), 57.
21. The scope of the work of the Bureau "Beauty of Labor" is discussed in detail in Shelley Baranowski, *Strength through Joy: Consumerism and Mass Tourism in the Third Reich* (Cambridge: Cambridge University Press, 2004).
22. Susanne Willems, *Der entsiedelte Jude: Albert Speers Wohnungsmarktpolitik für den Berliner Hauptstadtbau* (Berlin: Edition Hentrich, 2002), 40.
23. Ernst Neufert, *Bauordnungslehre* (Volk und Reich Verlag: Amsterdam, Prague, Vienna, 1943), 97.
24. Speer's colonizing ambitions are documented in Magnus Brechtken, *Albert Speer: Eine deutsche Karriere* (Munich: Siedler Verlag, 2017).
25. Günther Luxbacher, *DIN von 1917 bis 2017: Normung zwischen Konsens und Konkurrenz im Interesse der technisch-wirtschaftlichen Entwicklung* (Berlin: Beuth Verlag 2017), 256.
26. Letter reprinted in Ernst Neufert, "Das Oktameter-System," *Der soziale Wohnungsbau in Deutschland*, 13 (July 1, 1941): 452.
27. Witold Kula, *Measures and Men*, trans R. Szreter (Princeton: Princeton University Press, 1986), 18.
28. Ernst Neufert, *Bauordnungslehre*, ed. Albert Speer (Berlin: Volk und Reich Verlag, 1943), 3.
29. See Albert Farwell Bemis, *The Evolving House: Rational Design*, vol. 3. (Cambridge Technology Press, 1936), 53–54. For an excellent discussion of Bemis's ideas, see Andrew L. Russell, "Modularity: An Interdisciplinary History of an Ordering Concept," *Information & Culture* 47, no. 3 (2012): 257–87.
30. Ernst Neufert, *Bauordnungslehre*, 31.
31. Ernst Neufert, *Bauordnungslehre*, 35.
32. For a discussion of how the Nazis used modular systems to enforce racial norms and weaponize housing, see Nader Vossoughian, "The Birth of DIN 4171: Design, Forced Labor, and the Standardization of 'Widerspruchsfreiheit' in Nazi Germany," in *Mimetische Praktiken*

in der neueren Architektur, ed. Eva von Engelberg-Dočkal, Markus Krajewski, and Frederike Lausch (Heidelberg: Heidelberg University Press, 2017), 64–76.

33. Ernst Neufert, *Bauordnungslehre* (Volk und Reich Verlag: Amsterdam, Prague, Vienna, 1943), 467.
34. Ernst Neufert, "Das Oktameter-System," *Der soziale Wohnungsbau in Deutschland,* 13 (July 1, 1941), 463.
35. Quoted in Ernst Neufert, *Das Maßgebende* (Wiesbaden and Berlin: Bauverlag, 1965), 90.
36. Johannes Itten, "Bestätigung," May 3, 1947, Ernst Neufert Nachlaß, Archiv der Moderne, Bauhaus Universität Weimar, N/53/66.4.
37. See Werner Durth and Niels Gutschow, *Träume in Trümmern: Planungen zum Wiederaufbau zerstörter Städte im Westen Deutschlands 1940–1950.* 2 vols. (Braunschweig/Wiesbaden: Friedr. Vieweg & Sohn, 1988).
38. Ernst Neufert to the Ambassadors of the U.S.S.R, U.S.A, U.K., and Northern Ireland, French Republic, May 24, 1955. BArch, N 1340/107.
39. Ernst Neufert to Albert Speer, June 2, 1967. BArch, N 1340/41.
40. Albert Speer to Ernst Neufert, September 2, 1967. BArch, N 1340/41.
41. "Vereinbarung über Gemeinsame Architektenleistungen zwischen Professor Ernst Neufert Und Dipl. Ing. W. Rösel, Darmstadt Und Dipl. Ing. Albert Speer, Heidelberg," June 2, 1967 BArch, N 1340/41.
42. "Vereinbarung über Gemeinsame Architektenleistungen Zwischen Professor Ernst Neufert und Dipl. Ing. W. Rösel, Darmstadt Und Dipl. Ing. Albert Speer, Heidelberg," June 2, 1967. BArch, N 1340/41.
43. "Schrott in Kisten." *Der Spiegel* 19 (May 1, 1967): 102.
44. "Schrott in Kisten." *Der Spiegel* 19 (May 1, 1967): 103.
45. Ernst Neufert, *Industriebauten,* ed. Joachim P. Heymann-Berg, Renate Netter, and Helmut Netter (Wiesbaden-Berlin: Bauverlag GmbH, 1973), 274.
46. Wolfgang Rösel, "Aktennotiz Nr. 689/61," December 20, 1967. BArch, N 1340/41.
47. Wolfgang Rösel, "Aktennotize Betr.: Dortmunder Unionbrauerei (Besprechung am 26.7.1967 in Dortmund)," July 27, 1967. BArch, N 1340/41.
48. See Markus Krajewski, *Restlosigkeit: Weltprojekte um 1900* (Frankfurt a.M.: Fischer Taschenbuch, 2006).
49. Wolfgang Rösel, "Aktennotiz Betrf.: Dortmunder Unionbrauerei, Besprechung am 26.7.1967," July 27, 1967. BArch, N 1340/41.
50. Wolfgang Rösel, "Aktennotiz Betr.: Dortmunder Unionbrauerei," February 8, 1967. BArch, N 1340/41.
51. Wolfgang Rösel, "Aktennotiz Betr.: Dortmunder Union-Brauerei (Besprechung am 22.9.67 in Darmstadt)," September 22, 1967. BArch, N 1340/41.
52. Wolfgang Rösel. "Aktennotiz Nr. 689/127. Betr.: Besprechung am 21.2.1968 in Dortmund," February 22, 1968. BArch, N 1340/41.
53. Wolfgang Rösel, "Aktennotiz Nr. 689/127. Betr.: Besprechung am 21.2.1968 in Dortmund," February 22, 1968. BArch, N 1340/41.
54. Wolfgang Rösel, "Aktennotiz Nr. 689/61," December 20, 1967. BArch, N 1340/41.
55. Wolfgang Rösel, "Aktennotiz Nr. 689/61," December 20, 1967. BArch, N 1340/41.
56. Wolfgang Rösel, "Interne Aktennotiz (Vertraulich)," March 21, 1968. BArch, N 1340/41.

57. Interview with the author on October 25, 2015, at the home of Wolfgang Rösel.
58. For a cultural history of the shipping container, see Alexander Klose, *The Container Principle: How a Box Changes the Way We Think* (Cambridge, Mass.: MIT Press, 2015). For a technical account of the history of container shipping, see Marc Levinson, *The Box: How Container Shipping Made the World Smaller and the World Economy Bigger*, 2nd ed. (Princeton: Princeton University Press, 2016).
59. See Bernhard Siegert, *Cultural Techniques: Grids, Filters, Doors, and Other Articulations of the Real* (New York: Fordham University Press, 2015), 97–120.

Part III

Democracy

Perennially Deferred?

Who is the *demos*, the "people" who rule in a democracy? How is that *demos* constituted, and how is it represented? These are among the questions explored by the essays in this third part of the book. Each shows how a democratic political body becomes visible through architecture and urbanism—usually, however, in relation to those who are excluded.

Laura diZerega's "'The Fairness of Our Demands': Ecclesiastical Architecture, Bureaucracy, and Resistance in the Prussian Rhineland, 1815–1840" disarmingly locates a popular will, articulated through the limited agency of regional architects, in the problem of renovating Catholic parish churches in the Prussian Rhineland after 1815, following damage or disrepair from the Napoleonic occupation. This will, expressed in a contest over architectural styles and materials, was at odds with that of bureaucratic authorities in Berlin, chiefly Karl Friedrich Schinkel, who sought the basis for a national architecture. The ensuing dispute, carried out on the overlapping terrain of church and state, says a great deal about architecture's capacity to serve as a means by which a population recognizes itself and seeks indirect political recognition.

In Peter Minosh's "Metropolis against the State: Architectures of Violence after the Paris Commune," the bricolage of the barricades carries the material traces of two competing sovereignties: that of the communards who built them, and that of the newly ascendant bourgeoisie. In Minosh's account, the architect Hector Horeau, a self-described "minor functionary" during the Commune who was nevertheless imprisoned in the aftermath, provisionally transposes this antithesis into the architectural imagination, with his otherworldly plans for the reconstruction of Paris in the bloody aftermath, not to resolve the conflict in an illusory manner, or to memorialize it, but to reclaim the barricades as an architectural paradigm for a radically democratic *polis*. With Horeau, Minosh seems to suggest, the defeated *demos* reappears as an architectural dream.

In "The Racial Allegories of Frank Lloyd Wright's Prairie Style," Charles L. Davis II takes up a dramatic instance of ideological projection: Frank Lloyd Wright's much-discussed "architecture of democracy." Davis does so, however, not in the terms given by Wright or his apologists, but in terms of the racial narratives that governed Wright's world and their accompanying social and economic structures. What Davis calls "racial allegories" are devastatingly real; the multiple fireplaces around which Wright constructed an allegedly timeless, universal mythology of the hearth, doubled-up with the ideology of the frontier in such designs as the Darwin Martin house in Buffalo, turn out also to orchestrate performances of everyday life in which whiteness and its wages govern every step.

The ideological export of "democracy" as a form of soft power is the subject of Esra Akcan's "Democracy and War: The University of Baghdad between Collaboration and National Competition." Combining archival material with firsthand observation in what remains a conflict zone, Akcan weaves an account of the university project's conception, design, and realization under changing political and economic conditions from the perspectives of distinct, unevenly recognized actors. Working in translation literally and figuratively, Akcan shows how Walter Gropius and The Architects Collaborative learned from Iraqi architects, even as their orientalist design anticipated the notorious "clash of civilizations" discourse. Recovering voices and imaginaries, Akcan hints at how to translate the terms that govern perpetual war into those necessary for imagining perpetual peace.

Shifting scales the final essay in this part confronts two different notions of political subject. In "The Aesthetics of Resistance: Istanbul's Standing Man between the Body Politic and Bare Life," Can Bilsel contrasts the mass subject with that of the individual as a social figure nonetheless standing alone. In the wake of the Taksim Gezi Park protests in Istanbul, as the mass of protesters vanished, the "standing man" emerged, ambiguously calling attention to the failure of Turkey's secular state and of its neoliberal, authoritarian successor elected as a soft Islamist regime. Following the "standing man" in space and in public discourse, set anonymously against what he calls the "sublime state," Bilsel finds in this solitary figure an allegory of the *demos*, standing in opposition together.

Chapter 11

"The Fairness of Our Demands"

Ecclesiastical Architecture, Bureaucracy, and Resistance in the Prussian Rhineland, 1815–1840

Laura diZerega

Following the defeat of Napoléon in 1815, towns and villages across the majority-Catholic Rhineland consigned to Protestant Prussian rule found their ecclesiastical architecture suddenly subject to intrusive new bureaucratic constraints imposed from Berlin. Over the three decades that followed, marked by the suppression of liberal currents and the continued unwillingness of the Prussian monarch to address widespread demands for a constitution, bureaucratic disputes over these constraints on church building offered Rhenish provincial communities what official politics otherwise denied them: an institutional space in which they were able to muster resources to represent themselves, and to criticize and ultimately resist the rule of their new Prussian masters.[1]

By the time the Rhineland came under Prussian rule in 1815, Rhenish churches large and small urgently needed rebuilding. The French occupation of the Rhineland, from 1794 until Napoléon's defeat in 1815, inflicted an array of damages on church properties, including their secularization and use as barracks, grain storehouses, stables, and even slaughterhouses.[2] In addition, operating churches, often centuries-old, suffered from decades of deferred maintenance, and many had become far too small to house parishes that grew significantly over the eighteenth century.[3] Eager to reconstitute their ecclesiastical infrastructure in the wake of war and occupation, Rhenish parishes wasted no time in sending petitions to their new monarch, Prussian King Friedrich Wilhelm III, to request state funding for their building initiatives.

Rhenish petitions made their way through a recently constituted Prussian bureaucracy, created as part of the far-reaching reform initiatives beginning in 1807—a response to mounting losses in the Napoleonic Wars. Efforts to enhance government efficiency included the establishment of five separate bureaucratic ministries: Finance,

Foreign Affairs, Interior, Justice, and War. In 1810, Karl Friedrich Schinkel (1781–1841) began what would be a twenty-five-year tenure at the central Prussian state building authority, or *Oberbaudeputation,* and had the responsibility of reviewing architectural plans and budgets submitted to the government's ministries. Projects requesting five hundred Taler or more in state funds came to Schinkel for review and approval—a decidedly low cost-threshold that occasioned a steady flow of plans for modest Rhenish churches on Schinkel's desk.[4] Yet the reviews by Schinkel and his colleagues were far from cursory, and the Oberbaudeputation's demands for revisions and budget cuts often set in motion protracted and sometimes contentious exchanges between Rhenish provincial stakeholders (parish councils, municipal office holders, and architects) and Berlin-based bureaucrats.

Largely absent from these exchanges was the clerical hierarchy of the Catholic Church. Dismantled in the Rhineland during two decades of French occupation, the Rhenish Catholic administrative hierarchy began its reconstitution per the terms of an 1821 agreement negotiated between representatives of Pope Pius VII and Friedrich Wilhelm III. Funding of the Catholic Church in Prussia—for example, clergy salaries and parish maintenance—henceforth became the responsibility of the Prussian monarchy; in exchange, Prussia retained ownership of Church lands and properties seized by the French between 1794 and 1815. New Rhenish bishoprics were redrawn to conform with the jurisdictions of Prussian provincial government offices, further subjecting church administration to state rule. Correspondence between Prussian Catholic clergy and the Vatican was reviewed first by Prussian bureaucrats, a provision that remained in place until 1837. Prussian authorities retained influence over the appointment of bishops until the 1840s. All of which meant that the design and funding of ecclesiastic architecture in the quarter century between 1815–40 unfolded in a largely secular, bureaucratized milieu without significant input from the clerical hierarchy in either the Rhineland or Rome.

The repair and reconstruction of churches was particularly important for Rhenish Catholics, eager to rebuild the social and spatial order of their communities following the traumas of French occupation and the Napoleonic Wars. While Rhenish parishes acknowledged the need to secure state support for their church projects, they bristled at the requirement that they cede their autonomy in exchange. The Prussian regime, on the other hand, faced a quandary. While they wished to support piety in the new Rhenish territory, the Prussian monarchy was highly suspicious of its new province and viewed Rhinelanders "as carriers of foreign contagion, be it French, Habsburg, or Catholic."[5] In this tense environment, where the economically diverse, comparatively progressive character of the Rhenish "periphery" stood in stark contrast to the conservative, agrarian Prussian "center," Prussian efforts to control Rhenish building projects elicited ire from parish communities, producing the unintended effect of propelling these architectural initiatives into the sphere of critical discourse.[6]

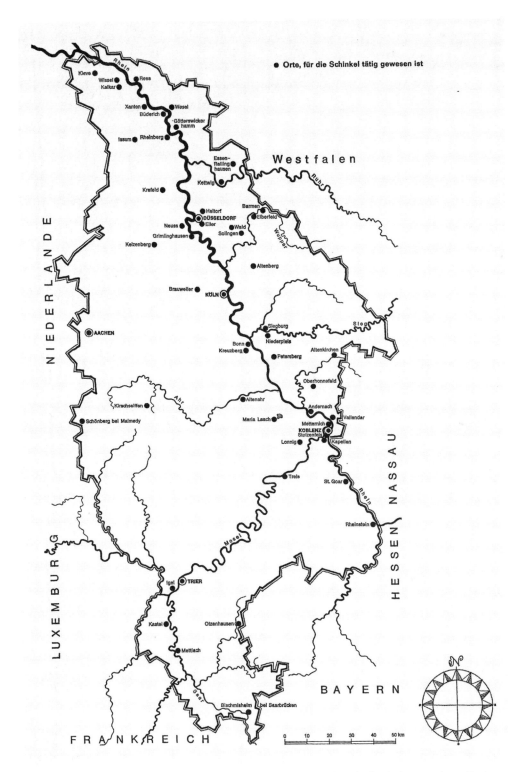

Figure 11.1. Map of the Prussian Rhineland in 1818. Black dots indicate towns where Karl Friedrich Schinkel engaged in provincial architectural initiatives. Eva Brües, *Die Rheinlande, Karl Friedrich Schinkel, Lebenswerk* (Berlin: Deutscher Kunstverlag, 1968). Courtesy Deutscher Kunstverlag GmbH, Berlin, Munich.

Starting with a brief overview of the history and conditions in the Prussian Rhineland between 1815–40, this essay will take as its point of departure events from a larger case study of the nearly two-decade struggle between the Prussian Oberbaudeputation and the Rhenish merchant community of Vallendar over the building of their new parish church. The case study will situate ecclesiastical architecture within the increasingly antagonistic milieu of center-province relations in the 1830s. Center-province tensions around church building were amplified in a polemical 1836 publication that excoriated the Prussian monarchy for its unfair treatment of the Rhenish Catholic population, particularly with regard to provincial architectural initiatives. The essay concludes by showing how provincial appeals for regional autonomy in church design, coupled with the central government's growing concerns about the potential for Rhenish unrest, incentivized Prussian authorities to allow Catholic parishes some leeway, at least in response to those who made steadfast demands. In this case, Rhenish publics learned to leverage Prussian bureaucratic frameworks as a regulating counterforce against arbitrary central governance and the attempts of a fervently Protestant monarch to suppress the growth of Roman Catholicism.

The Nineteenth Century's Bureaucratized Built Environment

Nineteenth-century European architecture was largely bureaucratic. Some of the greatest European architects of the first half of the nineteenth century, including Karl Friedrich Schinkel, Leo von Klenze, Henri Labrouste, John Nash, and Sir Robert Smirke, were employed by government bureaucracies where they worked on the broad spectrum of public architecture required by modern society: hospitals, prisons, theaters, military installations, museums, universities, libraries, palaces, and churches.[7] Through this bureaucratization of architecture, governments sought to shape their self-representation via the built environment; both in and beyond urban centers, buildings as well as the civic infrastructure of roads and bridges became potential emblems of the state and its power in the lives of often distant publics. Despite awareness of bureaucracy's role in nineteenth-century architectural production, little work has been done to consider *how* state bureaucratization fostered unprecedented critical spaces for exchange in which citizens, architects, and rulers alike increasingly negotiated public architectural environments. This paper aims to demonstrate how state architectural bureaucracies offer scholars an understudied channel through which to examine changing relations between central authorities and subject communities in early nineteenth-century Europe.

Prussian reform policies tasked the Oberbaudeputation in September 1809 with issuing judgments on the aesthetic merit of both court and public architectural plans. Prior to this change, aesthetics had been a concern chiefly in the realm of court architecture and was administered by the *Hofbauamt,* or Royal Building Office. In its reorga-

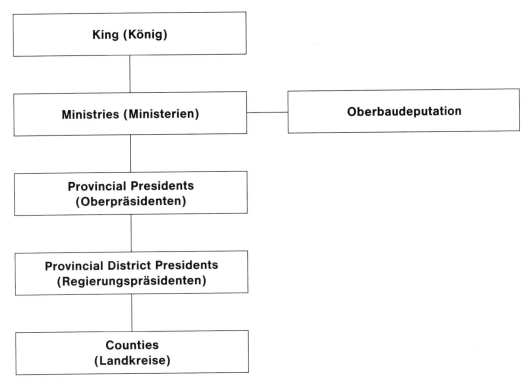

*Redrawn and translated from Strecke (2000), p. 226.

Figure 11.2. The position of the *Oberbaudeputation* in the Prussian bureaucratic hierarchy, 1809–48. From Reinhart Strecke, *Anfänge und Innovation der preußischen Bauverwaltung: Von David Gilly zu Karl Friedrich Schinkel* (Köln: Böhlau Verlag, 2000), 226. Created and translated by Laura diZerega.

nized form, Prussian bureaucrats at the Oberbaudeputation would henceforth regulate how ordinary buildings, as well as town- and cityscapes, *looked*. The types of provincial architecture subject to review by the Oberbaudeputation included churches and rectories as well as schools, military buildings, government office buildings, structures on royal lands, and infrastructure projects such as bridges and roads.[8] The reform signaled the state's understanding that the representational potential of a wide category of public structures merited state involvement. As of 1810, the bureaucrat leading this aesthetic oversight was Schinkel, as he and his Oberbaudeputation colleagues reviewed architectural plans submitted to Prussia's bureaucratic ministries by county and provincial government offices.[9] The expansion of the Oberbaudeputation's mandate also spoke to the mounting awareness among Prussian authorities that everyday environments, as much as officially representative ones, played a role in shaping the social, political, religious, and local identities of the populace. Bureaucratization embedded architecture within existing political frameworks and, by extension, created stakes for provincial publics as well as central authorities—all the more so during times of political unrest or regime changes.

For provincial publics, the growth of bureaucracies in the proto–nation-states of the early nineteenth century provided a mechanism by which they could convey their opinions to the state, particularly when they were at a geographical remove from the political center. In the Rhineland, bureaucratic channels functioned as a relatively level playing field on which parishioners, architects, and civil servants could engage in extended debates with Berlin over church building initiatives. New and different kinds of networks engaged in the systematization of architecture within the nation-state. In this sense, bureaucracy in this period constituted a kind of functional successor to eighteenth-century print culture, in which public criticism of official architecture had afforded ordinary citizens a rare forum in which they could also implicitly question and comment upon the conduct of the state.[10] Likewise, German architects, pastors, and parishioners of the early nineteenth century found in bureaucratic exchanges with state civil servants a means of voicing their often quite identitarian opinions on matters of church architecture, decades before the more famous campaign to complete Cologne Cathedral was launched in 1842.

For the Protestant Prussian state, the bureaucratization of Rhenish architecture had two objectives. The primary objective was state control of ideological differences with their Catholic subjects through regulation of new structures dedicated to a rival confession in a region distrusted for its liberalizing, foreign tendencies. The second objective, one in which Schinkel took particular interest, was to identify and preserve older structures that would represent the development of German architecture and validate Prussia's expanding territorial domination at the same time. When the Rhenish parish at Vallendar requested permission to replace their damaged thirteenth-century church with a new building, Schinkel rejected the idea, noting that the old church exemplified what he termed the Rhineland's distinctive "Byzantine" style (what today we would consider Rhenish Romanesque), and declared that its preservation would benefit a "Publikum" with an expressed interest in preserving old buildings.[11] Schinkel added that even as a ruin, incapable of fulfilling its original function, the old church at Vallendar would stimulate public interest for "several centuries."[12] In this and other instances, he privileged the cultural and historical validation conveyed by the region's crumbling churches over the needs of communities, who would also then be saddled with responsibility for maintaining these dilapidated structures. In Vallendar, however, Rhenish stakeholders persisted and successfully resisted the Oberbaudeputation's dictates.

Such bureaucratic exchanges over parish church design reveal the existence of "two communities of judgment" engaged in state-regulated, provincial ecclesiastical architecture, namely the local, impacted publics who felt real and imagined ownership for structures they lived with day in and day out, and the distant authorities who viewed architecture as part of their armamentarium to acculturate an abstracted provincial public into the burgeoning nation's fold.[13] Ecclesiastical architecture had civil stakes for both the autonomy of the ruled and the legitimacy of the ruler; its ensuing bureaucratic discourse galvanized newly constituted Rhenish publics, derived from across the secular and religious spheres of the community, to contest state power.[14]

The New Parish Church at Vallendar

In 1810, the priest at the Catholic church of Saints Marzellinus and Petrus in the market town of Vallendar wrote an urgent plea to the French authorities. He described his single-aisle, thirteenth-century church as being so crowded that two-thirds of the 3,000-member parish stood outside "in the rain, snow, or under the heat of the sun" during masses.[15] The situation was equally dire in the church cemetery, where bodies were stacked three to four on top of one another with the "last corpse reappearing" at subsequent burials.[16] After the fall of Napoléon, the parish priest continued to seek help from government authorities, turning now to the Prussian bureaucrats in the Koblenz regional government office. Pastor Dieter Reuter reported in 1819 that the size of the parish had grown to 5,000 with three-quarters of the worshippers having no choice but to stand outside during mass. The building had deteriorated further since his 1810 plea to the French authorities, and damage to the roof meant it was often "raining in several places inside the church."[17]

More than other state-funded building projects, the construction of churches brought community members into direct, often prolonged negotiations with the central government.[18] This process of petitioning and then eventually rebuilding the church at Vallendar was to consume the parish for more than two decades. (In addition to negotiations between parish elites and Prussian authorities, church-building projects also drew heavily upon a community's economic and human resources, including the use of local draught animals and corvée labor, and with an assessment of taxes across the socioeconomic spectrum.) Provincial church-building initiatives necessitated communication among five different constituents: (1) Rhenish townspeople serving on the church councils overseeing parochial building projects in their communities; (2) Rhenish architects who designed and managed the building projects as employees in the provincial offices of the Prussian government; (3) Prussian architect-bureaucrats employed by the Oberbaudeputation in Berlin; (4) other bureaucrats in Berlin, particularly those working in the large and powerful *Kultusministerium*; and (5) the Prussian monarch, King Friedrich Wilhelm III (reigned 1797–1840). In accordance with Prussian bureaucratic practice, a local architect would visit the site at the request of the parish community and issue a report. In the case of Vallendar, that architect was Johann Claudius von Lassaulx, who was Koblenz-born, self-taught, and, like many of his colleagues, had served as a building inspector during the French regime. After plans and budgets received local approval from the supervising architect, they were sent on to the Kultusministerium in Berlin, established in 1817 as a stand-alone ministry tasked to administer the collective spirits, minds, and bodies of the new Prussian state.[19] Following the Kultusministerium's review, the materials went to the Oberbaudeputation.

The Oberbaudeputation was not permitted to be in direct communication with provincial architects. The Kultusministerium served as the gatekeeper and routed communications between provincial actors, the Oberbaudeputation, and the monarch. The Kultusministerium's written bureaucratic orders knitted the distant ruling power into the local imagination, thereby inserting and normalizing the aims of central authority into the spatial field of the province.[20] Examples of the reach of the material culture in the Kultusministerium's bureaucracy are found in the myriad forms, tables, memoranda, and reports that functioned as "little tools of knowledge" binding center and province.[21] Requirements that budget templates, lengthy written justifications, and a series of architectural views be completed according to Kultusministerium and Oberbaudeputation directives and submitted for review reinforced the power asymmetry between Berlin and the Rhineland. Bureaucratic directives thus served to extend the state's reach beyond official government spaces to envelop everyday community sites such as parish churches, reinforcing a spatial regime of provinciality throughout the Rhineland.[22] Ministerial circulars regularly distributed across Prussia admonished local architects for a host of alleged offenses, such as making unapproved modifications to building plans, failing to provide accurate information on estimates, and exceeding budgetary parameters. Prussian bureaucratic ephemera effectively transmitted the regime's power with the specific intent to inhibit dialogic communications at the provincial level or between center and province. Beneath such bureaucratic apparatus and ephemera lay the Kultusministerium's ambivalence about the future of the Catholic Church in the Prussian Rhineland. Consequently, the physical buildings themselves were in some ways less crucial than the written discourse surrounding their creation, a discourse directed at disciplining the province and stymieing its autonomy.

The exchanges between von Lassaulx and the Oberbaudeputation concerning the design of the church at Vallendar illustrate how bureaucratic operations exerted central authority over the province as well as how the province resisted those attempts. Over eight drawings, four pages of textual description, and a seventeen-page, itemized budget, Lassaulx officially made his case for the design of a new church at Vallendar in 1824. Lassaulx was required to prepare standard architectural views, namely a ground plan, elevation, and cross section, along with a detailed written justification and cost proposal for the design. While the drawings are lost, the justification survives, providing a detailed description of his vision for the church. Lassaulx wished to incorporate new technology used in commercial architecture that he had seen on a recent trip to France. At the same time, his design drew upon the rich Rhenish Romanesque traditions of the former church as well as the surrounding region.

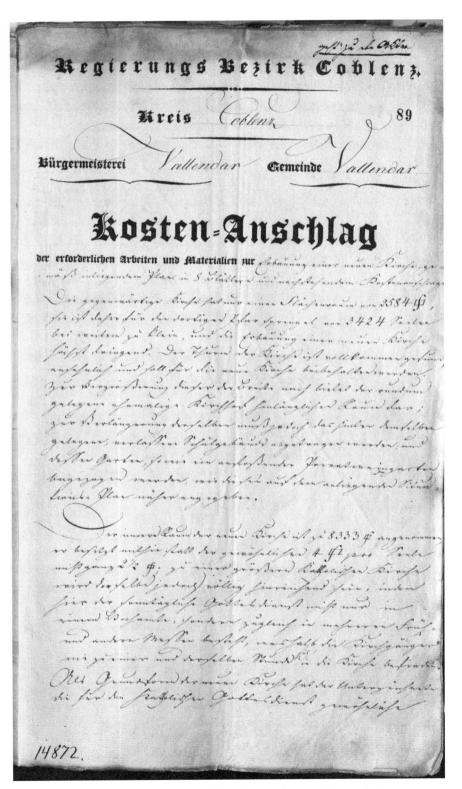

Figure 11.3. The first page of Johann Claudius von Lassaulx's twenty-two-page cost estimate for his design for the new church at Vallendar, dated May 1, 1824. Landeshauptarchiv Koblenz.

Taken together, these inspirations produced a boldly conceived modern sacred space, one technically advanced yet rooted in cultural memory. Lassaulx proposed a more than threefold increase in size from 2,584 square feet to 8,333 square feet. The church's interior featured a wide central nave separated from two narrow side aisles by rows of columns supporting arches. In keeping with the original church's design, he chose a Romanesque-inspired, round-arched style, in contrast to the pointed arch of the Gothic. He identified this style as most appropriate for a Catholic church, drawing upon Rhenish ecclesiastical traditions in buildings such as the Abbey Maria Laach or St. Peter's in Mainz. The interior featured three different vaulting methods: the side aisles were to have shallow, domical vaults, the organ gallery at the back of the church was to have a barrel vault, while over the nave he proposed a coffered ceiling "in the style of the magnificent old basilicas."[23] Illusionistic paintings were proposed to decorate the coffers over the nave, a cost-effective trompe l'oeil alternative to wood carvings. These helped link the church to the image of the great Roman basilicas, even as Lassaulx's round-arched style echoed the famous Romanesque abbeys of the Rhineland.

Lassaulx had equally ambitious plans for illuminating the altar. In contrast to his historicizing approach elsewhere in the building, Lassaulx's concept for the ceiling above the altar added a dramatic and technologically ambitious element at the building's most sacred point. Drawing his inspiration from the iron dome added by François-Joseph Bélanger to the Parisian *Halle aux blés* in 1811, Lassaulx proposed a translucent demi-dome to illuminate the altar from above through glass panels held in place by iron frames. To support the vault of a sacred space with iron was revolutionary in the 1820s; it was an experimental and expensive material.[24] Lassaulx's proposal predated Georg Moller's 1828 iron dome on the east tower of the Mainz cathedral and Karl Ludwig Althans's 1825 cast-iron supports in the main hall of the Sayner Hütte ironworks. Already anticipating Berlin's argument that illumination from above would prove insufficient, Lassaulx offered a poetic evocation of the interior of the *Halle aux blés* in his written justification, insisting that Bélanger's lantern, a soaring one hundred meters overhead, "bathes the interior with such a fullness of light that even the army of grain sacks do not disturb the marvelous impression."[25]

The Oberbaudeputation's two-page written assessment of Lassaulx's plan in November 1824 was unsparing in its criticism and rejected virtually every aspect of Lassaulx's design as being far too ambitious for a provincial church, even one with five thousand congregants. The maximum square footage they would permit was 5,000 square feet, while the budget of 20,000 Taler was deemed "completely impermissible" for a rural church.[26] The Oberbaudeputation instructed Lassaulx to replace the proposed coffering over the nave with a simple wooden truss ceiling and substitute what they termed his "ambitious" vaults over the side aisles and organ gallery with flat wooden ceilings. The dome was pronounced far too expensive, its construction and durability problematic, and, in any case, it did not fit the style of the building. In its place, they wrote, windows were to extend around the apse. Revised plans should be submitted to Berlin.[27]

Lassaulx addressed these criticisms in a June 1825 letter to his Koblenz superiors. First, he countered the Oberbaudeputation's argument that his budget was too high by presenting an itemized list of eight churches he had designed ranked according to cost per square foot. Vallendar's proposed costs fell right in the middle. Then he dared question the authority of the Oberbaudeputation, writing:

> As for the verdict of a royal, most honorable Oberbaudeputation, may I counter it with the perhaps all too favorable ones of Boisserée, Moller, Krahe, Vorhau, and Stieglitz? In any case, I must protest against the competence of the reviewers who regarded a plan I designed after much careful reflection and thorough investigation of many old churches with a nearly incomprehensible superficiality . . .[28]

Lassaulx's protest was thus inspired not only by the Oberbaudeputation's rejection of his design, but by their refusal of his efforts to evoke the Rhineland's Romanesque architectural history and Roman Catholic building traditions. His invocation of Stieglitz, Moller, and Boisserée pointedly countered the presumed authority of Schinkel and the Oberbaudeputation with the work of three theoreticians who identified the flowering of the Romanesque style in the Rhineland as a critical development in German architecture. Lassaulx likely consulted their work, among others, in his development of the Vallendar plans. Christian Stieglitz had published a collection of engravings entitled *Über altdeutsche Baukunst* in 1820, and Lassaulx seems to have drawn inspiration for the design of the portals at Vallendar from Stieglitz's elevation drawing of the façade of Saint Giovanni in Borgo in Pavia. Georg Moller, meanwhile, had published his *Denkmälern der deutschen Baukunst* in 1821, offering a compendium of lesser-known examples of German medieval architecture from the eighth to sixteenth centuries, including both a ground plan and façade elevation drawings of Koblenz's monumental Rhenish Romanesque *Kastorkirche* (the renovation of which Lassaulx himself had undertaken following the Napoleonic Wars). Sulpiz Boisserée, for his part, had argued in his 1823 history of Cologne Cathedral, *Geschichte und Beschreibung des Doms zu Köln*, that medieval ecclesiastical architecture was characterized by the juxtaposition of contradictory features; taking issue with what he saw as the limits of the label "gothic," he pronounced German medieval churches bold in size, fine and precise in workmanship, and highly imaginative in decoration. Boisserée's principle of contrary juxtaposition in medieval architecture arguably inspired Lassaulx's historicizing conception for Vallendar's mixture of distinctive vaulting styles animating each discrete space of the interior and its ethereal, otherworldly altar illumination, with modern materials and technology as its source. Lassaulx's protest against his Prussian judges defended not only his design, but also the Rhineland, its traditions, and history.

The Vallendar parish council also voiced their outrage. Their response was directed to Prussian government officials based in Koblenz, and, as Lassaulx had done, it drew upon Vallendar's civic and confessional attributes in order to defend their church building initiative in terms of Rhenish identity. In an April 1825 letter, they boldly asserted the "fairness of our demands," noting their right to proceed with a new church and their entitlement to state funding without further delays or conditions.[29] They acknowledged that while Vallendar lacked the official designation of a "city," it was nonetheless a prosperous market town with more than 2,600 citizens, larger than many official "cities" in Koblenz's administrative region. Like Lassaulx, they too backed up this statement with a list of fifteen officially designated "cities" nearby, each with a population smaller than that of Vallendar. They provided statistics from comparative church building projects in neighboring Rhenish towns to demonstrate that the cost estimates for Vallendar were in line with regional norms. Horchheim, for example, with only 800 citizens, had received 6,600 Taler in state funding for its church. If one were to use Horchheim's population as a measure, they argued, Vallendar's parish size of 3,800 merited a budget four times as large, or 26,400 Taler. They offered the examples of the nearby Rhenish towns of Neuwied and Altenkirchen, two municipalities to whom the king had donated generously for the building of new churches while Vallendar still waited for the state to approve their project. Needless to say, the authors of the letter pointed out in closing that the latter two examples concerned *Protestant* churches—a thinly veiled observation that the Oberbaudeputation's rejection of their plan occurred in part due to Prussian bias against Rhenish Catholics.

Prussian bureaucrats in Koblenz took the frustrations of Lassaulx and the Vallendar parish council seriously. In a blunt communication dated June 25, 1825, to their superiors in Berlin, they defended the arguments made by both Lassaulx and the parish council. They supported the parish council's argument that 3,800 parishioners could not fit in a 5,000 square foot church and argued that 20,000 Taler for a town church was fair. They even included Lassaulx's list of churches ranked by price per square foot, pointing out Vallendar's midrange position. They reiterated the slight felt by the Catholics of Vallendar with regard to the monarchy's support of Rhenish Protestant church building initiatives and warned that if the monarchy chose to support the building of Protestant churches in the Rhineland, no less could be done for Catholics without consequences. The administration of ecclesiastical architecture risked confirming Rhenish ire and suspicion of maltreatment by the Prussian authorities.[30]

Rhineland-based bureaucrats would repeat such warnings to Berlin in the decade to follow. In November 1836, for example, Rhenish governor Ernst Bodelschwingh warned Friedrich Wilhelm III that the vast majority of Rhenish Catholics "are of the opinion that their Protestant fellow citizens enjoy greater generosity from the state

Figure 11.4. Contemporary photograph of the south elevation of the Church of Saints Marzellinus and Petrus, Vallendar, Germany. Photograph courtesy of Laura diZerega.

when it comes to church matters."³¹ Employing the Oberbaudeputation's bureaucratic mode of written communications, Lassaulx and the parish council each continued to defend their vision of the project against obstruction from the Oberbaudeputation over the decade to come, honing and repeating the process until finally ground was broken on the new church in 1837. From their preference for octagonal columns in the nave to faceted vaulting over the ambulatory, they argued against Berlin's directives for changes; they also fought successfully against Berlin's directive to keep the old church for its historical value, which would have meant building their new church on another site. When it was finally dedicated in 1841, the finished church at Vallendar ultimately reflected much of Lassaulx's original conception: the fifteenth-century tower was retained and connected with the west façade of a new, larger church.

The discussions around building the church at Vallendar pitted claims of Prussian authority against counterclaims of provincial autonomy and identity. The bureaucratic directives issued by the Oberbaudeputation, while seeming to address only minor issues

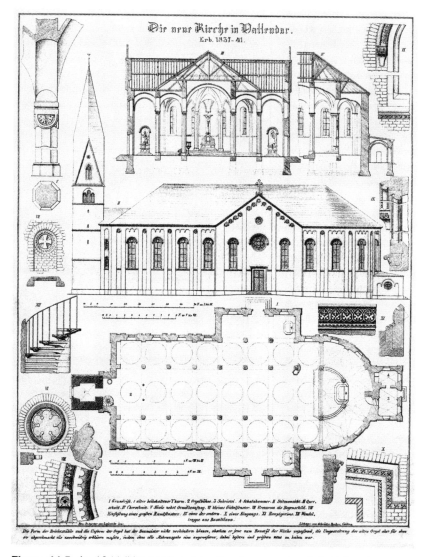

Figure 11.5. An 1841 lithograph celebrating the new church in Vallendar, including multiple architectural views.

such as the shape of a column or the placement of a baptismal font, were actually intended to provincialize Rhenish publics that Berlin viewed as foreign and French-inflected, and to assert Prussian political and cultural dominance in the region. In their responses to the Oberbaudeputation, Rhenish architects, and the parish councils with whom they collaborated, quickly learned to deploy their own bureaucratic rhetoric of rational justification to advance their preferred church designs. Using the same text-based, bureaucratic methods employed by the Oberbaudeputation, Rhenish architects and publics responded to the Oberbaudeputation's criticisms by making evidence- and data-based cases in support of their projects. Johann Claudius von Lassaulx and the parish council at Vallendar employed published technical sources, the latest Parisian architectural developments, population data, costs, figures, and statistics, proving themselves facile at countering Berlin's purportedly rational bureaucratic approach with one of their own fashioning. By comparison, the arguments in the architectural assessments issued by Schinkel and the Oberbaudeputation were of a different flavor, grounded in the abstract societal benefits offered by picturesque views, art historical significance, and an emphasis on "universals" such as harmony, symmetry, and clear disposition. In their exchanges with Prussian bureaucrats, and perhaps not fully aware of the process, Rhenish stakeholders nonetheless argued for the validity of their regional-based architectural preferences over attempts to align provincial plans with a "national" style acceptable to the Oberbaudeputation's arbiters of taste. The tensions between these two communities—Prussian bureaucrats eager to impose central authority on the distant spatial field of the province and Rhenish stakeholders engaged in immediate and quotidian struggles to bring their building projects to fruition—were given voice in a polemical 1836 publication entitled *Winter Evening Conversations among a Few Villagers by a Warm Oven*. The text recounted the many antagonisms Rhinelanders felt toward Prussian governance, and the numerous examples related to church building on its pages made clear that the events surrounding the new church in Vallendar did not represent an isolated incident.

Winter Evening Conversations among a Few Villagers by a Warm Oven (1836)

Published in Belgium to avoid Prussian censors, *Winter Evening Conversations among a Few Villagers by a Warm Oven (Winter Abend Unterhaltungen einiger Landleute am Warmen Ofen)* offers a vivid picture of the tensions experienced by Rhenish Catholics over the profound lack of state support for building and repair of their parish churches. It was brought to the attention of King Friedrich Wilhelm III by his interior and security minister Gustav von Rochow in 1837, who described the book as written in the "popular style for the lower classes" and posing a distinct threat to state security.[32]

Before even reading its content, the notation in the front matter that *Winter Evening Conversations* had been published in Belgium most certainly alarmed a Prussian monarchy fearful of the spread of revolutionary contagion from the Rhineland's neighbor to the west. Belgium and the Rhineland had both belonged to the French state on the left bank of the Rhine from 1795 to 1815. Following the Congress of Vienna, the Rhineland came under Prussian hegemony while Belgium went to the Kingdom of the Netherlands. Clear parallels existed in the situations of the two regions: in both, a politically active, self-confident merchant class had come to appreciate the liberal economic policies and legal system under Napoleonic rule; both were majority Catholic; both bristled at their transfer to rule under conservative Protestant monarchs.[33] The Belgian Revolution of

1830, part of the larger wave of revolutions that included the July Revolution in France and Greek independence from the Ottomans, came too close to home for Prussia, particularly when the Prussian army suppressed an uprising in Aachen just five days after the eruption of riots in Brussels. *Winter Evening Conversations* centers on the contrast between generous state support for Protestant churches and the cold disregard shown for Catholic building needs, and offers thereby another powerful example of how ecclesiastical architecture had become an important site of Rhenish Catholic resistance to Prussian rule.

Winter Evening Conversations is organized as a series of dialogues between rural neighbors in an unnamed village in the bishopric of Trier. Its long list of grievances endured by Rhenish Catholics at the hands of the Prussian regime took into account virtually every aspect of daily life in the Rhineland: the law requiring children of a mixed-confessional marriage be raised in the faith of the father (especially troublesome in the Rhineland, where Prussian soldiers or bureaucrats often married Catholic women); the requirement that Catholic soldiers in the Prussian army attend Protestant religious services instead of Mass; the unequal funding of Catholic schools relative to Protestant ones; the practice of filling bureaucratic posts with (Protestant) Prussians instead of (Catholic) Rhinelanders; and finally and most significantly for this essay, the consistent bureaucratic obstacles Catholic parish communities encountered in their church building initiatives.

At several points in the text, the conversation turns to the restraints the Prussian administration had placed on building and equipping Rhenish Catholic churches. Their first complaints are directed at the Prussian civil servants who regulated the amount parish councils could spend on supplies for masses. The "Protestant government" insists that parishes be *"sparsam,"* or thrifty. "We are often told how much wine, wax, or even hosts may be purchased."[34] Next, the group recounts the hardships of Catholic parishes whose requests to build new churches were denied by Prussian bureaucrats. They speak of the struggle of six hundred Catholics in the Silesian city of Görlitz, forced to travel two hours to attend Mass at the church of a neighboring village. After six years of petitioning the monarch in vain for permission to build their own Catholic church, their request was denied in 1829. (The denial granted them permission to rent a house in which to gather lawfully for Mass in Görlitz, but only nine times a year!) By comparison, they observe, the "Protestants of Görlitz own seven churches, six of which were originally Catholic and four of which are barely used."[35] They rail against a surfeit of recent Protestant church building in the province of Silesia, insisting that while Catholics went without, more than ten Protestant churches had been generously funded by the Prussian monarchy, some for congregations of barely thirty to forty people and none larger than two hundred.[36] In the Rhineland, they note, one had the "well-known example" of the town of Prumm, whose Catholics were spared a yearslong wait for permission to build a church because Prussian authorities simply denied their request immediately. Concerning the building and repairs for Catholic churches overall, "the state treasury was always empty or tightly locked when Catholics humbly requested something."[37] Finally, they observe with disgust that their "noble" Cologne Cathedral stood dark, while a new Protestant secondary school, for the "few Protestants that live there," collected the vast sum of 5,000 Taler annually in state funds.[38] The anonymous author(s) of *Winter Evening Conversations* deftly associated the Rhenish narrative of mistreatment with the similar experiences of Catholics in other regions of the Prussian state. Prussian authorities knew that the potential threat to the monarchical state could intensify substantially and rapidly if the outrage of millions of Catholics in the relatively prosperous and developed Rhineland were organized and extended to their confessional counterparts in the monarchy's eastern regions.

In the course of their tense exchanges concerning the style, site, and funding of ecclesiastical architecture, Rhenish civil servants and parish councils used Prussia's own bureaucratic framework to interact with Oberbaudeputation architects largely as coequals, with the liberty to judge, criticize, and advocate for their desired outcomes on building initiatives. More traditional political efforts to contest Prussia's lack of support for Catholic ecclesiastical architecture were to culminate in an 1837 petition introduced at the Fifth Rhenish Diet to compel the Prussian monarchy to fund church building on the Rhine's left bank. The petition was rejected outright by Minister of State von Altenstein, in a failure that both illustrates the limited political resources Rhinelanders had to contest Prussian hegemony and underscores the compulsion of Rhenish communities to contest the Prussians through bureaucratic means.[39] Indeed, even if not every parish was as successful as Vallendar in resisting Berlin, activism in Rhenish towns and villages on behalf of their church building projects ultimately provided a crucial training ground for political participation in an era otherwise lacking in meaningful popular representation. As such, these histories offer a salutary reminder that the emergent modernity of the early nineteenth century is as much to be sought in the hinterlands—in religious contexts and in traditional institutions—as it is in the more familiar settings of secular urbanity.

The battle lines were often blurred nonetheless. The Rhenish cause was not infrequently aided by civil servants in Prussian government service, who broke ranks with Berlin to advocate for Rhenish parish church initiatives. The events at Vallendar in the 1830s reveal the intricacy of bureaucratic processes and challenge the notion that the Prussian bureaucracy acted in monolithic fashion down the chain of command. To the contrary, one lesson of Vallendar is the growing incongruence between the priorities of bureaucrats on the ground, as it were, and those in the capital. State and province had different ideas about the objectives of their respective efforts, and complexities emerged as they attempted to define the "public" they served. Rhineland-based officials frequently aligned themselves with the "public" that comprised the immediate parish community over the tendency of their Berlin-based counterparts to consider the abstract "public" of the imagined "nation" beyond the Rhineland.[40] In this sense, the bureaucratization of ecclesiastical architecture may be said to have broadened community-based participation in public affairs generally, compelling members of the Rhenish public to serve as arbiters of their own interests vis-à-vis state power structures.

For Rhenish parishes, resistance to Berlin's mandates waned after the dissolution of the Oberbaudeputation in 1848 left decision-making largely in the hands of regional governments. The reconstituted Catholic Church hierarchy in the Rhineland would soon fill this vacuum in the 1850s and 1860s by appointing diocesan architects and explicitly mandating church style. In 1852, for example, the Archbishopric of Cologne stipulated that all new Catholic churches be designed in the neo-Gothic style. Likewise, in 1861 the *Eisenacher Regulativ*, a Prussian congress of Protestant clergy, stated its stylistic preference for neo-Gothic in Protestant church design.[41] In 1863, the diocese of Cologne officially hired a chief architect responsible for review of all parochial architectural plans.[42] In stark contrast to the wide and local variety of stylistic expression evident in provincial church designs under the Oberbaudeputation between 1815–48—from classicizing to neo-Gothic to Rhenish Romanesque Revival— the range of acceptable styles in the decades immediately following narrowed as *Kulturkampf* battles unfolded between the renewed Roman Catholic Church and an ascendant Prussia. The hegemony of neo-Gothic in the 1850–60s, sustained in part by enthusiasm for the completion of Cologne Cathedral, gave way in the last quarter of the nineteenth century to a renewed flourishing of Rhenish Romanesque Revival, the stylistic hallmark of so many of Lassaulx's Catholic church designs, including Vallendar.[43] This traditionally Catholic architectural language enjoyed favor even in Protestant church building, most notably at Berlin's monumental Kaiser-Wilhelm-Gedächtniskirche (dedicated 1895). The incorporation of *the* historical style of the Catholic Rhineland into monumental Prussian Protestant church design did more than just signal the end of the *Kulturkampf*; the adoption of such designs throughout Prussia helped give architectural form to the Prussian monarchy's achievement in unifying Germany in 1871, and, by association, their imperial claim to the cultural patrimony of lands now conjoined under their scepter.

The most obvious legacy of Rhenish parish council activism in the quarter century between 1815 and 1840 was the establishment of the Cologne Cathedral Building Society in 1842. Rhenish Catholics had been galvanized as never before to protest Prussian interference in provincial confessional affairs following the arrest in 1837 of the Archbishop of Cologne, who had refused to abide by the Prussian mandate that children born in Catholic–Protestant marriages be raised in the faith of the father. With twenty-five years' experience of Prussian bureaucratic impediments to parochial church building, Rhenish Catholics were by this time well conditioned to distrust the Prussian authorities, as evinced by texts like the 1836 *Winter Evening Conversations*. The roots of the widespread Rhenish enthusiasm that greeted the Cologne Cathedral project after 1842 are at least partly to be found in this legacy of distrust. Overwhelming Rhenish support for the annual lottery to benefit the Cologne Cathedral Building Society, and to lessen its reliance on donations from King Friedrich Wilhelm IV, should likewise be traced back to the weekly collections taken up between 1815 and 1840 at Masses across the Rhineland to fund church repairs—collections that did not just fund construction, but that also kept participants informed about the struggles facing Catholic parishes all across the region.[44] Thus an 1838 collection for the Rhenish parish of Spellen yielded parochial contributions not just from nearby Düsseldorf, but also from Cologne (60 miles away), Aachen (90 miles away), Koblenz (125 miles away), and even Trier (155 miles away).[45] Finally, these stories of bureaucratic conflict between Rhenish parishes and Berlin help us to better understand the Prussian monarchy's strong support for the completion of Cologne Cathedral, behind which lay the important lesson learned from the accumulated experience of hundreds of Vallendars.

Notes

1. This essay is based on my doctoral dissertation; see Laura diZerega, "Beyond Berlin: Karl Friedrich Schinkel, Bureaucracy, and Rhenish Ecclesiastical Architecture, 1815–1840" (PhD diss., University of California, Santa Barbara, 2021). On the relationship between institutions and the public sphere in eighteenth- and nineteenth-century German lands, see Jürgen Habermas, *The Structural Transformation of the Public Sphere: An Inquiry into a Category of Bourgeois Society*, trans. Thomas Burger (Cambridge, Mass.: MIT Press, 1991), 31–43. For the history of the Prussian building bureaucracy, see Reinhart Strecke, *Anfänge und Innovation der preußischen Bauverwaltung: Von David Gilly zu Karl Friedrich Schinkel* (Köln: Böhlau Verlag, 2000) and Eckhard Bolenz, *Von Baubeamten zum freiberuflichen Architekten: Technische Berufe im Bauwesen (Preußen/Deutschland, 1799–1931)* (Frankfurt am Main: P. Lang, 1991). For a history of Prussian interventions in Rhenish ecclesiastical architecture under architect Karl Friedrich Schinkel, see Eva Brües, *Die Rheinlande*, in the Karl Friedrich Schinkel Lebenswerk series, ed. Margarete Kühn (Berlin: Deutscher Kunstverlag, 1968). See James M. Brophy, *Popular Culture and the Public Sphere in the Rhineland, 1800–1850* (Cambridge: Cambridge University Press, 2007) for a study of the role of popular culture, including religion, and the development of modern political publics in the Rhineland during the first half of the nineteenth century.
2. Udo Liessem, "Bau- und Kunstgeschichte der Kirchen und Gemeindezentren in den evangelischen Gemeinden Koblenz und Pfaffendorf," in *Pragmatisch, preußisch, protestantisch: Die evangelische Gemeinde Koblenz im Spannungsfeld von rheinischem Katholizismus und preußischer Kirchenpolitik*, ed. Markus Dröge, Erich Engelke, Andreas Metzing, Ulrich Offerhain, Thomas M. Schneider, and Rolf Stahl (Bonn: Rudolf Habelt Verlag, 2003), 148–49.
3. On the economic conditions attending eighteenth-century population growth in German lands, see Ernest Benz, "Population Change and the Economy," in *Germany: A New Social*

and Economic History, vol. 2, ed. Sheilagh Ogilvie (London: Arnold, 1996), 39–62; see also David Blackbourn, *History of Germany 1780–1918: The Long Nineteenth Century,* 2nd ed. (Oxford: Blackwell, 2003), 20–23, and James J. Sheehan, *German History, 1770–1866* (Oxford: Oxford University Press, 1989), 74–78.

4. A single-aisle village church cost a few thousand Taler; five hundred Taler might cover repairs to a roof or bell tower. The cost threshold was raised to one thousand Taler in an updated guidance document for the Oberbaudeputation dated October 23, 1817.

5. Michael Rowe, "The Napoleonic Legacy in the Rhineland and the Politics of Reform in Restoration Prussia," in *Napoleon's Legacy: Problems of Government in Restoration Europe,* ed. David Laven and Lucy Riall (Oxford, New York: Berg, 2000), 136.

6. Of the contrasts between Rhinelanders and their new Prussian rulers, their divergent legal systems may have been the starkest. Napoléon's Code Civil was introduced in the Rhineland during the French occupation in 1804; it theoretically recognized all citizens as equal before the law. In Prussia, by contrast, the legal framework of the Prussian General Code of 1794 contained more than one hundred and fifty paragraphs for offences against noble honor; see Rowe, "The Napoleonic Legacy," 137. For further reading on the sociocultural, confessional, and political tensions between Prussia and the Rhineland in the first half of the nineteenth century, see also Michael Rowe, *From Reich to State: The Rhineland in the Revolutionary Age, 1780–1830* (Cambridge: Cambridge University Press, 2003); Karl-Georg Faber, *Die Rheinlande zwischen Restauration und Revolution: Probleme der Rheinischen Geschichte von 1814 bis 1848 im Spiegel der zeitgenössischen Publizistik* (Wiesbaden: Franz Steiner Verlag, GmbH, 1966); Volkmar Wittmütz, "Preußen und die Kirchen im Rheinland, 1815–1840," in *Preußens Schwieriger Westen: Rheinisch-preußische Beziehungen, Konflikte und Wechselwirkungen,* ed. Georg Mölich, Meinhard Pohl, and Veit Veltzke (Duisburg: Mercator Verlag, 2003); and Jürgen Herres and Bärbel Holtz, "Rheinland und Westfalen als preußischen Provinzen (1814–88)" in *Rheinland, Westfalen und Preussen: Eine Beziehungsgeschichte,* ed. Georg Mölich, Veit Veltzke, and Bernd Walter (Münster: Aschendorff Verlag, 2011).

7. Eckhard Bolenz, *Von Baubeamten,* 6; David Van Zanten, "Nineteenth-Century French Government Architectural Services and the Design of the Monuments of Paris," *Art Journal* 48, no. 1 (Spring 1989): 16. See also David Van Zanten, *Building Paris* (Cambridge: Cambridge University Press, 1994).

8. Geheimes Staatsarchiv Preußischer Kulturbesitz (GStA PK) I HA Rep 76 Kultusministerium IX Sekt 1, Nr. 10, Bd. 1, 41–44, "Die Instruktionen für die Landbaubeamten betreffend" dated May 10, 1817.

9. Strecke, *Anfänge und Innovation,* 165.

10. On public debates surrounding eighteenth-century French architecture and their function as a framework for the social participation of ordinary people in civil society, see Richard Wittman, *Architecture, Print Culture, and the Public Sphere in Eighteenth-Century France* (New York: Routledge, 2007).

11. Landeshauptarchiv Koblenz (LHA-Ko), Abt. 441, Nr. 16004, 408–9.

12. LHA-Ko, Abt. 441, Nr. 16004, pages 410–11.

13. Wittman, *Architecture, Print Culture, and the Public Sphere,* 120–22.

14. For a useful discussion on the nature of publics, see Michael Warner, *Publics and Counter-*

publics (New York: Zone Books, 2002), particularly pp. 65–124. Warner broadly defines a public as a "multicontextual space of circulation, organized not by a place or an institution but by the circulation of discourse." As will be developed later in this essay, the discursive bureaucratic record of Prussia's ongoing impediments to Rhenish church-building initiatives circulated widely throughout the Rhineland via such varied channels as print publications and the regular collections taken up at church services to support the region's cash-strapped church-building projects.

15. LHA-Ko, Abt. 441, Nr. 16015, 23. Letter dated September 24, 1810.
16. LHA-Ko, Abt. 441, Nr. 16015, 23. Letter dated September 24, 1810.
17. LHA-Ko, Abt. 441, Nr. 16015, 27.
18. Prussian schools were strictly segregated by confession, and school construction was marked by similar antagonisms between local stakeholders and state authorities. To economize and standardize school building, the Oberbaudeputation issued design templates for schools of varying sizes to all its provinces. In 1821, the Oberbaudeputation chastised the Düsseldorf regional government and its architects for disseminating its own set of template school designs without prior authorization from Berlin. See GStA PK I HA Rep 93 B Ministerium der öffentlichen Arbeiten Nr. 2480, 41–162 and GStA PK I HA Rep 76 Kultusministerium IX Sekt 1 Nr. 4, Bd. 1.
19. From its inception in 1817, the Kultusministerium had three divisions; the first division dealt with religious affairs, the second with educational affairs, and the third with medical affairs. As of 1841, the Kultusministerium was formally divided into four departments: Protestant Affairs, Catholic Affairs, Educational Affairs, and Medical Affairs. While the Protestant Affairs department of the Kultusministerium was dissolved in 1849, the Catholic Affairs department existed until its dissolution by Otto von Bismarck in 1871. Bärbel Holtz, "Stellenstruktur, Binnenorganisation, und Zunahme des Geschäftsbetriebes," in *Acta Borussica, Preussen als Kulturstaat, Band 1.1* (Berlin: Akademie Verlag, 2009), 103–5.
20. On this concept, see Arindam Dutta, *The Bureaucracy of Beauty: Design in the Age of Its Global Reproducibility* (New York: Routledge, 2007), 71.
21. Peter Becker and William Clark, *Little Tools of Knowledge: Historical Essays on Academic and Bureaucratic Practices* (Ann Arbor: University of Michigan Press, 2001), 1–34.
22. See Tania Sengupta, "Between Country and City: Fluid Spaces of Provincial Administrative Towns in Nineteenth-Century Bengal," *Urban History* 39, no. 1 (2012): 56–82, and Tania Sengupta, "Between the Garden and the Bazaar: The Visions, Spaces and Structures of Colonial Towns in Nineteenth-Century Provincial Bengal," *Visual Culture in Britain* 12, no. 3 (2011): 333–48, https://doi.org/10.1080/14714787.2011.613732.
23. LHA-Ko, Abt. 441, Nr. 16015, 90.
24. Albrecht Mann, *Die Neuromanik* (Köln: Greven Verlag, 1966), 18.
25. LHA-Ko, Abt. 441, Nr. 16015, 91.
26. To put this in perspective, a small village parish church typically cost between 6,000–8,000 Taler, while a moderate church in a medium-sized town required 15,000–25,000 Taler or more. The Protestant church of Werden an der Ruhr, completed in 1834, had a budget of nearly 12,000 Taler for a church to fit a congregation of 1,400, comparatively smaller than the Vallendar congregation.
27. LHA-Ko, Abt. 441, Nr. 16005, 122–23.

28. LHA-Ko, Abt. 441, Nr. 16015, 135–36.
29. LHA-Ko, Abt. 441, Nr. 16015, 133.
30. LHA-Ko, Abt. 441, Nr. 16015, 139–44.
31. GStA PK IHA Rep 89 Nr. 23014, 50–51, letter from Bodelschwingh to Altenstein dated November 22, 1836.
32. Letter from Interior Minister Gustav Adolf von Rochow to the monarch, May 24, 1837. GStA PK IHA Rep 89, Nr. 23036, 1–5.
33. Klaus Pabst, *Belgien und Rheinland-Westfalen seit dem 19 Jahrhundert: Beziehungen zweier Nachbarländer.* Geschichte im Westen, Jahrgang 1990, Heft 1, 26–37.
34. *Winter Abend Unterhaltungen einiger Landleute am Warmen Ofen,* 1836, 28. See the copy sent by Interior Minister Rochow to Friedrich Wilhelm III, GStA PK IHA Rep 89, Nr. 23036, 6–58.
35. *Winter Abend Unterhaltungen,* 48–49.
36. *Winter Abend Unterhaltungen,* 51.
37. *Winter Abend Unterhaltungen,* 51.
38. *Winter Abend Unterhaltungen,* 94.
39. GStA PK I HA Rep 77 Ministerium des Innern Titl 523h, Nr. 22, Bd. 1, 69.
40. See Richard Wittman's argument on the development of publics in debates surrounding eighteenth-century French architecture in *Architecture, Print Culture, and the Public Sphere,* 120–22.
41. See Willy Weyres, "Katholischen Kirchen im alten Erzbistüm Köln und im rheinischen Teil des Bistums Münster," in *Kunst des 19 Jahrhunderts im Rheinland, Band 1: Architektur I, Kultusbauen,* ed. Eduard Trier and Willy Weyres (Schwann: Düsseldorf, 1980), 76–77.
42. Willy Weyres, "Katholische Kirchen," 76.
43. On the Rhenish Romanesque Revival in late nineteenth-century Prussia, see Wolfgang Cortjaens, "Sprache des Materials, Politik der Form: Die katholische Kirchenbau in den linksrheinischen Teilen der preußischen Rheinprovinz und im Rhein-Maas-Gebiet, 1815–1914" in *Historism and Cultural Identity in the Rhine-Meuse Region/Historismus und kulturelle Identität in Raum Rhein-Maas,* ed. Wolfgang Cortjaens, Jan De Maeyer, and Tom Verschaffel (Leuven: Leuven University Press, 2008) 276–79. See also Kathleen Curran, "The German Rundbogenstil and Reflections on the American Round-Arched Style," *Journal of the Society of Architectural Historians* 47, no. 4 (December 1988): 351–65.
44. For the politics of Cologne Cathedral's rebuilding, see chapter two of Michael Lewis's indispensable study, *The Politics of the German Gothic Revival* (Cambridge, Mass.: MIT Press, 1993).
45. GStA PK IHA Rep 89, Nr. 22016, 169.

Chapter 12

Metropolis against the State
Architectures of Violence after the Paris Commune

Peter Minosh

On January 27, 1871, the French Government of National Defense—established upon the fall of the Second Empire in September 1870—formally surrendered to the Prussian Army. The French Second Empire was defeated at the Battle of Sedan in September 1870 where its leader, Napoléon III, was taken prisoner. From September to January, Paris was under siege by the Prussian army. A conversation between two soldiers opens Eugène Emmanuel Viollet-le-Duc's 1871 book *Mémoire sur la défense de Paris*—a sprawling work published in the wake of the Commune, encompassing military history, tactics, and discipline as well as national character and public education—all under the guise of a technical treatise on fortifications.[1]

> **27 January 1871**
>
> X... What fatal destiny weighs on us? How can we conceive such a succession of disasters, and what will happen to our unfortunate country?
>
> XX... it is not fate, my dear friend; if a nation suffers disasters, they are theirs alone to fix... We are defeated today, and our disasters were long anticipated by anyone with any foresight. The misfortunes that overwhelm us could have been delayed, or less severe, or less overwhelming; but they were inevitable given our social conditions.
>
> We have complained, with no lack of bitterness, of the indifferent attitude of Europe. But did we consult Europe or those powers to whom we rendered service before beginning this fatal war? Without having done so, wouldn't the help that one or more of these powers might have given us proved more humiliating than defeat? We invaded Italy: since then,

we have never ceased to reproach the Italians for their ingratitude, they couldn't possibly see our recent setbacks without a certain satisfaction, as is the axiom of politics: we abandon the unfortunate because they are no longer to be feared.

X ... Your reasoning regarding the Prussians, it seems to me, is that might makes right.

XX ... Let us understand each other, please, because this is not the time to mix sentiment with politics, or, if you will, to do politics with sentimentality, let us not mince words or throw around eloquent phrases of empty meaning. Let us use reason; especially in the presence of an enemy whose reason is sound. At the origin of every society, force alone establishes right, and there are few rights that have not been brought about through conquest. Property rights, political rights, civil rights, the rights of nations, are all of conquest, that is to say, the results obtained by the use of force on a force that has been weakened, or chaos, or anarchy. The civilized nations then establish among themselves certain conventions that they name the Law of Nations, of neutrals, of belligerents, etc., but there is also the right of war. And right now, that supersedes all others.[2]

This dialogue between the anonymous XX and his interlocutor X plays out repeatedly in diverse contexts on this particular day. The terms are familiar from Hobbes's *homo homini lupus* to Schmitt's sovereign exception: war supersedes both the rights of man and the laws of nations because both are born of violence. We can assume the Socratic voice, X, to be that of Viollet-le-Duc himself. Viollet-le-Duc served as a lieutenant colonel in the *Garde Nationale*—the French volunteer force—in Adolphe Alphand's Legion of Engineering. He oversaw a group of architects—Gabriel Davioud, Théodore Ballu, Ambroise Baudry, and Anatole de Baudot, among others—working as sappers in the Auxiliary Corps of Civil Engineers, charged with the construction of trenches and batteries, the clearing of roads to aid the artillery, the construction of barricades, and the serrating of walls.[3] XX, then, could be any of the architects or builders in his unit, but speaks more broadly to the sentiment of the *Garde Nationale* at the moment that the government had abandoned the city, leaving its residents to fend for themselves against the Prussian army.

XX observes that France never invoked any law of nations when Napoléon marched across Europe; in fact, it had taken the same liberties with Prussia after the Battle of Jena that Bismarck was taking in turn. Even with the defeat of Napoléon, France never repudiated his policies, and his battles were still celebrated in popular culture. "Beaten and abandoned by our allies at Leipzig, defeated at Waterloo," XX explains, "we have never taken these defeats as the fair reprisal of law against force." Taking the conquest of Alsace and Lorraine as an exemplar of this right of the strongest, if France could not protect these provinces, then by all rights, they belong to the conqueror. X protests:

> X... A Population has rights and cannot be taken, ceded, or conquered, in the nineteenth century like a flock of sheep.
>
> XX... As long as people will behave like sheep, they cannot refuse to be treated as such by the shepherds and the wolves.

France, according to XX, has been a "docile flock" since the absolute monarchy. State centralization was a form of conquest, not by an outside power, but by a sovereign, Louis XIV being the "first instigator of our misfortunes by his spirit of conquest and his manic domination of everything and everyplace." The French had become well-penned sheep, "grazing at the discretion of a master in the name of national unity." State power, consolidated and centralized by Louis XIV, did not resist the rule of force but furthered it. The obligations of citizenship, paying taxes, conscription into the army, voting, holding political offices, and serving on juries all represent passive acquiescence to state power. XX then frames an alternate politics to both the right of force and rule of the state, or, of Prussia and the French government in exile: "it is up to us to guard ourselves, without the shepherd and without the wolves." One's real responsibility is to utilize all productive capacity over and above civic obligations, to actively contribute all physical and mental means to the cause of liberty. Rights are not issued through the distribution of obligations; they are actively formed through collective action.

After a slapdash election, a conservative National Assembly claimed power on February 16, 1871, and formally surrendered to Prussia ten days later. The people of Paris rejected this capitulation and refused the government entry to the city, exiling the government to Versailles. This chapter examines a set of debates spanning the Paris Commune: seventy-two days from March 18 to May 28, 1871, in which the people of Paris barricaded the city against both the invading Prussian army and the government of France to build—under the most precarious conditions—a revolutionary society. The dialog opening Viollet-le-Duc's *Mémoire sur la défense de Paris* reflects the terms of these debates (which had already begun taking place in the workers clubs at the end of the second empire) regarding sovereignty in the absence of the sanction and protection of the state. I examine how architects negotiated the absence of traditional modes of sovereignty and in that space built new social and political configurations.

Viollet-le-Duc was no Communard; the Central Committee of the *Garde Nationale* resigned on March 28. "Threatened with arrest by the Commune if I refused to march under its orders, as an officer of engineering, I left Paris on 29 March." He retired to Pierrefonds to build his own response to the Second Empire: an atavistic medieval utopia recalling organic social relations before the appropriation of secular, spiritual, and political power by the nobility, organized religion, and the bourgeoisie.[4] I will instead focus on the work of Hector Horeau, a contemporary of Viollet-le Duc, who participated in the Commune and whose projects from the end of the Second Empire to the aftermath of the Commune highlight a capacity to negotiate revolutionary desires through architecture.

Horeau is best known for his unrealized projects for voluminous cast-iron and glass pavilions.[5] Sigfried Giedion considered him to be a prophet who anticipated the architectural forms of technologies yet to be implemented.[6] In 1851 he won the open competition for the Great Exhibition in London with an entry for a vast and sweeping pavilion that would have been the first of its kind—had the commission not been given to Joseph Paxton for his Crystal Palace, a scaled-down version of Horeau's scheme. In 1863 he designed the favored project for the Halles Centrales de Paris, a commission that was ultimately given to Victor Baltard. By 1871 Horeau had amassed a lifetime of unfeasible and unrealized projects. Giedion observed, "Whenever the nineteenth century feels itself to be unobserved, it grows bold." Horeau's architecture, which remained stubbornly autodidactic throughout the Beaux-Arts institution-building of the Second Empire, provided a platform to reimagine the metropolis in the wake of the Commune.

Iron Utopias

Billowing glass and steel canopy structures populate the utopian fantasies of the 1860s, most deriving from the spectacle of London's Crystal Palace. Best known among these are Vera Pavlovna's dream in Nikolay Chernyshevsky's 1863 *What Is to Be Done?* and Fyodor Dostoyevsky's response to Chernyshevsky in *Notes from Underground* published the following year. The stakes of Chernyshevsky's modernization fantasy with the Crystal Palace as a site of utopian liberation and Dostoyevsky's rebuke of this vision—where the Crystal Palace stands in for the totalizing oppression of instrumental reason—have been well rehearsed in urban history.[7] In examining Horeau's glass and steel structures (and the writers and events with which they were in dialogue) I hope to shift the terms of modernization in the metropolis away from the terms, on the one hand, of Chernyshevsky's anti-urban fantasy in which endless Crystal Palaces serve as self-enclosed sites of production and habitation that resolve and replace the crisis of the metropolis, and, on the other hand, of Dostoyevsky's fear of losing the city as a site of struggle, suffering, and desire.

The French Second Empire imposed strict censorship on speech deemed political; direct criticism of the Church or the government was prohibited, forcing writers to sublimate political critique within other literary and artistic forms. Futurist visions of Paris were a popular mode: some described a future city while others looked at the present from the standpoint of some future civilization.[8] Tony Moilin's 1869 novella, *Paris in the Year 2000*, did both in positing the rise of socialist government after revolution.[9] While Moilin's Paris is among those set in the distant future—the year 2000—unlike them, his future is clearly anchored in the Paris of the 1860s. It is a city of iron, glass, and cobblestone, powered by coal and steam, where well-heeled residents promenade along *Grands Boulevards*. By extension, then, the revolution does not presuppose speculative future conditions but springs from the means, imaginaries, and conditions of Second Empire Paris.

Paris in the Year 2000 commences in the immediate aftermath of a revolution that brought a socialist government to power. The first act of this new revolutionary government is architectural: to appropriate the city's private houses and hand them over to the architects to build gallery streets for the new society. To fill out this vision of a speculative utopia, Moilin turned to the work of Horeau by describing the transformation of Haussmann's boulevards into vast covered passageways.

> On the first floor of each house they took over all the rooms overlooking the street and demolished the intermediary partitions; then they opened large bays in the party walls and thus obtained gallery-streets that had the height and width of an ordinary room and occupied the entire length of a block of buildings ... Similar bridges, but much longer, were even extended over the various boulevards, over the squares and over the bridges crossing the Seine, so that the gallery-street did not suffer any break in continuity.[10]

Horeau's rendering of an 1862 project to enclose Rue de l'Impératrice—he would draw several similar schemes throughout the decade—shows a glass arcade with a clearstory cupola supported by filigreed cast-iron beams spanning the entire width of the boulevard. They are anchored on the façades of the existing buildings and adorned with flowerpots and chandeliers that hang from their curbs and ridges. The hybrid section-perspective drawing shows the lower floors of the existing buildings taken over by iron galleries, extending the public space of the street into the private interior. This recalls contemporaneous utopian socialist projects, such as André Godin's *Familistère de Guise*, whose iron canopy transformed the residential block into a space of social relation.

Horeau's accompanying commentary is largely technocratic, describing the project's mechanical systems such as fire prevention, ventilation, climate control, and sanitation. No indications of these systems exist in the drawings; ducts, vents, basins, and furnaces do not interrupt his voluminous spaces. As technologies still under development, they remain speculative assemblages of biopolitical control.

These iron and glass structures play out as hypothetical social-space arrangements on the urban scale in Horeau's 1868 treatise on urbanism, *Assainissement, embellissements de Paris, ou Édilité urbaine mise à la portée de tout le monde* [Consolidation and Embellishment of Paris, or Urban Administration to be put into Practice throughout the World][11] in the *Gazette des architectes et du bâtiment*, edited by Viollet-le-Duc's son Eugène-Louis and Anatole de Baudot. While framed as a critique of Haussmann's

Figure 12.1. *Projet pour la rue de l'Impératrice,* 1862. *Catalogue des dessins,* 200. Académie d'Architecture.

Second Empire city, Horeau laid out his own utopian vision for Paris by developing his architectural sensibilities into an overarching modernization.

Édilité urbaine is structured as a model for civic improvement with sections for circulation, entry to the city, security, hygiene, and art. Within these prosaic categories of urban amelioration Horeau describes a space of urban luxury. Many proposals stem from unrealized designs that would gain a second life in his utopian city.[12] He would remove the walls to the north of the Archives de France and the gates at the Jardin de Tuileries, Parc Monceau, and the Jardins du Luxembourg to allow for the extension of roadways that would cut wide swaths across the city from north to south. He would remove the fortifications that cut Paris off from its surroundings and replace them with a railway to encircle the city. The circulation of goods and traffic was to be complemented by the circulation of people. He offered his studies for glass enclosures of the city's boulevards to propose a network of glass structures allowing for continuous movement independent of the hour or the weather. These boulevards would pass under the Seine and tunnel through the Butte Montmartre. Glass roofs would cover traditional sites of aristocracy such as the old courtyard of the Louvre and the garden of the Élysée Palace, opening them to the public. He would remove the gates surrounding any private or enclosed gardens of Paris, such as at the Place Royale, illuminate these spaces, and offer amenities such as cafés and gymnasiums for public use both day and night; Place Vendôme would be filled with mats, seats, and illuminated fountains. Lastly, the city was to be devoid of all industry to make way for circulation and consumption. Granaries, arsenals, barracks, hospitals, hospices, prisons, warehouses, boulangeries, and the old ateliers of Saint-Thomas-d'Aquin would move to the outskirts of the city and be replaced by schools for professional, industrial, and commercial training, as well as libraries and conference centers.[13]

The Destruction of Monuments

Walter Benjamin takes the Haussmannization of Paris to be paradigmatic of nineteenth-century phantasmagoria—those "magic lanterns" that suspended the masses between technological mediation and estranging illusion—the essence of a modernity "incapable of responding to new technological capabilities with a new social order."[14] David Harvey has shown that Haussmann's city enabled greater ease of communication and transportation by creating a networked economy to facilitate production, industry, and finance. The workers' quarters that had been strongholds of revolutionary association became townhouses for the bourgeoisie. As the city became an instrument of state liberalism, urban space was itself monetized as financial instruments to fuel a real estate speculation bubble along the corridors of bourgeois habitability.[15] The demolition of the spaces of traditional association were never intended to disempower regimes of privilege; they were to render the entrenchment of bourgeois values as progress. Benjamin described boulevards screened off by canvases to ceremonially unveil some civic monument. He then observed, "the burning of Paris is the worthy conclusion to Baron Haussmann's destruction."[16]

For Benjamin, the barricade destroyed both the physical order of Second Empire phantasmagoria as well as its hold over the masses.

> The barricade is resurrected during the Commune. It is stronger and better designed than ever. It stretches across the great boulevards, often reaching a height of two stories, and shields the trenches behind it. Just as the *Communist Manifesto* ends the age of professional conspirators, so the Commune puts an end to the phantasmagoria that dominates the earliest aspirations of the proletariat.[17]

The phantasmagoria of revolutions from 1789 until the Commune was the illusion that the revolutionary capacity of the proletariat stood apart from any other mode of labor power. The bourgeoise built its political standing upon the alienation of this revolutionary capacity.

Victor Hugo recognized the barricade to be disruption of architectural order in his description of the Revolution of 1848:

You might say: Who built that? You might also say: Who destroyed that? It was the improvisation of ferment. Here! That door! That grating! That shed! That casement! That broken furnace! That cracked pot! Bring everything! Throw on everything! Push, roll, dig, dismantle, overturn, tear down everything! . . . This barricade, chance, disorder, bewilderment, misunderstanding, the unknown, had opposed to it the Constituent Assembly, the sovereignty of the people, universal suffrage, the nation, the republic; it was the Carmagnole defying the Marseillaise.[18]

A door, a casement, a furnace; all are stripped of architectural identity as they become components of the barricade. As Kristin Ross describes the barricade, "Monumental ideals of formal perfection, duration, or immortality, quality of material and integrity of design are replaced by a special kind of *bricolage.*"[19] While many of the barricades produced under the Commune were engineered with remarkable precision, they nevertheless present a soritical paradox (from the Greek *soros,* meaning "heap") wherein an object whose determination as an assemblage of parts cannot be defined according to its constituent makeup.[20]

Hugo and Benjamin both tie the destruction of architectural order by the barricade to the destruction of the political order of the state. For Hugo (a proponent of the conservative revolution) it represents the wanton destruction of political sovereignty by the revolutionary masses. For Benjamin it is the destruction of the phantasmagoria that portray class alliance between the bourgeoisie and the proletariat.

Little is known about Horeau's activities during the Commune. He claimed to have served as "Architect-conservator of public buildings" with an office in the attic of the Hôtel de Ville. Any official records of his tenure would have been lost when the building burned during the *Semaine Sanglante,* the "Bloody Week" in which the government of France brought a brutal end to the experiment of the Paris Commune, destroying much of the city in the process. Only a small collection of drawing fragments, sketches, and thirdhand accounts offer a glimpse of his activity. With the fall of the Commune, Horeau became a political prisoner of the Third Republic, accused of collaboration with the Commune. He denied having any political role in the Commune, describing himself as a minor functionary much like a librarian or an archivist.[21]

Horeau drew a series of vignettes depicting some of the key moments of the Commune, its fall, and his imprisonment.[22] All are of fleeting moments captured in his quick and loose graphic style. In the first scenes, Napoléon III declares war on Prussia "against the public will," and the *Garde Nationale* assembles in Paris. These are followed by the bombardment of Strasbourg, which capitulated to Prussia on August 12, 1870, followed by a demonstration on September 27 in homage to Strasbourg on Place de la Concorde. The next scenes depict the city during the Commune: food shortages, the residents of the radical proletarian neighborhood Bellevue marching on the Hôtel de Ville, and the *Garde Nationale* encamped there. The final set of images depict some of the most notable events of the Commune. The personal residence of Adolphe Thiers, president of the Third Republic, is torn down on orders of the Commune. The next panel shows the felling of the Vendôme Column, ordered destroyed by Gustave Courbet as a "symbol of brute force and false glory." Alfred Darcel places Horeau directly at the scene:

> Presiding over these preparations, I regret to say, was an eminent architect, always the hothead, especially in those times when no one was sure of their own good sense—Mr. Hector Horeau, who only the old cosmopolitans can forgive. Citizen of the universe; for more than thirty years anything that happened in Paris with a foreign air passed through his studio.[23]

The next scene shows the explosion of the *cartoucherie,* a powder magazine on the Champs de Mars, believed to be carried out by the government troops, the *Versaillais*, in retaliation for the Vendôme Column. Lastly, Horeau depicts the barricades around the Tour Saint-Jacques. These vignettes are more than just episodes in a historical moment; their subject is the city itself and its transformation into a radical milieu, beginning with Napoléon III commanding a crowd and ending with the city barricaded by the citizens against the state in exile. They depict a transformation of lived and symbolic space of the city from the occupation of the public realm, to the destruction of monuments, to the architectural defense of the revolution. They describe the gradual realization of the city as a site of radical potentiality. The next set of sketches shows the end of the Commune and its aftermath. Paris smolders from the fires of the *Semaine Sanglante,* following the detention of prisoners and Horeau's own transfer to a raft on the Orne River followed by the military prison at Île-d'Aix.

Only one architectural drawing by Horeau survives from the period of the Commune; it was drawn on the verso of the frontispiece of a copy of his 1841 *Panorama de l'Égypte et de Nubie*.[24] It shows a partial plan and elevation, addressed to the "Citoyens membres de la Commune," of a project to turn the Church of the Madeleine into an "urban omnibus bureau." It is a partial reprise of an 1869 proposal to transform the Madeleine from a monument to Napoléon to a church. There he explained, "The Madeleine, a former temple built for military glory, in no way accommodates Christian ceremony."[25] He had proposed to strip the building of its Napoleonic representation and transform it into a functioning church and civic space. His 1871 proposal goes further to strip the Madeleine of both its imperial and religious significance by turning it into the centerpiece of a civic agglomeration. As Matthew Page points out in his brief on this drawing, we can take this project as an extension of the felling of the Vendôme Column to rid the city of its monuments to imperial domination.[26]

illustration des évenemens de Paris depuis le 4 7bre 1870
a bour de meatouze a de couruption

Napoléon III déclare la guerre aux prussiens contrairement à la volonté publique

La Statue de Strasbourg

démolition de l'hôtel Thiers

rue nationale

la sortie de faubourg d'edmont les parisiens vivres anglais autels déguisés donneur au ?

Colonne vendôme abattue

les hommes conservent les institutions que les régisseurs ?

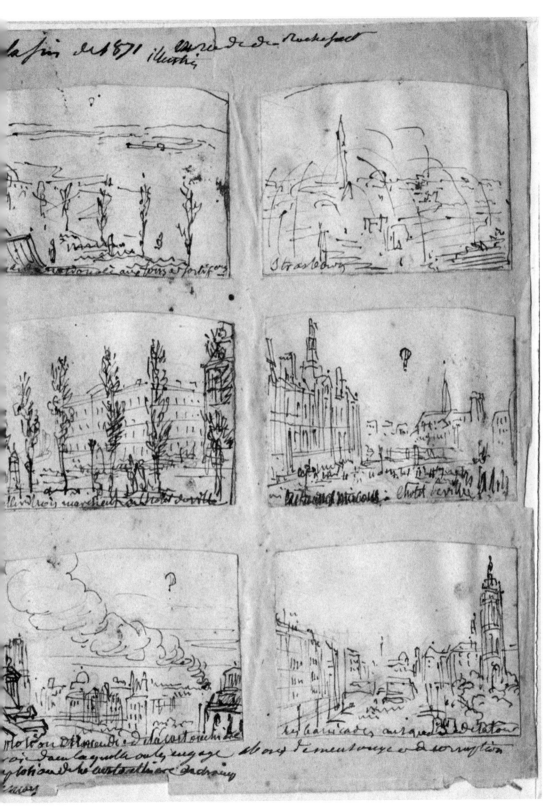

Figure 12.2. Sketches of the Paris Commune, 1871–72. Fonds Hector Horeau, 403j. Archives départementales de la Seine-Saint-Denis.

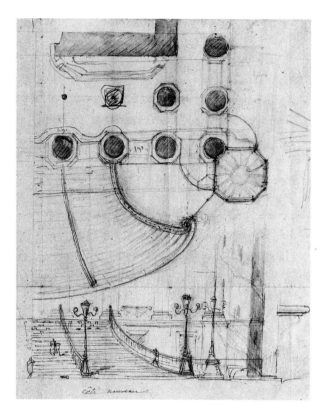

Figure 12.3. Design for converting La Madeleine to an omnibus office, 9 April 1871. DMC 1968.2. Drawing Matter.

Reconstructions

After the Commune, Viollet-le-Duc was a natural choice to lead a survey of the damages to the official buildings and churches of the city.[27] He opened the first issue of the *Encyclopédie d'Architecture* with a call to arms. His article "Les monuments incendie de Paris" opens with an admonition of the Commune and "the despotism of a drunken populace, a permanent orgy, and, after them, or more properly with them, the end of the civilized world."[28] It goes on to fault the complacency of the nation for its humiliating defeat and to call on France to place all of its material and intellectual efforts towards reconstruction.

Under the guise of a reformist proposal for the reconstruction of the city, Viollet-le-Duc then offers a wide-reaching rebuke of the Second Empire. He proposed restoring only the original central building of Hôtel de Ville, "one of the chief works of the late renaissance," and razing the two wings that crowded the original edifice. All superfluous programs, such as its reception rooms and apartments, could someday be placed elsewhere, "when we are once again wealthy and have time to consider such diversions."[29] He had similar advice for the Ministry of Finance, whose compromised autonomy during the Second Empire caused the credit downturn that precipitated the financial crash of 1869.[30] The Conseil d'État held a dubious function in a reconstructed state. Intended to serve as the legal advisor to the executive branch, it became a key instrument of Napoléon III's monopoly on power.[31] In Viollet-le-Duc's estimation the Palais would better be left in ruins: "The Conseil d'État . . . Will there be a Conseil d'État? Meanwhile leave, if you like, these ruins to remain until we find a use for them."[32] As for the Tuileries, Viollet-le-Duc proposed to stop the wings of the Louvre at the pavilions Fleurs and Marsan, preserving only the ground floor of the Palais built by Philibert de l'Orme and the two pavilions by Jean Bullant. "Without prejudging the question of knowing if France will conserve a republican form of government or whether it will once again attempt a monarchy (which we dare not wish for)," he offered "a proper palace to house the president of the Republic."[33]

For Viollet-le-Duc, the collapse of the Second Empire was an institutional failure that could be remedied through architecture. In each case the reconstruction was an opportunity for political reform. He would remove political influence from ministerial functions. Ceremonial spaces would be replaced by efficient civic administration, ministries compromised by the Second Empire would have no place in the reconstruction, and France would remain a republic.

As a prisoner of the Third Republic, Horeau rendered his criticisms of Haussmann's Paris as counterprojects to the reconstruction. He proposed to transform Charles Garnier's Opéra—a building that was not yet complete—from an opulent work of Beaux-Arts eclecticism into an iron and glass structure. He would remove the loggia facing the Boulevard de l'Opéra and replace it with a uniform curtain wall; replace the side domes and carriage entrances with windows to illuminate and ventilate the interior; remove the central dome to improve drainage; install elevators at the corners and replace the monumental staircase with lateral stairs serving the entire building; and improve visibility and acoustics in the theater. Shops would be located on the ground floor, cafés and enclosed gardens in the attic. The expanded theater would accommodate assemblies of 12,000 people.[34] Horeau proposed to democratize the formal and cultural properties of the building. He would eliminate the monumental markers of bourgeois culture—the classical façade with its projected balcony at the *piano nobile*, the central dome, and the ceremonial entrance and staircase—and replace them with public amenities throughout the building and spaces for mass gatherings. Administration of the Opéra and all other public buildings would take place at Horeau's proposed Central Office for the City of Paris to be located on the site of the old Salle Le Peletier, Paris's Opera until 1821.[35]

Horeau also offered a counterproject for the Hôtel de Ville that left the ruins of the old Hôtel in place while proposing a new building in the adjoining Place de l'Hôtel de Ville—which he had earlier depicted as a site of revolutionary assembly during the Commune. Horeau called his Hôtel de Ville a "monumental fantasy," a vast interior garden enclosed

Figure 12.4. *Projet pour un hôtel de ville.* Ville de Paris, 1871. Bibliothèque historique, MS-3460(2).

within "durable, incombustible, polychromatic materials, metals, granite, terracotta, majolicas, crystals, and large-scale enamels."[36] It would be a vast enclosure of disparate elements buttressing a billowing dome tethered to the volume by stalactite iron lamps.

Kristen Ross offers a notion of "communal luxury," a term taken from the manifesto by Eugène Pottier of the *Fédération des Artistes* under the Commune who spoke on behalf of the artist, architects, and decorative artists of Paris.[37] For Pottier, communal luxury was the democratization of the arts—breaking the distinction between high and low arts by granting decorative artists the same copyright protections reserved for painters and sculptors and bringing it out of the salons to make it available and accessible to the people. For Ross, communal luxury makes a broader demand that beauty become a public utility, shared in common through the engagement of art into everyday life.[38] The practice of the Commune allowed Parisians the opportunity to bring the debates taking place in the worker's clubs and the practice of revolutionary association taking place in the metropolis to the factory floor. Writing on the Commune, Marx noted that "with labor emancipated, every man becomes a working man, and productive labor ceases to be a class attribute."[39] The general form of labor only appears through the particular form of its alienation via surplus or stockpiling.[40] Ending the alienation of labor ends the category of labor as such, leaving in the metropolis a new signification of work. The elevation of the decorative arts (having nearly been relegated to mere labor under the Second Empire) to art as such stands in here for the general elevation of labor in general under the Commune. Similarly, considering this art as a public utility marks a shift for labor to the public good rather than private interest. In the end, it is the liberation of labor in general that provides, per Pottier, the "future splendors and the Universal Republic."

In the final years of the Second Empire, Beaux-Arts architecture began to exhibit a montage of motifs that theorists such as Paul Sédille would promote as "universal eclecticism": the absolute synthesis of historical styles as the fullest realization of Beaux-Arts style (take, for instance, Ballu's Sainte-Trinité). These now read less as synthesis than as crisis. As the ossification of Republican values under the imperial regime, they display an incapacity to maintain and convey meaning—representing an anguished desire to mean without the capacity to do so. The metals, granite, terracotta, majolicas, and enamels that fill Horeau's iron and glass halls after the Commune both elevate the decorative arts and integrate them into the public realm of the metropolis. They fulfill the call of the *Fédération des Artistes* to do both, and in doing so re-signify the investment of the worker in the space of the metropolis. Moreover, the bricolage of these elements to create a lush civic interior repudiates the syntheses of universal eclecticism that marks a late style of Beaux-Arts architecture. Like the barricade's destruction of a coherent relation between constitutive elements, decorative surfaces of differing materials stand in indeterminate relation to each other, privileging bricolage over formal unity.

Metropolis against the State

Horeau's drawings through 1870 are populated by leisurely figures of a bourgeois class. They ride on horseback or in carriages; they stroll the boulevards, alone or in pairs, with hats and canes; couples dance in lush atmospheres enclosed within high iron canopies. After the Commune, the inhabitants of Horeau's architecture change. The carriages are no longer out for leisurely strolls but ride with determination down the busy boulevards. Individuals become nondescript, solitary figures rendered in vague black smudges and barely distinguishable from the shadows cast at their feet as they wander aimlessly through giant iron volumes and across wide boulevards.

Reconstruction of Paris after the Commune—both political and architectural—pursued a policy of forgetting; no trace of it was to remain in the public imaginary.[41] The reconstruction of the Hôtel de Ville—the political center of the Commune—by Théodore Ballu and Édouard Deperthes is a key example; it suppressed the historical memory of the Commune while adhering to Viollet-le-Duc's call for administrative reform. The architects completely razed the burnt-out building and built a nearly exact replica in its place. While differences in the exterior of the current building are nearly indiscernible from historical photographs of the original, the interior underwent a complete renovation. The old Hôtel was assembled piecemeal from the sixteenth century on. Ballu and Deperthes determined that it had suffered from too many functions jammed together and decided to remove the ceremonial functions such as reception rooms and apartments for ministers

Figure 12.5. *Vue perspective et cavalière de Paris avec les principaux monuments projetés par Horeau*, 1871. *Catalogue des dessins*, 227. Académie d'Architecture.

to allow for a more efficient administration. No traces of the revolutionary city were to remain as reconstruction-as-reform would be generalized throughout the city.

Horeau rendered his Hôtel de Ville as a cutaway perspective such that the viewer can see both its tiered exterior enclosure and its vast interior volume. A low fence marks the cut line of the drawing, as if the building itself was to be left agape and an architectural element was needed to keep visitors from wandering across the graphic divide. Recalling Horeau's covered arcades of the previous decade, this opening of the building's interior to the surrounding city integrates space into the metropolitan circuits of exchange. Where the rationalized administration of Ballu and Deperthes's Hôtel de Ville sits autonomously from its context, Horeau's project engages the vast labor, commercial, industrial, and consumer assemblage that is the metropolis. The metropolis penetrates the envelope of the building, occupying its interior. This is the metropolis that Horeau depicts in its general form in his 1871 *Plan de Paris*.

Horeau's Hôtel de Ville, Opéra, and Central Office were to be just three components of a larger alternative to the reconstruction of Paris. Horeau's plan for reconstruction is projected as an oblique panorama in his 1871 *Plan de Paris*, a rendering that appears at first glance to be a graphic depiction of his *Édilité urbaine*.[42] Like his 1869 project, it describes a combination of existing buildings and his built and unbuilt works of the prior forty years. I would argue that the stakes of Horeau's 1871 *Plan de Paris* differ fundamentally from his *Édilité urbaine*. The earlier proposal showed the utopian amelioration of the class antagonisms of the industrial metropolis. After the Commune this was no longer possible.

The bold and frantic lines of Horeau's *Plan de Paris* transform Haussmann's linear *Grands Boulevards* into sweeping curves that show a dynamic city.[43] He replaces the ruins of Haussmann's urban agglomeration with covered galleries, fantastical iron and glass volumes, and illuminated arcades. Horeau's Hôtel de Ville is shown at the site of the ruined building; his proposals to renovate the Opèra and the Madeleine as well as his project for the Central Office are all present; an 1843 project for the Tuileries is marked in bold where the destroyed building had stood. The Vendôme Column remains absent. Rather than offer a utopian rationalization of the urban agglomeration through a redress of the Second Empire city's shortcomings, Horeau monumentalizes the destruction of the city. He encases Paris within iron and glass structures whose plush decoration marks them as commons of labor, extending the vicissitudes of the metropolis to its erstwhile sites of administration and control. At the moment of the Commune's erasure, Horeau demands the maintenance of its aims and objectives.

I am not arguing that the Commune somehow radicalized Horeau in such a way that he began to replace his utopian visions for Paris with revolutionary ones. Rather, I suggest that the lived practice of the Commune and the reconfigurations of urban space by its constituents formed a notion of the metropolis that would have been unthinkable under the Second Empire. If the Metropolis is, in the last instance, a mechanism of capitalist development, then its logic is inexorably linked to the bourgeois state. Massimo Cacciari argues that the enlistment of the state to resolve class conflict through the organization of capital brings about the condition of the metropolis. "A Metropolis without a State, a Metropolis outside of a rationally organized State, is an impossibility."[44] I would argue that in Horeau we find an alternative metropolis-as-such that does not amount to the subject's dissolution by capital but rather becomes a site of alterity and the production of alternate subjectivities.

The experience of the Commune made possible a vision of the metropolis as an indeterminate political space. Paolo Virno describes a "subjectivity of the multitude" distinct from that of the people. Following Hobbes, he adopts the category of the people as formed through the absolute right of a sovereign to determine the ground of subjectification through the form of the state. The multitude, by contrast, is a self-forming body engaged in the collective transformation of the poetic, political, and productive grounds of individuation—an open participation formulating the general intellect. This formation of the subject is the continuous engagement with the indeterminate ground of subjectification. This subjectivity as self-formation of the self, for Virno, can never be transferred or delegated to a sovereign.[45] Drawing on Virno, Michael Hardt and Antonio Negri describe the Metropolis as "*the inorganic body,* that is, the body without organs of the multitude."[46] Per Cacciari, the Metropolis is the organization of productive life, and as such, the instrument of alienation.[47] But it is also the site of happenstance, the unpredictable and the aleatory—for Hardt and Negri, it is the continuous encounter with alterity.[48] These circuits of cultural and productive exchange fashion a proletarian common.

I propose that this notion of the *common*—a space of encounter in which aleatory relations continuously reconfigure the grounds of an ongoing process of subjectification—is on display in Horeau's drawings after the *Commune*. While formally similar to the *grands magasins* of the next decade—as well as his own work through the previous decade—they are different in intent. Filigreed luxury elevates labor into art. The circuits of movement that penetrate the interior of civic administration render the autonomy of biopolitical control of the metropolis impossible. The sweeping boulevards of the city in Horeau's *Plan de Paris* do not dismantle the metropolitan circuits of exchange, but speed them up. Along these corridors, "architectural fantasies" and sites of alterity stage the sites of encounter that fashion the proletariat as a multitude and open a space for new forms of political sovereignty.

Notes

1. Eugène-Emmanuel Viollet-le-Duc, *Mémoire sur la défense de Paris, Septembre 1870–Janvier 1871* (Paris: A. Morel, 1871).
2. Viollet-le-Duc, 1–4.

3. Jean Baptiste Massillon Rouvet, *Viollet-le-Duc et Alphand au siège de Paris* (Paris: Librairies-imprimeries réunies, 1892), 45.
4. Paul Gout, *Viollet-le-Duc, sa vie, son oeuvre, sa doctrine* (Paris: É. Champion, 1914), 136–39.
5. Two major surveys of Horeau's work were published in 1979 and 1980. Jacques Barda, Vincent Folléa, and Pierre Granveaud, eds., *Hector Horeau, 1801–1872* (Paris: Centre d'études et de recherches architecturales, 1979); Paul Dufournet, *Hector Horeau, précurseur: Idées, techniques, architecture* (Paris: Académie d'architecture, 1980). In 1991 Marcel Cerf and Jacques Zwirn published a collection of sketches by Horeau produced during and after the commune: Marcel Cerf and Jacques Zwirn, *L'architecte et la Commune: Les dessins d'Hector Horeau* (La Garenne-Colombes: Espace européen, 1991).
6. Sigfried Giedion, *Building in France, Building in Iron, Building in Ferroconcrete*, trans. Duncan Berry (Santa Monica: Getty Center for the History of Art and the Humanities, 1995).
7. I employ Marshall Berman's terms, which remain central to this scholarship. Marshall Berman, *All That Is Solid Melts into Air: The Experience of Modernity* (New York: Viking Penguin, 1988), 212–48; Peter Sloterdijk, *In the World Interior of Capital: For a Philosophical Theory of Globalization*, trans. Wieland Hoban (Cambridge: Polity Press, 2013), 169–76.
8. Brian Stableford, "Introduction," in *Paris in the Year 2000* (Tarzana: Black Coat Press, 2013).
9. Tony Moilin, *Paris en l'an 2000* (Paris: Librarie de la Renaissance, 1869); Tony Moilin, *Paris in the Year 2000*, trans. Brian Stableford (Tarzana: Black Coat Press, 2013); Nathaniel Walker discusses Moilin in relation to Haussmann's Paris: Nathaniel Robert Walker, "Lost in the City of Light: Dystopia and Utopia in the Wake of Haussmann's Paris," *Utopian Studies* 25, no. 1 (2014): 24–51.
10. Moilin, *Paris in the Year 2000*.
11. Hector Horeau, "Assainissement, embellissements de Paris, ou Édilité urbaine mise à la portée de tout le monde," *Gazette des architectes et du bâtiment* 6, no. 6 (1868): 41–48; no. 7 (1869): 49–57.
12. Boudon and Loyer detail the works from Horeau's oeuvre in *Édilité urbaine*. Françoise Boudon and François Loyer, "Catalogue Des Dessins et Des Œuvres Figurées d'Hector Horeau," in *Hector Horeau, 1801–1872*, ed. Jacques Barda, Vincent Folléa, and Pierre Granveaud (Paris: Centre d'études et de recherches architecturales, 1979), 23–137.
13. Horeau's proposals in *Édilité urbaine* beg comparison to Le Corbusier's 1922 Ville Contemporaine, which proposed to resolve class antagonism through the rational distribution of urban amenities and, particularly, his Plan Voisin three years later, that like Horeau proposed this utopian schema in the heart of Haussmann's city. It is at the moment of revolution's avoidance that these projects diverge.
14. Walter Benjamin, "Paris, Capital of the Nineteenth Century," in *The Arcades Project*, ed. Rolf Tiedemann, trans. Howard Eiland and Kevin McLaughlin (Cambridge, Mass.: Belknap Press of Harvard University Press, 1999), 26.
15. David Harvey, *Paris, Capital of Modernity* (New York: Routledge, 2003).
16. Benjamin, "Paris, Capital of the Nineteenth Century," 24–25.
17. Benjamin, "Paris, Capital of the Nineteenth Century," 24.
18. Victor Hugo, *Les Misérables,* trans. Lee Fahnestock and Norman MacAfee (New York: New

American Library, 1987). The Carmagnole was a satirical revolutionary hymn named after the short jackets worn by the sans-culottes.
19. Kristin Ross, *The Emergence of Social Space: Rimbaud and the Paris Commune* (Minneapolis: University of Minnesota Press, 1988), 36.
20. Dominic Hyde, "Sorites Paradox," in *The Stanford Encyclopedia of Philosophy*, ed. Edward N. Zalta, 2014, http://plato.stanford.edu/archives/spr2014/entries/sorites-paradox/.
21. Hector Horeau letter to Bailly, May 30, 1871, in *Hector Horeau, précurseur*, 232–33.
22. These images are reproduced in Cerf and Zwirn, *L'architecte et la Commune*. I follow their historical notes on these sketches.
23. Alfred Darcel, "Les Musées, les arts, et les artistes pendant le siege (3e article)," *Gazette des Beaux-Arts* 5, no. 175 (January 1, 1872): 149.
24. Matthew Page, "Aux Citoyens Membres de La Commune Attachés à La Commissions Des Services Publiques," Drawing Matter, September 7, 2018, https://www.drawingmatter.org/sets/drawing-week/hector-horeau/.
25. Boudon and Loyer, "Catalogue Des Dessins," 126.
26. Page, "Aux Citoyens Membres."
27. Eugène-Emmanuel Viollet-le-Duc, "Etat des dégradations causées tans à l'extérieur qu'à l'intérieur de la Cathédrale de Paris par suite du commencement à incendie alluminé le 24 Mai 1871" (Paris: Archives Nationale de France, 1791), F21 496, Beaux-Arts.
28. Eugène-Emmanuel Viollet-le-Duc, "Les monuments incendie de Paris," *Encyclopédie d'architecture: Revue mensuelle des travaux publics et particuliers* I (1872): 1.
29. Viollet-le-Duc, "Les monuments incendie," 1
30. Roger Price, *The French Second Empire: An Anatomy of Political Power* (New York: Cambridge University Press, 2001), 60–61.
31. Price, *The French Second Empire*, 79–80.
32. Viollet-le-Duc, "Les monuments incendie," 5.
33. Viollet-le-Duc, "Les monuments incendie," 2.
34. Commentary by Horeau for a "Project to Redress the Opera." In Boudon and Loyer, "Catalogue Des Dessins," 128.
35. Boudon and Loyer, "Catalogue Des Dessins," 129.
36. Horeau's commentary on his 1871 project for a Hôtel de Ville. In Boudon and Loyer, "Catalogue Des Dessins," 130.
37. Kristin Ross, *Communal Luxury: The Political Imaginary of the Paris Commune*, English-language edition (London: Verso, 2015); Commission Fédérale des Artistes, "Rapport de La Commission Fédérale Des Artistes (Peintres, Sculpteurs et Graveurs En Médailles, Architectes, Graveurs et Lithographes, Artistes Industrielles), Au Citoyen Vaillant, Délégué à l'instruction Publique, Sur Les Réformes á Apporter Dans l'administration Des Beaux-Arts," *Journal officiel de la République française sous la Commune*, May 10, 1871.
38. Ross, *Communal Luxury*, 54.
39. Karl Marx, "The Civil War in France," in *The First International and After* (London: Verso, 2010), 212.
40. Gilles Deleuze and Félix Guattari, *A Thousand Plateaus: Capitalism and Schizophrenia*, trans. Brian Massumi (Minneapolis: University of Minnesota Press, 1987), 490–91.

41. Colette E. Wilson, *Paris and the Commune, 1871–78: The Politics of Forgetting* (Manchester: Manchester University Press, 2007).
42. Boudon and Loyer reach this conclusion. They argue, however, that the revised project doesn't go nearly as far as his earlier iteration. "Urbanistically, the document is disappointing. It is less the figuration of an original project than the representation of official and unrealized schemes. All or nearly all the streets traced by Horeau are or will be executed by the Haussmann administration." Boudon and Loyer, "Catalogue Des Dessins," 133.
43. Horeau based his *Plan de Paris* on Marie-Hilaire Guesnu's 1867 map *Excursion dans Paris sans voitures,* a tourist map employing an elevated perspective view to show the prominent monuments of the city arrayed around an axis defined by the Champs-Élysées, running from the Louvre to the Arc de Triomphe. Boudon and Loyer, "Catalogue Des Dessins," 133. Following the tradition of Paris maps up to the middle of the eighteenth century, it takes an east–west rather than north–south orientation.
44. Massimo Cacciari, *Architecture and Nihilism: On the Philosophy of Modern Architecture,* trans. Stephen Sartarelli (New Haven: Yale University Press, 1993), 31; Correspondingly, for Tafuri the end point of the metropolis is in Hilberseimer's dissolution of the architectural object to abstract coordinates across infinite dimensions. Manfredo Tafuri, *Architecture and Utopia: Design and Capitalist Development,* trans. Barbara Luigia La Penta (Cambridge, Mass.: MIT Press, 1976).
45. Paolo Virno, *A Grammar of the Multitude: For an Analysis of Contemporary Forms of Life* (Cambridge: Semiotext(e), 2003).
46. Michael Hardt and Antonio Negri, *Commonwealth* (Cambridge, Mass.: Belknap Press of Harvard University Press, 2009), 249.
47. Cacciari, *Architecture and Nihilism,* 3–22.
48. Hardt and Negri critique Cacciari's "negative thought" as identifying relentless subjugation of reason to power without recognizing the capacities of resistance to power to form new subjectivities. *Commonwealth,* 114.

Chapter 13

The Racial Allegories of Frank Lloyd Wright's Prairie Style

Charles L. Davis II

> A free America, democratic in the sense that our forefathers intended it to be, means just this *individual* freedom for all, rich or poor, or else this system of government we call democracy is only an expedient to enslave man to the Machine and make him like it.
>
> —Frank Lloyd Wright, *Modern Architecture* (1930)

Reassessing the Racial Politics of Wright's Prairie Style

From his birth in 1867 to his death in 1959, Frank Lloyd Wright's life and career was entirely circumscribed by the racial attitudes of the Jim Crow era, a period in American politics that reversed the constitutional gains made by African Americans after the Civil War.[1] During the late nineteenth century, white supremacist ideologies animated the resentment of retrenched southern whites, fueling urban segregation in the North and the violence of lynching on Black subjects who tried to preserve their status as equal citizens. American politicians would not legally secure the full rights of African Americans again until the passage of the Civil Rights Act of 1964, almost a full century after the Civil War ended. And this legal precedent has been destabilized by recent Supreme Court decisions that place Black rights in newly precarious positions.[2] While this backdrop strongly suggests that American democracy was heavily curtailed by a racially exclusive conception of the citizen-subject, this period also gave birth to one of the most influential American architecture movements ever to develop in the United States. Wright's Prairie Style has been praised by architectural historians past and present for developing a "democratic architecture" that materializes the inherent promise of America.[3] How are we to reconcile the apparent discrepancies that exist between a progressive interpretation of national politics in Wright's architecture and the constrained racial politics for Black Americans in this very same era? What did it mean to create an architectural representation of American democracy during the Jim Crow era? And is Wright's architecture, which is meant to express the very best of American democracy, compromised in any way by its pragmatic limitations?

The answers to these questions cannot be found by considering Wright's architecture as a simple material exponent of the racial politics of the Jim Crow era. Wright often challenged the politics of his day to favor the birth of a suburban and agrarian nation that did not fully exist in his time. Nor can the answers be found via an isolated examination of the architect's words. Wright, like his mentor Louis Sullivan, was fond of poetic expressions and philosophical incantations that had little meaning outside of architectural discourse. Instead, one must find answers by identifying the racial politics that Wright inherited from his forefathers at the turn of the twentieth century when he first authored the Prairie Style of architecture. Despite his own personal belief, Wright was continuing a long tradition of white material culture within the United States that argued for its status as a new form of autochthonous culture. By returning to the racial politics established by the founding fathers of this nation, it is possible to limn the deeper meaning of Wright's democratic architecture in both its progressive and regressive manifestations. I argue that Wright's Prairie Style simultaneously constitutes one of the most politically progressive portraits of "democratic architecture" that could have been defined in the Jim Crow era, while also constituting an architecture against democracy insofar as his architecture fails to decolonize the interpretation of the body politic that dehumanized and discriminated against racial minorities seeking to belong as equal citizens. Instead of dismissing or minimizing the racial animus of Wright's architecture as an anomaly of the Jim Crow era or retroactively purging it of its inconvenient content, the following chapter uses the lens of settler colonial theory to examine the ways that Wright's Prairie Style materializes the deep racial commitments of American democracy from its founding. Placing Wright's architectural designs within this longer political context reveals the numerous ways that his buildings operated as diachronic symbols of universal American progress while synchronically embodying the practical limitations of Jim Crow politics in the late nineteenth and early twentieth centuries.

The often-cited notion that Wright established a democratic architecture reflective of the common culture of the United States in part stems from textual references to "democracy" within the pages of his writings. An early example of this appears in the essay "A Home in a Prairie Town," published in 1901 in *Ladies' Home Journal*, officially announcing the maturation of his Prairie Style.[4] He wrote more books in the 1930s and 40s in which he developed a Usonian system of design and a projective utopian plan for remodeling American conurbations in an exhibit entitled "Broadacre City."[5] New titles such as *An Organic Architecture: An Architecture of Democracy* and *When Democracy Builds* revised the architect's earlier notions.[6] But what did it mean when Wright claimed that his architecture was democratic? Did it constitute a physical space for engaging in the political practices of American governance, an interpretation that would place his work on the same register as the White House or the Capitol? Or did he intend for his architecture to operate as a humbler and more metaphorical symbol of the common values of the American public? Over the course of his career, both of these modalities get implicated in Wright's architecture. Yet he characteristically gives an entirely architectural explanation for the formal idioms he established. Building upon the organic philosophy of his mentor Louis Sullivan, Wright claims that only architectural forms that emerge directly from the everyday conditions of American culture can ever formally reference this culture. Just as the flora and fauna of the Midwestern prairie naturally emerged from the landscape, he reasoned, so must an indigenous architecture that was worthy of the label "American architecture." Of course, in retrospect Wright was probably equally indebted to the historical precedents found in Chicago's Oak Park neighborhood. These included newly constructed Victorian houses that had a documented history of flowing interior spaces anchored by a fireplace for regulating important social functions.[7] What is unique about Wright's architecture is its novel integration in interior and exterior forms, all commonly found in earlier architectures, but cleverly synthesized into an *ur-form* expressive of the trends of its time.

Settler colonial theory provides a unique analytical lens for outlining the racial politics that Wright inherited from the political structures established at the founding of the republic. Such a reading traces the hegemonic function of whiteness that continued to operate in the late nineteenth century when Wright was beginning to articulate his idea of the Prairie Style. As Lorenzo Veracini and Patrick Wolfe note in their studies of settler colonial history, the United States used great violence and oppression to secure its status as a wealthy democracy. Its adherence to racial capitalism is not an incidental event established by the taking of Indigenous lands or the enslavement of African laborers but a fundamental structure of American politics. As the historical strategy of limiting the freedoms of people of color ran in opposition to the purported national ideals of universal freedom for all, white elites created a series of national mythologies and new white racial identities that would serve as ideological cover for this protracted tradition of democracy. Within the political context of a settler colonial state, Wright's Prairie Style architecture operates as a material analogue of the national myths behind democratic culture that legitimize the settler colonial politics that stoked the racial divisions that have subtended American liberalism from its founding.

The Settler Colonial Politics of the American Prairie

Veracini and Wolfe define *settler colonialism* as a form of colonial government that establishes a permanent political structure to preserve the rights and privileges of a settler group over those of existing Indigenous and subsequent immigrant groups.[8] The feature that distinguishes settler colonial states from other types of colonial powers is the occupational form it takes: it seeks to transform the colony into a permanent home, which in turn regulates the historical pattern of land ownership and sovereignty rights established therein. Another important feature of settler colonial states is the common rubric of national myths and propagandistic narratives it generates to legitimize the settler groups' monopolization of natural resources. According to Veracini, settler groups aim to replace the existing Indigenous population, both literally and metaphorically, in order to make their new home permanent.[9] This occupational strategy is distinct from those taken by traditional western colonies, which operate as temporary extensions of a metropole or homeland. Settler colonists then secure their political rights through a combination of overt state violence (i.e., through actions that target the land and sovereignty rights of existing Indigenous groups) and the formulation of soft forms of political propaganda to legitimize their control of contested local amenities and resources.[10] Contemporary scholars of settler colonial states tend to concentrate their research on state propaganda and the political narratives invented to depict the settler as either a new type of Indigenous subject or a naturally superior race or ethnicity. In the United States, nationalist propaganda has taken many forms, from the political doctrine of Manifest Destiny to the demonization of Indigenous and immigrant groups. Another form we should consider is the hegemonic role of "American architecture" movements that have operated as political propaganda, especially by romanticizing the material culture and social practices of white settler communities. An examination of these cultural forms would extend the scholarly examination of media associated with settler colonial propaganda.

During the nineteenth century, the notion of a wide-open prairie was a common trope within narrative depictions of Manifest Destiny. It is rendered as a bucolic and peaceful setting that could emerge only after the domestication of the hostile frontier. This natural trope was not accidental, as such imagery offered settler groups a discursive tool for depicting themselves as new indigenes.[11] An obvious example of this is the structural opposition maintained between representations of seemingly virtuous but hardened "Cowboys" against the savage and lawless "Indians" of early Westerns, even as the names, customs, and aesthetic motifs of Native Americans were appropriated in real time to designate the names of new settler communities. The frontier was perceived to require civilizing, and within the paradigm of Manifest Destiny the main civilizing forces were Christianity, Enlightenment rationalism, and European notions of capitalist land ownership and development. This historical pattern of literal and symbolic erasure of Indigenous peoples became a leitmotif of the nineteenth-century search for an autochthonous or "aboriginal" style of architecture in the United States.[12] Even as late as 1945, Wright celebrated the continued momentum of America's Manifest Destiny in the form of his evolving architectural style.[13] As Veracini notes, the parallel strategies of literal and symbolic Indigenous replacement coexist within the nation's political framework by renewing themselves throughout the life of the settler colony.

These recurring cycles of mythmaking deflect and neutralize the counterclaims of sovereignty made by the previous native populations or competing immigrant groups. This phenomenon helps explain the historical endurance of white nativist myths in the United States, even during the Jim Crow era, as the Constitution has undergone revisions through amendments, juridical interpretations, and new laws expanding and contracting its powers.

As discussed above, the political structure inaugurated within the settler colony of the United States established legal protections for the initial waves of European settlers that elevated their sovereign rights over those of the previous Indigenous population, most notably in the racialized patterns of land ownership and self-governing rights. However, this political structure also works against the guaranteed rights of subsequent waves of immigrants deemed incapable of assimilating the social norms and political values of the ruling elite, even if these social groups are also white and European. Wolfe and Veracini's refinements of settler colonial theory, which began in the fields of anthropology, sociology, and American studies in the 1970s, accounts for the discrimination of subsequent waves of "exogenous" groups that arrive after the first wave of immigrants, both literally and in national myths.[14] These outsiders have historically included white ethnic immigrants that arrived from Central Europe, Eastern Europe, and other lands outside of the protestant-controlled Anglo-Saxon migrants of the original thirteen colonies—places such as Poland, Ireland, Italy, and other non-Germanic lands. Another group of citizens with contingent status in the United States includes most nonwhite laborers brought to the nation to serve as a captive and inexpensive labor force, such as African slaves and Chinese laborers. While any group of immigrants can theoretically be absorbed into the body politic, their status as equal citizens depends upon their perceived level of assimilation of certain cultural norms, which has historically been contingent upon elite perceptions of racial and class fitness of an individual.[15] Over time, the initial restrictions for white land tenure established to dispossess Indigenous occupants have been expanded to limit the rights of other nonassimilable exogenous groups, such as the protective covenants used against African Americans in housing deeds during the interwar and postwar periods.[16]

The triadic structure of Indigenous, settler, and exogenous groups within settler colonial states requires constant interaction and negotiation to maintain the stability of the state. In terms of racial identity, the initial acts of settler dominance over Indigenous and exogenous groups institutes a pattern of symbolic replacement that requires the settler to perform their native and immigrant status, even when these identities conflict with one another. Within the political context of the United States, this ritual creates a complex field of possibility for performing whiteness as a racial identity: a true citizen not only belongs to the heartland of America but also values his European lineage for connecting him to the most civilized states of the globe. The polarization of Indigenous and exogenous identities in settler origin myths requires the state's social elites to internalize a contradictory sense of self to maintain their legitimation of exclusive legal rights and privileges.

Veracini and Wolfe's schematic model of settler colonial politics enables us to more competently assess the latent hypocrisies inherent to democratic liberalism as a governing philosophy in the United States, both at a national level and at the level of artistic representation. Despite the emancipatory claims associated with American democracy as the beacon of freedom and individualism in the Western world, the long history of white supremacy appears to maintain the purported aims of a settler colonial regime: the dominance of a white settler hegemony is maintained against all other counterclaims of shared governance. In addition, the principle of assimilation guarantees that the social inclusion of exogenous groups will not structurally alter the social hierarchies established (and symbolically maintained) by the nation-state. Within the field of architectural history, a settler colonialist reading of American architecture movements complicates a pluralistic interpretation of Wright's Prairie Style buildings, as they rarely challenge the founding mythology of the nation-state. This structural consistency provides an opportunity to explore the hidden ways that Wright's architecture operates as ideological cover for the whiteness of our existing system of governance.

The Fireplace as Indigenous Replacement

Wright's organic interpretation of style establishes a mode of design that synthetically integrates the political, economic, and aesthetic elements of the site into an integrated representation of prairie culture. This tableau establishes a horticultural plinth for Wright's buildings that analogically recalls the horizontal orientation of agricultural activities of the agrarian state. A representative case study of this arrangement is the Darwin D. Martin complex in Buffalo, New York. The Martin complex is a collection of buildings that brings together at least three discrete scales of domesticity: the single resident's apartment (for the chauffeur), a gardener's cottage, and a single-family home both with servants (Martin house) and without them (Barton house).[17] Wright's consistent separation of the symbolic functions of the fireplace (as a symbol of the family hearth) from the stove (as a literal space for cooking food in the kitchen), even when the living space is reserved for a servant, provides a unique context for the white homeowner to symbolically replace the premodern modes of living stereotypically associated with the Indigenous subjects of the past.

The importance of the hearth in the Martin complex is anticipated by several nineteenth-century pictorial representations of national belonging. George Caleb Bingham's *Daniel Boone Escorting Settlers through the Cumberland Gap* (1851–52) tellingly portrays white settlers claiming the Indigenous expertise required to navigate the frontier. Boone, who is centralized in the frame, figuratively provides the guiding light required to move through the dark terrain. Bingham's use of light projects Boone to

Figure 13.1. Winslow Homer, *Campfire*, 1880 (public domain). The Metropolitan Museum of Art, Gift of Josephine Pomeroy Hendrick, in the name of Henry Keney Pomeroy, 1927.

the foreground of the composition as he literally provides a light for the eye to navigate the darkness beyond. Winslow Homer's *Campfire* (1880) is another vivid painting that represents the rustic and romantic setting of the white frontiersman, this time using an open fire to warm the interior of a makeshift tent. Again, the separation of foreground and background is accomplished by highlighting the mountain man's implements, from his raging fire to his open tipi. These images establish a mythological origin point for the beginning of American culture, one that rebrands the white settler as a new origin point for a modernist American culture. Homer's image unifies the symbolic and pragmatic functions of the hearth that are subsequently separated in the Victorian interior to fit a later stage of cultural development.

It is fruitful to read the Martin complex as a material codification of a modern stage of American civilization, one that exists beyond the practical realities of the untamed frontier with all of its dangers to one that develops the spatial practices of white cultural elites in the now-domesticated prairie. At least one architectural historian has characterized Wright's site strategy for the Martin complex as an aggregated campsite intended to collect every relocated member of the Martin family in Buffalo, New York.[18] Martin's occupation of the landscape recalls the caravan of wagons depicted in romantic portraits of frontier life, where Euro-American settlers struggled to establish new homesteads that would become the basis of a new town. As a complex, Wright transforms Martin's family retreat into an encyclopedic catalog of what his Prairie Style could accomplish: "You have the very large Martin house, for the wealthy; the Barton house, appropriate for a middle-class family; an apartment in the Carriage House; servants' quarters in the main house; and the very compact Gardener's Cottage."[19] In this higher phase of civilization, the white native develops a Euro-American modernity that advances the current state of American arts and letters, one that leaves behind the rustic state of Native American society (at least as popularly depicted within American mythology).

The racial embodiment of whiteness in the Martin house is specifically enacted by a metaphorical transformation of the homeowner into a native subject of the Americas, one who can recall the early stages of frontier life as a prelude to reengaging with the present. These performances take place within the combined areas of the Victorian home where the fireplace anchors important social activities. Within the Martin house, a massive freestanding fireplace immediately across from the front entrance anchors a combined space that connects the living room, dining room, library, and sitting rooms near the northernmost projecting porch of the floor plan. While this space is massive in terms of its horizontal extents, a sense of warmth and coziness is achieved by placing a band of horizontal molding overhead to create a datum that reduces the interior scale. Within this dimly lit area, an open fireplace serves as a natural focal point of the room, which provides a unique source of light to the interior. The dark-colored interior Roman brick and gilded mortar lines of the primary walls amplify the phenomenal effects of firelight within the interior, much as Homer's campfire would have done in the great outdoors.[20] However, in this new context Darwin Martin could emulate the naturalism of his ancestors' frontier life without endangering his personal safety or that of his family. Everything was provided within a cozy interior. Wright's design is an American version of the domestic ethnography the French architect Viollet-le-Duc established at Villa la Vedette.[21]

And what meaning did Wright's ornamentation develop, as it consisted of geometrical simplifications of Japanese and pre-Columbian artistic motifs?[22] These visual references would have provided the Martin family with a virtual catalog of mankind's natural history, which would have been useful for comparing the mythological origins of the white settler native with those of other indigenes across time:

> The appreciation of beauty on the part of primitive peoples, Mongolian, Indian, Arab, Egyptian, Greek and Goth, was unerring. Because of this their work is coming home to us today in another truer Renaissance, to open our eyes that we may cut away the dead wood and brush aside the accumulated rubbish of centuries of false education ... Then, having learned the spiritual lesson that the East has the power to teach the West, we may

Figure 13.2. Martin House reception room with Sunburst fireplace. Darwin D. Martin Photograph Collection, University Archives, University at Buffalo, The State University of New York.

build upon this basis the more highly developed forms our more highly developed life will need.[23]

The open fireplace contrasts with the aesthetically grounded position of the southerly oriented Sunburst fireplace within the foyer/sitting room. This space receives sunlight throughout the day and gives off warmth in the evening hours when the sun recedes from view. Wright's arrangement here creates a material representation of nature that mimes the white settler's orientation to the open landscape. It is within this space that the modern-day Anglo-American can imagine what it was like for his ancestor to rise and retire each day with the sun.

Curiously, the wall containing the Sunburst fireplace heavily demarcates the connectivity of the reception room to other spaces within the Martin house. The living room, dining room, library, and reception room all flow into one another, forming an enfilade of spaces that constitute the open plan celebrated in Wright's architecture. As one walks through these spaces, there is no indication of what lies beyond on the first floor except for the spaces connected to the main staircase rising and regressing from the entry hall below. Thus, it may surprise you that the Sunburst fireplace is situated immediately in front of a fireplace that was originally located in the very large kitchen on the other side of the wall. The geometrical alignment between these two fireplaces is so great that they form a massive chase space on the second-floor plan that finally opens up into a nearly fifteen-foot-wide chimney that rises above the roofline. Yet each fireplace was meant to be accessed by means of two separate entries on the ground floor: a servant's door along the back and the main door at the front. Most historians have accounted for this functional separation by referencing the class-based division of space in the Victorian home. In Great Britain where this style first originated, it was important to distinguish between the classes of people entering the "upstairs" and "downstairs" spaces of the home, with the homeowners privileged in the main spaces and the servants resigned to the metaphorical back of house. However, the continuity of this class separation would have been transformed by its location within the political context of the settler colony. One of the first challenges to this notion would have been the false presumption that the United States operates as a class-free society. In addition, in the place of class-based divisions, many upper-middle-class homes in the United States also used race to distinguish who was expected to be a servant in well-to-do neighborhoods. This expectation was so strong that it persisted into the 1950s in Levittown, Pennsylvania, a suburb created for first-generation homeowners who wanted the privileges of living in an "all-white" community.[24]

How might the racial politics of American suburbia complicate Wright's metaphorical interpretation of the upper-middle-class home as the American prairie? What nationalist themes are played out through the separation and segregation of various bodies within the interior of the settler colonial home? And what might a breakdown of the strongly policed division of spaces on the first floor have meant within this political context? Given the clear demarcation of owner and servant space Wright channels in his design, it is important to note that at least one floor plan generated by his office finally connects these two fireplaces. This drawing, completed by an apprentice in Wright's office during a busy time in June 1916, was created to satisfy Isabelle Martin's persistent requests to modify the servant's wing to provide greater proximity to her private quarters as she needed help managing the home with her diminishing eyesight. Among the many changes noted by previous scholars, Wright's office provided a more formal registration between the Sunburst and kitchen fireplaces that essentially registered their mutual use of the chase spaces common in the first-floor plan. If one reads this formal feature through the lens of settler colonial theory, the clear separation of the fireplaces in the owner and servant spaces provides a symbolic distinction between the settler subjects who eventually took command of the open prairie and subsequent waves of immigrants whose position within the body politic was much more contingent. As a wealthy

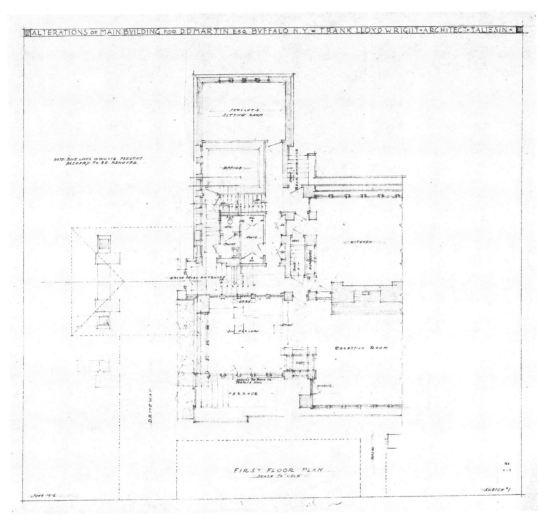

Figure 13.3. First-floor plan of the Martin House with alterations. Architectural Drawings of the Darwin D. Martin House, University Archives, University at Buffalo, SUNY. Copyright 2023 Frank Lloyd Wright Foundation, Scottsdale, Arizona. All rights reserved.

homeowner, Martin finally affirmed his role as a white elite in American society—at least as it was performed within the architectural frame that Wright provided his clients. Any breakdown of the racially inflected class divisions between "homeowner" and "servant" within this framing symbolically challenged the structural rules that undergirded Wright's metaphorical interpretation of citizenship and belonging within the American empire. In practice, there was a constant blending of owner and servant spaces within the home. This was especially true on the second floor, where no clear partition separated the sleeping quarters of those present within the home. However, this division was rigorously maintained at a formal level on the first floor, where the family spent most of their waking hours. A proposed integration of amenities between these formal enclaves would have acknowledged the common structural rules that bound owner and servant spaces and constituted a modest challenge to the rhetorical efforts to mythologize who belongs within the nation-state.

The Back Entry as Exogenous Containment Space

The existing archive of business correspondence and personal records extant from the Martin family suggests that they maintained the racial and class distinctions expected of a proper Victorian family even as they were living in the United States. In class terms, they matched the social distinctions of hereditary-based elites from Europe while performing the social norms of white Anglo-Saxon protestant elitism. A decidedly American attitude in business was clearly evident in Martin's comments upon the thrift, diligence, and hard work expected of members of the entrepreneurial class. In racial terms, Martin and his family strove to project the stability and social sophistication of global white elites while grounding their personal identity within a uniquely American interpretation of merit. The whiteness of American wealth was further codified by the conspicuous nature of its leisure practices and the literal placement of racial bodies within the home. The European cast of life at the Martin house complex is perhaps most evident in the Victorian customs of dress and grooming captured in period photographs. As an example, Isabelle Martin often sat in corseted dresses within the home, and the children were staged in period toddler dress. In architectonic terms, everything from the social division of interior spaces to the horticultural practices that sustained the gardens surrounding the home was meant to fortify the whiteness of the Martin family stock. Business records show that Darwin Martin hired English gardeners with explicit knowledge of Continental horticultural practices to maintain the grounds of the Martin family complex and the summer house, Graycliff. At least two existing photographs reveal the intimacy with which garden staff interacted with the Martin family children at both homes.

Insofar as Victorian houses traditionally separated people by their racial and class affiliations with front doors for white elites and back doors for everyone else, Wright's architecture skillfully manipulates the spatial trajectories of social groups living in Martin's America. This is true even in symbolic terms. White settler and exogenous subjects were metaphorically channeled and segregated into different areas of the home while the entire structure carefully maintains the organic fiction of an integrated architectural form inside and out. In the context of the front door/back door of the Martin house, the prominent front entry is reserved for all "free" white individuals, or those who own property in a Jeffersonian model of citizenship. All others, be they upwardly mobile whites or nonwhite servants, are restricted to using the back or servant entry. This class division of space was inherently racialized by the segregation patterns of

Figure 13.4. Mr. Sprague, the gardener, pushing Darwin M. and Margaret Foster in "Gray Cliff" wheelbarrow in front of Graycliff garden wall. Darwin D. Martin Photograph Collection, University Archives, University at Buffalo, SUNY.

suburban Buffalo, which informally reserved the use of back doors for nonwhite visitors to the home. To complicate this situation, the racial segregation of bodies in the interior did not require the domestic interior to be emptied of all references to nonwhite material culture. Instead, the Martin house introduced formal geometries to the windows and wooden built-ins within the family spaces that were directly inspired by pre-Columbian material culture. These "Indigenous" and "immigrant" elements of the home are conspicuous because they display a knowledge of Indigenous subjects, but merely as a ghostly presence. This reflection upon indigeneity operates as a symbolic erasure of the lost Indian native, which by extension constitutes a celebration of the indigeneity introduced by white settler culture.

The back door of the Martin house operates as a voyeuristic portal for interpreting the essential characteristics of the citizen-subject: the aspirant servants can look to the primary spaces of the home to understand what it takes to become properly "white" and "wealthy" in nineteenth-century America. A clear hierarchy is evident in the architectural finishes and spatial access provided throughout these spaces. The use of white marble finishes to underscore the cleanliness of servant spaces has long been commented upon by architectural historians as a punitive means of policing race-based and class-based health fears in the late nineteenth century. Some of these fears are manifest in a photograph of servants kept within the Martin family archive. It is not clear whether this image was of servants who worked in the Martin family home or in the home of an acquaintance, but the fact that it was valuable enough to keep is important. This servant image is curious for the ways it both attempts to emulate the social norms of Victorian photography while projecting the wanting elements of those who seemed unable to emulate the characteristics of the white wealthy elite. In this sense, even the working-class white subject is viewed with suspicion within the private spaces of the elite home. While we might consider them to be nominally white today, nineteenth-century elites often viewed white immigrants from Southern, Central, and Eastern Europe with suspicion. If one remembers the multiple waves of Irish, Italian, and Polish immigrants coming into Buffalo, New York, at this time, it is reasonable to infer that a symbolic coordination of old settler and new exogenous subjects complicated the performance of whiteness in the Darwin D. Martin home. As Noel Ignatiev reveals to us with his research on Irish American integration in the United States, certain groups of white ethnics were accepted as equals only after generations of discrimination.[25] Whiteness was a premier category of exclusion that has preserved its exclusivity over time by gradually expanding to include subsequent waves of European immigrants. So, while the separation between working-class and elite white subjects only registers as a class issue today, it was considered through a racial lens in the nineteenth century. One way of interpreting the white racial embodiment of these spaces, then, is to interrogate the ways each object—from the Indigenous-inspired ornamentation and the

Figure 13.5. Unidentified group of servants, late 1800s. Darwin D. Martin Photograph Collection, University Archives, University at Buffalo, SUNY.

metaphorical vistas created by the interior fireplaces to the front/back entryways and the low-hanging eaves that frame the landscape—enabled one to perform the social positionality of an elite white homeowner.

An interesting fact about the history of the Martin house is the racial identity of the family's servants. In contrast to the expectation that they may have hired people of color as the help, at no time does it appear that the Martins employed nonwhite servants. Instead, they seem to have ventured in the other direction by always employing servants, particularly gardeners, from England. On its surface, this might suggest that race has nothing to do with the everyday customs of the Martin house. However, if we consider the fact that Martin's commissioning of this house cemented his status as a member of the white elite, then it makes sense to understand his hiring of Old World servants as a visual sign of his connection to the cultural standards of Europe, which in this case related specifically to the gardening practices used in his home. In one instance, perhaps as an expression of goodwill, the Martins permitted one of their servants to get married within the primary spaces of the home. In addition, the Martins would regularly visit some of their upwardly mobile servants after they settled in other areas of the United States and abroad. Of course, not every servant experienced such close relations, but those who did simultaneously benefited from the Martins' largesse while managing their connectivity to their transatlantic origins. Surviving photographs of these servants demonstrate the degree to which the Martins considered themselves to be Victorians, as well as their ascent socially alongside Old World subjects with the assets gained from entrepreneurial wealth. Again, it is important to remember that whiteness in the 1880s and 1890s was an expanding concept in its own right: the Irishman had only recently gained acceptance as white shortly before this time, and the American Jew would have to wait until the postwar period for fuller acceptance.[26] The upper and lower rungs of whiteness were still heavily contested and segregated in ways that combined ethnic and class identity, ways that would be unthinkable today.

Darwin D. Martin, as a poor Midwesterner who slowly made his way up the social ladder, was not immune to the anxieties associated with white identity. He allayed such fears at least once by soliciting a phrenological reading of his racial character from Orson Squire Fowler, a leading theorist on biological character.[27] Fowler's theory of phrenology purported to be able to read the psychological importance of the geometry of the skull, which he later translated into architectural principles in his treatise on the octagon house. He created a profile for Darwin D. Martin in January 1886, nearly seven years before construction on the Martin House complex began. In this profile, Fowler interprets Martin's abnormally large skull as a physical indication of his penchant for business—the very quality that Martin relied upon for entry into the upper-middle class.[28]

Clues to the hegemonic definition of whiteness in this period can also be found in Wright's architectural writings, which directly compare the material culture of Euro-Americans with Japanese, Puerto Rican, and African American peoples.[29] In each case,

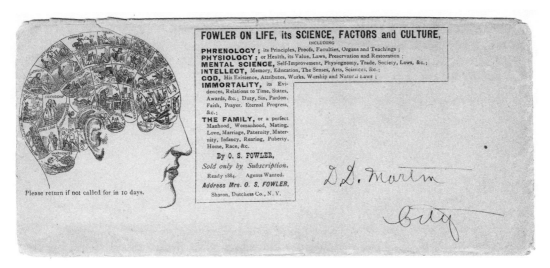

Figure 13.6. Envelope used to relay O. S. Fowler's phrenological reading of Darwin D. Martin's head. Darwin D. Martin Photograph Collection, University Archives, University at Buffalo, SUNY.

the long historical traditions of nonwhite peoples are compared negatively as primitive to the progressive modernity of white Americans. Wright would combine his romantic love of the prairie with a progressive vision of construction and geometrical expression that was quite unique in the United States, what he called an autochthonous national style of American architecture. Martin would become one of Wright's first clients in the northeast, which would open up new grounds for disseminating his architectural style there.

After Darwin Martin suffered a serious financial reversal, the house lay abandoned until an Italian American architect saved it from demolition. The architect, Sebastian Tauriello, likewise used it to confirm his status among the city's elite, a situation that reflects the expansion of white racial identity via the rising status of the city's Italian community in the 1950s and 1960s.[30] For both the Martins and the Tauriellos, Wright's design for the Martin house served as a physical emblem of their ascension into the city's cultural elite.[31]

When Frank Lloyd Wright set out to design a democratic architecture for America, he inherited the cultural politics of a settler colonial government that constructed a white settler narrative for the nation-state. This mythology anticipated the white nativist ideologies that were on the rise during the Jim Crow era; the period of Wright's entire career as an architect. Within a settler colonial context, self-proclaimed movements for an "American architecture" operate as ideological constructions of the nation-state, or as a soft form of propaganda, as Lorenzo Veracini and Patrick Wolfe have defined the political narratives invented to legitimize the excesses of settler colonial states. Looking back toward the nation's founding, it becomes possible to understand the racial politics that undergirded Wright's American architecture. It is described here as both an architectural portrait of individual freedoms in Jim Crow America and one that ultimately operates as an architecture against democracy in the longer history of pluralizing American race relations. Wright is a stop along the way, a portrait of Anglo-American contributions to the nation-state that does not give a proper nod to the contributions of nonwhite subjects. This interpretation acknowledges the presence of Indigenous and Japanese precedents in Wright's houses and in his personal writings. However, it critiques the social contexts for which they were created, which was not to demonstrate the assimilable nature of these nonwhite subjects, but to metaphorically replace the "native" status of these subjects by demonstrating white settlers' comparable position in American history. Thus, Wright's gaze (and those he establishes with his Prairie Style architecture) privileges the orientation of the white homeowner, regardless of who is watching. The solipsism of this phenomenon must be recognized if we are to develop an appropriate reading of the racial politics embodied by Wright's democratic architecture.

Notes

1. The Jim Crow era began with the repeals to federal laws supporting Southern Reconstruction in 1877 and ended with the passage of the Civil Rights Act in 1965. See, for example, Dianne Harris, "Where Was Jim Crow? Frank Lloyd Wright, Broadacre City, and the All-White American Suburb," in *Segregation and Resistance in the Landscapes of the Americas*, ed. Eric Avila and Thaisa Way (Washington, D.C.: Dumbarton Oaks, 2023), 161–82.
2. Adam Liptak, "Supreme Court Invalidates Key Part of Voting Rights Act," *New York Times*, June 25, 2013. https://www.nytimes.com/2013/06/26/us/supreme-court-ruling.html.
3. See for example William Storrer, *Frank Lloyd Wright: Designing Democratic America* (Traverse City, Mich.: WineWright Media, 2015); Robert Fishman. *Urban Utopias in the Twentieth Century: Ebenezer Howard, Frank Lloyd Wright, Le Corbusier* (Cambridge, Mass.: MIT Press, 1982), 104; Naomi Tanabe Uechi, *Evolving Transcendentalism in Literature and Architecture: Frank Furness, Louis Sullivan, and Frank Lloyd Wright* (Cambridge Scholars Publishing, 2013), 125–40; Joseph Siry, *Unity Temple: Frank Lloyd Wright and Architecture for Liberal Religion* (Cambridge: Cambridge University Press, 1996); and Neil Levine, *The Architecture of Frank Lloyd Wright* (Princeton: Princeton University Press, 1998)
4. Frank Lloyd Wright, "A Home in a Prairie Town," *Ladies' Home Journal* 18 (February 1901): 17.
5. This 1935 exhibit has caused great confusion amongst many Wright scholars. See Lewis Mumford's negative critique in the article "The Skyline: Mr. Wright's City—Downtown Dignity," *New Yorker* (April 27, 1935): 63–66; and Anthony Alofsin's summation of its critical reception in "Broadacre City: The Reception of a Modernist Vision," in *Modernist Visions and the Contemporary American City*, a special issue of *Center: A Journal of Architecture in America* 5 (1989): 8–43.

6. Frank Lloyd Wright, *An Organic Architecture: An Architecture of Democracy* (1939; repr., London: Lund Humphries & Co. Ltd., 1970) and *When Democracy Builds* (Chicago: University of Chicago Press, 1945).
7. See, for example, James O'Gorman, *Three American Architects: Richardson, Sullivan, and Wright, 1865–1915* (Chicago: University of Chicago Press, 1991), 150; and Vincent Scully, *The Shingle Style and the Stick Style: Architectural Theory and Design from Downing to the Origins of Wright* (New Haven: Yale University Press, 1955), 5–9.
8. See Lorenzo Veracini, *Settler Colonialism: A Theoretical Overview* (London: Palgrave Macmillan, 2010), and Patrick Wolfe, *Settler Colonialism and the Transformation of Anthropology: The Politics and Poetics of an Ethnographic Event* (London: Cassell, 1999).
9. Veracini, *Settler Colonialism*, 16–21.
10. Veracini, *Settler Colonialism*, 16–21.
11. Joanna Merwood-Salisbury, "Western Architecture: Regionalism and Race in the *Inland Architect*," in *Chicago Architecture: Histories, Revisions, Alternatives*, ed. Charles Waldheim and Katerina Rüedi Ray (Chicago: University of Chicago Press, 2005), 1–14.
12. Kenneth Frampton, *Wright's Writings: Reflections on Culture and Politics, 1894–1959* (New York: Columbia Books on Architecture and the City, 2017), 133–37.
13. Wright, *When Democracy Builds*, 7–9.
14. Veracini, *Settler Colonialism*, 1–4.
15. One of the best studies of contingent citizenship rights for nonwhite groups in the United States is Claire Jean Kim's essay "The Racial Triangulation of Asian Americans," *Politics & Society* 27, no. 1 (March 1999): 105–138. In addition, many scholars in Whiteness Studies have examined the religious and class restrictions that kept Central and Eastern Europeans marginalized in the mid- to late-nineteenth century. See for example Noel Ignatiev, *How the Irish Became White* (New York: Routledge, 2009).
16. Of course, African Americans were just one of several groups discriminated against. A full list can only be arrived at by studying the racial and class anxieties of cultural elites during specific periods in time. Other examples include Jewish Americans, Catholics, and certain types of mentally and physically disabled individuals. See for example Antero Pietila's study of anti-Black and antisemitic attitudes in Baltimore in *Not in My Neighborhood: How Bigotry Shaped a Great American City* (Chicago: Ivan R. Dee, 2010).
17. See Jack Quinan, *Frank Lloyd Wright's Buffalo Venture: From the Larkin Building to Broadacre City* (Petaluma, Calif.: Pomegranate Communications Inc., 2012); and Jack Quinan, *Frank Lloyd Wright's Martin House: Architecture as Portraiture* (New York: Princeton Architectural Press, 2004), 81–83.
18. Quinan, *Frank Lloyd Wright's Martin House*, 187: "The plan of the Martin complex can only be fully understood and appreciated in light of the events and experiences that shaped Darwin Martin's life . . . The epicentral motif of this ambition was a home, one that would reunite the dispersed Martin family. . . . He was able to begin to formulate a plan to build a housing complex of such transcendent beauty and tranquility that it would draw his siblings to him, where together they could live out the rest of their lives in luxury and blissful reminiscence."
19. Douglas J. Forsyth, "When Less Is More: Frank Lloyd Wright's Buffalo Cottages," *American Bungalow* 77 (Spring 2013): 18

20. This architectural effect came at great cost as Mrs. Martin, who suffered from poor eyesight, constantly complained that Wright's design greatly deteriorated her eye condition. See Quinan, *Frank Lloyd Wright's Martin House,* 208–14.
21. See Jacques Gubler's "In Search of the Primitive," in *Eugène Emmanuel Viollet-le-Duc, 1814–1879,* ed. Penelope Farrant, Brigitte Hermann, and Ian Latham (London: Academy Editions, 1980), 80–83.
22. Wright's exploration of non-Western sources for geometrical principles is explained in Kevin Nute, *Frank Lloyd Wright and Japan: The Role of Traditional Japanese Art and Architecture in the Work of Frank Lloyd Wright* (London: Chapan & Hall, 1993); and Anthony Alofsin, *Frank Lloyd Wright: The Lost Years, 1910–1922: A Study of Influence* (Chicago: University of Chicago Press, 1993).
23. Frank Lloyd Wright, *Ausgeführte Bauten und Entwürfe,* ed. Ernst Wasmuth (Berlin: Ernst Wasmuth, 1910), 7.
24. This expectation was so strong that news of the first Black homeowner in the all-white suburb of Levittown, Pennsylvania, caused a riot that was covered in national newspapers. For a full accounting of this, see David Kushner, *Levittown: Two Families, One Tycoon, and the Fight for Civil Rights in America's Legendary Suburb* (New York: Walker & Co., 2009).
25. Ignatiev, *How the Irish Became White,* 1–4, 144–168.
26. For more monographs on the evolution of whiteness in the United States, see David Roediger, *The Wages of Whiteness: Race and the Making of the American Working Class* (London: Verso, 1999), and Nell Irvin Painter, *The History of White People* (New York: W. W. Norton, 2010).
27. See Quinan, *Frank Lloyd Wright's Martin House,* 20, 52; and Christopher Castiglia, *Interior States: Institutional Consciousness and the Inner Life of Democracy in the Antebellum United States* (Durham: Duke University Press, 2008), 179.
28. This report is stored in the Darwin D. Martin papers at SUNY Buffalo. This report opens with the following summary: "Your brain Sir, is large in size and extra good in quality and these conditions in conjunction render you a decidedly smart man and too smart for your own good for you are a little top heavy."
29. Examples of this can be found in Wright's autobiography. See Frank Lloyd Wright, *An Autobiography* (New York: Horizon Press, 1977), 75, 117–123, 209.
30. Marjorie L. Quinlan, *Rescue of a Landmark: Frank Lloyd Wright's Darwin D. Martin House* (Buffalo: Western New York Wares, Inc., 2000), 29–46.
31. Italian immigrants were one of the last groups to gain acceptance in the elite classes of Buffalo, New York, in part due to the fact that Buffalo has remained a white ethnic working-class town, which exacerbated the Anglicization of white ethnic names up to (and in some cases through) the postwar period when white suburbanization was on the rise. See for example Virginia Yans-McLaughlin, *Family and Community: Italian Immigrants in Buffalo, 1880–1930* (Urbana: University of Illinois Press, 1982).

Chapter 14

Democracy and War

The University of Baghdad between Collaboration and National Competition

Esra Akcan

No event has given democracy a worse name after the end of the Cold War than the U.S.-led invasion of Iraq in 2003, conducted with the pretext of bringing democracy. Ample evidence has exposed that Western powers waged an unjust war against Iraq by not being truthful about its nonexistent weapons of mass destruction. This realization has not resulted, however, in accountability either for the initial violence or for the continuing failure in post-conflict healing. Scholars have explained this war as resulting from different types of greed, including oil revenue control, war capitalism, or disaster capitalism. Whatever the incentive, the war was claimed as a democratizing act.[1]

Why was it so easy to build consent for war by playing the democracy card? After the war, many blamed the failure of postwar reconstruction on Iraqis' unwillingness to accept the rule of democracy, and by extension found therein a justification for the dominant clash-of-civilizations argument.[2] But why was Baghdad's experience with self-governance and municipal undertaking, going back to its status as an Ottoman province, excluded from established urban history? When U.S. companies planned to reconstruct Iraq after the invasion, they imported concrete materials and labor. Why did they not draw instead from Iraq's own advanced concrete industry, an industry that produced some of the world's most architecturally qualified, albeit underacknowledged concrete buildings? The U.S. military is a bigger polluter than 140 other countries,[3] as the numbers on economic and ecological waste spent on Iraq's conflict and post-conflict reconstruction confirm.[4] Why was ignorance of passive cooling techniques in Iraq, developed before air-conditioning became the norm, so widespread? These questions about economic, global, and environmental injustice can be partially addressed through the history of the University of Baghdad's design.

The University of Baghdad was part of a larger modernization and construction leap in Iraq.⁵ Modernization efforts during the late Ottoman Empire (ca. 1850–1915) and the British mandate (1917–32) had already left durable marks. With the steep increase in oil revenues as a result of the 1951 agreement that diminished British profits, local and foreign architects carried out a comprehensive translation movement that differed from the mandate period by virtue of the fact that these architects were invited by a new set of Iraqi elites and the Iraqi government. I use the term *translation* here to describe a process of transformation during the act of transportation. I refer to an earlier book in which I developed a terminology to write geopolitically conscious intertwined histories of modern architecture. In that same book I defined *translation* as the multidirectional migration not only of people but also of objects, ideas, technologies, information, and images from one place to another and their transformations in new locations. This work came from my discomfort with narratives about global modernism that do not sufficiently problematize the interrelated violence of Eurocentrism and nationalism. Eschewing the conservative definition of *translation* as a secondhand copy or a smooth bridge between cultures, the book demonstrated how translation makes history with the participation of multinational individuals often trivialized by historians hunting for "geniuses" and "originals."⁶

This chapter also takes issue with the recent formulaic global history of architecture that has created a simplified narrative about the colonization and decolonization of the world based mostly on the history of Spanish, British, and French colonization. While correcting earlier accounts and exposing the entanglement of modernity, capitalism, and coloniality, this history nonetheless excludes large sections of the globe and differences between lands both before and after they were colonized by either of the European imperial powers. More nuanced and layered researches into other empires, nation-states, and communities, and a better confrontation with other dark sides of global modernity such as xenophobic nationalism, authoritarianism, and enforced "democracy" are overdue. Postwar Iraq provides one such example. Below, I focus on the design process of the University of Baghdad and explain how it mattered to different protagonists for different political reasons that ranged from antifascist democratization to cultural imperialism, and from international solidarity to nationalist propaganda. In the context of this push and pull of competing political agendas, I demonstrate that the encounter between Iraqi, American, British, and German architects, scholars, rulers, elites, and policymakers resulted in an architectural language with passive climate control techniques that have been trivialized due to the rise of fuel-energy dependent buildings.

This translation story begins with a group of Iraqi architects asking for self-determination after the British mandate, during which all government buildings had been designed by military engineers with personnel who had served British colonization in India.⁷ In their attempt to take matters into their own hands, a group of architects in Iraq opted to replace the British mandate's cultural symbolism with another

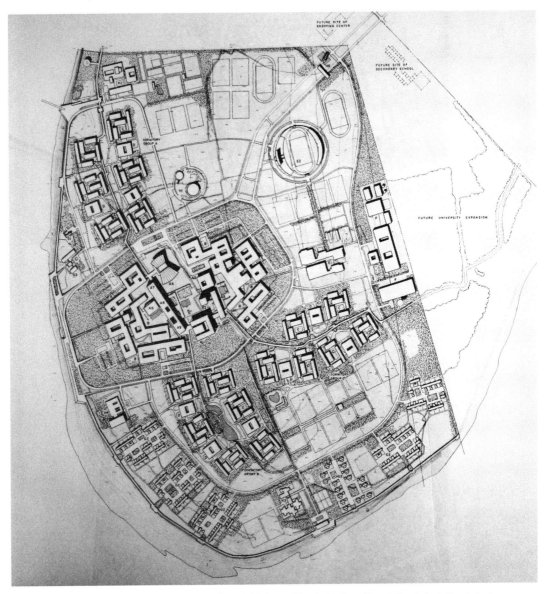

Figure 14.1. Walter Gropius and TAC and Hisham Munir, University of Baghdad, Baghdad, 1954–81, site plan. Canadian Centre for Architecture (CCA). Courtesy Zaydoon Munir.

that would come out of their collaboration with international architects. As part of this context, German American architect Walter Gropius visited his former students, Ellen and Nizar Ali Jawdat, in Baghdad in 1954. This couple in turn helped convince King Faisal II to commission Gropius for the University of Baghdad.[8]

Originally designed for twelve thousand students, the University of Baghdad was located on a prestigious site surrounded by the Tigris River on three sides. The commission

Figure 14.2. University of Baghdad. View of network of walkways that provide shade and connect academic departments. Photograph by author.

resulted from an international collaboration between Gropius (who was the chair of the Graduate School of Design at Harvard University), his Boston-based architectural firm TAC (The Architects Collaborative), a large team of experts from Harvard, and the so-far uncredited Iraqi architect Hisham Munir. Munir also cofounded the Department of Architecture at the University of Baghdad and continued his productive practice until 1996, when he emigrated. His monumental reinforced concrete buildings constitute a unique genre of Baghdad brutalism and testify to the sophisticated concrete industry that existed in Iraq before the U.S. occupation. The University of Baghdad's concrete buildings were designed between 1954 and 1981 and have endured three political regimes and six rulers.

The Theory: Democracy, Collaboration, Education

To discuss the University of Baghdad in relation to democracy and U.S. involvement in Iraq is not arbitrary. Its lead architect, Gropius, was preoccupied with the relation between three concepts at this time: democracy, collaboration, and education. In articles collected in *Apollo in the Democracy* in 1968, Gropius declared that these thoughts were the result of his trips around the world and his opportunity "to compare the development of architecture in South America and in Oriental countries with our own."[9] In a speech to Harvard alumni in 1959 (the same year that the Baghdad project's preliminary plans were approved), he declared:

> I should be infinitely sorry if Americans did not see through, in the field of building and planning, the task they originally set for themselves in this world: the introduction of democratic standards for all aspects of life, including the cultural.[10]

He repeated this call at the American Institute of Architects (AIA) convention the same year: "We stand at a moment in history that calls for a bold, imaginative interpretation of the democratic idea."[11] In the context of the Cold War, the word *democracy* meant being against both communism and fascism, as Gropius could not have been unaware or uninterested, but the architect sought to extend this meaning from a form of governance to a state of mind: "When I am speaking of democracy" he said, "I am speaking of the modern form of life which, without political identification, is slowly spreading over the whole world, establishing itself upon the foundation of increasing industrialization, of growing communication- and information-services and of broad admission of the masses to higher learning and the right to vote."[12] Two years before his death, he added, "For me democracy begins with the tie between you and me and with the emphasis that every individual must, according to his capacities, have the possibility to take part, to speak up about what he wants to do—when we can begin mutual cooperation."[13]

This relation between the democratic state of mind and collaboration also reflected Gropius's defense of teamwork at TAC. Founded in 1946 with eight partners, TAC's office structure was promoted as democratic and collaborative:

> As democracy obviously hinges on our ability to cooperate, I urged that the architect as a coordinator by vocation should lead the way toward developing a new technique of collaboration in teams. The essence of such technique should be to emphasize individual freedom of initiative instead of authoritative direction by a boss.[14]

In a special interpretation then, Gropius associated democracy with a collective intelligence that could be achieved in true collaboration, as opposed to the "nineteenth-century idea of individual genius" or the ego of a designer.[15]

None of this would have improved quality of life, in Gropius's mind, if the public did not receive an education. On the contrary, without education, democracy would have produced a tyranny of banal design.[16] So, having spent his entire career thinking about design education in Weimar, Dessau, and Cambridge, Massachusetts, Gropius could not have found a better opportunity than to design both the educational approach and the buildings of a large university in Baghdad, at a time when he thought the American architect was responsible for the democratization of the world, and in collaboration with a large team of architects and engineers at TAC, experts on the Middle East and higher education at Harvard University, as well as colleagues from Iraq.

Working for ten months in 1957, the Harvard team prepared an extensive report that laid down the education and design principles, including the sizes and programs of all academic disciplines, the university's administrative structure, the design and engineering of buildings, traffic and landscape, sewage disposal, irrigation systems, and cost estimates.[17] The University of Baghdad was a unique amalgam of interdisciplinary university structure and campus design. The team criticized both the educational and architectural approaches of the British, German, and American universities because they created specialization and departmentalization at the expense of an integrated education. To foster academic dialogue between departments, the Harvard education team suggested mixing classrooms and labs. Consequently, the architecture team designed a campus without departments located in separate buildings.[18] They divided the campus into common, academic, and residential zones and designed it with a centrifugal arrangement in which buildings would get gradually more compact as they extended from the center toward the river. Programs to be shared by all fields, including the administration building, faculty club, library, auditorium, theater, student union, and mosque would be placed at the core of the first ring on a central floating plaza with open vistas. The departments at the periphery of the ring would be collected around relatively smaller civic-scaled green courtyards with fewer vistas. Elevated streets and shaded paths would create a continuous web of circulation that would knit the learning spaces together. Even though each department had its own headquarters, they would share infrastructural facilities, classrooms for 20, 40, 80, and 200 students, and even some labs to foster interdisciplinary dialogue. The midrise gender-specific dormitories would define tighter courtyards for a capacity of 5,600 men and 2,400 women, whereas a compact fabric of low-rise individual houses for the president, faculty, and research fellows would be situated on the periphery along the river. These dormitory zones would be placed by following the existing dikes that had been built during late Ottoman modernization to regulate water flow and prevent flooding. The team also suggested an irrigation network and a sewage treatment system so that bacteriologically safe water could be used for landscape irrigation.

Even though the University of Baghdad was designed as an alternative to American campuses, Gropius made sure the project was not linked to anything close to anti-Americanism. For example, Giulio Carlo Argan wrote an extensive article for *Casabella* after talking to Gropius in 1960. Handmade corrections to Argan's manuscript, most

Figure 14.3. University of Baghdad. Comparison of mosque design. First version *(top)* and second version *(middle)*. Canadian Center for Architecture (CAA). Courtesy Zaydoon Munir, The Architects Collaborative (TAC). Photograph as constructed *(bottom)* by Esra Akcan.

likely by Gropius, Americanizes Gropius by erasing any possible socialist or Western Marxist association from his designs. When Argan wrote "in sharp departmentalization class distinction usually develops," Gropius corrected "rigid departmentalization tends to impair the unity and breadth of education"; when Argan praised "Gropius, the theoretician of classless society," the architect preferred "Gropius, the theoretician of an integrated society"; when Argan criticized "discrimination of class and worse race still to be found in European and American universities," Gropius softened the words as "University of Baghdad will foster a much more intimate contact between the various departments than to be found [sic] in European and American universities."[19] In addition to erasing socialism, this last edit represents conscious whitewashing of racism in European and American universities. It is an open question as to whether Gropius felt insecure in his new country of residence, where he had arrived as an exile and maneuvered his way out of conflicts with such adjustments, or whether he intentionally carried the torch of Americanization with all its guises.

The Expert: Democracy, Orientalism, Area Studies

In their first report to the University of Baghdad, the project team noted that they had started by thoroughly learning about the Middle East, Islamic architecture and art, and Arab literature and area studies, and they did so by working with "consultant experts" at Harvard University.[20] Who were these experts? The most established was Hamilton Gibb, the British Orientalist who started his career at Oxford and came to direct Middle Eastern Studies at Harvard University. In his seminal critique, *Orientalism,* Edward Said acknowledged that Gibb produced the best scholarly work of his time, albeit one that recalibrated the stereotypical Oriental–Western divide into a world no longer shaped by official European colonization.[21] In 1945, Gibb was still talking about the "lack of a sense of law" in Islam that was premised on his inaugural bias about the untranslatability between Islam and the modern world. In Said's words, "If Islam is flawed from the start by virtue of its permanent disabilities, the Orientalist will find himself opposing any Islamic attempts to reform Islam, because, according to his views, reform is a betrayal of Islam."[22] At the time of his consultancy to Gropius, Gibb penned *Islamic Society and the West,* where he divided the history of Turkey and Arab provinces of the Ottoman Empire (including Baghdad) into three phases. Westernization divided this history into a before and an after, bringing a sharp, unabsorbable break into these societies, a break that could be observed (for example) in the modernization of their urban architecture.[23] It was a challenge for an Orientalist to explain self-determined modernism in the Ottoman Empire and the nations that came out of it; Gibb wanted to see the world separated into an Orient and a West and was anxious lest the distance between them disappear. Given Gibb's fundamental theory of Islam as interest in the Unseen (i.e., the nonmaterial and spiritual), he was bound to regard modernism as a "dislocation" and a fundamental crisis. For the same reasons, Gibb opposed secular nationalism because it would presumably "corrode the inner structures" of Muslim societies.[24] This was nothing but a common conviction about the perceived untranslatability between the modern and the Islamic, the American and the Iraqi, which continues to this day as the Orientalist conviction on the impossibility of democracy in the Middle East.[25]

Despite Gropius's good intentions, this paradigm of Orientalism echoed in his writings, as he claimed that modern technological progress caused a "split personality" between "inner" and "outer" self in "Oriental countries."[26] Vocabulary premised on the Western–Oriental divide and perceived Oriental backwardness in modern progress but forwardness in spirituality appeared in the University of Baghdad's report: "A great gain might be made if the University of Baghdad were somehow to synthesize the materialistic and scientific gains and knowledge of the West with the mysticism, philosophy and aesthetics of the East."[27]

The second "consultant expert" was William Polk, the assistant director under Gibb in Middle Eastern Studies at Harvard during the writing of the report, but who also worked for the U.S. State Department as a consultant to the Kennedy and Johnson administrations between 1961 and 1965. Polk eventually became more involved with the university project, following Gropius to Baghdad in 1959, joining in the conversations about mosque design, and introducing Gropius to Egypt-based architect Hassan Fathy, for whose book *Architecture for the Poor* Polk wrote the foreword.[28] Fathy also designed Polk's house in Aspen, Colorado. Even though Gibb and Polk directed Harvard's Center for Middle Eastern Studies together, they had different methodological approaches. The turn of the directorship in this department is a case in point for the transformation from Orientalism as an academic discipline in Europe to policy-oriented area studies in the United States. Polk was a social scientist convinced by Weberian modernization theory that all societies would walk on the same Western path to progress. He held to the mission of democracy against communism. In other words, the distinction for Polk was less about the West and the Oriental (as it was for Gibb) and more about the opposition of the modernist against the traditionalist.[29] Polk used this distinction to define necessary actions in the fight for democracy against communism. In his books *What the Arabs Think* (1952) and *Backdrop to Tragedy: The Struggle for Palestine* (1957), both included in the bibliography of the University of Baghdad's report, Polk warned that U.S. experts were behaving like European colonialists while communism was increasingly being associated with the idea of change that Iraqis wanted.[30] In other words, Polk wanted U.S. foreign policymakers to recognize modernization demands from the ground for the sake of the U.S. victory in the Cold War. Years later, Polk objected to the U.S. occupation of Iraq in 2003 because he knew that Iraqis would perceive it as imperialism. Instead, he wanted to maintain power without the risk of nationalist backlash for the sake of U.S. interest in oil.[31] He suggested that post-conflict reconstruction projects be carried out by Iraqis, not foreigners, "as they were in the past."[32] When Polk referred to the past, he must have had in mind his own consultation days when he, Gropius, and TAC worked together with local officials and architects that experts like Polk used to call "change agents." This maintained his conviction in modernization theory and the need for soft power (and soft imperialism) rather than guns for the making of the world in the image of the U.S.-style democracy.

The Meeting: Cold War, Republic, Revision

Building a university in Iraq during the Cold War was, however, situated in a new power dynamic that went beyond reading Orientalist literature, practicing modernization theory, or visiting these lands as a tourist. No scene represents this dynamic better than a meeting in Baghdad in 1959. While the U.S. design team was finalizing the first version of the university, the republican revolution of July 14, 1958, put an end to King Faisal II's monarchy in Iraq and placed Abdul Karim Qasim in charge of representing the Iraqi people's sovereignty. The revolution pushed Gropius's former students Ellen and Nizar Jawdat, who had originally helped him get the commission, into temporary exile. In their continuing correspondence, they compared the Iraqi situation to Gropius's own experience with fascist Germany.[33] According to his own recollection, Hisham Munir acted quickly to prevent the cancellation of the project by the new regime (as other projects had been) and contacted the university president; he also sent a telex to Gropius to urge him to come to Baghdad to meet the new president.[34]

In the United States, meanwhile, Polk published a debut article in *The Atlantic* about which Gropius wanted to converse. "Let us not forget that our essential policy interests are identical with those of the Arabs," Polk wrote, arguing that the best policy to preserve U.S. interest in the region was to quit supporting the former ally—the king who had turned paternalistic and frustrated the Western-educated Iraqi experts—and instead cooperate with the new regime, backed by the young generation that Polk characterized as "our intellectual foster children."[35] He continued: "What, in effect, do we want from the Middle East? . . . At the present, the answer seems to me to be sufficient peace to prevent a world war and a sufficient flow of oil."[36] Polk was never dishonest about the fact that his motivation was U.S. interests in oil, not necessarily the Iraqi people's sovereignty, and that his aim was to win the Cold War, not necessarily democracy, collaboration, education, or anything that implies perpetual peace based on global equality. Whether Gropius shared Polk's motivations or not, he followed his and Munir's suggestions. Gropius and Polk were soon on their way to Baghdad.

In Baghdad, Gropius told Polk that the new context reminded him of Hitler's Germany, where "megalomania was state policy."[37] TAC architect Louis McMillen also has vivid memories of the meeting:

> It was intimidating to visit him [Qasim] at the Ministry of Defense. One entered the building and passed through a large hall, at the end of which a grand staircase led to the ruler's office. At the head of this staircase a soldier sat behind a machine gun that was aimed directly down the stair; one had to walk up hoping for the best. In General Qasim's office, a huge square room, there was a soldier stationed in each corner at attention and holding a sub-machine gun.[38]

The guns, in other words, had now reversed hands after the end of the British mandate and the kingdom it had established. In Polk's reading, Qasim had deliberately prepared an intimidating scene to show who was in power, including positioning fake cameras as if the meeting were being broadcast. Everyone had a big laugh when it was understood that the cameras were just a stage, after which the sides shook hands over the architects' fee and moved the project toward construction.[39]

Qasim wanted at least one major change, however: a tall building added to the central plaza so he could see it from his office miles away (according to McMillen) and the public could see the government was building the country (according to Munir).[40] In 1960, the architectural team submitted the revised and extended version in an impressive portfolio with detailed drawings of each building; lively ruled perspectives showing the central area, academic departments, and dormitories; and a thorough description of the step-by-step implementation of the entire campus.[41] Construction began in 1963 with the faculty office tower and the entrance gate in the form of a freestanding arch left unfinished to symbolize an "open mind."[42]

The site and design of the mosque also changed in the second version. Placed in the central plaza in the first version, within the urban fabric of university buildings, the mosque was shifted out of the first ring to a detached site where it stood as a freestanding object in the second. This decision fitted the aspirations of secular nationalism more than Orientalism à la Gibb, who saw Islam at the core of everything in Middle Eastern societies. The architectural design of the first version had followed classical Sunni typology, with an entrance courtyard and a dome placed on top of a square base, whereas the second version consisted of a uniquely shaped concrete shell dome placed directly on the ground. During this transformation, a mosque design by Munir composed of three shell domes rising directly from the ground as a way of integrating new technology and materials served as a reference point.[43] According to Munir, it was "one of the greatest moments of his career" that his design thesis as a student influenced TAC in "changing their traditional mosque into a new form."[44] Judging from the photographs of Gropius's visits to the University of Baghdad to oversee its construction, Munir's claim is plausible. Munir stands at the center of these photographs, explaining to Gropius and a group of architects who listen to him alertly. Munir lived in Baghdad for the entire design and construction phases, ensuring the continuity and quality of construction despite periodic halts during times of turmoil, corruption, and frequent regime changes.[45] When TAC was commissioned for an extension in 1981 (third version) as part of a new development leap with international architects hired now by Saddam Hussein, most of the academic buildings inside the first ring had been built (except the auditorium). Four clusters and two dining halls in each of the three dormitory zones as well as the mosque in its new location had been completed.[46]

The History: Collaboration, Climate, Nationalism

The question of the translatability or untranslatability of architecture from another country to Iraq occupied the architects continuously. Even though the British Mandate had ended, influential architects such as Ihsan Fethi and Rifat Chadirji considered the ongoing foreign presence in Iraq in the 1950s as a continuing legacy of the Mandate in cultural issues.[47] Contrary to the claims of his critics, these concerns did not escape Gropius. Ellen Jawdat, in touch with Gropius throughout the process, had already introduced some of them in her article written in 1957. She reported that Iraqi architects were critical of foreign architects both when they did not add something beyond their "rational discipline" and "functional approach" and when they used forms unintelligently just because they were employed in the past. "It is no narrow nationalism" she said, when Iraqi architects ask their colleagues from abroad to "collaborate with local architects."[48] Jawdat probably considered herself one of the unofficial local collaborators, as she often sent comments about the choice of materials and climatic concerns in her letters.[49] Gropius and TAC was one of the earliest firms at the time to designate an associate local architect.[50]

The University of Baghdad was composed of freestanding clusters with ample green spaces between buildings rather than the tight urban fabric associated with traditional Baghdad neighborhoods. The exposed concrete buildings with modular façades recall the aesthetic of industrialization. But the campus did not result from foreignizing translation. On the contrary, the design team consciously sought for appropriating translations from early stages[51] and put particular emphasis on passive climate control techniques by studying traditional construction methods.[52] The team specifically referenced "old Baghdad houses" for this purpose. Buildings were placed close to each other in their own clusters in order to provide maximum shade as in traditional urban fabric. Meanwhile, the green areas between secured the air flow and cross ventilation. The ramps and covered streets-in-the-air that connected classrooms to foster interdisciplinarity also provided a network of shaded spaces. Extensive cantilevers created shadows beneath; deep set-back façades protected the interior from the sun's rays. In gender-specific dormitories, the buildings created a courtyard with an L-shaped street circling two sides of the square cluster so that outdoor spaces were shaded and rooms had correct orientation and privacy. Vertical screens with bricks were meant to cast shade on

Figure 14.4. Munir, Gropius, and TAC members at the construction site of the University of Baghdad. The Architects Collaborative (TAC). Busch Reisinger Museum, carton 71, folder untitled. Harvard Art Museums Archives, Harvard University, Cambridge, Massachusetts.

inner walls and protect them from excessive sun, like the windows of *ursi* rooms in traditional houses. Courtyards and water fountains in courtyards replicated the climate control techniques of *tarma* houses in Baghdad.[53] The roofs were to be irrigated with a vaporized water sprinkler system, which the team associated with the local custom of pouring water to cool down in dry heat.[54] An air cooling system would be placed in window openings to drip water and allow the prevailing wind to blow inside, like the *bagdir* openings in traditional houses. It is ironic that the third version of the campus of 1981, designed after Gropius's death, amplified air conditioning in lieu of passive climate control techniques at a time when references to cultural identity had become the norm in architectural discourse.

Gropius and TAC referred to "traditional houses" and "old Baghdad" when they spoke of the historical customs and architectural elements that guided them in modern passive climate control techniques. But what exactly were the architectural attributes of these houses? How did the design team know about them? How were their histories written—by who and for whom? Was climate control really a concern for their builders, or did these houses grow into how they were found in the 1950s due to different

Figure 14.5. University of Baghdad. Façade articulation and courtyard. Photograph by author.

historical dynamics? Any reader who has followed the "Islamic city" or "Arabic architecture" debates would know that the answer to these questions is highly inflected by the historian's orientalist, imperialist, nationalist, or religious perspective. Even the name of Baghdad's original settlement differs in different accounts: "Garden of Justice" for the Ottomans, "City of Peace" for the British.[55] Suffice it to say that there are at least Iraqi, British, Ottoman/Turkish, French, and German accounts of the historical "Baghdad house" that also change over time.

To fill the gaps in our story, the question is: what could the design team have known about these houses, and which history books would they have read? By the mid-1950s, "Islamic architecture" as an Orientalist art historical field had produced thick tomes that appeared in the team's bibliography. These were not specific to Baghdad, however, and they did not include anonymous houses.[56] Histories of Baghdad had been written in the Ottoman yearbooks, but these documents have not been integrated into scholarship on Baghdad even today. The *City of Peace* was written from the British colonialist perspective in 1927, treating Baghdad's history as nothing but a broken link between al-Mansur's Round City and the British Empire.[57] According to this narrative, the times in which "old Baghdad houses" had been built were nothing but a decline. The University of Baghdad design team's chosen inspiration went against the grain of British historiography.

A likely source for ideas about the Baghdad house is Oscar Reuter's *Das Wohnhaus in Bagdad* (1910).[58] Gropius's knowledge of German architectural scholarship and the fact that TAC gave this book to Harvard Library years later suggest as much. The extensive typological study of ground plans, façades, ornaments, and materials provided a reference source for what was named as *tarma* houses as specific variations on courtyard dwellings. In the 1970s and 1980s, Iraqi scholars documented and described the typological and taxonomic histories of the *tarma* houses, which simply stood for the "Iraqi house."[59] In the context of nationalist historiography, some of these historians omitted the influence of Persia and the Ottoman Empire, and the history of Jewish and Christian builders and residents, even though they used the same drawings published in Reuter's book.[60] Many historians did, however, add a much more attentive analysis of climate-specific concerns and passive cooling techniques, which Reuter had not emphasized. While extensive studies by Iraqi scholar Ihsan Fethi on this topic were becoming better known, local architects were exploring sun-protected façades, such as Ihsan Kamil's honeycomb sun-shade in Khan Pasha residence (1957). Gropius, TAC, and Munir must have been learning and inventing modern climate control techniques while also observing the as-found versions of the traditional houses in Reuter's book, speaking to Iraqi colleagues, and seeing new buildings designed by local architects.[61] Namely, the invention of a new midcentury modernist vocabulary that emphasized sun-protected surfaces and shaded outdoor spaces, covered walkways, sun shading devices at the facade, courtyards, and umbrella roofs—a vocabulary often credited to "great modernist masters" such as Gropius, Josep Lluís Sert, and Le Corbusier—was actually the result of a multidirectional and multinational translation process with many agents in Baghdad.

To conclude, the translation history of the University of Baghdad shows that the campus design mattered to different protagonists for different reasons. For members of the Iraqi elite such as Ellen Jawdat during the post-Mandate/post-colonial kingdom and before the popular revolution, it was a crowning artifact of Iraqi modernization, an international project of self-determination against the British Mandate. For Iraqi architect Munir, it resulted from a collaboration with his own significant input. For the area studies scholar Polk, it epitomized U.S. soft power in the name of winning the Cold War and controlling oil revenue. For Iraqi leader Qasim after the popular revolution, it symbolized his own success in modernizing and nationalizing Iraq as an independent country. Gropius seems more conflicted, as both a German exile in America and an American expert in Iraq. When speaking with the ideas of Gibbian Orientalism, he saw his task as a Western reformist bringing progress and democracy to a land that could presumably not modernize itself. During his conversations with Polk, he was left with the choice between refusing to collaborate with a dictator and agreeing to be an arm of American aid in democratizing the world. Hints of cosmopolitan translations and openness beyond national interests nevertheless emerged at some moments against significant odds. As a matter of fact, the elaboration of a new modern language with passive climate control techniques was indeed the result of cosmopolitan moments in this translation process.

During the U.S. occupation, the University of Baghdad became the target of large-scale attacks and was used as a military camp by American forces. During the research and writing of this article, the university functioned only half a day, delaying academic reconstitution and healing through education. Rather than representing the complex history and taking accountability for the violence produced through this history, the simplistic accounts in North American and European media still disseminate clash-of-civilizations rhetoric. When one compares the ubiquity of political analyses and media coverage of conflict with the scarcity of art and architecture books on Iraq, one might recall that ignorance about culture and failure in international relations often reinforce each other. Contrasting international relations before, during, and after the Cold War therefore reveals hypocrisies in the dominant geopolitical order that identified a "clash" with civilizations that had been deemed allies in need of "developmental" support just a couple of years earlier. If perpetual wars rely on the conscious production of ignorance about the history of the world, historians can respond by writing more histories while turning historiography into a self-critical discipline that constantly checks and reevaluates its previous accounts.

Notes

Primary documents of the University of Baghdad are split between Walter Gropius Papers, Houghton Library, Harvard University, Cambridge (hereafter HL); Canadian Centre for Architecture, Montreal (hereafter CCA); Frances Loeb Special Collections, Harvard Graduate School of Design, Cambridge (hereafter FLSP); MIT Museum Archives, Cambridge (hereafter MIT-M); Harvard Art Museum Archives, Somerville, Boston (hereafter HAM); Hisham Munir Archive, Aga Khan Documentation Center, MIT, Boston (hereafter AGD). The Ottoman yearbooks are also primary sources for Baghdad's history (Cengiz Eroğlu, Murat Babuçoğlu, Orhan Özdil, *Osmanlı Vilayet Salnamelerinde Bağdat* [Ankara: Global Strateji Enstitüsü, 2006]). I have conducted on-site observations and conversations with faculty in Baghdad in December 2018. I would especially like to thank my colleagues in Baghdad Saba Sami and Mohammed Kassim for their continuing generosity, and Caecilia Pieri for facilitating my introduction to Iraqi colleagues, as well as her work on the architecture of Baghdad. For more illustrations and discussion of a broader context, see Esra Akcan, *Abolish Human Bans: Intertwined Histories of Architecture* (Montreal: CCA Singles, 2021).

1. "To protect our Nation and honor our values, the United States seeks to extend freedom across the globe by leading an international effort to end tyranny and to promote effective democracy." "The National Security Strategy of the United States of America," Section II, "Champion Aspiration for Human Dignity" (2006): http://www.whitehouse.gov/nsc/nss/2006/index.html.
2. See, for example, Ralph Peters: "We did give Iraqis a chance to build a rule-of-law democracy . . . [But they preferred] to indulge in old hatred, confessional violence, ethnic bigotry and culture of corruption. It appears that cynics were right. Arab societies cannot support democracy as we know it." Ralph Peters, "Last Gasps in Iraq," *USA Today,* November 2, 2006.
3. "US military is a bigger polluter than as many as 140 countries—shrinking this war machine is a must," *The Conversation,* June 24, 2019, https://theconversation.com/us-military-is-a-bigger-polluter-than-as-many-as-140-countries-shrinking-this-war-machine-is-a-must-119269.
4. Naomi Klein, *The Shock Doctrine: The Rise of Disaster Capitalism* (New York: Metropolitan Books, 2007), 325–384.
5. On architecture in Baghdad during this time, see Ihsan Fethi, "Contemporary Architecture in Baghdad," *Process Architecture* (May 1985): 112–32; Hoshiar Nooraddin, "Globalization and the Search for Modern Local Architecture: Learning from Baghdad," in Yasser Elsheshtawy, ed., *Planning Middle Eastern Cities* (London: Routledge, 2004), 59–84; Pedro Azara and Laura Iglesias Martinez, eds., *Irak Restored: City of Mirages; Baghdad from Wright to Venturi* (Barcelona: Polytechnical University of Catalonia, 2008); Magnus T. Bernhardsson, "Faith in the Future: Nostalgic Nationalism and 1950s Baghdad," *History Compass* 9–10 (2011): 802–817; Caecilia Pieri, *Baghdad: La construction d'une capitale moderne (1914–1960)* (Beyrouth: Damas, 2015); Ridha Al Chalabi, موسوعة العمارة العراقية, (Encyclopedia of Iraqi Architecture), 3 vols. (Baghdad, 2018). On the University of Baghdad, see Gwendolyn Wright, "Global Ambition and Local Knowledge," in Sandy Isenstadt and Kishwar Rizvi, eds., *Modernism and the Middle East: Architecture and Politics in the Twentieth Century* (Seattle: University of Washington Press, 2008), 221–54; Mina Marefat, "The Universal University," in Azara and Martinez, eds., *Irak Restored,* 157–166; Fiona MacCarty, *The Man Who Built Bauhaus* (Cambridge, Mass.: Belknap Press of Harvard University Press, 2019); Michael Kubo, "Companies of Scholars: The Architects Collaborative, Walter Gropius, and the Politics of Expertise at the University of Baghdad," in Ines Weizman, ed., *Dust and Data: Traces of the Bauhaus across 100 Years* (Spector Books, 2019).
6. Esra Akcan, *Architecture in Translation: Germany, Turkey, and the Modern House* (Durham: Duke University Press, 2012).
7. Khalid Sultani, "Architecture in Iraq between Two World Wars, 1920–1940," *UR* no. 2 (1982): 92–105. See also Mark Crinson, *Modern Architecture and the End of Empire* (Burlington: Ashgate Publishing Company, 2003).
8. Nizar Jawdat's father was the Iraqi Ambassador in Washington who then became the prime minister under King Faisal II, Ali Jawdat Al-Aiyubi. In a letter, Ellen Jawdat wrote to Gropius: "We are more than ever convinced that we must find some way for you to make your contribution to this country." Rifat Chadirji, Abdulla Ihsan Kamil, and Qahtan Awni

also had important roles in the selection of architects. Ellen Jawdat to Gropius, October 3, 1954, Box 25, No. 956, MS Ger 208, HL; Louis McMillen, "Notes for Gropius Book" Manuscript, April 6, 1989. Box "The university of Baghdad: the master plan = Jami'at Baghdad, 1981" Rare LG 338.B33/U641X, FLSP; T. Bernhardsson, "Faith in the Future"; Mina Marefat, "The Universal University." Current scholarship considers two rather than three versions. I took Gropius's first visit to Baghdad in 1954 as the start date, and I studied three submissions from 1957, 1960, and 1981.

9. Walter Gropius, *Apollo in the Democracy: The Cultural Obligation of the Architect* (New York: McGraw-Hill, 1968), vii. The photographs that Walter and Ise Gropius kept from these trips are in the Busch-Reisinger Museum, Gropius Archive, Feininger and Beuys material, 1906–1991 HUAM Records 2009.14. Carton 73, HAM; and the Busch-Reisinger Museum, Walter Gropius Papers, BRM 4, Box1, HAM.

10. Walter Gropius, speech to Harvard alumni in New Orleans, June 24, 1959, Manuscript, Box 9, No. 243, MS Ger 208, HL.

11. Walter Gropius at AIA Convention, New Orleans, June 25, 1959, Manuscript, Box 9, No. 244, MS Ger 208, HL.

12. The term "universal suffrage" stood instead of "right to vote" in the manuscript. Walter Gropius, "Apollo in the Democracy," in *Apollo in the Democracy*, 3–14, quotation: 3; "Unity in diversity (the lesson of Bauhaus)" 1961, Manuscript, Box 9, No. 262, n.p., MS Ger 208, HL.

13. Walter Gropius, "A conversation with Walter Gropius," September 1967, Box 10, No. 291, p. 2, MS Ger 208, HL.

14. Walter Gropius, "Speech on the occasion of the award of the gold medal of the Architectural League of NY to the Architect's Collaborative for its design of the Harvard Graduate Center, NY," May 1957, Manuscript, Box 9, No. 230, p. 4, MS Ger 208, HL.

15. Walter Gropius, "The Architect in Society. Speech delivered at Columbia University," March 1961, Manuscript, Box 9, No. 256, p. 20, MS Ger 208, HL. On voluntary teamwork, see Walter Gropius, "On Teamwork," 1961, Manuscript, Box 9, No. 265, MS Ger 208, HL. On respect for each individual's ideas and expertise within a democratic structure, see Walter Gropius, "The Architects Collaborative and the technique of collaboration," August 9, 1961, Manuscript, Box 9, No. 259; Walter Gropius, "Speech at TAC Annual Meeting" 1967, Manuscript, Box 10, No. 293, MS Ger 208, HL; and Walter Gropius, "Unity in Diversity," *Apollo in the Democracy*, 21–35.

16. Walter Gropius, "Basic attitudes towards constructive town planning," March 4, 1964, Manuscript, Box 10, No. 280, MS Ger 208, HL; Walter Gropius, "Tradition and Continuity in Architecture," *Apollo in the Democracy*, 71–104, esp. p. 71.

17. Walter Gropius, Louis McMillen, and Robert McMillan worked as the responsible TAC principals; Hisham Munir became the associated architect in Baghdad. Morse Payne and George Connelly drew the expressive perspectives of the first version, and Helmut Jacoby drew those of the second. Frank Basil took on the engineering of cooling machines, Jon Nocton the landscape design, and the Harvard School of Education headed by Cyril Sargent, Donald Mitchell, and Keyes Metcalf (from Harvard Library) developed the educational program. "Report on the University of Baghdad Designed by Architects Collaborative, Cambridge, Massachusetts," 1957, FLSB; John Harkness, *The Walter Gropius Archive*,

Volume 4: 1945–1969; The Works of the Architects Collaborative (New York: Garland Publishing, 1991).

18. "Report on the University of Baghdad" 1957, 10.
19. Giulio Carlo Argan, "Walter Gropius and the design of the University of Baghdad, Iraq," Rome, 1960, Manuscript and handmade corrections, Box 10, No. 314, MS Ger 208, HL.
20. Argan, "Walter Gropius," 4–6.
21. Gibb defended Orientalist study to prevent overspecialization and nationalist self-centeredness. Edward Said, *Orientalism* (New York: Pantheon Books, 1978), 257.
22. Said, *Orientalism*, 106.
23. "Since the beginning of the nineteenth century the study of the city takes on an increasing importance. The expansion of the cities and their external transformation, the breaking down of old divisions, the establishment of municipalities and municipal services, form one aspect of this; the other, and even more important, is connected with the rise of the middle class, the development of intellectual life in the cities." Hamilton Gibb, *Islamic Society and the West: A Study of the Impact of Western Civilization on Moslem Culture in the Near East* (Oxford: Oxford University Press, 1963), 8.
24. Said, *Orientalism*, 263.
25. Said's and my criticism against Gibb for failing to see modernism on the ground does not whitewash the violence in the name of modernization of Iraqi or other tyrannical rulers.
26. "Western mind, in its restless desire to seek new horizons in the physical world, would do well to learn a lesson in spiritual intensification from the Oriental mind. i.e. how to seek new horizons in the inner world." Walter Gropius, "Architecture in Japan," in *Apollo in the Democracy* (earlier version published in *Perspecta* in 1955), 107–138. Quotation: 108. Gropius was following European Orientalism that he inherited from Germany. See Akcan, *Architecture in Translation*; Itohan Osayimwese, *Colonialism and Modern Architecture in Germany* (Pittsburgh: University of Pittsburgh Press, 2017).
27. "Report on the University of Baghdad" 1957, 8.
28. William Polk, *Understanding Iraq* (New York: HarperCollins Publishers, 2005); William Polk, "Gropius and Fathy Remembered," *Architectural Design* 174, no. 6 (2004): 38–45; William Polk, "Foreword," Hassan Fathy, *Architecture for the Poor* (Chicago: University of Chicago Press, 1973), ix–xiii. Fathy was collaborating with Doxiadis at the time for Baghdad. See especially Panayiota I. Pyla, "Ekistics, Architecture, and Environmental Politics, 1945–1976: A Prehistory of Sustainable Development" (PhD diss., MIT, 2002).
29. Richard Bulliet's memoirs give hints to the dynamics in the Middle Eastern Studies at Harvard University. Richard Bulliet, "Memoir—Harvard College." https://www.academia.edu/8142163/PAGES_FROM_A_MEMOIR_HARVARD_COLLEGE.
30. "What is significant for Americans is that the Arabs are increasingly accepting the idea that communism is equated with change, while democracy is equated with *status quo*." William Polk, *What the Arabs Think. Headline Series*, no. 96. November–December 1952, quotation: 45, 55. See also William Polk, *Backdrop to Tragedy: The Struggle for Palestine* (Boston: Beacon Press, 1957).
31. "From their long experience with foreign exploiters and with their recent memory of 'crude oil politics,' Iraqis almost certainly will react against 'oil imperialism' with unending hostility." Polk, *Understanding Iraq*, 202–3.

32. "Step by step, health care, clean water, sewage, roads, bridges, pipelines, electric grids, housing, etc., could be mainly provided by the Iraqis themselves." Polk, *Understanding Iraq*, 212.
33. Ise Gropius to Ellen Jawdat, September 29, 1958, Box 25, No. 956; Nizar Jawdat to Walter Gropius, October 4, 1958, Box 25, No. 957, MS Ger 208, HL.
34. Hisham Munir, "When Politics and Architecture Collide," lecture at MIT, October 15, 2015.
35. William Polk, "The Lesson of Iraq," *Atlantic* (December 1958), https://www.theatlantic.com/magazine/archive/1958/12/the-lesson-of-iraq/306494/.
36. Polk also said, "Our reasons for identifying ourselves with [the former Iraqi government] were three: it existed, it was prepared to agree to join our side in the Cold War, and it was able to assure the flow of oil." Polk, "The Lesson of Iraq."
37. Polk, "Gropius and Fathy Remembered," 39.
38. McMillen, "Notes for Gropius Book," Manuscript, 1989, n.p.
39. Polk, *Understanding Iraq*, 111. Gropius to Lily Hildebrandt, February 3, 1959, Box 23, No. 884, MS Ger 208, HL. Gropius visited Baghdad in the upcoming years without tension. Walter Gropius, "Speech at London University," manuscript of notes, October 17, 1967, Box 10, No. 292, MS Ger 208, HL.
40. McMillen, "Notes for Gropius Book"; Munir, "When Politics and Architecture Collide."
41. The Architects Collaborative, "University of Baghdad. Preliminary Drawings and Specifications," 1960. CCA Collections. The individual drawings of the portfolio and some of their negatives are situated in MIT-M; Busch-Reisinger Museum. Gropius Archive. Feininger and Beuys material, 1906–1991 HUAM Records 2009.114. Card File Box 77 HAM.
42. Gropius posed in front of this gate for his profile in *Life*. "Close-up: Walter Gropius at 85. All-Purpose Old Master of Design," *Life*, June 7, 1968: 49–64.
43. Both McMillen and Polk emphasized the research and discussion process.
44. Hisham Munir, Manuscript explaining "Thesis: Mosque 1953," AGD.
45. I use the word *corruption* because of a confidential letter in which McMillen asks Gropius whether they should pay off Nouraddin (first name not given) by secretly giving him 5% of their fee, as Nouraddin had threatened he would tell the authorities that the firm did not follow the directions. McMillen was concerned that the project would be tied up because it would be hard to explain directly to the planning board that they "did the right thing." From Louis McMillen to Walter Gropius, "Confidential letter—no copies made," August 1, 1962, Box 27, No. 1151, MS Ger 208, HL.
46. "The university of Baghdad: the master plan = Jami'at Baghdad, 1981" Rare LG 338.B33/U641X, FLSP. The site plan and placement of dormitory zones went through some changes because the existing dikes lost their relevance.
47. Ihsan Fethi, an influential architectural historian who returned to Baghdad after earning his doctoral degree from the University of Sheffield, characterized the 1950s as "a hasty experimental phase during which Iraqi architects abandoned their cultural roots in favor of catching up with the western bandwagon." Rifat Chadirji, Iraq's most well-known architect, who has taken important posts for over four decades, evaluated buildings with the criteria of technical, physical, and cultural perfection; he argued that the work of TAC, like most of the international architects, was excellent in the first two criteria but "indifferent

to the indigenous cultural environment." Scholar Mina Marefat also held this viewpoint. Most of these comments were made in the context of the 1980s, when architects leaned toward cultural identity issues, but the question of appropriate translation and Iraqi agency were important concerns in the 1950s as well. Ihsan Fethi, "Urban Conservation in Iraq," 3 vols. (PhD diss., University of Sheffield, 1977); Ihsan Fethi, "Contemporary Architecture," 124; Rifat Chadirji, "The State of Arab Architecture," *UR* no. 4 (1981): 61–67, quotation: 66; Mina Marefat, "The Universal University;" Mina Marefat, "Wright's Baghdad: Ziggurats and Green Visions," in *Irak Restored*, 144–155.

48. Ellen Jawdat, "The New Architecture in Iraq," *AD* 27 3 (1957): 79–80.
49. Ellen Jawdat to Gropius, May 1958; May 9, 1966, Box 25, No. 956, MS Ger 208, HL.
50. McMillen, "Notes." Nizar Jawdat told Mina Marefat that he introduced Gropius to Munir; Mina Marefat, "The Universal University." Munir had recently graduated, returned to Baghdad, and partnered with Midhat Ali Madhloom, who already had a relatively big practice.
51. In *Architecture in Translation,* I define "appropriating translation as the tendency to assimilate or absorb a foreign idea or artifact into the local norms, and foreignizing translation as the tendency to resist domestication, to expose the differences between two places and to introduce a discontinuity. Needless to say, every actual translation exists somewhere between these two ends of the spectrum," 16.
52. The Architects Collaborative. University of Baghdad, *Architectural Record* (April 1959): 147–154; Argan, "Walter Gropius and the design of the University of Baghdad, Iraq." The 1957 Report also refers to Doxiadis's "Low Cost Housing Study for Iraq"; John Harkness, *The Walter Gropius Archive, Volume 4*.
53. "Most traditional houses have inner courts, with water that evaporates for a cooling effect, . . . which works well as the temperature in the courts are always lower." McMillen, "Notes for Gropius Book" Manuscript, 1989, n.p.
54. "This will incorporate by improved technical methods the old habit of pouring out water in excessive dry heat. Small water basins or water channels with fountains are distributed as beautiful cooling features throughout the campus . . ." "Report on the University of Baghdad," 31.
55. The attributes of "Iraqi house" shifted with modifications in official history of changing powers during the time that Gropius, TAC, and Munir designed versions of the University, and later.
56. These tomes included Creswell's *Early Muslim Architecture* (1st ed., Oxford, 1932) and Arthur Pope's *Survey of Persian Art* (Oxford, 1938–39). Eric Schroeder of Harvard University's Fogg Museum must have suggested these books.
57. Richard Coke, *Baghdad: City of Peace* (London: Thornton Butterworth, 1927).
58. Oscar Reuter, *Das Wohnhaus in Bagdad und Anderen Städten des Irak* (Berlin: Verlag von Ernst Wasmuth, 1910).
59. Fethi, "Urban Conservation in Iraq," 1977; Ihsan Fethi and John Warren, *Traditional Houses in Baghdad* (Sussex: Coach Publishing House, 1982); John Warren, "Traditional Houses in Iraq" *UR* no. 1 (1983): 5–11; Mu'ath Dhafir al-Alusi, "The Baghdad School of Architecture," *UR* (Autumn 1979): 10–25; Subhi al-Azzawi, "Oriental Houses in Baghdad: Concepts, Types, and Categories," 3-part essay, *UR* no. 1 (1985): 2–25; no. 2 (1985): 30–41;

no. 3 (1985): 7–21; Layth Rauf, "Tradition and Continuity in the Modern Iraqi House," *UR* no. 1 (1985): 15–24.

60. See also Caecilia Pieri, "Editing Out the Architectural History of Modern Iraq: Aspects of the Academic Discourse (1950–1980)" *International Journal of Contemporary Iraqi Studies* 9, no. 1 (2015): 7–20.

61. Gropius's colleague at Harvard University, Josep Lluís Sert, whose design for the American Embassy in Baghdad is one of the most cited examples of climate-specific midcentury modernism, must have also joined the conversation, although I did not find documents of direct correspondence.

Chapter 15

The Aesthetics of Resistance

Istanbul's Standing Man between the Body Politic and Bare Life

Can Bilsel

The Figures of Resistance

> What positive and specific images will remain as the enduring icons of the global revolution of 2011? What monuments will commemorate the series of democratic insurgencies that swept the world from the self-immolation of a fruit vendor in Tunisia to the occupation of the Tahrir Square to Occupy Wall Street?[1]

Written in the wake of the occupation of Cairo's Tahrir Square, W. J. T. Mitchell's question haunts us today, not least because the urban uprisings, which he greeted then, have since been overshadowed by the political catastrophes that ensued. It is not certain if the occupation of public spaces in Cairo, Sana'a, New York, Tel Aviv, Madrid, Istanbul, and Rio de Janeiro between 2011 and 2013 can reasonably be grouped under an international Occupy movement, much less a "global revolution." Yet, these urban uprisings unmistakably left behind a peculiar iconography. Mitchell observes that the pictures that have become the enduring icons of New York's Zuccotti Park and Cairo's Tahrir Square are not of individual faces, but of anonymous figures of resistance. Although these figures interpolate a subject position to be assumed by others, they are often depicted as a lone figure in the public square. The way the occupiers of 2011–13 inhabited spaces as isolated individuals presented a departure from the spatial practices of earlier labor and civil rights activists who marched by closing ranks. Resistance in public space is now often depicted as the stoicism and vulnerability of an individual body.

This chapter tackles the loneliness of the figure of resistance in the public square—the sublime gesture of an isolated, vulnerable, and distant protester. How shall one read

Figure 15.1. A figure of resistance in Taksim Square during the Gezi Park protests, May 31, 2013. Photograph by and courtesy of Yücel Tunca.

this iconography at the nexus of collective memories of resistance and a politically engaged history of specific architectural and urban spaces? How to tease out of this iconic figure of resistance a social critique of aesthetic culture while doing justice to the antihegemonic promise of these urban insurgencies?

The Gezi protests of 2013 in Istanbul and many other cities in Turkey may be as good a place to start as any.[2] They also present an unusual case. Unlike the "hard revolutions" taking place in Tunis and Cairo, saving a green public space in Istanbul and rejecting top-down urban redevelopment remained among the key demands of the Gezi Protests.[3] "Resistance" amounted to the occupations of contested public spaces by thousands of bodies in motion—to such an extent that a prominent political commentator had to remind her readers that the Gezi protests were not "just about protecting urban greenery."[4]

Critics have aptly interpreted "the visual emergence of the Occupy Gezi movement": the back talk of the protestors who appropriated the epithet *çapulcu* (looters, thugs, loafers) the prime minister used to describe them as their proud nom de guerre; their "disproportionate wit" in countering and evading the disproportionate force deployed by the police; and the exceptionally diverse range of performances, from the carnivalesque to solemn vigils for the victims of police violence.[5]

Photojournalists, themselves participants in the events, produced the iconic imagery which frequently returns to the aesthetics of the sublime: the solemn dignity of a body of the resistance against the crushing forces unleashed by the state: the guitar player who stood against armored TOMAs (the Turkish acronym for Mass Incident Intervention Vehicles), the woman in red, the woman in black, to name only a few.[6] Gezi's soundscape was equally important, with entire neighborhoods banging on pots and pans in protest and the occupiers "playing" the barricades to the tune of a protest hip-hop. All this was made instantly available on social media: choreographed and edited videos have since been running endlessly to the tune of the hymns of resistance.[7]

I begin with the question: to what extent does "the aesthetics of resistance"[8] articulate with a new citizen, a new body politic, and a new *demos*? What is the potential of this aesthetic figure in consolidating a new collective subject position after decades of neoliberal policies and authoritarianism have ruthlessly dismantled organized labor and replaced the welfare state with precarity and crony capitalism in Turkey and elsewhere? Conversely, does the aestheticization of resistance—both a translation of this specific conflict to the aesthetics of the political in general, and in the sense of "aestheticization of politics" that Walter Benjamin warned against[9]—unwittingly reproduce the neoliberal notion of a global "individual" who is unable to organize and take decisive action?

The unmatched aesthetic production of the Occupy movements have been interpreted through Chantal Mouffe's and Ernesto Laclau's theory of hegemony and radical democracy and Judith Butler's nonfoundationalist feminist theory as emblematic of an expanded field where "the political" and performance art are no longer distinguishable.[10] Aesthetics is no longer understood as a rarefied domain but as an art of bodies performing spontaneously and collectively as they occupy public spaces. I also take my clues from Zeynep Gambetti who, in a compelling commentary, writes that "Gezi was a spatial, situational, and relational reconfiguration that territorialized ethics in a *site* structured in such a way as to enable multiple encounters."[11] The aesthetic praxis in the park embodied and situated the ethics of political emancipation.

My essay both engages with and departs from these positions. Mouffe's and Butler's turns away from an ontic theory of politics to an ontological condition of "the political" establishes aesthetics—bodies performing in space—at the core of its model of society, thus seeking to supersede critical theory's perennial skepticism of "the aestheticization of politics." Yet the turn from politics to the "political" overlooks how the state *appears* in the square as a symbolic and aesthetic form.

My project here is to historicize the precariousness, the indeterminacy of this aestheticized subject—and how an anonymous figure, "an ordinary citizen," stands against and thus aesthetically reconstitutes the dignity of the state. I wish to emphasize the ambiguity and the opacity of the visual images of this "ordinary citizen" and show how the reception of a protest/performance as an allegory may have contradictory meanings: defiance against the state, or an aesthetic reconstruction of the sublime state.

Secular Bodies

Let me begin with the allegory *duran adam* or "standing man." It began on June 17, 2013, around six in the evening, when a 34-year-old man wearing a long-sleeved white shirt and carrying a backpack was seen in Istanbul's Taksim Square. He stood near the subway exit, facing the AKM Building across giant flagpoles, and froze.[12]

Emblematic of the legacy of Turkish modernism, the Atatürk Culture Center (AKM) once lent an austerely elegant façade to Istanbul's most important public square. Designed in the early 1950s and completed in 1969, the program combined Istanbul Opera and Ballet, a theater, and a children's cinema with a grand foyer for the plastic arts. Architect Hayati Tabanlıoğlu's design masterfully veiled all this behind a glass and aluminum curtain wall. The AKM projected an image of transparency and lightness to Taksim Square.[13]

For a decade beginning in 2007, this building stood in near-ruins, abandoned while a legal battle ensued between the AKP (the Turkish acronym for Justice and Development Party) government intent on demolishing it and the preservationists. When mass demonstrations engulfed Taksim Gezi Park in May and June 2013 and the riot police retreated from the square on June 1, a group of activists temporarily occupied the building, posing as victorious communards on the roof. The façade served as a billboard for the diverse, competing, and coexisting banners of the protesters.[14]

When the euphoria of newfound freedoms ended badly in Gezi Park and the police repossessed Taksim Square on June 11, most banners hanging from the building were cleared. The building emerged from a thick cloud of tear gas with only a Turkish flag and a portrait of Mustafa Kemal Atatürk, the founder of the Republic of Turkey, intact.[15]

In the next days, the portrait and flag composition was changed more than once. When standing man began his performance, the AKM Building was draped in two giant flags symmetrically arranged around a larger portrait of Atatürk.[16]

The man stood in Taksim Square motionless, staring straight at the AKM for eight hours and saying nothing. Plainclothes police, vigilant and befuddled, searched his pockets, pulled down his backpack, and went through his belongings. A television crew couldn't tempt him to break his silence: "Is this a silent [act of] resistance?"[17] An absent gaze, an untucked shirt, a dropped backpack: the iconic image of standing man was produced.[18]

Five hours into the performance, others in the square started joining standing man silently. The hashtag *#duranadam* (standing man) "went viral" on Twitter. Around 1:00 a.m., a "standing woman" stood motionless in Ankara's central Kızılay Square, marking the scene where the Gezi protestor Ethem Sarısülük had been shot by the police.[19] As the police began arresting the silent bystanders in Istanbul, the original standing man slipped away around 2:00 a.m.[20] The following morning a new practice was born: hundreds who went about their daily business in Taksim and across Turkey suddenly froze and stood motionless in public spaces. A group stood in the spot where Gezi

Figure 15.2. Students, members of labor unions, civil society organizations, women's groups, LGBT bloc, and soccer fans gather at Taksim Square and at the AKM Building on the twelfth day of the Gezi protests, June 8, 2013. Photograph by and courtesy of Mehmet Kaçmaz.

Figure 15.3. Erdem Gündüz performs *duran adam* or "standing man" for eight hours in Taksim Square, June 17–18, 2013. Photograph by and courtesy of Adnan Onur Acar.

protestor Abdullah Cömert was killed; others stood where Turkish Armenian journalist and public intellectual Hrant Dink had been assassinated in 2007; standing men and women performances were reenacted in front of news channels that failed to cover the mass protests.[21]

The Turkish and international press reported that Taksim's standing man was the performance artist and choreographer Erdem Gündüz.[22] A native of Ankara, he studied theater and dance in Izmir and Istanbul and was a graduate student of stage arts at Istanbul Mimar Sinan University.[23] Even though he was mute throughout the happening, Gündüz's presence in the square was universally understood as a stand-against: the body of an individual against an authoritarian regime. It has been described either as a vigil in remembrance of the fallen during the anti-government protests or more commonly as an act of "civil disobedience."

In a video interview recorded shortly after the event, Gündüz walks a fine line. He describes the performance as personal response to the unfolding events, an individual act of resistance:

> I am a performance artist. I tried to express frustration I felt. The news channels either did not report on the mass protests that took place on Istiklal Avenue, Taksim Square, and Dolmabahçe, or portrayed the events inaccurately. Everywhere, the streets . . . have been repaired and cleaned with an incredible speed, and presented back to the public as if nothing had happened there . . . And yet the resistance that started with Gezi Park was in its 18th or 19th day. All I did was to express myself like one of young protesters out there . . .
>
> *I stood alone in the square.* But let us not forget: everyone, every individual who joined the resistance at Gezi Park did so in defense of their own liberty . . . The cleaning of the streets as if nothing happened is the greatest violence of all . . .
>
> . . . Did I stage it? I didn't—not quite.
>
> Today I stood up in resistance. Some may call it civil disobedience . . . I am an ordinary person . . . I am an ordinary citizen of this country. If I stand down, someone else will replace me . . .[24]

Accusations of narcissism have often been leveled against performance and new media artists since the 1970s.[25] Within Turkey's collective urban protest movement, appearing as a self-promoting artist would have been untenable. Gündüz qualifies his act as an individual act of disobedience, and, paradoxically, retreats from authorship. He wishes, instead, to remain "an ordinary citizen."

If this event was a performance in which the artist effectively turned his mute body

Figure 15.4. A standing woman in Taksim Square, July 2, 2013. Photograph by Can Bilsel.

and his absent gaze into a work of art in public space, we need to consider the possibility that the message may not be as transparent as it appears.

There is at least one more reading, shared by a significant segment of the audience, that Gündüz was paying his respect to Kemal Atatürk, the founder and architect of the secular Turkish Republic, by standing at attention in front of his portrait.[26] For decades Turkish school children stood silently for a minute every November 10 at 9:05 a.m. to commemorate the moment Atatürk died. Some of the reenactments of standing man in the following days by "ordinary citizens" recalled the secular ritual of *saygı duruşu* (standing at ready, to remember, to pay respect).

The site of the standing man performance reactivated the ceremonial function of Taksim as "Cumhuriyet Meydanı" (Republic Square). Designed by Henri Prost in 1939, the monumental stairs and elevated podium between the Gezi Park and Taksim Square served as the front row for spectators to Republic Day processions.[27] In the 1940s both the square and the park presented a "modern" way of life, where the sexes were desegregated and where women became "visible." The public space prescribed a secular subject position for the "citizens of a nation-state."[28]

Thus performing standing man can be read in diametrically opposite ways: asserting the rights of the individual who is in the public square in defense of his/her/their individual rights, or a retreat from individuality in which the subject seeks to be integrated with the body of the nation and therefore becomes ground on ground.

In both readings, the potential identification of the irreducible presence of the standing man's body with the collective body of the nation poses a threat to the AKP. Since 2002, the ruling party has manufactured consent for its top-down neoliberal policies with a brand of populist identity politics that ranges from cultural conservatism to antisecular Sunni-Islamist majoritarianism. It is not surprising that those who wish to discredit Gündüz have done so by either dismissing his performance as a parody, or, worse, by claiming that he is an agent provocateur, an agent of a foreign service (e.g., the CIA).[29] Only if he can be presented as an agent will he be dismissed as "foreign" to the body of the nation. For his retreat from subjectivity, and his bare presence, have proven far more dangerous to AKP's authoritarian rule than anything he could enunciate in the public square.

The three competing identities projected upon Gündüz's body—a performance artist, a resistance fighter, and a spy—are not mutually exclusive. During the standing man performance, all Gündüz provided was an immobile body, a silent expression, and an absent gaze. Few signs of a preconstituted identity were in sight. What his original motives may have been are, therefore, beside the point. The questions are why so many people have been eager to project an identity on his otherwise mute body. How can we explain standing man's unprecedented potency in reaching out to (or angering) multiple audiences?

A small scandal erupted in the pro-government press when it was discovered, courtesy of Facebook, that Erdem Gündüz had participated nine years earlier, in 2004, in another protest-performance.[30] This was in the very early years of the AKP government, when the secularist ban on wearing the Islamic headscarf in Turkish universities was still in effect. Women who covered their hair were asked to remove their headscarves or risked being denied access to university campuses. The headscarf controversy remained the central front in the political and culture wars of the 1990s and early 2000. Opposition to the ban became the cause célèbre of the Turkish Islamists and the liberal critics of secularism alike. Erdem Gündüz's performance of 2004—or rather, his provocation—consisted of wearing a woman's Islamic headscarf and showing up at the university with two friends (a man and a woman also wearing headscarves). The "protest" took place in the class "Principles of Art," and they were not kicked out. Gündüz later related that theirs was a protest against rules that discriminated against women: only women were banned from wearing symbols of Islamic identity.[31]

The pro-AKP commentators were not impressed with this discovery, to say the least. They did not greet Gündüz as a defender of the right of religiously observant women to veil themselves if they so choose. If the pictures are any measure, Gündüz, in Islamic women's headscarf, looked more like a cross-dresser. While trying to ridicule an authoritarian brand of Turkish secularism and offer a liberal critique in 2004, he donned not a religious but a sexual stigma.

The Gezi protests of June 2013 gave a brief reprieve to transgender women in public spaces. A new LGBT bloc, which included transgender activists and others who gathered under the rainbow flag, played a prominent role in the protests.[32] Zeynep Gambetti describes the spontaneous camaraderie that developed between the LGBT bloc, the leftists, and (more surprisingly) Istanbul's otherwise homophobic soccer fans as they defended the barricades together. The camaraderie was such that the soccer fans could at once hurl the usual homophobic insults at the police but also praise the bravery of "a boy in a skirt" in combat.[33] Gambetti argues that the transgendered activists, often seen as more organized and prepared than other protestors, could register a claim for the collective self at Gezi rather than fall back to the usually ascribed role of "the constitutive Other."[34] For the urban masses subjected to indiscriminate police violence, the figure of transgender bodies transitioned from perceived vulnerability to resilience, and then to resistance.

Coming in the immediate aftermath of the Gezi events, standing man retreats into a secular regime in body politics, where the "ordinary" is the normative body and expressions of difference in public space (sexed, gendered, ethnic, or religious) are frowned upon. In spite of Gündüz's presentation of "standing man" as an "ordinary citizen"—or rather because of it—his performance commits the Gezi resistance to collective memory through repetition. It also exposes fault lines in the Turkish body politic, and more specifically in Turkish secularism (*laïcité* or *laiklik*) at a moment when secularism came under sustained attack by the AKP government.

Why, we must ask, has a young male of dominant ethnicity come to define "a stand-against" (or standing at attention with indignation) whereas the iconography of women, such as "woman in red" at Gezi Park (not unlike "woman with the blue brassiere" in Cairo) is shown on the receiving end of police violence? The standing man's staging of masculinity as "bare life" and the retreat from subjectivity has posed a challenge to the government's attempt to reshape the architecture of prominent public spaces by fiat.

Urban Transformations

The "urban transformation" (*kentsel dönüşüm*) of Istanbul and other cities in Turkey has been, for the last two decades, the primary theater in which a bargain between global finance and AKP's project of social engineering was effectuated, visiting upon the people the consequences of eminent domain, privatization, urban gentrification, and the destruction of remaining green spaces. For years, Istanbul's Kurdish and Roma residents, undocumented transient migrants, and transgender women were routinely subjected to forced relocation and police violence.[35]

The AKP government "conquered" one neighborhood after another, and "the conquest of Istanbul" has been the operational metaphor.[36] Grandiose plans such as the International Financial Center in Ataşehir or a mega-Friday mosque in Çamlıca (the city's nineteenth-century recreational grounds) have gone hand in hand with an attempt to brand an "Ottoman"-themed city made safe for the flow of international capital.

To establish its own hegemony in Taksim, which has long been identified with the secular republican regime, is the spatial-symbolic culmination of a view that has long seen the city as a ground for political conflict against the legacy of the modernizing republic in the twentieth century. By 2013, AKP-led administrations had undertaken a near systematic demolition of Turkish modernist architecture and public spaces.[37] The proposed destruction of Gezi Park for the reconstruction of the nineteenth-century Ottoman Artillery Barracks epitomized this vision. The construction in 2020 of a monumental mosque overlooking Taksim following decades of controversy suggests that the governing party remained committed to this vision years after the Gezi events.

The ideological significance of reconstructing the Ottoman Artillery Barracks thus outweighed any practical financial consideration. The promise to "recover" the lost Ottoman building and its self-Orientalizing "Islamic" language came to serve AKP's antisecularist authoritarian vision.[38] Paradoxically, when the AKP government regained control of Taksim on June 11, it was not an Islamic Ottoman imperial symbolism but the insignia of a sovereign nation state—the Turkish flag and the portrait of the founder of the secular republic—that were presented to the people.

By gazing at the AKM Building from the square for eight hours and simultaneously vacating the agency of the viewer, the standing man—a man who looks but who does not see—revealed a fatal contradiction in the government's representation of space. On the one hand, the AKP government understands Taksim Square and Gezi Park as a territory it unconditionally controls as a sovereign power. The ruling party sees ideological reconstruction as its inherent right of self-representation. On the other hand, the AKP's urban-spatial policy, like all neoliberal regimes that finance their operations with the flow of international capital and need to return a surplus on the investment, entails the deliberate confusion between public and private spaces. So, for instance, the police removed the protesters from the public park for a project that sought to privatize its revenues.[39] Confusion reigned among officials about the intended function of the reconstructed Artillery Barracks: a shopping mall or some other commercial venture that reified "Ottoman" heritage.[40]

I therefore contend that the power of Taksim's standing man resides in the ambiguity of spectatorship and presence that both assumes the place of the spectator and negates it. When we start asking for whom this composition of portrait and flags is intended, the visual expression of a supposed national consensus (a return to the iconography of the secular republic), which the government reverted to in a moment of crisis, is revealed to be vacuous.

It suffices to have the public pause, look at a building, and refuse to see it in order to destabilize the idea of architecture as a singular representation. How can a building and a park embody overlapping symbolisms—a nation and international capital; liberty and its suppression; "anarchy" and the sovereign state—from one day to another? Architecture can be destabilizing to a government when it encounters an "ordinary" body it cannot identify or locate as a subject.

But the question remains: did standing man, in his solitude and bare presence, become constitutive of the rights of others (e.g., the displaced transient workers, the undocumented migrants, the Roma, the Kurds, and the transgendered women) all at once? Or, conversely, did standing man become a near obsession for both the supporters and critics of the protest movement because it embodied what the subject has so commonly become—a body, visible, and yet without rights?

The Return of the Political

"Everywhere is Taksim, resistance is everywhere" has been the motto of the Turkish protestors.[41] Although the Gezi protests erupted spontaneously in every major city in Turkey, Taksim is imbued with the symbolism of a legendary site, one that mirrors all other sites of resistance. Since the 1970s Taksim has been identified with May 1st Labor Day rallies and with Turkey's left and socialist movements.[42]

In the first ten days of June 2013, during the occupation of Taksim Square and Gezi Park, the participants engaged in performative acts, including interventions in public spaces, site-specific art, dance, musical performances, and guerrilla agriculture. This entailed transforming one edge of Gezi Park into a community vegetable garden, a *bostan* for the people. There was a piano in the square, a band performing in gas masks, and the youth orchestra and chorus. The park featured a library with donated books and a field clinic with donated medications. The occupiers volunteered in shifts for the upkeep and cleaning of the park.[43]

Many have therefore arguably experienced Gezi Park as an aesthetic commune: a place where class and gender differences appeared not to matter; where sexual orientations and gender identities could be lived without repression; where ethnic conflict came to an end; where architectural monuments could be taken over and tagged with ephemeral counter-monuments and the aesthetic performances of the occupiers; where public interest overcame the private interests of global capital; and where the people established, if only for ten days, an aesthetically performed form of democracy. The message of Gezi Park was clear: the society emancipated from oppression is beautiful.

In a survey conducted by KONDA (a research and consultancy company specializing in surveying national trends) with a sample of 4,411 people who occupied Gezi Park on June 6–7, 2013, a large majority of the respondents described themselves as "ordinary citizens" unaffiliated with a political party or a civil society organization. The majority of the occupiers of Gezi Park were women (50.8 percent), and the average age was 28.[44]

Although the Gezi protests were spontaneous and the participation of millions unexpected, they also brought together activists and members of various organizations. The politics of some of these groups was (and is) not only in competition but also at times anathema to each other. The interviews conducted by the political psychologists Özden Melis Uluğ and Yasemin Gülsüm Acar with the Gezi protestors in a number of cities feature a stunningly diverse group: Alevi activists, "Anticapitalist Muslims," Çarşı (the fans of the Beşiktaş soccer club), feminist activists, the LGBT bloc, Kurdish activists, members of labor unions and professional organizations, socialists, Kemalists, Ülkücüler (Turkish ultranationalists), and Taksim Solidarity (the platform of civil society organizations founded to preserve the square against privatization and urban transformation). Of these, the editors of the survey subdivided "the socialists" into six socialist or communist parties: EMEP, ESP, ÖDP, SDP, SYKP, and TKP. It is clear that the editors' attempt to classify the activists by affiliation is itself ripe for potential controversy.[45] Başak Ertür observed that, whereas the organized left was a minority in the occupied park and the square, they formed about half of those who attended the meetings of the umbrella group, Taksim Solidarity, which met outside the occupied zone.[46]

Uluğ and Acar's interviews document the ways the activists negotiated their newfound solidarity. The activists describe their experience of becoming aware of and coming to accept the others, often reserving their strongest criticism for the parties closest to their own affiliation. For instance, the socialists often provide a critical assessment of other socialists. The self-described "Anticapitalist Muslims" seems to have attracted the most attention, as they promised to break from the AKP government's hegemonic bloc and challenge its claim to represent the pious majority. The displays of solidarity continued after the riot police violently repossessed the square and then the park. The "Anticapitalist Muslims" invited all the components of the resistance to *iftar* during the Ramadan of July 2013. A miles-long street potluck, *Yeryüzü Sofrası* ("Terrestrial" or "Whole Earth Banquet") extended from Galatasaray to Taksim.

How did people of such diverse political worldviews come together? An interview with an activist identified as "male, 25-year-old, high-school graduate," from "Tuzluçayır Solidarity in Ankara" weaves together a compelling narrative. Despite being characterized as an "Alevi activist," he did not join the resistance in defense of the rights of a religious minority but in opposition to the AKP government's "neoliberal policies." He describes neoliberalism as all of these at once: "the commodification of public spaces and the environment," "the privatization of public services (education, healthcare, transportation, housing)," "the precarization of the working class" into contract workers (*taşeronlaştırma*), "the proletarianization" of the professionals and of the "petit-bourgeoisie," the restrictions imposed on women's "reproductive freedoms" and on abortion, the "ecological disaster" that has unfolded across the land. He adds that AKP's ongoing oppression of the religious and ethnic minorities, too, is indicative of its project to forge a "homogeneous" subject under neoliberalism.[47]

The strong counterhegemonic discourse, with all these disparate demands coming together in their opposition to an authoritarian neoliberal regime, has the potential of forming a new hegemony as Ernesto Laclau and Chantal Mouffe have argued since 1985, and which Mouffe describes in her more recent book, *For a Left Populism:*

> A left populist strategy is informed by an anti-essentialist approach according to which the "people" is not an empirical referent but a discursive political construction. It does not exist previous to its performative articulation and cannot be apprehended through sociological categories.[48]

Gezi, like all Occupy movements, reveals a profound distrust in the representations of society as a totality. On June 27, 2013, Hazal Halavut published in the feminist news portal *5Harfliler* a critique of those "experts of expertise" who pass sociological, political, and psychological judgments about who the protestors are and what they want without leaving their "expert-armchairs." All "objective" analysis detached from the immanence of the events is suspected of trying to make the protests intelligible to the state. And when the protestors dispute those judgments to pass their own, they, too, forget about all that violence and begin "speaking as the citizens of the state."[49] Halavut writes:

> We were an ambiguous subject—and the ambiguity of "us" was as disturbing as the police and tear gas. As we chanted "shoulder to shoulder against fascism," it was already obvious that the person with whom you now stand together, may tomorrow embrace fascism—or perhaps he already has—a fascism that he shall call patriotism or honor. Then you will have to find other allies to form another "us" to fight against his fascism.[50]

A nonfoundationalist theory, which is strongly represented among the Turkish protestors and the interpreters of the Gezi movement, equates resistance with the performance of the political. As Leticia Sabsay has shown, both the theory of hegemony as described by Laclau and Mouffe and the feminist theory of Judith Butler depend on the antagonistic and unstable construction of subject positions against a "constitutive other." Both positions depend on the assumption that any totality or stable, integrated body—be it the society, the masses, the crowds, the nation—is ontologically arbitrary.[51] Alliances constantly change, and one group's political "demands" take precedence over those of the others, forming a new hegemony.

Yet, hegemony is not always consolidated through short-term alliances as Mouffe, Laclau, and Butler have suggested. It persists in the *longue durée,* and in Turkey, what is hegemonic is the organicist and communitarian idea of the nation that both belongs to and owns a sovereign state. In her book *"Makbul Vatandaş"ın Peşinde (In Search of the Acceptable Citizen)*, Füsun Üstel traces the history of the "good citizen" in public school curricula since the late Ottoman Empire, documenting its transformations since 1908 when it appeared in the textbooks.[52] Despite significant transformations, the notion of ethno-culturalist citizenship with duties toward the nation-state continues to be embraced today by large segments of the society, the supporters of the governing bloc and the opposition alike.

Not all the subject positions are equally distant to the state as "floating signifiers"[53] vying for hegemony on a leveled semantic field. The state exists not just in relation to its citizens but also against the bodies it excludes, as articulated in Giorgio Agamben's analysis of "bare life" and "the state of exception."[54]

Both Butler and Gambetti criticize Agamben's "bare life" in their respective readings of the occupations of the Tahrir Square and Gezi Park. Gambetti rightly contends that Agamben essentializes biopolitics and reduces politics into sovereignty.[55] Butler returns to a critique of Agamben's "bare life" in her assessment of Gezi:

> There is no sovereign power jettisoning the subject outside the domain of the political as such; rather, there is a renewal of popular sovereignty outside, and against, the terms of state sovereignty and police power, one that often involves a concerted and corporeal form of exposure and resistance.[56]

By turning to Agamben's "bare life" to understand the mute gesture of standing man, I do not wish to subscribe to his truly disconcerting thesis that it is the prison camp, not the *polis*, that is the "biopolitical paradigm of the West." Agamben's "bare life" brings to a logical conclusion the ontological turn toward the political. When pushed to an extreme, reading the political as performative and embodied in the "constitutive other" leads to an ahistorical theory of biopolitics in which law is defined by a "state of exception."

It is in the affinity Agamben finds between the appearance of "bare life" and the aesthetics of the sublime[57] that I find a clue for reading the allegory of standing man. In an essay reflecting on Walter Benjamin's earlier work on Goethe's *Elective Affinities* (on the relation of the "veil and the veiled, appearance and essence"), Agamben writes:

> This is human nudity. It is what remains when you remove the veil from beauty. It is sublime because, as Kant claims, the impossibility of presenting the idea through the senses is reversed at a certain point by a presentation of a higher order where what is being presented is, so to speak, presentation itself . . . The sublime, then, is an appearance that exhibits its own vacuity and, in this exhibition, allows the inapparent to take place.[58]

Figure 15.5. A gathering in Taksim Square in remembrance of the demonstrators who perished during the Gezi Park protests, June 13, 2013. Photograph by and courtesy of Yücel Tunca.

A vast empty space was left behind in June 2013 after the riot police dispersed the protestors. Taksim Square amounted to all of these at once: a concrete slab devoid of occupants; an infrastructure space with underground motorways, metro entrances, and a giant flagpole; a staging ground for the police; a perpetual construction zone. Taksim, repossessed by the state, amounted to a tabula rasa swept clean of the conflicting and competing collective memories of the square. The AKM Building itself was in ruins and being used as a logistical hub for the riot police and their terrifying TOMAs. (The AKM Building was demolished in 2018 and replaced.) At night, stadium-grade lights flooded the square, pinning the occasional person strolling to the concrete floor with multiple shadows.

When he stood in Taksim, Gündüz was perceived as reigniting resistance by simply defying the ban of *being* in the square. He did not resume the playful performances of the Gezi commune. Nor did he seek solidarity with the crowds. For the first five hours, Gündüz stood alone against the crushing emptiness of this space. He unveiled himself to the state, which revealed nothing. He stripped himself of the "grace" of the beautiful resistance (the harmony of collective bodies performing earlier in Gezi) and assumed a lonely gesture. He inverted the overwhelming forces unleashed by the state into an unidentified and vulnerable body.

In Taksim the state is not limited to a logistical entity. Its sovereignty is not made manifest in police powers and the mechanized, overwhelming force it unleashed against the masses. Sovereign power once embodied in the person of the ruler migrated under the republic to the replaceable and nondescript body of the anonymous "ordinary citizen."[59] The sovereign state *appears* in the square as what I shall call the *sublime state* in relation to this unidentified body.

The appearance of standing man in front of the insignia of the sovereign power, the denuding of this body from communal identities, upholds a higher order: the *secular republican state*. In this relation the sublime state is thus elevated back to a "disinterested" aesthetic field and is absolved from the biopolitical transgressions of a government acting in its name.

"Every individual who joined the resistance . . . did so in relation to their own liberty" declared Gündüz in 2013. He added: "If I stand down, someone else will replace me . . ."[60] In the final analysis, standing man is an allegory of the *demos* rather than of individual. This lone figure of resistance—its bare presence in the square—presents secular republican body politics as a sine qua non of liberty.

Notes

This chapter draws from many years of research on the iconography of "resistance" since the Gezi events of May–June 2013. An earlier, shorter version was delivered on October 24, 2013, for SANART's Aesthetics Congress of Turkey at Mersin University. The text has since expanded and evolved in response to a series of seminars and invited talks and is published for the first time here. I wish to thank the organizers and the participants in these conversations: F. Cânâ Bilsel, Belgin Turan Özkaya, İpek Akpınar, Nathalie Clayer, Panayiota Pyla, Alona Nitzan-Shiftan, Sally Yard, Molly McClain, Patricia Blessing, and Ali Yaycıoğlu. I am grateful to Reinhold Martin and Claire Zimmerman for raising the questions articulated in this book.

1. W. J. T. Mitchell, "Image, Space, Revolution: the Arts of Occupation," *Critical Inquiry* 39, no. 1 (2012): 14.
2. The Taksim Gezi Park protests (or the Gezi resistance) started shortly before midnight on May 27 and the early hours of May 28, 2013, when a group of environmental activists stopped bulldozers at Gezi Park. A peaceful occupation to shield the park from redevelopment escalated into mass protests after the police raided the encampments. For a citizen-journalist's account see Timur Danış, *Yaşam İçin Gezibostan Direnişi: Taksim 2013 Mayıs-Haziran; Ve Meşeye Su Verildi* (Istanbul: Cadde Yayınları, 2013). On June 2, 2013, the Turkish Medical Association reported that hundreds of protestors were injured during two days of protests in Istanbul, Ankara, and Izmir by police-operated water cannons and tear gas canisters fired at close range or in confined spaces. Türk Tabipleri Birliği, "Uygulanan

Orantısız Güç Kabul Edilemez," June 2, 2022, www.ttb.org.tr, archived at webarchive.org. Public revulsion against police violence spread through the social media: thousands (cumulatively millions) of protestors arrived in Istanbul Taksim Square, and in parks, squares, and public spaces in Ankara, Izmir, Mersin, Konya, Adana, Bursa, Eskişehir, Antakya, and numerous other cities in Turkey.

3. For the citizen platform Taksim Solidarity and its efforts to save Gezi Park and stop the "pedestrianization" (privatization) of Taksim Square, see the interview with Mücella Yapıcı, "Evet, Mesele 3–5 Ağaç Değil," *soL*, September 16, 2013, haber.sol.org.tr. See also the press release and website of Taksim Dayanışması archived on June 5, 2013 at https://web.archive.org/web/20130605105631/http://taksimdayanisma.org.

4. Seyla Benhabib writes that saving Gezi Park must be "a small grievance" when compared to the people's discontent with the policies of the ruling Justice and Development Party (AKP), which has systematically eroded the secular character of the republic and intruded into the private lives of citizens. "Turkey's Authoritarian Turn," *New York Times*, June 3, 2013. Political commentary on the Gezi protests are too numerous to list here. For a collection of essays written during or shortly after the protests, see the monthly socialist culture review *Birikim* 291–292 *#gezidirenişi Bir Yanımız Bahar Bahçe* (July–August 2013) and Cihan Tuğal, "'Resistance Everywhere': The Gezi Revolt in Global Perspective," *New Perspectives on Turkey*, 49 (2013): 157–72. For a critical review of the literature published in the five years following the Gezi protests, see Kaan Ağartan, "The Politics of the Square: Remembering Gezi Park Protests Five Years Later," *New Perspectives on Turkey* 58 (2018): 201–17.

5. Christiane Gruber, "The Visual Emergence of the Occupy Gezi Movement" in "'Resistance Is Everywhere': The Gezi Protests and the Dissident Visions of Turkey," ed. Anthony Alessandrini, Nazan Üstündağ, and Emrah Yıldız, special issue, *JADMAG* 1, no. 4 (Fall 2013): 29–36; Jeremy F. Walton, "'Everyday I'm Çapulling!' Global Flows and Local Frictions of Gezi," in *Everywhere Taksim: Sowing the Seeds for a New Turkey at Gezi*, ed. Isabel David and Kumru F. Toktamış (Amsterdam: Amsterdam University Press, 2015); Ezgi Bakçay Çolak, "Gezi Parkı Eylemleri Özelinde Toplumsal Muhalefet ve Estetik Politik Eylem" in *Sokağın Belleği: 1 Mayıs 1977'den Gezi Direnişi'ne Toplumsal Hareketler ve Kent Mekânı*, ed. Derya Fırat (Ankara: Dipnot Yayınları, 2014); Aygün Şen, "Street Art: Gezi Parkı ve Direnişin Estetiği," *Yeniyol* (July 2013), archived at academia.edu.

6. City planner and academic Ceyda Sungur was photographed by Osman Orsal (Reuters) as she stood defiantly in Gezi Park. A police officer in riot gear is shown firing pepper spray on her face. Named "woman in red," the picture circulated internationally. Max Fisher, "The Photo That Encapsulates Turkey's Protests and the Severe Police Crackdown," *Washington Post*, June 3, 2013, www.washingtonpost.com, archived at webarchive.org. See also *Gazeteci Gözüyle Direniş / Through the Eyes of Journalists: Resistance and Gezi Park Photographs* (Istanbul: Kırmızı Kedi, 2013); Özcan Yurdalan, ed., *Bir İsyanı Fotoğraflamak* (Istanbul: Agora, 2014). For a list of photojournalists and reporters injured during the protests, see "Habercinin İsim İsim 33 Gezi Günü," https://m.bianet.org/biamag/medya/148689-habercinin-isim-isim-33-gezi-gunu.

7. See A. Nüvit Bingöl, "Gezi Havası/Gezi Tune," June 4–17, 2013, video, 4:20, https://vimeo.com/68917094; Hakan Vreskala, "Dağılın Lan," June 8, 2013, video, 2:56, https://

www.youtube.com/watch?v=cjfoXoz69sw; Kardes Türküler, "Tencere Tava Havası/ Sound of Pots and Pans," June 6, 2013, video, 4:22, https://www.youtube.com/watch?v=o-kbuS-anD4.

8. *Die Ästhetik des Widerstands,* Peter Weiss's three-volume historical novel about the German socialist resistance against Hitler, was translated into Turkish in 2005 by Çağlar Tanyeri and Turgay Kurultay (2nd edition, Istanbul: İletişim, 2013). The Turkish title *Direnmenin Estetiği* ("the aesthetics of resisting" more than "resistance") duly describes an allegory more than specific events. The novel begins with a description of the Gigantomachy Frieze in Berlin's Pergamon Museum, vividly depicting the agony, bodily pain, and defeat of the earthly giants by the Olympian gods. The narrator explains how the enslaved and dehumanized workers of Pergamon were forced to build the Great Altar, a victory monument dedicated to their own defeat: the frieze is an allegory of class struggle. Peter Weiss, *The Aesthetics of Resistance,* vol. 1, trans. Joachim Neugroschel (Durham: Duke University Press, 2005). The Turkish word *direniş* (resistance) describes specific labor movements and strikes since the 1970s. The Gezi events were immediately described as a *direniş* or *#direngezi* (resist Gezi).

9. Walter Benjamin, "The Work of Art in the Age of Mechanical Reproduction," *Illuminations,* trans. Harry Zohn, ed. Hannah Arendt (New York: Schocken Books, 2007), 217–52.

10. Judith Butler, "Rethinking Vulnerability and Resistance," in *Vulnerability in Resistance,* ed. Judith Butler, Zeynep Gambetti, and Leticia Sabsay (Durham: Duke University Press, 2016), 13–27. See also Chantal Mouffe, *For a Left Populism* (London: Verso, 2018) and Leticia Sabsay, "Permeable Bodies: Vulnerability, Affective Powers, Hegemony," in *Vulnerability in Resistance,* 278–302.

11. Zeynep Gambetti, "Risking Oneself and One's Identity: Agonism Revisited," in *Vulnerability in Resistance,* 28–51, esp. 47. See also Zeynep Gambetti, "Occupy Gezi as Politics of the Body," in *The Making of a Protest Movement in Turkey: #occupygezi,* ed. Umut Özkırımlı (New York: Palgrave Pivot, 2014), 89–102.

12. Erin B. Mee and Erdem Gündüz, "Standing Man and the Impromptu Performance of Hope: An Interview with Erdem Gündüz," in "Performing the City," special issue, *TDR* 58, no. 3 (Fall 2014): 69–83.

13. Sibel Bozdoğan and Esra Akcan, *Turkey: Modern Architectures in History* (London: Reaktion Books, 2012), 128–129; Esra Akcan, "Bir cepheyi paylasmak: Parşömen Olarak AKM ve Toplumsal Bellek," *Mimarist* 13, no. 48 (Fall 2013): 85–92.

14. Esra Akcan describes the visual appropriation of the AKM as a "countermonumental gesture," an example of "participatory design" and of the "radical or plural democracy." Esra Akcan, "How Does Architecture Heal? The AKM as Palimpsest and Ghost," *The South Atlantic Quarterly* 119, no. 1 (January 2019): 88.

15. See a photograph by Lam Yi Fei, June 11, 2013, "Turkish Police Attempt to Clear Taksim Square of Protestors," Getty Images, www.gettyimages.com.

16. "'Standing Man' Inspires a New Type of Civil Disobedience in Turkey," June 19, 2013, https://www.hurriyetdailynews.com/standing-man-inspires-a-new-type-of-civil-disobedience-in-turkey--48999.

17. For a video clip of the standing man performance edited into eight minutes and three

seconds, see "Duran Adam Şaskın Polisler," June 18, 2013, https://www.youtube.com/watch?v=hQlvRjJHWZE.

18. For the iconic image of standing man, see https://resistology.org/tag/duranadam, accessed September 25, 2022.
19. "Ankara'da 'Duran Kadın,'" *Sözcü,* June 18, 2013.
20. Mee and Gündüz, "Standing Man," 79.
21. Mee and Gündüz, "Standing Man," 70; Pieter Verstraete, "The Standing Man Effect," IPC-Mercator Policy Brief, Istanbul Sabancı University (July 2013), 8, https://ipc.sabanciuniv.edu.
22. "Kim Bu Duran Adam? İşte Geçmişi," *Internet Haber,* June 18, 2013, www.internethaber.com; "Kim Bu Duran Adam?," *Milliyet,* June 18, 2013, milliyet.com.tr.
23. See the artist's website http://www.erdemgunduz.org, accessed September 25, 2022.
24. "Taksim'deki Duran Adam Erdem Gündüz Konuştu" ("Interview with Erdem Gündüz"), June 18, 2013, 13:44, www.hurriyet.com.tr, video clip accessed on September 13, 2022 on youtube.com. Translation mine.
25. Anne Wagner, "Performance, Video, and the Rhetoric of Presence," *October* 91 (Winter 2000): 59–80.
26. In an interview with Erin Mee, Gündüz states that he "misses" the founding principles and values of the republic under Kemal Atatürk, with secularism, equal rights, and women's rights being among them. Gündüz reproached the AKP government for eroding these values: "The AKP tells women how many children to have." Mee and Gündüz, "Standing Man," 78.
27. For Henri Prost's design of Taksim Republic Square and İnönü Esplanade (Gezi Park), see F. Cânâ Bilsel, "Espaces Libres: Parks, Promenades, Public Squares . . . ," in *From the Imperial Capital to the Republican Modern City: Henri Prost's Planning of Istanbul 1936–1951,* ed. F. Cânâ Bilsel and Pierre Pinon (Istanbul: Istanbul Araştırmaları Enstitüsü, 2010), 349–80, esp. 356.
28. İpek Akpınar, "Remapping Istanbul: Taksim after Gezi" in *The Case of Beyoğlu, Istanbul: Dimensions of Urban Re-development,* ed. Gülden Erkut and Reza Shirazi (Berlin: TU-Berlin, 2014), 31–38. For a discussion of modernizing "secular ideology" in Prost's Istanbul plan, see Akpınar, "The Rebuilding of Istanbul Revisited: Foreign Planners in the Early Republican Years," *New Perspectives on Turkey,* no. 50 (2014): 59–92.
29. Personal attacks on standing man in the pro-government press are too numerous to cite here. The pro-AKP columnist Abdülkadir Selvi wrote a particularly egregious one in *Yeni Şafak* on June 20, 2013.
30. "Aper Alpözgen'den Açıklama," June 20, 2013, www.trthaber.com.
31. Mee and Gündüz, 75; see also Pieter Verstraete, "The Standing Man Effect," IPC-Mercator Policy Brief, Istanbul Sabancı University (July 2013), https://ipc.sabanciuniv.edu.
32. Başak Ertür, "Barricades: Resources and Residues of Resistance," in *Vulnerability in Resistance,* 97–121.
33. Zeynep Gambeti, "Risking Oneself and One's Identity: Agonism Revisited," in *Vulnerability in Resistance,* 37–47.
34. Gambetti, "Risking Oneself," 38.

35. For urban gentrification in the early years of AKP, see Jean-François Pérouse, *İstanbul'la Yüzleşme Denemeleri: Çeperler, Hareketlilik ve Kentsel Bellek* (Istanbul: Iletişim, 2011), esp. 281–82; and Tuna Kuyucu and Özlem Ünsal, "'Urban Transformation' as State-led Property Transfer: An Analysis of Two Cases of Urban Renewal in Istanbul," *Urban Studies* 47, no. 7 (June 2010), 1479–99. For the mass eviction of transsexuals in 1995 from the "back streets" of Taksim shortly before the UN Habitat Conference, see Mary Robert and Deniz Kandiyoti, "Photo Essay: Transsexuals and the Urban Landscape in Istanbul," *Middle East Report*, no. 206 (1998): 20–25.
36. For the politics of "conquest commemoration," see chapter 6 of İpek Türeli, *Istanbul, Open City: Exhibiting Anxieties of Urban Modernity* (London, New York: Routledge, 2018). Eray Çaylı argues that the reification of heritage into "a thing belonging to a proprietor" was reinforced, not challenged, by the Gezi protests; Eray Çaylı, "Inheriting Dispossession, Mobilizing Vulnerability: Heritage amid Protest in Contemporary Turkey," *International Journal of Islamic Architecture* 5, no. 2 (July 2016): 359–78.
37. Zafer Akay, "Gezi'de Örtülü Bir Yıkım Politikasının Baltası Taşa mı Vuruldu?," *Mimarist* 13, no. 48 (Fall 2013): 80–84.
38. Ahmet A. Ersoy, "Topçular Kışlası ve Bir Kitlesel Tüketim Aracı Olarak Tarih," *Toplumsal Tarih* 235 (April 2013): 72–76; Can Bilsel, "The Crisis in Conservation," *Journal of the Society of Architectural Historians* 76, no. 2 (June 2017): 141–145.
39. Mücella Yapıcı recalls that the employees of a private contractor attempted to remove protestors from the park. Yapıcı, "Evet, Mesele 3–5 Ağaç Değil," *soL*, September 16, 2013, haber.sol.org.tr.
40. Ahmet Ersoy, *Architecture and the Late Ottoman Historical Imaginary: Reconfiguring the Architectural Past in a Modernizing Empire* (Farnham Surrey, UK: Ashgate, 2015), 246–51.
41. Cihan Tuğal, "Resistance Everywhere."
42. May Day celebrations resumed in Taksim in 2010–2012 until the government closed the square for impending "pedestrianization." Mehmet Ö. Alkan, "Osmanlı'nın, Cumhuriyet'in, Islamcıların, Kemalistlerin ve Sosyalistlerin Taksim'i: Taksim'in Siyasi Tarihine Mukaddime," *Birikim*, nos. 291–292 (2013): 146–152; Tanıl Bora, "Taksim, 1 Mayıs 1977 ve Yüzleşme," *Birikim* no. 253 (2010): 8–10.
43. For the occupation of Gezi Park as "an aesthetic and political action," see Ezgi Bakçay Çolak, "Gezi Parkı Eylemleri Özelinde Toplumsal Muhalefet ve Estetik Politik Eylem," in *Sokağın Belleği: 1 Mayıs 1977'den Gezi Direnişine Toplumsal Hareketler ve Kent Mekânı*, ed. Derya Fırat (Ankara: Dipnot, 2014). For the ephemeral architectures and spatial practices, see Belgin Turan Özkaya, "Akışkan Coğrafyalar," in *İnci Aslanoğlu için Bir Mimarlık Tarihi Dizimi*, ed. T. Elvan Altan and Sevil Enginsoy Ekinci (Ankara: Kalkan/METU, 2019), 1–6.
44. KONDA, "Gezi Parkı Araştırması: Kimler, neden ordalar ve ne istiyorlar?," https://konda.com.tr.
45. For the interviews with the activists, see Özden Melis Uluğ and Yasemin Gülsüm Acar, *Bir Olmadan Biz Olmak: Farklı Gruplardan Aktivistlerin Gözüyle Gezi Direnişi* (Ankara: Dipnot, 2014).
46. Ertür, "Barricades," 106.
47. Uluğ and Acar, *Bir Olmadan Biz Olmak*, 21–33.
48. Mouffe, *For a Left Populism*, 62; see also Ernesto Laclau and Chantal Mouffe, *Hegemony and*

Socialist Strategy: Towards a Radical Democratic Politics (London: Verso, 1985); Mouffe, *The Democratic Paradox* (London: Verso, 2005); Laclau, *On Populist Reason* (London: Verso, 2005).

49. Hazal Halavut, "Gezi ya da Uzanıp Kendi Yanaklarından Öpmenin İhtimali" *5Harfliler*, June 27, 2013, www.5harfliler.com.
50. Halavut, "Gezi ya da Uzanıp," www.5harfliler.com.
51. Leticia Sabsay, "Permeable Bodies: Vulnerability, Affective Powers, Hegemony," in *Vulnerability in Resistance*, 278–302.
52. Füsun Üstel, *'Makbul Vatandaş'ın Peşinde* (Istanbul: İletişim, 2004).
53. Laclau, *On Populist Reason*, 129–38.
54. Giorgio Agamben, *Homo Sacer: Sovereign Power and Bare Life* (Stanford: Stanford University Press, 1998).
55. Zeynep Gambetti, "Occupy Gezi as Politics of the Body" in *The Making of a Protest Movement in Turkey #Occupygezi*, ed. Umut Özkirimli (Palgrave-Pivot, 2014), 89–102; see also Gambetti, "Foucault'dan Agamben'e Olağanüstü Halin Sıradanlığına Dair Bir Yanıt Denemesi," *Cogito* 70–71 (2012).
56. Judith Butler, "Rethinking Vulnerability and Resistance," in *Vulnerability in Resistance*, 26.
57. For a critique of Agamben's reframing of the sublime, see Carlo Salzani, "The Notion of Life in the Work of Agamben," *CLCWeb: Comparative Literature and Culture*, 14, no. 1 (2012).
58. Giorgio Agamben, "Nudity," in *Nudities* (Stanford: Stanford University Press, 2011), 85–86.
59. Compare with Rosalyn Deutsche, "Agoraphobia," in *Evictions: Art and Spatial Politics* (Cambridge, Mass.: MIT Press, 1996), 272–73.
60. "Taksim'deki Duran Adam Erdem Gündüz Konuştu," www.hurriyet.com.tr, video clip accessed on September 13, 2022 on youtube.com.

Conclusion

Democracy Now?

Reinhold Martin and Claire Zimmerman

Wherein lie the maladies this volume seeks to expose? We might distinguish the insufficient corpus of political architectural history, practically speaking, from different ways of reading that corpus. With few exceptions, for example, we do not yet have a robust, teachable archive of truly "soviet" architecture, its relatives, or of its descendants in the more modest, local, and democratic sense emphasized by Hannah Arendt.[1] Nor does the architecture of county courthouses, town halls, council chambers, meeting houses, Freedmen's Bureaus, Rathausen, hôtels de ville, and so on feature with any real prominence in accounts of modern architecture's emancipatory project. Whereas, for example, the distinct political meanings of two radically different cases as the planning and design of Brasilia, a national capital, and Chandigarh, the capital of the Punjab, were collapsed into the "new monumentality" of the postwar order, at least for modernist avant-gardes, if not for their traditionalist contemporaries or for the more anonymous designers and builders of everyday institutions.

While necessary, adding the Federalist courthouse on Main Street or the Gothic Revival town hall on the village square remains insufficient to help readers of the built environment grasp the larger dynamic shaping architecture and politics. Such buildings have received considerable attention not just from critical historians of vernacular architecture but also from guardians of national and subnational "tradition" (in the latter case, often with ethnoracial overtones), as well as from the unsung devotions of countless historical societies.[2] Nor will it suffice to scale down even further to the architecture of voting itself as the bare minimum requirement of any democratic process. Here the hegemonic scene of the voting booth, a comparative luxury, is perhaps overshadowed by "election ink" applied the world over to voters' fingers to verify participation, a mark that testifies poignantly to democracy's hard-won intimacies on the one hand and to the inherent fragility of representation on the other.

Expanding the inquiry to public institutions more generally, we can assess any number of subnational museums, libraries, schools, and civic buildings realized worldwide for their eclectic efforts to speak to differentiated publics and, in many (but not all) cases, to offer those publics an opportunity to speak in turn. We can also recognize how, in the Soviet bloc, a relative loosening of architectural languages afforded opportunities for public speech—and in some cases public gathering—that had been otherwise constrained by totalitarian force.[3] But rarely do we see in these examples the cultivation of a *demos* that a thinker like Arendt would recognize, a body able to maintain the political autonomy that is indispensable to democratic deliberation, and to fend off the incursions of what she called the "social" via the entrepreneurial consumer to whom so many postmodern efforts to communicate were addressed.[4]

Still, our wager here remains that if we continue collectively to invoke such a *demos*, articulate its possible modes more fully, and render it legible, that *demos* may be easier to build. To the question of how to read the built environment, the volume also adds crucial material. If we are able to see in buildings the physical marks of hegemony, technocracy, *and* democracy, as essayed in the Introduction, these may provide society with a useful diagnostic device, whether after the fact or prior to building. As part of the public realm, buildings can be legible to anyone who might wish to read them. A few additional tools are indeed required. In the chapters above, and the material below, some of those tools are laid out.

Political Architecture from the Nineteenth to the Twentieth Century

This volume's conclusive framing began where its editors are, in today's United States, with an instantly infamous scene. Thousands of angry protestors, convinced by their political party and affiliated mediascapes that the 2020 U.S. presidential election had been stolen, storm the U.S. Capitol Building in Washington, D.C. Overwhelming police, hundreds violently force their way in, shout threats at elected officials gone into hiding, clash with guards, and mill about the halls and chambers posting videos to the internet. In one of these videos, taken in the Senate chamber, a helpless guard can be heard pleading to the insurrectionists to please respect this most "sacred" of civic spaces. The insurrectionists more or less comply.[5]

The sacralization of civic monuments has long been a hallmark of nationalism, an architectural version of political theocracy. The neoclassical U.S. Capitol Building, begun in 1793 to designs by William Thornton and carried out by several others, made vivid use of one of the two available idioms, classical and Gothic, with which a "battle of the styles" would later be waged over civic buildings in the British metropole and elsewhere. In a sign of its imperial character, that battle raged most famously over the design of the British Foreign Office and India Office in London, which began on paper in 1855 as a Gothic Revival monument rendered by George Gilbert Scott and was realized by Scott in 1868 in a neo-Renaissance style, with an orientalist "Sultan's Court" supplied by Matthew Digby Wyatt. Although Scott modeled the ultimate building on the secular palazzi of early modern merchants, and despite their use here and in countless other secular monuments, the classical orders that punctuated its bureaucratic façade retained, like the Gothic, the faint aura of their sacred origin—even if less pious and more triumphant in character.

While the British imperial office complex was under construction, the U.S. Capitol dome was being rebuilt under the supervision of Thomas Ustick Walter. Walter's design replaced the formerly wooden central dome with a much taller, iron-framed cupola, the construction of which proceeded against all odds during the Civil War with the Union Army's Eighth Massachusetts Regiment encamped below. When all was done, a triumphal, side-lit fresco nestled between the oculus of the coffered inner dome and the structural outer shell. The design recalls Jacques-Germain Soufflot's Church of Ste-Geneviève in Paris, which the revolution later secularized as the Panthéon, in a renaming that evokes both buildings' distant sacred archetype. But where the U.S. Capitol's predecessors (Christopher Wren's St. Paul's Cathedral in London among them) shaped daylight into an otherworldly glow, Walter's version used gaslight (later electrified) to illuminate an allegorical image: Constantino Brumidi's *Apotheosis of [George] Washington*, with the national patriarch as Christ, ascending to the heavens.[6]

Brumidi's fresco contributes to the sacralization of the vestibule below, the congressional spaces adjacent, and indeed the entire building in a manner that abandons any pretense to treat the nation's seat of democratic government as anything other than a church. In that respect, the Senate guard read the signs correctly in January 2020: the Capitol Building was sacred ground. Not, however, because it housed the organs of democracy, but because its architecture pledged allegiance to "one nation, under God," under a double dome.

A nation here is an imagined community, though not only in the sense defined by Benedict Anderson as a circle of readers sharing the wealth of print capitalism.[7] Under the new Capitol dome, the imagined nation was a federated body held together by force, a body that had just survived a civil war, the scars of which would not fade with time. Although it may seem that the dome's anticlimax as a mere lobby for lawmakers gives literal, anachronistic form to the thesis promulgated a century later by the philosopher Claude Lefort that democratic power occupies an "empty place," there is nothing empty about the myth propagated there.[8] That myth, of the nation as democratic body, is neither simply ideological cover for antidemocratic action nor a necessary fiction to prevent dissolution. It is, instead, a powerful but contradictory ideal, invoking racial, ethnic, or regional identity as a hedge against internationalist empire, yet paradoxically combining such an identity with elusive notions of equality among citizens. Since the nineteenth century, varieties of nationalism have often gone hand in hand with political democratization in Europe, North America, Latin America, and later in the postwar, postcolonial world. Yet the nation as sacred apotheosis is ultimately incommensurable with secular democracy and with the *demos* optimistically called forth by the Capitol's halls.

In ancient Athens, the gods dwelt on an acropolis while the people governed from the Pnyx, adjacent. During the modern period, nationalists, perceiving that what the people's representatives represent (whether they are elected or not) is ultimately antithetical to the very idea of a nation, have repeatedly attacked the state and its representatives as a matter of principle. "Nationhood" is mythical as well as historical; evidence for its existence resides in language, habits, and other cultural forms, the internal coherence and closure of which are manufactured, or "hailed" as Louis Althusser might have put it.[9] As such, a nation is part political theology. The example of the United States is unexceptional in this as in other regards, just as the architecture of its civic buildings exchanged styles and signifiers freely with those of the British and French imperium as well as with their Spanish predecessors, and through them Rome in its republican, imperial, and (for the Romanesque) "holy" forms. This has been especially true when architecture is enlisted to bind race and nation together.[10]

In contrast, Timothy Mitchell has argued for a different spatial effect resulting from the modern growth of the nation-state, when he notes in *Carbon Democracy* that national representative democracies were foundational to the excesses of capitalism and empire that unfolded beyond their borders. Representative democracy, he points out, came into being as a function of large populations pooled in the industrial cities that grew to exploit the growth of fossil fuels and modern industry. Political representation provided a way to control large urban populations even as it gave them rights. Mitchell drew attention to the borders of nation-states as the outer limit of any given democratic regime, beyond which capitalism provided a powerful technique of colonization and then empire-building without representation.[11] Thus, nationalism both authorizes antidemocratic practices beyond the borders of the nation, as many of our authors also show, and limits the scope of democratic ones even while associating itself with jingoism and xenophobia. If the nation-state provided the setting within which democracy came into being in the modern period, it also signaled its limits from the beginning.

Just as the nation embodies irresolvable contradictions between ethnic hegemony and democratic enfranchisement, so are its buildings equally riven by Roman and Greek models, as if a combination of Greek democracy and Roman empire might result from their adaptation. Led by Beaux-Arts academicians, a nominally secularized neoclassicism and its variants won the battle of the styles when it came to Euro-American political buildings throughout the nineteenth and twentieth centuries. Indeed, rejecting alternatives offered by a modernist vanguard, even the transnational League of Nations headquarters donned neoclassical garb on the shores of Lake Geneva in the late 1920s.

The 1927 design competition for the League of Nations headquarters resulted in a building designed by a team consisting of the Italian Carlo Broggi, the Swiss Julien Flegenheimer, the French Camille Lefèvre and Henri-Paul Nénot, and the Hungarian József Vágó, all of whom either trained at the Parisian École des Beaux-Arts or were associated with its traditions. Though historians have tended to treat this design team's modernist opponents more sympathetically, all sides of the contest belonged to a wider effort to attach architectural expression, or style, to political program. Such an effort was typical of the interwar period, especially in Europe and its faltering empires, echoing the earlier style debates referenced above.

Classical architecture as a purported signifier of democracy thus recurs in government buildings throughout the twentieth century within many national boundaries. Indeed, the association of classical culture with democracy is a familiar trope that often serves to brand as democratic those revolutions that are decidedly not so. Classical architecture is also the select style of authoritarian regimes at both ends of the ideological spectrum, as it has been historically. References to ancient culture invoked in twentieth-century global politics, as historian Jeanne Morefield points out, continued to provide a persistent foil for Western imperial practices as they had done since the rise of the Roman Empire (if not before). The finally constructed League of Nations building, for example, invoked classical order for the mandate system of international governance whose "constitution" was largely written by Jan Smuts, architect of South African apartheid. As Morefield notes, Smuts "ushered in both the extension of formal imperialism into the age of internationalism and set the stage for the informal imperialism that followed."[12] The project of international governance authored by Western imperial powers was designed thus to provide the means for their continued dominion. The "stripped neoclassical" League of Nations provides a first outpost of declining British and rising U.S. empires; the modernist slab of the United Nations Building in New York provides a second—correlating the work of such different figures as Edwin Lutyens and Wallace Harrison. This pairing reveals just how style matters to the architecture of international governance. For the British in India, modified classical architecture provided a sufficiently "international" style that functioned nonetheless as a signifier of Britishness; international modernism provided the same kind of passport for the United States, coming as it did from U.S. institutions staffed by cosmopolitan European émigrés. In neither case was building style incidental to the claims made for empire; rather, embassies, agencies, and hotels often functioned as national flags planted in the soil of a symbolically conquered land. Buildings of a certain scale and with a certain official profile perhaps inevitably lend themselves to styles that attempt to signify hegemonic domination—Persuasion P with Coercion C.

Neoliberalism after 1945

For Arendt, public assemblies, from the ward system proposed by Thomas Jefferson to the twentieth century's workers' councils and soviets, were the true legacy of the revolutions that defined the modern period.[13] Such assemblies were a potential bulwark not only against totalitarian organization, but also (we can add today) against the capture of the public realm by private interests in the neoliberal counterrevolution that followed.

There is no shortage of assembly halls, parliaments, and other spaces for democratic deliberation in the architectural annals of the postwar period, of which the United Nations Headquarters remains vividly representative. The historiography rightly singles out many of these as instruments of self-government for recently decolonized nations or, as in Latin America and elsewhere, for nations seeking geopolitical and economic autonomy.[14] Less remarked by architectural historians but visible within the fledgling United Nations itself is a political tension among the three organs of global governance projected by the Bretton Woods Agreement of 1944. Where the interests of wealthier nations and of global capital were disproportionately represented in the International Monetary Fund (IMF) and the World Bank, the more democratic International Trade Organization (ITO) was eventually scrapped, as was its successor, the New International Economic Order (NIEO) proposed to the United Nations by anticolonial nationalists across the global South.[15]

Neoliberalism was therefore not just a matter of deregulation and privatization; it was a matter of building a postwar global order within which political and economic sovereignty were decoupled, as the example of Berlin makes clear.[16] Neoliberalism, in other words, rebuilt the political distinction between public and private life that the Keynesian welfare state had eroded, but in reverse. Rather than subordinate private interests to the public good or the interests of individual nations to those of the globe as a giant *polis,* neoliberalism sought to render the private sphere sovereign and capital borderless. Using Arendt's terms, we might say that neoliberalism reversed the "rise of the social" by which she perceived the classical distinction between public and private to be threatened, but it did so in a manner that diminished the sovereignty of the *demos* as represented by the state, both domestically and internationally.[17]

Recent scholarship on architecture and neoliberalism has offered crucial insight on the transvaluation of everyday life that this entailed, from the transformation of housing to the development of shopping centers.[18] Dialectically, however, as the methods of architects, urban designers, and planners became more inclusive and participatory in response to the antidemocratic excesses of urban renewal and postwar reconstruction in the North, and of five-year plans and other sweeping instruments of nation-building in the South, they may have invited neoliberalism in through the back door. The most salient characteristic of antidemocratic praxis in this regard is the designation of markets as self-governing, autopoetic agents. This stipulation is the basis for many deregulatory programs; it is also the autonomic heartbeat of neoliberalism's archetypal subject, *homo economicus* reborn, whose sovereignty is enshrined in public-private partnerships and other instruments of governance designed to bypass local assemblies and maximize return on investment.[19]

This project, of utilizing the visible hand of the state to unchain the invisible hand of the market, is not new. Nor does it lack architectural distinction, from John Soane's Bank of England onward. But too often, the capitalist state's libertarian alter-ego is mistaken for a genuine alternative to the undemocratic rule of one, few, or many. To recast small as beautiful, or to seek solace only in extraparliamentary formations, is to misread Arendt's cautiously revolutionary message: that only when the *demos* assembles in public with a corresponding architecture will the neoliberal counterrevolution be turned back and democracy be rebuilt.

In the aftermath of popular movements that shook empires and transformed the world order, from anticolonial uprisings—peaceful or not—to the U.S. Civil Rights movement, and leading up to the convulsive events of 1968, it appeared to many that the *demos* had reclaimed the street and the public square. From Algiers to Paris, what Arendt called the "space of appearance" had acquired a political and strategic significance for which even the paramilitary planning of Baron von Haussmann's boulevards seemed no match. But with a few temporary exceptions, like the Chilean interlude or, more ambiguously, post-apartheid South Africa, the day after the revolution did not see democracy flourish. Nor did the popular revolts around 1989, from Wenceslas Square to Tiananmen, result in the uniformly liberal order dreamed of by the false prophets of history's "end."[20]

In the architectural academy, the new vengeful "spirit" of capital unbound had meanwhile been captured in hymns to Wall Street like Rem Koolhaas's *Delirious New York*, or in Robert Venturi and Denise Scott Brown's celebration of Las Vegas casinos. It was also found in the softer form of a "heritage" curated by elites who now claimed to represent on the global stage the nation-states formed out of the ashes of European colonialism's later phases.[21] In the United States, where (with the United Kingdom) neoliberalism's cultural logic may be most apparent, architects and urbanists proved more than willing to collaborate with these forces by adapting ancient and modern languages of social belonging, from classical symmetries to functionalist transparencies, into entire corporate complexes. In the single-family house, an object of artistic experimentation from Le Corbusier to the New York Five, were new machines for living: fossil-fueled mechanical ones to get around and fossil-fueled electronic ones to stay put. This is what the autopoesis of markets looked like by the millennium's turn: a traffic jam in which commuters stewed in their cars listening to talk radio while others furiously communicated on their devices as Arendt's antipolitical, antidemocratic "rise of the social" became the rise of social media.

Democracy Now?

We began writing the introduction to this book soon after the U.S Capitol riots of January 6, 2021. We conclude at a moment of heightened conflict and great political uncertainty. In solidarity with those who struggle to build democracy worldwide, the modest tools we provide from within our own field are simply these:

1. Understand that buildings operate hegemonically; they demand that we consent to and comply with decisions generally made by *others.*
2. Recognize the regime of technocratic knowledge that authorizes specific spatial and material decisions without reference to their larger effects, and decipher those effects.
3. Consider how buildings and spaces might nonetheless operate democratically to advance public goods over private ones; how public places *can* represent the interests of the *demos;* how buildings, cities, and environments remain sites from which a new, more democratic order might one day spring.

Notes

1. Hannah Arendt, *On Revolution* (New York: Penguin Books, 2006), 245–73.
2. Standing out among many examples of critical scholarship on vernacular architecture is Dell Upton, *Holy Things and Profane: Anglican Parish Churches in Colonial Virginia* (New York: Architectural History Foundation / Cambridge: MIT Press, 1986).
3. Vladimir Kulić, ed., *Second World Postmodernisms: Architecture and Society under Late Socialism* (New York: Bloomsbury, 2019).
4. On the "rise of the social," see Hannah Arendt, *The Human Condition* (Chicago: University of Chicago Press, 1958), 38–49.
5. Luke Mogelson et al., "A Reporter's Footage from Inside the Capitol Siege," *New Yorker*, January 17, 2021. The scene runs from 4:00 to 9:24. https://www.newyorker.com/news/video-dept/a-reporters-footage-from-inside-the-capitol-siege.
6. William C. Allen, *History of the United States Capitol: A Chronicle of Design, Construction, and Politics* (Washington, D.C.: United States Government Printing Office, 2001), 322, 338–39.
7. Benedict Anderson, *Imagined Communities: Reflections on the Origin and Spread of Nationalism* (London: Verso, 1983).
8. Claude Lefort, *Democracy and Political Theory* (Cambridge, UK: Polity Press, 1988), 17ff.
9. Louis Althusser, "Ideology and Ideological State Apparatuses," in *Lenin and Philosophy and Other Essays*, trans. Ben Brewster (New York: Monthly Review Press, 1971), 127–88.
10. Irene Cheng, Charles L. Davis II, and Mabel O. Wilson, *Race and Modern Architecture: A Critical History from the Enlightenment to the Present* (Pittsburgh: University of Pittsburgh Press, 2020).
11. Timothy Mitchell, *Carbon Democracy: Political Power in the Age of Oil* (London: Verso, 2011).
12. Morefield cites the nearly seamless continuity between this moment and *The Project of a Commonwealth* (1915), in which Lionel Curtis, representing a group known as "The Round Table," theorized British imperialism as a new form of international cooperation among "commonwealth" nations. Just as ancient Greece had developed the city-state as a commonwealth, so had Britain done the same for the sovereign nation, creating the nineteenth-

century commonwealth within the borders of Great Britain. The next step in the twentieth century was to be an international commonwealth under the Union Jack—freed of the stigma of colonialism but still operating like empire. See Jeanne Morefield, *Empires without Imperialism: Anglo-American Decline and the Politics of Deflection* (Oxford: Oxford University Press, 2014), 101, 173; Lionel Curtis, *The Project of a Commonwealth: An Inquiry into the Nature of Citizenship in the British Empire, and into the Mutual Relations of the Several Communities Thereof* (London: Macmillan, 1915); Mark Mazower, *No Enchanted Palace: The End of Empire and the Ideological Origins of the United Nations* (Princeton: Princeton University Press, 2009).

13. Arendt, *On Revolution*, 245–73.

14. See for example: Ayala Levin, *Architecture and Development: Israeli Construction in Sub-Saharan Africa and the Settler Colonial Imagination, 1958–1973* (Durham: Duke University Press, 2022); Łukasz Stanek, *Architecture in Global Socialism: Eastern Europe, West Africa, and the Middle East in the Cold War* (Princeton: Princeton University Press, 2020); Patricio del Real, *Constructing Latin America: Architecture, Politics, and Race at the Museum of Modern Art* (New Haven: Yale University Press, 2022); and Luis E. Carranza and Fernando Luis Lara, *Modern Architecture in Latin America: Art, Technology, and Utopia* (Austin: University of Texas Press, 2014).

15. Quinn Slobodian, *Globalists: The End of Empire and the Birth of Neoliberalism* (Cambridge, Mass.: Harvard University Press, 2018), 125–145. Where the International Monetary Fund (IMF) would help stabilize currencies and the World Bank would fund infrastructure and development, the proposed International Trade Organization (ITO) would oversee trade. Slobodian emphasizes that representation in the ITO was to be more democratic, on the principle of one-country-one-vote. A large number of those votes would have been cast by new nations, many of whom sought to develop autochthonous industry and to protect domestic production from competition from the industrial North. Advocates of an incipient neoliberal project in Europe and North America objected fiercely to this "economic nationalism," as it was called. The ITO was scrapped in favor of a regime designed to enhance the global mobility of capital, thereby restoring the liberal principles on which the League of Nations was based while protecting foreign assets from nationalization. As Adom Getachew has explained, the ITO's historical successor, the New International Economic Order, suffered a similar fate for many of the same reasons. See Getachew, *Worldmaking after Empire: The Rise and Fall of Self-Determination* (Princeton: Princeton University Press, 2019), 142–75.

16. Slobodian, *Globalists*, 125–45.

17. Arendt, *The Human Condition*, 38–49.

18. Kenny Cupers, Catharina Gabrielsson, and Helena Mattsson, eds., *Neoliberalism on the Ground: Architecture and Transformation from the 1960s to the Present* (Pittsburgh: University of Pittsburgh Press, 2020).

19. On markets as autopoetic agents, see especially F. A. Hayek, *The Road to Serfdom: Text and Documents*, ed. Bruce Caldwell (Chicago: University of Chicago Press, 2007). On neoliberalism and *homo economicus*, see Michel Foucault, *The Birth of Biopolitics: Lectures at the Collège de France, 1978–79*, ed. Michel Senellart, trans. Graham Burchell (New York: Picador,

2004) and Wendy Brown, *Undoing the Demos: Neoliberalism's Stealth Revolution* (Brooklyn, NY: Zone Books, 2015).
20. Francis Fukuyama, *The End of History and the Last Man* (New York: Avon Books, 1993).
21. Rem Koolhaas, *Delirious New York: A Retroactive Manifesto for Manhattan* (New York: Oxford University Press, 1978); Robert Venturi, Denise Scott Brown, and Steven Izenour, *Learning from Las Vegas* (Cambridge, Mass.: MIT Press, 1972). For the postcolonial recalibration of architectural heritage see, for example, the journal *Mimar* (Singapore: Concept Media, 1981–92).

Contributors

Esra Akcan is professor in the Department of Architecture and resident director of the Institute for Comparative Modernities at Cornell University. She is coauthor of *Turkey: Modern Architectures in History* and author of *Landfill Istanbul*; *Architecture in Translation: Germany, Turkey, and the Modern House*; *Open Architecture: Migration, Citizenship, and the Urban Renewal of Berlin-Kreuzberg by IBA-1984/87*; and *Abolish Human Bans: Intertwined Histories of Architecture*.

Can Bilsel is professor of architecture and art history and founding director of the architecture program at the University of San Diego. He is author of *Antiquity on Display: Regimes of the Authentic in Berlin's Pergamon Museum* and coeditor of *Architecture and the Housing Question*.

José H. Bortoluci is professor of social sciences at the Getulio Vargas Foundation (FGV-EAESP) in Brazil.

Charles L. Davis II is associate professor of architectural history and criticism at the School of Architecture at the University of Texas at Austin. He is coeditor of *Race and Modern Architecture: A Critical History from the Enlightenment to the Present* and author of *Building Character: The Racial Politics of Modern Architectural Style*.

Laura diZerega is an editor of scholarly and museum publications. She received her PhD with distinction from the Department of the History of Art and Architecture at the University of California at Santa Barbara.

Eve Duffy is associate vice-provost for global affairs at Duke University and author of *The Return of Hans Staden: A Go-Between in the Atlantic World*.

María González Pendás is assistant professor in the history of architecture and urban development at the College of Architecture, Art, and Planning at Cornell University.

Paul B. Jaskot is professor of art history and director of the Digital Art History and Visual Culture Research Lab at Duke University. He is author of *The Nazi Perpetrator: Postwar German Art and the Politics of the Right* (Minnesota, 2012) and *The Architecture* *of Oppression: The SS, Forced Labor, and the Nazi Monumental Building Economy*, and coeditor of *Beyond Berlin: Twelve German Cities Confront the Nazi Past*.

Ana María León is associate professor of architecture at the Harvard University Graduate School of Design. She is author of *Modernity for the Masses: Antonio Bonet's Dreams for Buenos Aires* and *Bones of the Nation / A Ruin in Reverse*.

Ruth W. Lo is assistant professor of architectural history in the art history department at Hamilton College.

Reinhold Martin is professor of architecture in the Graduate School of Architecture, Planning, and Preservation at Columbia University. His books include *The Organizational Complex: Architecture, Media, and Corporate Space*; *Utopia's Ghost: Architecture and Postmodernism, Again* (Minnesota, 2010); *The Urban Apparatus: Mediapolitics and the City* (Minnesota, 2016); and *Knowledge Worlds: Media, Materiality, and the Making of the Modern University*.

Peter Minosh is associate teaching professor of architectural history at Northeastern University. He is author of *Atlantic Unbound: Architecture in the World of the Haitian Revolution* (forthcoming).

Itohan Osayimwese is associate professor of the history of art and architecture at Brown University and author of *Colonialism and Modern Architecture in Germany*.

Kishwar Rizvi is Robert Lehman Professor of the History of Architecture at Yale University. She is author of *The Transnational Mosque: Architecture and Historical Memory in the Contemporary Middle East* and *The Safavid Dynastic Shrine: Architecture, Religion, and Power in Early Modern Iran*. She is editor of *Affect, Emotion, and Subjectivity in Early Modern Muslim Empires: New Studies in Ottoman, Safavid, and Mughal Art and Culture* and coeditor of *Modernism and the Middle East: Architecture and Politics in the Twentieth Century*.

Naomi Vaughan is a translator of German and coffee shop proprietor. Her dissertation investigates the production, popular aesthetics, and legacy of National Socialist architecture in film and visual media.

Nader Vossoughian is professor of architecture at New York Institute of Technology and an adjunct associate professor of architecture at Columbia University.

Mabel O. Wilson is the Nancy and George E. Rupp Professor of Architecture, Planning, and Preservation and professor of African American and African diaspora studies at Columbia University. She is author of *Begin with the Past: Building the National Museum of African American History and Culture* and *Negro Building: Black Americans in the World* of Fairs and Museums, and coeditor of *Race and Modern Architecture: A Critical History from the Enlightenment to the Present.*

Claire Zimmerman teaches history of architecture and the built environment at the University of Toronto. Her books include *Photographic Architecture in the Twentieth Century* (Minnesota, 2014), *Albert Kahn, Inc.: Architecture, Labor, Industry, 1905–1961* (forthcoming), and, as coeditor and contributing author, *Detroit–Moscow–Detroit: An Architecture for Industrialization, 1917–1945.*

Index

Page numbers in italics refer to figures.

abolitionist movement, 20, 27
Abu Dhabi, United Arab Emirates, 117n19
A.C. (journal), 202n1
Acar, Yasemin Gülsüm, 332
Accíon Popular, 205n34
Acrópole (journal), 87–88
"aesthetics of resistance," 323, 338n8
African Americans. *See* Blacks
Africa orientale Italiana (AOI). *See* Italian East Africa
Agamben, Giorgio, 99, 334, 334
Aggregate Architectural History Collaborative, 14n24
Agrupacíon Espacio, 206n39
airports, 92
AKM Building, Istanbul. *See* Atatürk Culture Center (AKM)
AKP (political party), 324, 328, 329–30, 337n4, 339n26
Alabbar, Muhammad, 117n22
Al Arrab Motor City (restaurant), 113
Aldar Headquarters Building, Dubai, 115
Ali, Syed, 103
Alianza Popular Revolucionaria Americana (APRA). *See* APRA
alienation, 275
allegories, 234, 323, 324, 334, 336, 338n8
Allen, Rose Mary, 143
Alphand, Adolphe, 258
alterity, 275
Althans, Karl Ludwig, 244
Althusser, Louis, 346

aluminum, 68, 69, 177, 178, 179
American Anti-Slavery Society, 27
American Popular Revolutionary Alliance (APRA). *See* APRA
Anderson, Benedict, 345
Ángel, Eduardo Zuleta, 204n27
"Anticapitalism Muslims," 332
antidemocracy, 1, 6, 10–11, 119, 348. *See also* democracy
apartments: Brazil, 85, 87; Peru, 205n38; United Arab Emirates, 101, 104, 117n19
Apollo in the Democracy (Gropius), 303
Apotheosis of Washington (fresco) (Brumidi), 345
APRA, 191, 205n36, 206n40
Arabian Ranches, Dubai, 100, 108, 109–11, *109*, 115, 118nn33–34
Arango, Jorge, 196
archaeology: Roman, 65
architects: competition for projects, 189, 193–94; fascism and, 59–61, 62, 63, 77n12, 164, 171, 176, 180; local, in collaboration with international, 191, 192, 199, 300–301, 310, 318n47; star, 117n26
Architectural Design (journal), 199
Architectural Forum (journal), 164, 199
architecture, 2–3, 11, 82, 83, 201, 263–64, 331, 344, 350; "American," 234, 282, 284, 294–96; Arab, 310–13; autarchic, 18, 66; Baghdad brutalism, 302; Beaux-Arts, 271, 346; bureaucratization of, 238–39, 241–42, 244–49; church, 235, *235*–36,

357

240, 241–42, 244–49, 252; classical, 41, 57n48, 163–64, 165, 176, 347; competitions, 167, 175–77; "democratic," 279–81, 343; discourses about, 2–4, 202, 236, 240, 241, 245–49, 281; fascist, 3–5, 8, 60, 67, 120, 163–80; formalism in, 163–64; German, 240, 245; government, 167, 175–77, 343, 347; history, 1, 2–5, 284, 300, 343; imperial, 164; International Style, 211; Italian, 59–60, 63, 66, 72, 75; Italian Rationalism, 62, 63; media and, 17–18, 38, 45–46, *46, 47, 50, 51,* 52, 56nn45–46, 58n71, 66, 67, 79n30; modern, 1–4, 9–10, 41, 44, 57n48, 91, 163–64, 191, 194, 204n20, 206n39, 343; National Socialist, 17, 38–53, 121–35, 138n38, 212–13, 214, 226; neoclassical, 41, 79n36, 121, 212–13, 344, 346; neo-Gothic, 252; neo-Renaissance, 344; nineteenth century European, 238, 252; political and political history of, 1–4, 343, 344–47; politics and, 1–4, 6–7, 8, 11, 38–39, 59–60, 87, 94–95, 121, 163–66, 175–80, 186, 187, 191, 343; Prairie Style, 279, 280, 284–90, 292, 294–95, 296; propaganda and, 3–4, 38–39; public/civic, 1, 2, 3–4, 5, 6, 10, 17, 19–20, 21–22, 176, 178–80, 238, 343–45, 346; rationalism, 62, 119, 171; Rhenish/Rhenish Romanesque, 240; Rhenish Romanesque Revival, 252; Romanesque Revival, 23, 26; *stile littorio,* 67; styles, 17, 20–21, 23, 35n22, 41, 344, 346, 347; technology and, 126, 163–64, 178, 281; Victorian, 281, 285, 286, 288, 290. *See also* built environment
Architecture and Politics in Germany, 1918–1945 (Miller Lane), 3–4, 8, 212
Architecture and Utopia (Tafuri), 8
Architecture d'Aujourd'hui, L' (journal), 199
Arendt, Hannah, 4–5, 12n8, 180, 343, 347, 349
Argan, Giulio Carlo, 304, 306
Argentine, 202n9, 203nn10–11
Arnold, Eve, 103–4

Arquitecto peruano, El (journal), 205n34
Arrese, José Luis, 173; *New Organic Law of the Movement* (proposal), 173, 174
articulation, 82–83
Artigas, João Vilanova, 18, 82, 83–84, 86, 87, 95n6
Assainissement, embellissements de Paris, ou Édilité urbaine mise à la portée de tout le monde (Horeau). See *Édilité urbaine* (Horeau)
assembly lines, 217, 224
assimilation, 283, 284, 296
Ästhetik des Widerstands, Die (Weiss), 338n8
Atatürk, Mustafa Kemal, 324, 327, 339n26
Atatürk Culture Center (AKM), Istanbul (Tabanlıoğlu), 324, 330, 331, 335, 338n14
Augé, Marc, 100
Augustan Exhibition of Romanità, 62
Autarchic Exhibition of Italian Minerals. *See* MAMI
autarchy, 18, 59, 62, 63, 64, 76n1, 77nn11–12; architecture and, 63, 66, 77n12
autoconstruction, 85
autocracy, 15n38
autonomy, 344
Auxiliary Corps of Civil Engineers, 258
Azienda Carboni Italiano (ACaI). *See* Italian Coal Company
Azienda Generale Italiana Petroli (AGIP). *See* General Italian Oil Company

Backdrop to Tragedy (Polk), 307
Baghdad, Iraq, 310, 311–13
Baghdad, City of Peace (Coke), 312
Baird, Spencer, 30, 31
Bajo Belgrano, Buenos Aires, 193
Baker, Herbert: British Raj headquarters, New Delhi, 10
Baker-Finch, Ian: Links Golf Club, Dubai, 111
Ballu, Théodore, 258, 271, 274
banality of evil, 4–5, 12n8, 120

Banco Nacional de Habitação (BNH), 84, 85, 89, 90, 93
Barbero, Manuel: SEAT Auto-Industry Warehouse, Barcelona, *167*
"bare life," 329, 334
barricades, 263–64, 265, 323
Batista, Fulgencio, 181n2, 200
Battistia, Eugenio, 207n47
Baudot, Anatole de, 258, 261
Baudry, Ambroise, 258
Bauentwurfslehre (Neufert), 212
Baukunst, Die (journal), 126
Bauordnungslehre (Neufert), 212, 213, 216, 217
Baur, Max, 56n46
Bayut.com, 108
beauty, 270
beer: bottles, 221, *222*; hygiene and, 221, 224–25
Bélanger, François-Joseph, 224
Belaúnde Terry, Fernando, 191, 201, 205n34
Bell, Duncan: *Political Theory and Architecture*, 3
Bemis, Alfred Farwell, 216, 217
Benhabib, Seyla, 337n4
Benjamin, Walter, 263, 323
Bense, Max, 8
Berlin, Germany: architecture, 37–58, 121; memorial district, 37, 54n3; reconstruction (Soviet), 49–50, 52, 53; redevelopment, 37–38, 56n47; redevelopment plans (National Socialist), 127
Bimillenario Augusteo, 62
Bingham, George Caleb: *Daniel Boone Escorting Settlers through the Cumberland Gap* (painting), 284
biology, 213
biopolitics, 99, 172, 275, 334, 336
Blacks, 6, 17, 20, 22, 27, 33, 279–80, 283; Washington, D.C., population, 27; white Americans fear of, 29
blocks, 70, 72, 217
BNH. *See* Banco Nacional de Habitação (BNH)

Bodelschwingh, Ernst, 246
Bodmer, Karl, 30, 31
body politic. See *demos*
Bogotá, Colombia: burning/destruction of, 195–96, 197, *197*; opposition to plan, 196, 197, 199; plan, 194–95, 196, 197, *198*, 199, 201, 208n57, 208n59, 208n61, 209n76; Plaza Bolívar, 199; public squares/city voids, 196, *198*, 199, 201, 209n72
"Bogotazo, el," 195, 196, *197*, 199
Boisserée, Sulpiz: *Geschichte und Beschreibung des Doms zu Koln*, 245
Bonaparte, Napoléon, 1, 258; Code Civil, 254n6
Bonet, Antonio, 190, 193, 205n29, 205n32, 207n47, 209n72
bonifica, 66, 79n29
Boone, Daniel, 284–85
Boring, William, 146, 151
Borsig Palace, Berlin, 39, 41
boulevards, 261, 263
bourgeoise, 263, 264, 269, 271, 275
Brasilia, Brazil (Niemeyer and Costa), 201, 343
Brazil, 186, 188–90, 192; building programs, 189, 204n20; coup d'etats, 84, 188, 189, 190; economy, 84–85; First National Development Plan, 84; governmental control, 189, 204n24, 207n46; housing, 6, 18, 84, 86–97, 189, 204nn18–19; industrial development, 83, 85, 90–91, 95n6; job creation, 84–85, 90; labor force, 84, 85, 87; military, 203n10; nationalism, 189; political parties, 189; urban planning, 188–89, 204nn18–19; World War II diplomatic relationships, 186, 188, 202n9, 203n11
Brazil Builds (exhibition), 193, 203n17
Bretton Woods Agreement, 185, 348
breweries and bottling complexes, 212, 221–26, *225*
bricks, *215*, 217
bricolage, 271
British Foreign Office and India Office, London, 344–45

Index 359

British Raj headquarters, New Delhi (Lutyens and Baker), 10
British West Indies, 143
Brito, Fernando Saturnino de, 189
broadsides, 27, *28*
Broggi, Carlo: League of Nations headquarters, Geneva, 346–47
Brown, Tammy, 142
Brumidi, Constantino: *Apotheosis of Washington* (mural), 345
Brutalität im Stein (film) (Kluge), 5
Buenos Aires, Brazil, 193
Buffalo, New York, 298n31
built environment, 1, 2, 3, 6–7, 82, 83, 91–92, 94–95, 105–6, 107–15, 217, 274, 344, 350; bureaucratization of, 238, 241–42; identity and, 17–18, 239, 240–41, 245–46, 247–48; reforms, 22, 238–39. *See also* architecture
Bullant, Jean, 269
bunkers, 37, 38, 39, 47–48, 49, 55n35, 57n61
bureaucracy: Franquismo, 176–80; National Socialist, 39, 44, 55n34, 56n42; Prussian, 9, 235–36, 240, 241–42, 245–49; Prussian hierarchy of, 238–39, *239*
Burj al-Arab, Dubai, 104
Burj Khalifa, Dubai (Skidmore, Owings, and Merrill), 105
Bustamante y Rivero, José Luis, 191, 206n40
Butler, Judith, 323, 333, 334
Byrd, Jodi A., 27

Cacciari, Massimo, 275, 278n44, 278n48
Cali, Colombia, 196
Cameron, Gilbert, 28
Campfire (painting) (Homer), 285, *285*
Camprubí, Lino, 171
canopies, 261, 263
capital, 348, 351n15
capitalism, 5, 6, 7, 10–11, 98, 101, 102, 274–75, 329–30, 346, 348–49; racial, 281; welfare, 22
carbon, 72

Carbon Democracy (Mitchell), 346
Carbonia, Italy, 75
Carroll, Charles, 34n4
Casanova, José, 172, 175, 182n21
casinos, 349
Castro, Fidel, 207n53
Catlin, George, 31
Cecap, São Paulo (state), 86–87, 93
Cecap Cumbica, São Paulo (state). *See* Cecap Guarulhos, São Paulo (state)
Cecap Guarulhos, São Paulo (state), 18, 83, 86–97, *93*, *94*; advertisements, 89; amenities and infrastructure, 88–89, 91–92, *94*; apartment buildings, 90–91, *93*; Community Center, 92; Community Council, 92; flooding of, 91; funding, 90; land, 86, 90; opinions about, 92–94; research on potential buyers, 88–89; residents, 88–90, 91–94; security, 93, *94*; structural problems, 93
Cecap Zezinho Magalhaes, São Paulo (state). *See* Cecap Guarulhos, São Paulo (state)
cement, 63, 70
Center Market, Washington, D.C., 26
Centro Superior de Investigaciones Cientificas (CSIC). *See* National Research Council (Spain)
Césaire, Aimé, 164
Chadirji, Rifat, 310, 310n47
Chandigarh, India, 343
Chatterjee, Partha, 9
Chernyshevsky, Nikolay: *What Is to Be Done?*, 260
child welfare, 62
Chile, 201, 203n11, 209n77
Chimbote, Peru: local plan team, 191, *192*; plan, 190, 191, *192*, 193, 201, 206n43; population, 192, 206n44
churches (Rhineland): building costs, 236, 254n4, 255n26; building funding requests, 235, 240, 241–42, 244–49, 250–51; Catholic vs. Protestant, 235, 236, 246, 250–51, 252; regional autonomy vs.

government restrictions, 233, 238, 241, 242, 244–49, 251–52; review of petitions, 236, 241–42, 244–45
Church of Saints Marzellinus and Petrus, Vallendar, 238, 240, 242, 244–49, *247, 248*; cost estimate for rebuilding, 242, *243*, 244, 245, 246; local protests against Prussian rejection of design, 245–49; plans, 244–46
Church of Ste-Geneviève, Paris (Soufflot). *See* Panthéon, Paris (Soufflot)
Church of the Madeleine, Paris, 265, *268*
CIAM, 186, 188, 190, 201, 208n66; Chapter for Relief and Postwar Planning, 204n26
CIAM 6, 190–91, 192
CIAM 7, 193–94; Latin American delegations, 196, 207n47; projects displayed, 193, 207n47
CIAM 8, 199–200
Circus Maximus, Rome, 61, 67; borehole, 72, 80n49
citizenship, 20, 27, 33, 114, 152, 157, 327, 334, 345; contingent rights and, 283, 288–89, 297n15; United Arab Emirates, 98, 99, 101, 114
City of Motors, Brazil, 188–89, 190, 204nn18–19, 204n21, 205n31
civil disobedience, 326
Civil Governments (CD), Spain, 176
civil rights, 279, 283, 331
civil servants, 173–74
cladding, 70
classical orders, 345
classicism: Roman, 5
coercion, 6–7, 17, 47, 102
Coke, Richard: *Baghdad, City of Peace,* 312
Cold War, 179, 303, 307, 313, 318n36
collaboration, 303, 310, 313
collective action, 142, 251, 259
collective life, 83, 92, 94
Cologne Cathedral, 245, 251–52
Cologne Cathedral Building Society, 252
Colombia: burning/destruction of cities, 195–96, *197*; coup d'etats, 199; government, 194, 197, 199, 208n64; Law 88, 196, 208n62; Le Corbusier and, 194–95, 196, 207n47, 208nn57–58, 208n61; migration within, 196, 197; military, 208n64; nationalism, 193; political unrest and violence, 195–96, 199, 207nn54–55, 208n67; urban planning, 194–97, *198*, 199, 208n57, 208n62, 208n63, 208n66
Colombian Society of Architects, 194
colonialism, 6, 8; Italy, 62, 64, 73, 75; National Socialist, 124, 127; United States, 17, 29, 282
colonization, 21, 73, 127, 164, 300, 306, 307, 346
"color line," 9
Cömert, Abdullah, 326
commonwealths, 350n12
"communal luxury," 270
Communism: Arabs and, 307, 317n30
Communist Party, 156, 189, 192, 204n23, 207n53, 208n67
communities: utopian/experimental, 21–22
community life, 21–22, 87, 91, 92, 100, 113
Compagnia Mineraria Etiopica (COMINA). *See* Ethiopian Mining Company
Compañía de Aceros del Pacifico (CAP), 209n77
Compromise of 1850, 29
concentration camps, 157, 218
concrete, 59, 63, 70, 87, 90, 91, 299, 302
Confederate States of America, 33
Conjunto Urbano Nonoalco Tlatelolco, Mexico City, 83
Conseil d'Etat, Paris, 269
consent, 6, 17
construction, 211; industrialization of, 87, 88, 90–91, 95; management, 212, 217–18; standardization, 212, 213, 214, 215, 216–19; traditional, 85, 90, 310; weaponization of, 121, 217; wood, 67, 70, *71*, 72, 80n46, 215, 218. *See also* modular systems; prefabrication

Index 361

construction industry: Brazil, 84, 85, 90–91, 95n6; Fordist approaches to, 217; Germany, 213; mechanization of, 217; standardization of, 212, 213, 214, 216–19; Taylorist approaches to, 217; vertical integration of, 213

consumerism, 101, 113–14

Contiero, Davide, 132

Contributions to Knowledge (Smithsonian Institution), 31

control. *See* coercion

conveyor systems, 224

Coop Himmelb(l)au: European Central Bank, Frankfurt, 5

Corona, Eduardo, 87

Corporación de Fomento de Chile, 209n77

Corporación Nacional de la Vivienda (CNV). *See* National Housing Corporation (Peru)

Corporación Peruana del Santa (CPS). *See* Peruvian Corporation of Santa

Corrales, José Antonio: New Headquarters for the Ministries of Industry and Commerce Competition, Madrid, *170*

cosmopolitanism, 113

Costa, Lúcio, 181n2, 185, 189; Brasilia, Brazil, 201

cotton, 62

Courbet, Gustave, 265

courtyards, 176, 311, 313

Crystal Palace, London, 260

CSIC. *See* National Research Council (Spain)

Cuba, 200

curtain walls, 7, 120, 163, 165, 166, 167, 169, 178, 179, 180, 181n2

Curtis, Lionel, 350n12

DAMAC Real Estate, 105

Daniel Boone Escorting Settlers through the Cumberland Gap (painting) (Bingham), 284

Darcel, Alfred, 265

Darwin D. Martin complex, Buffalo, 234, 284–90, *287, 289,* 292, 294–95, 297n18; back entryway, 288, 290, 292, 294; division of space, 288, 289–90; fireplaces, 281, 284, 286–88, *287;* gardens and gardeners, 290, *291,* 294; lighting, 286, 298n20; life at, 289, 290; open plan, 287–88; ornamentation, 286–87, 292; servants at, *291,* 292, *293,* 294; servant's wing, 288, 289, 292; site, 285–86

Davioud, Gabriel, 258

Davis, Alexander Jackson, 23

decorative arts, 270–71

Delegación de Hacienda, La Coruña (Sota, Tenreiro, and Molezún), 178–80

Delirious New York (Koolhaas), 349

democracy, 1–2, 6–7, 8–9, 10–11, 15n38, 98, 99, 102, 103, 115, 165, 179, 234, 279, 280, 284, 299, 303, 315n1, 344, 345, 347, 349, 350; fight against communism and, 307; Middle East and, 306–7, 313; radical, 323; representational, 346; technology and, 163–64. *See also* antidemocracy

demographics: United States, 152

demos, 4, 9, 10, 18, 83, 89, 95, 174, 233, 234, 239–40, 251–52, 275, 323, 333, 336, 344, 345, 348, 349, 350

Denkmalern der deutschen Baukunst (Moller), 245

Deperthes, Édouard, 271, 274

deportation, 154–57

deregulation, 348

De Renzi, Mario, 61, 62, 67; Pavilion of Arms, MAMI, *60, 61,* 67, 70, 80n45

Desole, Angelo Pietro, 80n51

destruction, 121

Deutscher Werkbund, 214

Deutsche Stahlbauverband. *See* German Steel Construction Association

Deutsches Volk – Deutsche Arbeit (exhibition): Hall of Energy and Technology, 78n28

developmentalism, 83, 84–85, 120, 167–68, 174, 188

Dickens, Charles, 19

dimensional coordination, 214, 216, 221; four-inch system, 216; octametric system, 216–17, 228

DIN 4171, 218
Dink, Hrant, 326
direniş, 338n8
Direnmenin Estetiği (Weiss). See *Ästhetik des Widerstands, Die* (Weiss)
discourses: architectural, 202, 236, 240, 241, 245–49, 281; clash-of-civilization, 299, 314. See also information
Dolmage, Jay, 150, 151, 160n52
domes, 270, 270, 345
domesticity, 57n50, 111–12, 284, 286
dominance, 6
Dopolavoro Exhibition, 62
Dorich, Luis, 191, 205n35, 205nn38–39
dormitories, 304, 310, 318n46
Dortmund, Germany, 223
Dortmunder Union-Brauerei (DUB), Dortmund, 225; expansion plan (Speer, Neufert, and Rösel), 212, 221–26, 225; signage, 223, 226, 227
Dostoyevsky, Fyodor: *Notes from Underground*, 260
Dred Scott v. Sandford, 27, 33
DUB. See Dortmunder Union-Brauerei (DUB), Dortmund
Dubai, United Arab Emirates, 6, 99, 102, 103–6, 104, 105, 107, 117n19; apartments, 104; beachfront, 104–5, 105; business district, 105; construction, 105–6, 105; freeholds, 99, 103, 108–12, 113–14; property ownership, 18, 108, 114; real estate development, 104–5, 108–13; surveillance in, 101, 110; zones, 106, 114
Dubai Holdings, 118n31
Dubai International Finance Centre (DIFC), Dubai, 105, 106
Dubai Land Development (DLD), 108
Dubai Marina, Dubai, 104
Du Bois, W. E. B., 9, 152
Duhart, Emilio: Villa Presidente Ríos, Talcahuano, Chile, 201, 209n77
duran adam. See standing man
Durth, Werner, 220

Dutch Antilles, 143
Dutra, Eurico Gaspar, 189, 204n24

Eastern Europe: National Socialist occupation of, 121–35
East Germany, 52
Echaide, Rafael: SEAT Auto-Industry Warehouse, Barcelona, 167
Eckhardt, Felix, 212, 223, 225–26
Eco, Umberto, 180
economic markets, 348–49
economic mercenaries, 103, 108
economic mobility, 99, 103, 109, 114
ecosystems, 150
Édilité urbaine (Horeau), 261, 274, 278n42
education, 21, 22, 25, 303–4
efficiency, 173, 226
Eichmann, Adolf, 4, 12n8
Eliécer Gaitán, Jorge, 195
Ellis Island, 119–20, 140–41, 145–47, 148–49, 150–51, 154–57, 160n52; described as concentration camp, 156–57; design, 145–47, 148–49, 150–51; detention and deportation at, 8, 144, 146, 151–52, 154–57, 159n23, 159n25; graffiti, 151; islands of, 145, 147, 148–49; land instability, 150; land reclamation and infill, 145–46, 147, 150; Main Building, 146, 151; Railroad Ticket Office, 147; Registry Room, 144, 145, 155; segregation at, 154, 155, 156; site plan, 148–49
Emaar Properties, 105, 108
emancipation, 20, 22
embassies, 10
empire building, 62, 64, 70, 164, 174, 345, 346
enclaves, 106–7; Caribbean, 143; residential, 99, 100, 101, 103, 107, 108–13
Encyclopédie d'Architecture (journal), 268
enfilades, 41, 44, 45, 56n45, 287
engineering tolerances, 221–22
Engineer Management Automation Army Reserve. See Emaar Properties
enslavement, 20, 144. See also slavery

environmentalism, 112
equality, 102, 345
erasures, 49–50, 53, 271, 274, 282, 292
Ertür, Başak, 332
Escorial, El (Spain), 164–65, *165*
Escrivá de Balaguer, José María, 171, 172, 175, 184n52
Esposizione Universale Roma (EUR), 59, 67; Palazzo dei Congressi, 67; Palazzo della Civiltà Romana, 67
Ethiopia, 62, 64, 77n11
Ethiopian Mining Company, 64
EUR. *See* Esposizione Universale Roma (EUR)
European Central Bank, Frankfurt (Coop Himmelb(l)au), 5
European Committee for Standardization (CEN), 221
evangelization, 165, 171, 172, 174, 175, 179
exclusion, 119, 150, 152, 334
Excursion dans Paris sans voitures (Guesnu), 278n43
Exhibition of National Textiles, 62
Exhibition of Sardinian Extractive Industries, 75
Exhibition of the Fascist Revolution, 62
expansionism: France, 259; Germany, 214, 217, 240; United States, 17, 20, 29, 31–32, 179, 282
expatriates, 98, 99, 101, 102–3, 107, 114–15; freehold properties and, 108–9, 114; memories of, 99, 100–101, 113; residence visas, 108, 113–14
experts, 7, 120, 171–72, 200
Export–Import Bank, 203n17, 209n77
exurbs, 101, 108–12, 113

façades, 40–41, 45, 68, 69, 163, 176, 177–79, 312
factories: power of foremen, 217; standardization, 214
Faisal II, King, 301, 308
Falange (political party), 173, 174
Familistère de Guise, Guise (Godin), 261

fantasies: utopian, 233, 260–63, 274, 275
fasci, 62, 68, 69, 72
fascism, 1, 2–3, 164, 170–71, 180, 189, 208n64, 220
fascism (Italy), 6, 18, 59–60, 62, 65, 66, 80n51; after-work activities and, 62; agriculture and, 70, 72; architects and, 59–61, 62, 63, 77n12; assertion of legitimacy, 65; colonialism, 63, 64, 73, 75; conquests, 62, 64, 77n11; economic policies, 59, 60, 62; exhibitions, 56–76; militarism, 63, 70; mineralogists/geologists and, 61, 62, 65; population campaign, 62, 64, 65–66, 77n9; race and, 61, 62, 64–65, 75. *See also* Partito Nazionale Fascista (PNF)
fascism (Spain), 8, 164, 165, 168, 172–73; architects and, 164, 171, 176, 180; architecture and, 164, 175–76, 179–80. *See also* Franquismo
Fathy, Hassan, 307
Feder, Gottfried, 126
Federal University, Rio de Janeiro, 185, 202n4
Fédération des Artistes, 271
Fernández-Cebrián, Ana, 171
Ferrari-Hardoy, Jorge, 191, 193, 205n32, 207n47
Ferry, Elizabeth Emma, 65
Fest, Joachim, 212
Fethi, Ihsan, 310, 313, 310n47
Finance Delegations (FD), Spain, 176–78
Finley, Cheryl, 144
fireplaces, 234, 281, 284, 286–88, *287*
Fisac, Miguel, 175
Flächsner, Hans, 213
Flegenheimer, Julien: League of Nations headquarters, Geneva, 346–47
Folha de São Paulo (newspaper), 93–94
For a Left Populism (Mouffe), 333
forgetting, 271
Foster, Darwin M., *291*
Foster, Margaret, *291*
Foucault, Michel, 8, 14n24
Fowler, Orson Squire, 294

France, 233, 257–75; censorship, 260; financial crash, 268; Ministry of Finance, 268–69; Second Empire, 260, 263, 268, 269; state centralization, 259; Third Republic, 269

Franco, Francisco, 164, 172–74, 182n12, 202n7

Frank, Hans, 121–22, 124

Franklin and Armfield (firm), 27

Franquismo, 120, 166, 171, 172–74, 175–76, 180, 181n8; building program, 8, 175–80; governmental control, 172–73; government offices, 176, 178–80

freedom, 99, 101–2, 103, 114–15, 163–64, 281

freeholds, 99, 103, 108–12, 113–14

Friedländer, Saul, 123

Friedman, Jeffrey: *Power without Knowledge*, 7

Friedrich Wilhelm III, King, 235, 236, 246–47, 249

Friedrich Wilhelm IV, King, 253

frontiers, 234, 282, 286

Führerbunker, Berlin, 37, 38, 55n35, 57n61, 58n67

furniture: Alpine-style, 218

Gaitán Cortés, Jorge, 199, 201, 207n47, 208n62, 209n70

Gama, Ruy, 86, 88

Gambetti, Zeynep, 323, 329, 334

García Canclini, Néstor, 188, 203n15

Garde Nationale, 258, 259

gardens, 269–70

Garnier, Charles: Opéra de Paris, 269

Garvey, Marcus Mosiah, 143, 144

gated communities: Brazil, 93, 94; United Arab Emirates, 99, 108, 108–13, 115, 117n28

G.A.T.E.P.A.C., 202n1

Gazette des architectes et du bâtiment (journal), 261

Generalbebauungsplan von Krakau, Der. *See* General Reconstruction Plan for the Building of Krakow

Generalgouvernement (Poland), 121–22, 124; Baudienst, 125

General Government (Poland). *See* Generalgouvernement (Poland)

General Italian Oil Company, 72

General Reconstruction Plan for the Building of Krakow, 125–32, *128*, *129*, *133*, 134; digital visualization, 119, 132, *133*, 134; goals, 127; Jewish ghetto location, 129, *133*; model, 129, *129*; phases, 132, *133*, 134; plans and photographs, 128–29, *128*; presentation version, 126–27; text, 126, 127, 129, 134, 138nn30–31, 138n35

genocide, 121, 122

Gentile, Giovanni, 8

geologists, 65

geopolitics, 155, 300, 314

German Institute of Standardization, 214, 216

German Steel Construction Association, 218

Germany, 4, 5, 40, 214; Bureau "Beauty of Labor," 214; General Building Inspectorate of the Imperial Capital of Berlin (GBI), 213, 214, 223. *See also* National Socialism

Geschichte und Beschreibung des Doms zu Köln (Boisserée), 245

Gezi resistance. *See* Taksim Gezi Park protests

ghettos, 122, 136n7; Dubai, 107; Jewish, 122, 132, 134, 137n17, 139n39

Gibb, Hamilton, 306, 317n21, 317n25; *Islamic Society and the West*, 306, 317n23

Giedion, Sigfried, 185, 193, 202n3

Gillett, Aaron, 65

Giménez Caballero, Ernesto, 165

Glanvill, Mark, 154–55

glass, 70, 168, 177, 178, 262

Godin, André: Familistère de Guise, Guise, 261

golf courses, 111

Gómez, Laureano, 208n64

Gorgonio, Ottorino, 70

governance: international, 347

governmentality, 8

Gramsci, Antonio, 6, 13n13
Graña Garland, Francisco, 206n40
Gran Madrid (journal), 168
Graycliff, Derby, New York, 290
Green Community Motor City, Dubai, 100, *100*, 108, 111–12
Greenough, Horatio, 28–29; *The Rescue* (sculpture), 29, 33
Gregori, Romeo, 68, 70, 72
grids, 163, 165, 168, 169, 177, 178–79, 228
Griffin, Roger, 164, 171
Gropius, Walter, 78n28, 185, 217, 202n3, 214, 234, 301, 302–3, 310, *311*, 313, 319n51; Americanization and, 304, 306; *Apollo in the Democracy*, 303; on collaboration, 303; on democracy, 303; on education, 303–4; on Iraq after 1958 revolution, 308; meeting with Qasim, 308–9; United States Embassy, Athens, 10; University of Baghdad, Iraq, 301–4, *301*, 306, 309–11, *311*, *312*, 313, 318n45
Großmarkthalle, Frankfurt, 5
Grottacalda, Italy: sulfur mines, 75
Guarulhos, Brazil, 86
Guerin, Ayasha, 150
Guerrini, Giovanni, 67; Pavilion of Art, MAMI, 67; Pavilion of Solid Combustibles, MAMI, 64
Guesnu, Marie-Hilaire: *Excursion dans Paris sans voitures*, 278n43
Guevara, Che, 207n53
Guha, Ranajit, 6
Gündüz, Erdem: headscarf protest-art performance, 328–28; identities projected onto, 327–28; as standing man, 324, *325*, 326–28, 329, 335, 336, 339n26
Gutschow, Niels, 220

Habermas, Jürgen, 5
Hácha, Emil, 46–47
Haitian Revolution (1791), 142
Halavut, Hazal, 333
Halle aux blés, Paris, 244

Hampton Normal and Agricultural Institute, 33
handbooks: standards, 212, 213, 216
Hardensett, Heinrich, 66
Hardt, Michael, 275, 278n48
Harrison, Wallace, 347
Harvard University: experts for University of Baghdad plan, 302, 306–8; Graduate School of Design (GSD), 185, 188, 200, 202n3
Harvey, David, 263
Hausbaumaschine. *See* House Building Machine
Haussmann, Georges-Eugène, 261–62, 263
hearths. *See* fireplaces
Heck, Marina, 89
hegemony, 2, 6–7, 11, 13n13, 17–18, 82–83, 95, 117n26, 281, 323, 330, 333–34, 336, 343, 347, 350. *See also* power
Henry, Joseph, 25, 30
Herf, Jeffrey, 66, 79n33, 171, 212
heterotopias, 101, 160n52
Hilberseimer, Ludwig, 278n44
Hines, Lewis, 147
Hints on Public Architecture (Owen), 23, *24*, 25
historicism, 62
historic preservation: Germany, 240, 247; Turkey, 324
Historikerstreit, 3, 5
historiography, 314
Hitchcock, Henry-Russell, 200
Hitler, Adolf, 3, 17, 38–40, 47, 55n18, 56n40; architecture and, 38–39, 121; renovation of his homes, 38–39
"Hitler Cities," 126, *127*
Hobsbawm, Eric, 8
Holocaust, 122, 123, 135
Holstein & Kappert (firm), 225
"Home in a Prairie Town, A" (Wright), 280
home ownership, 89, 108, 113–14
Homer, Winslow: *Campfire* (painting), 285, *285*

366   Index

homo economicus, 348
Horeau, Hector, 233, 260, 261, 264, 265, 269–71, 274–75; Church of the Madeleine, Paris, conversion drawing, 265, *268*; *Édilité urbaine*, 261, 274, 274n42; figures within his drawings, 271; imprisonment, 264, 269; Paris Commune sketches, 264–65, *266–67*; Paris reconstruction plan, 269–71, *272–73*, 274, 278nn42–43; *Plan de Paris, 272–73*, 278nn42–43
Hôtel de Ville, Paris, 268, 269–70, *270*, 271, 274
House Building Machine, 217, *218–19*
houses: back entryways, 288, 290, 292, 294; fireplaces, 281, 284, 286–88, *287*; Iraqi, 310, 311–13, 319n53, 319n55. *See also* villas
housing: agencies, 85; discrimination and, 283, 288, 298n24; low-income, 85; middle-class, 85, 89, 103, 108–12; upper-class, 85, 101, 284, 285–90, 292, 294–95; weaponization of, 217
housing projects: Brazil, 6, 18, 83, 86–97, 189, 204nn18–19, 207n47; Germany, 126; Peru, 191–93, 201, 205n34, 205n38, 207n46; United Arab Emirates, 98, 108
Hübsch, Heinrich: *In welchem Style sollen wir bauen?*, 23
Hudnut, Joseph, 202n3
Hugo, Victor, 263–64
Hull, Cordell, 186, 202n8, 203n11
human scale, 189, 204n21
"Human Scale in City Planning, The" (Sert), 204n21
Hyde, Timothy, 9
hyperrealism, 72

IBM, 225
identity: exogenous, 283–84, 292, 294; Germany, 6; Indigenous, 283–84, 292; individual, 151; Iraq, 310, 318n47; Italy, 6, 18, 61, 62, 65, 66, 75; National Socialist, 17–18, 126; racial, 20, 21, 23, 28, 33, 63, 79n33, 126, 213, 216, 279–87, 288; Rhineland, 240–42, 246, 247–48; Turkey, 328, 333–34; United States, 17, 19, 20, 21, 23, 26, 33, 150, 152, 279, 281–84, 288–90, 292, 295–96, 298n24, 345; working-class, 83, 298n31. *See also* Blacks; Native Americans; whiteness
Ifill, Vera Clark, 144, 159n23
Ignatiev, Noel, 292
immigrants, 8, 119, 99, 150, 283, 288, 292; African-descended, 140–42, 152; Afro-Caribbean, 142–45, *142*, 152, 154, 157, 157n6; Algerian, *153*; deportation and internment of, 154–57; discrimination against, 283, 292, 297n16; illegal, 154; Irish, 292; Italian, 295, 298n31; Jamaican, 152–53; Somalian, *141*
immigration (U.S.), 119, 140–42; exclusionary policies, 119, 150, 152; laws, 142, 152, 154; politics and, 155–57; quota system, 142, 152
imperialism, 7, 8, 10, 32, 15n38, 172, 180, 308, 347, 350n12; British, 350n12; oil, 307–8; Spain, 172, 180; United States, 307, 317n31. *See also* colonialism; colonization; empire building; expansionism; Manifest Destiny
impermanence, 99
indigenes, 282
individuals, 234, 328; global, 323; rights of, 328, 330
infill, 150
information: circulation of, 240, 249–51, 254n14; control of, 223, 226, 228. *See also* knowledge
infrastructure, 91–92, 111
insurrections: Black, 20
interior decoration, 176
International Bank for Reconstruction and Development, 186
International Conference of American States (9th, Bogotá), 195

Index   367

International Congress for Modern Architecture (CIAM). *See* CIAM
International Institute of Administrative Sciences (IIAS) (10th, Madrid), 173
International Monetary Fund (IMF), 186, 348, 351n15
International Petroleum Company (IPC), 206n40
International Trade Organization (ITO), 348, 351n15
internment, 155
In welchem Style sollen wir bauen? (Hübsch), 23
Iraq: British mandate, 300, 310; corruption in, 318n45; democracy and, 9, 234, 299, 306–7, 313, 315n2, 317n30; Gropius and Polk's meeting with Qasim, 308–9; local architects and international collaboration, 300–301, 310, 318n47; post-war reconstruction, 299, 308, 318n32; power and, 309; republican revolution (1958), 308; United States imperialism and, 307, 317n31; United States invasion of, 299, 313, 315n1
Iraq War, 299, 313, 315n1
Irish Americans, 292
iron, 244, 261
Islam, 306–7
Islamic Society and the West (Gibb), 306, 317n23
Istanbul, Turkey, 329–30; mosque, 330; Ottoman-themed vision of, 330; public squares/city voids, 335. *See also* Taksim Gezi Park, Istanbul; Taksim Square, Istanbul (Prost)
Istituto Luce, 79n30
Istrian peninsula, 64
Italian Coal Company, 64
Italian East Africa, 64
italianità, 65
Italy: fascist empire building, 62, 64, 70; material scarcity in, 6, 59; propaganda, 68, 78n18; trade sanctions on, 59, 62, 63, 67, 77n11. *See also* fascism (Italy)
Itten, Johannes, 219–20

Jackson, Andrew, 20
James, C. L. R., 119–20, 144, 155–56; *Mariners, Renegades, and Castaways*, 156
James, Winston, 142
James Birch (firm), 27
Jaskot, Paul, 213
Jawdat, Ellen, 301, 308, 310, 313, 315n8
Jawdat, Nizar Ali, 301, 308, 315n8, 319n50
JBR, Dubai, 104
Jebel Ali, United Arab Emirates, 107
Jefferson, Thomas, 29
Jews, 122, 123, 125, 126, 129, 130
Jim Crow era: racial attitudes, 279, 288, 295, 296n1, 298n24
Jones, Claudia, 156–57
Joya, Rafael de la: SEAT Auto-Industry Warehouse, Barcelona, *167*
Jucho (firm), 218, 226
Jumeirah Beach Residences, Dubai. *See* JBR, Dubai
Jumeirah English Speaking School (JESS), Dubai, 111
Justice and Development Party (AKP). *See* AKP (political party)

Kaiser-Wilhelm-Gedächtniskirche, Berlin, 252
Kamil, Ihsan: Khan Pasha residence, Baghdad, 313
Kanna, Ahmed, 107
Kasinitz, Philip, 142
Kastorkirche, Koblenz, 245
Khan Pasha residence, Baghdad (Kamil), 313
Kızılay Square, Ankara, 324
Klenze, Leo von, 238
Kluge, Alexander: *Brutalität im Stein* (film), 5
knowledge: dissemination of, 21, 22, 28, 29–32. *See also* information
KONDA (firm), 331
Koolhaas, Rem: *Delirious New York*, 349
Krakow, Poland, 119, 123–39; building goals (Ritter's long-term vs. Frank's short-term), 124–26, 129–31, 134, 135; construction within, 125, 127, 130–31, 134–35,

136n6; "Germanization" of, 119, 121, 124, 125–26; Jewish ghetto/ghettoization of, 8, 122, 129, 130, 132, *133*, 134–35; National Socialist administration, 8, 124–25, 128, 129, 130, 132, 138n35; National Socialist building plans, 122–23, 124–25, 136n10; National Socialist genocidal policy for, 125, 127, 130; National Socialist housing policy, 130; occupation of, 123–24; populations, 123, 126, 127; Ritter's reconstruction plan, 126–32, *128, 129, 133,* 134; spatial relationships of communities, 132, *133,* 134; transportation network, 125; Wawel Castle, 124, 127, 128–29, 130–31, *131,* 132, 138n31

Krier, León, 56n47
Ku Klux Klan, 33
Kula, Witold, 216

labor, 20, 65, 221, 270–71; Brazil, 85, 87; forced/prison, 125, 132, 134–35, 213, 217–18, 283; Germany, 125, 213; management, 85, 213, 214, 221, 223–24; manual, 217; non-white, 283; organized, 88, 90, 213, 221, 224, 226; United Arab Emirates, 113, 114
labor camps: Jewish, 134; United Arab Emirates, 99, 108, 118n29
Labrouste, Henri, 238
Laclau, Ernesto, 82, 323, 333
land grants, 32
land occupation, 282–83
land reclamation, 72, 80n48, 145–46, 147
land surveys, 31, 32
Lane, Barbara Miller. *See* Miller Lane, Barbara
Larraín, Sergio: Villa Presidente Ríos, Talcahuano, Chile, 201, 209n77
Lassaulx, Johann Claudius von, 241, 242, 244–46; cost estimate for Vallendar church, 242, *243,* 244, 245, 246; design for Vallendar church, 244–46
Last of Their Race, The (painting) (Stanley), 31, 33

Las Vegas, Nevada, 349
Latin America, 185–210
Latin American Architecture Since 1945 (exhibition), 200
Latour, Bruno, 83
League of Nations headquarters, Geneva, 346–47
Lebensraum. See expansionism: Germany
Le Corbusier, 181n2, 186, 189, 190, 193–94, 202n5, 204n20, 204n25, 204n27, 313; Brazil and, 193; Colombia and, 194–95, 196, 207n47, 208nn57–58, 208n61; Plan Voisin, 276n13; telegraph cable from Sert/Wiener to, 195, *195*; Ville Contemporaine, 276n13
Lefèvre, Camille: League of Nations headquarters, Geneva, 346–47
Lefort, Claude, 345
Legion of Engineering, 258
Lenape nation, 145
Lesueur, Charles A., 30
Levittown, Pennsylvania, 288
Levy, Lawrence H., 203n13
Ley, Robert, 214
LGBT, 329
Libera, Adalberto, 62, 67; Palazzo dei Congressi, EUR, 67
liberalism, 284
liberty, 259, 336
lies, 4, 12n8
lighting, 226, 286, 298n20, 345
Lima, Attilio Corrêa, 204n18; Ministry of Education and Health Building, Rio de Janeiro, 189, 204n20
Lima, Peru, 193, 205n38, 206n41, 206n43
Links Golf Club, Dubai (Baker-Finch and Nicklaus Design), 111
logistics, 213
Long Way from Home, A (McKay), 144
López Rodó, Laureano, 172, 173–74, 175, 179
L'Orme, Philibert de, 269
Lotz, Wilhelm, 214
Louis XIV, King, 259
Louvre, Paris, 269

Index 369

Luccichenti, Ugo: Pavilion of Marl, MAMI, 63
Lutyens, Edward, 347: British Raj headquarters, New Delhi, 10
Luwa Firm, 224
Luxbacher, Günther, 214

Macià plan, Barcelona, 202n1, 209n75
Maclure, William, 30
Madhloom, Midhat Ali, 319n50
Madinat Jumeirah resort, Dubai, 104
Madison, James, 34n4
Magalhães de Almeida Prado, José Maria, 86
"Makbul Vatandas" in Peşinde (Üstel), 334
Maktoum, Mohammed bin Rashid Al, 108, 118n31
MAMI, 59–68, *60–61, 69,* 70, *72–73,* 75–76; advertisements, 65, 78n25; colonnades, 67; construction, 67, 70, *71,* 72; displays, 59, 65–66, 68, 72; eagle relief, 68, *69;* exhibition catalog, 70, *71,* 80n46; façades, 68, *69;* marble quarry, 72, *74;* oil derrick, 72, *73,* 80n49; Pavilion of Arms (De Renzi), *60, 61,* 67, 70, 80n45; Pavilion of Art (Guerrini), 67; Pavilion of Autarchy, Research, and Invention (Puppo and Vitellozzi), 68, *69,* 70; Pavilion of Land Reclamation, 72; Pavilion of Liquid and Gas Combustibles (Paniconi and Pediconi), 72, *73;* Pavilion of Marl (Luccichenti), 63; Pavilion of Solid Combustibles (Montuori and Guerrini), 64; pavilions, 59, *60, 61,* 63, 64, 67, 68, *69,* 70, *71, 72–73, 73, 74,* 81n55; photography and newsreels, 66, 67, 79n30; purpose, 60, 64–65; scale models, 75; sculpture of Italia, 70, *71,* 80n47; Ufficio tecnico-artistico, 67; water pump, 72
Manifest Destiny, 17, 29, 282
marble, 45, 48, 49, 52, 56n46, 57n63, 72, *74,* 80n47
March on Rome, 62
Marefat, Mina, 318n47, 319n50
Mariners, Renegades, and Castaways (James), 156

marl, 63
Marshall, George, 207n53
Martin, Darwin D., 290, 294, 297n18; family, 285, 297n18; phrenological reading of, 294, *295*
Martin, Isabelle, 288, 290, 298n20
Martínez, Fernando, 208n58
Martínez Jiménez, Carlos, 194
Marx, Karl, 270
masculinity, 329
masonry, 72, 79n36, 176, 178, 179
material culture, 123; autochthonous, 280; white, 280, 282
materials: autarchic, 59–76; building, 59, 66, 68, 70, 75; industrial, 91; reflective, 45, 57nn48–49
Mbembe, Achille, 101–2
McKay, Claude: *A Long Way from Home,* 144
McMillen, Louis, 308–9, 318n45
Medellín, Colombia, 196
megapolises, 104
megaprojects, 105
Melville, Herman: *Moby-Dick,* 144
Mémoire sur la defense de Paris (Viollet-le-Duc), 257–59
memory: collective, 144, 329; cultural, 38, 48, 62, 113
men (as a concept): capitalist vs. technical, 66, 79n33
Mendes da Rocha, Paulo, 86
merchant marines, 143–44
metropolises, 274–75, 278n44, 278n48
Meyer, Adolf, 217
Mies van der Rohe, Ludwig, 78n28, 178, 179
migration: Caribbean, 142–45, 157n6; Colombia, 196, 197; Peru, 192, 207n46
Miller Lane, Barbara: *Architecture and Politics in Germany, 1918–1945,* 3–4, 8, 212
Mills, Robert, 23, 25, 35n22
mineralogists, 62, 65
minerals: abundance and, 65–66, 78n28; autochthonous, 18, 59, 65; extraction of, 61–62, 65; transformation of, 65–66, 68
mining, 61–62, 64, 65, 72–73, 75

Ministry of Education and Health Building, Rio de Janeiro (Costa), 189, 204n20
Ministry of Education Building, Brazil, 181n2
Miró Quesada, Luis, 206n39
Mitchell, Timothy, 7; *Carbon Democracy*, 346
Mitchell, W. J. T., 321
Moby-Dick (Melville), 144
Modern Art in the United States (exhibition), 179
Moderne Bauformen (journal), 138n38
modernism, 8, 120, 179, 194, 200–201, 203n15, 212, 306–7, 347; constitutional, 9; fascism and, 164, 170–71, 189; global, 300; localized, 201, 306; Middle East, 306–7; reactionary, 66, 171, 212; Turkey, 330
modernity, 303; Euro-American, 286, 290; global, 300
modernization, 6, 167–68, 170–71, 173, 175, 179, 180, 200, 203n15, 307; Iraq, 299–300, 313–14
modularization, 216, 223, 224, 228
modular systems, 169, 178–79, 216, 223, 224, 228; bricks and, *215*, 216
Moilin, Tony: *Paris in the Year 2000*, 260–61
Molezún, Ramón Vázquez: Delegación de Hacienda, La Coruña, 178–80; New Headquarters for the Ministries of Industry and Commerce Competition, Madrid, 170
Moller, Georg, 244; *Denkmalern der deutschen Baukunst*, 245
Mondragón, Hugo, 201
Montecatini (firm), 64
Montuori, Eugenio: Pavilion of Solid Combustibles, MAMI, 64
monuments, 164, 344
Morefield, Jeanne, 347
Moreton, Bethany, 172
Morgenthau, Henry, 185, 186
Morrison, Toni, 29
mosques, *305*, 309, 330
Mosse, George, 171
Mostra Augustea della Romanità (MAR). *See* Augustan Exhibition of Romanità
Mostra autarchica del minerale Italiano (MAMI). *See* MAMI
Mostra del Dopolavoro. *See* Dopolavoro Exhibition
Mostra della Rivoluzione fascista (MRF). *See* Exhibition of the Fascist Revolution
Mostra delle industrie estrattive della Sardegna. *See* Exhibition of Sardinian Extractive Industries
Mostra nazionale delle Bonifiche. *See* National Exhibition on Land Reclamation
Mostra nazionale delle colonie estive e dell'assistenza all'infanzia. *See* National Exhibition of Summer Camps and Assistance to Children
Mostra nazionale del tessile. *See* Exhibition of National Textiles
Mouffe, Chantal, 82, 323, 333; *For a Left Populism*, 333
Moya, Luis, 163–64, *165*; *Sueno arquitectonico para una exaltacion nacional* (unbuilt monument), 164
Müller, Jan-Werner, 8
Mumford, Lewis, 163
Munir, Hisham, 302, 308, 309–10, *311*, 313, 319n50
Murray, Martin J., 107
Museum of Modern Art (MoMA), New York: *Brazil Builds*, 193, 203n17; *Latin American Architecture Since 1945*, 200; *Modern Art in the United States*, 179
museums, 62
Muslim Brotherhood, 116n13
Mussolini, Benito, 62, 64, 65; Ascension Day speech, 62, 77n9; dictum, 68; empire building of, 62, 64, 70; images of, 64, 73, 75, 80nn51–52; pronatalism of, 62, 77n9
myths and mythmaking, 17–18, 38, 48, 49–50, 52–53, 164, 282–83, 345

Nahyan, Zayed Al, 113
Napoléon III, Emperor, 257, 269
narcissism, 326
Nash, John, 238

National Catholicism, 166
National Council of Architectural Registration Boards (NCARB), 202n7
National Exhibition of Summer Camps and Assistance to Children, 62
National Exhibition on Land Reclamation, 80n48
National Factory of Motors, 188–89, 203n17
National Fascist Party. *See* Partito Nazionale Fascista (PNF)
National Housing Bank. *See* Banco Nacional de Habitação (BNH)
National Housing Corporation (Peru), 191, 205n37
nationalism, 6, 59, 66, 164–65, 189, 192, 193, 288, 346; economic, 351n15; ethno, 59; secular, 307, 309. *See also* identity
nationalist international, 1, 12n2
National Research Council (Spain), 172, 174
National Socialism, 3–5, 8, 39–40, 44, 127, 213, 216, 220; architecture and, 3–5, 121–39; bureaucracy, 39, 44, 55n34, 56n42; construction and, 214, 216–18; dissolution of governance, 39, 40, 44, 56n42; economy, 132, 134; infrastructure projects, 214; internecine rivalries, 124, 130, 137n17, 214; polycratism, 124; propaganda, 3–4, 12n8, 39, 40, 41, 45, 46, 48, 53, 55n36, 56n45, 124; race and, 124, 125, 126, 135, 217
National University of Colombia: School of Architecture, 194
nations, 17, 345–46
nation-states, 7, 10, 98, 157, 240, 284, 290, 295, 296, 327, 334, 345, 346, 349; borders, 346
Native Americans, 17, 20, 27, 29, 32–33, 145, 282; dispossession/forced removal, 20, 21, 29, 31–32; erasure of, 282, 292; images of, 31–32; reservations, 33; sovereignty, 20, 21, 32, 33, 145, 282, 283
natural history, 286
naturalists, 30–32
natural resources, 282

Navarro Rubio, Mariano, 174
Nazism. *See* National Socialism
necropolitics, 164
Negri, Antonio, 275, 278n48
neighborhoods: master-planned, 59, 193, 205n38; Peru, 201, 210n78; private, 101, 108, 117n28
Nénot, Henri-Paul: League of Nations headquarters, Geneva, 346–47
neoliberalism, 6, 11, 18, 98, 101, 114, 174, 234, 323, 328, 332–33, 347–49, 351n15
Nervi, Pier Luigi, 59
Neufert, Ernst, 120, 212, 213, 216, 219–20, 221–26, 228; *Bauentwurfslehre,* 212, 213; *Bauordnungslehre,* 212, 214, 216; Dortmund, 212, 221–26, 225; Dortmunder Union-Brauerei (DUB) expansion plan, octametric system of, 216–18, 228; relationship and collaboration with Speer, 212–13, 216, 220–26, 228; support of Speer and National Socialism, 219–20
Neumeyer, Fritz, 178
Neutra, Dione, 214
Neutra, Richard, 213–14; *Wie baut Amerika?,* 213
New Finance Headquarters Competition, Valencia (Sota), 177, *177*
New Harmony, Indiana, 21–22, 23, 30
New Headquarters for the Ministries of Industry and Commerce Competition, Madrid, *166,* 168–70, *169, 170,* 180
New International Economic Order (NIEO), 348, 351n15
New Lanark, Scotland, 21, 22
"new monumentality," 9, 343
New Reich Chancellery, Berlin (Speer), 17, 37–53, *42–43, 47, 50, 51*; bombing of, 57n56; building functionality, 41, 44, 48, 55n34, 56n40; construction, 39, 40, 55nn25–28; demolition, 37, 38, 48–50, *50, 51,* 52; de-mythologization/erasure of, 49–50, 53; enfilade, 41, 44, 45, 56n45; façade, 40–41, 45; Führer block, 41, 44; garden, 41, 55n35; hallways, 41, 44;

Hitler's office, 41, 45–46, *46, 47,* 49, *50*; Honors Court, 56n47; Marble Gallery, 41, 44, 45, *46,* 49–50, *50,* 55n36; mythology of, 6, 38, 48, 49–50, 52–53; offices, 44, 56n40; Party Chancellery, 41, 44, 57n56; photographs (post–WWII/Soviet), 38, *50, 51,* 52, 58n71; photographs and newsreels (National Socialist), 17–18, 38, 45, *46, 47, 50, 51,* 52, 56nn45–46; plan, 40–41, *42–43,* 44; provisional nature, 40, 55n31; purpose, 40, 44; Reception Hall, 41, 55n36; Reich Chancellery, 41, 44; reuse of its material parts, 48–49, 52, 57n63; site visits to, 48, 52–53, 58n72; vacancy within, 47–48, 57n55
new towns, 72, 75
New Urbanism, 100
Ngai, Mae, 152
Nicklaus Design: Links Golf Club, Dubai, 111
Niemeyer, Oscar, 185, 189, 204nn19–20, 204n23; Brasilia, Brazil, 201
nonfoundationalist theory, 333
"non-places," 100
Notes from Underground (Dostoyevsky), 260
Nuestro Tiempo (journal), 174
Nuremberg Race Laws, 213, 216

Obelisk of Axum, 68
Occupy movements, 321, 322, 323, 331–34. *See also* Taksim Gezi Park protests
octometer, 216–17, 226
Odría Amoretti, Manuel, 191, 192, 206n40
oil: United States interests in Iraq and, 306–7, 308
oil derricks, 72, 73
Old Fort Walla Walla (painting) (Stanley), 32
Ollantaytambo, Brazil, 206n41
Opéra de Paris (Garnier), 269
Opus Dei, 171–72, 174–75, 182n21
Orientalism, 306–7, 313–14
Orientalism (Said), 306
Orsal, Osman, 337n6
Ortega y Gasset, José, 199, 209n72

Ortiz-Echagüe, Cesar, 174; SEAT Auto-Industry Warehouse, Barcelona, *167*
O'Sullivan, John, 29
Ottoman Artillery Barracks, Istanbul, 330
Owen, David Dale, 23, 24, 25, 30
Owen, Richard, 21
Owen, Robert, 17, 21
Owen, Robert Dale, 17, 20, 21, 22, 30; *Hints on Public Architecture,* 23, *24, 25*
Owenites, 21

Paesani, Eugenia, 88
Page, Matthew, 265
palazzos, 67, 176
palingenetic myth, 164
pallets, 221, 222, 223, 224, 226, 228
Palm Dubai, Dubai, 104
Pan-American States Conference (3rd, Rio de Janeiro), 186, 188, 202n9
Paniconi, Mario, 67; Pavilion of Liquid and Gas Combustibles, MAMI, 72, 73
Panthéon, Paris (Soufflot), 345
Paris, France, 257, 258, 261–62, 263, 264–65, 272–73, 274–75; futurist visions, 260–63, 276n13; Haussmann and, 261–62, 263; map (Horeau), 272–73, 278n43; *Plan de Paris* (Horeau), 271, *272–73,* 274, 278n42; reconstructions, 268–71, *272–73,* 274–75, 278n42
Paris Commune, 9, 233, 259, 264, *266–67,* 271, 274; barricades, 233, 263; erasure of, 271, 274
Paris in the Year 2000 (Moilin), 260–61
parking, 92
parks, *100,* 322, 336n2; occupation of, 322, 331, 332, 336n2, 337n4
Parque Cecap, São Paulo (state). *See* Cecap Guarulhos, São Paulo (state)
Partito Nazionale Fascista (PNF), 61–62
Pasotti, Legnami, 70, 80n45
passageways, 261
passive climate control, 299, 300, 310, 313, 319nn53–54
patios, 192, 206nn41–42

patrimony, 65
Peabody, George F., 33
Pediconi, Giulio, 67; Pavilion of Liquid and Gas Combustibles, MAMI, 72, 73
Pegler-Gordon, Anna, 155
Penteado, Fábio, 86, 90
people, the. See *demos*
Pérez Jiménez, Marcos, 200
performance art, 323, 324, 325, 326–28, 329
permanence, 99, 109, 114
Perón, Juan, 193, 207n53
Perpiñá, Antonio: New Headquarters for the Ministries of Industry and Commerce Headquarters Competition, Madrid, 166, 169, 169
persuasion, 6
Peru, 191–93; coup d'etats, 192; General Office of Planning and Urbanism, 191; governmental control, 192–93; land property management, 192; migration within, 192, 207n46; Ministry of Public Works, 193, 206n43; nationalism, 192–93; political unrest and riots, 191, 206n40; PREVI housing project, 201; urban planning, 190–92, 205n38, 207n46
Peruvian Corporation of Santa, 191, 193, 205n33
Pestalozzianism, 22, 25
Peters, Ralph, 315n2
Petrucci, Franco, 64
photographs: New Reich Chancellery, Berlin (National Socialist), 38, 45, 46, 47, 53, 56nn45–46; New Reich Chancellery, Berlin (post–WWII/Soviet), 38, 49, 50, 51, 52, 58n71
photography: architectural, 44–45, 48, 57n49; media, 323, 337n6; Victorian, 292, 293
phrenology, 294, 295
Pius VII, Pope, 236
PNF. See Partito Nazionale Fascista (PNF)
political science, 3, 7
Political Theory and Architecture (Bell and Zacka), 3

politics, 6, 8, 83, 300, 323, 334; aesthetics of, 323; architecture and, 1–2, 6–7, 8, 11, 38–39, 59–60, 87, 94–95, 102, 121, 163–66, 175–80, 186, 187, 191, 281, 343, 347; Black, 142–43, 279–80; Cold War, 179, 303, 307, 318n36; immigration and, 155–57; leftist, 87, 155; performative, 333–34; propaganda and, 282, 295, 299, 314; racial, 281, 288, 296, 298n24; Soviet, 38
Polk, William, 307–8, 313; *Backdrop to Tragedy*, 307; meeting with Qasim, 308–9; on United States interest in Iraq and oil revenue, 306–7, 308, 313; *What the Arabs Think*, 307
pollution, 299, 315n3
populace. See *demos*
porphyry, 70
Posner, Eric, 102–3
Pottier, Eugène, 270
power, 6, 102, 278n48; asymmetry of, 242; concentration of, 39, 55n18, 213, 217; industrial, 217, 223; resistance to, 278n48, 349; soft, 6, 234, 308, 313; standardization and, 216, 217, 223, 228; symbols/images of, 45, 48, 68, 69. See also hegemony
Power without Knowledge (Friedman), 7
Prado, Manuel, 191
prairies, 282
precision, 222–23
prefabrication, 87, 91, 214, 217–18
PREVI housing project, 201
Prins der Nederlanden (ship), 143
prisoners of war: non-Jewish, 217
Proa (journal), 194, 196, 197, 199, 201
productivity, 224, 226
proletariat, 87, 263, 264, 275
property ownership, 33, 108, 113–14, 282, 283
proselytism, 175
Prost, Henri: Taksim Square, Istanbul, 327
protesters, 321–23, 322, 324, 325, 326, 330–31, 337n4
protests. See resistance
provinciality, 242, 248

Pruitt–Igoe housing project, St. Louis, 95n5
Prussia: army against Paris, 257, 258; bureaucracy, 235–36, 240, 241–42, 245–49, 251–52; Hofbauamt, 238; Kultusministerium, 242, 255n19; legal system, 254n6; Oberbaudeputation, 236, 238, 242, 245, 247–49, 251, 252, 255n18; rule/state control, 235, 240, 242, 248, 249–50, 251
Prussian General Code, 254n6
public assemblies, 347–48, 349
public-private partnerships, 348
publics, 238, 240, 248, 254n14
public squares: Bogotá, 196, *198*, 199, 201, 209n72; Istanbul, 321–22, 324, *325*, 326, 327
Pulitzer-Finali, Gustavo, 64
Puppo, Ernesto: Pavilion of Autarchy, Research, and Invention, MAMI, 68, *69*, 70

Qasim, Abdul Karim, 308–9, 313
Qasimi Foundation, Al, 104
Qatar, 103
quality control, 222–23
quarries, 72, 74
Queensbridge Houses, New York, 95n5

railroads, 31
Rand, Erica, 147
Ratio Structures (firm), 202n5
Rattinger, Richard, 125
Rava, Carlo Enrico, 64
real estate development, 104–5, 108–13
real estate market, 85; branding, 106; speculation, 98, 106, 109, 263; United Arab Emirates, 98, 103, 106, 109, 117n19
reclamation. See *bonifica*
Rediker, Marcus, 143
reflections, 45, 57nn48–49
Regis, Flavio, 207n47
Reich, Lilly, 78n28
Reidy, Affonso Eduardo, 204n20, 207n47
Renwick, James, 17, 26, 35n26; Smithsonian Institution, Washington, D.C., 20–21, 23, 25–26, *25*, 30, 33, 35n26

replacements, 283, 284
Rescue, The (sculpture) (Greenough), 29, 33
residency: permanent, 98, 109
resistance, 9, 234, 321, 322, *322*, 323, 331, 333, 334, 335–36, 338n8, 349, 350; individual, 326, 331, 335–36; urban, 321–23, 330–31
restaurants, 113
Restlosigkeit, 224
Reuter, Dieter, 241
Reuter, Oscar: *Das Wohnhaus in Baghdad*, 313
Revista Nacional de Arquitectura (RNA) (journal), 165, 176, 178
Revolution of 1848, 263–64
revolutions, 249–50, 259, 263–64
Rhenish Diet (5th), 251
Rhineland, 9, 235–53; built environment and identity, 233, 239; Catholicism of, 235, 246; church building, 233, 235–36, 240, 241–42, 244–49, 252; church funding petitions (Catholic), 235, 240, 241–42, 244–49, 250–51, 253; church funding petitions (Protestant), 246–47, 250–51; cities, 246; legal systems, 254n6; map, *237*; parish councils, 246, 247; protests, 245–49, 249–51; provincial constituents vs. Prussian state officials, 235, 236, 239–41, 241–42, 244–49, 251–52; Prussian bureaucracy in, 235–36, 240, 241–42, 245–49, 251–52; Prussian rule/state control, 235, 240, 242, 248, 249–50, 251; review of architectural petitions, 236, 239, 240, 244–45; schools and school design, 251, 255n18
ribs: wood, 70, *71*, 80n46
Richards, James, 192
Riefenstahl, Leni, 4
Ritter, Hubert, 122–23, 125–26, 137n23; Großmarkthalle, Leipzig, 126; Krakow reconstruction plan, 126–30, 132, *133*, 134, 138nn30–31, 138n35; "Rundling" housing estate, Leipzig, 126
Ritter Echeverry, Herbert, 194, 195, 196, 208n57

Rochow, Gustav von, 249
rocks, 65–66, 68
Roediger, David, 140
Rojas Pinilla, Gustavo, 199, 208n67
Roman Catholicism, 120, 171, 174, 238; bias against, 246–46; clerical administration of, in Rhineland, 236, 252; funding for, in Prussia, 236; mandated church architectural style, 252
Roman-ness, 62
Romany, José: New Headquarters for the Ministries of Industry and Commerce Competition, Madrid, *170*
roofs: wood, 70, *71*, 80n46
Roosevelt, Warren, 150
rootedness. *See* permanence
Rösel, Wolfgang, 212, 221; Dortmunder Union-Brauerei (DUB) expansion plan, Dortmund, 212, 221–26, *225*
Ross, Kristen, 264, 270
Rue de l'Impératrice, Paris, 261, *262*
rule of force, 258–59
"Rundling" housing estate, Leipzig (Ritter), *126*

Sabsay, Leticia, 333
sacralization, 344, 345
Sáenz de Oiza, Francisco Javier, 178, 180; New Headquarters for the Ministries of Industry and Commerce Competition, Madrid, *170*
Said, Edward: *Orientalism*, 306
Saint Giovanni in Borgo, Pavia, 245
Sajwani, Hussain, 117n22
Samper, Germán, 199
Sandalo, Rudolf de, 56n46
Santoro, Ernesto, 70
São Paulo, Brazil, 84, *85*, *86*
Sarısülük, Ethem, 324
Say, Thomas, 30
saygı duruşu, 327
Schinkel, Karl Friedrich, 233, 236, 238, 239, 240, 245
Schmidt, Joost, 78n28

Schnapp, Jeffrey, 62
schools, 22, 25, 251, 255n18
Schulenburg Palace, Berlin, 38, 40, 55n34, 57n56; balcony, *39*; National Socialist renovation, 38–39; salon, *39*; "Service Building"/addition, 38, 54nn7–8, 57n56
science, 21, 29–32
Scott, Dred, 27
Scott, George Gilbert, 344–45
Scott Brown, Denise, 349
SEAT Auto-Industry Warehouse, Barcelona (Ortiz-Echagüe, Echaide, Barbero, and Joya), *167*
secularism: Turkey, 328–29, 330
security states, 101–2
Sédille, Paul, 271
segregation, 101, 107, 111–12, 114, 115, 288, 290, 292, 298n24
self-formation, 275
self-sufficiency, economic. *See* autarchy
sense of belonging, 99, 114
Serpieri, Arrigo, 80n48
Serrano, Gabriel, 196
Sert, José Luis, 120, 185–201, *187*, 320n61; architectural degree, 202n7, 204n25; architectural works, 209n75; in Brazil, 188–89; in Colombia, 194–99; CIAM and, 188, 190–91, 201; his house, 206n42, 209n75; "The Human Scale in City Planning," 204n21; lecture tours in South America, 186, 188, 191, 203n13, 209n75; partnership relationships, 185–86, 189–91; in Peru, 191–93; relationship with Le Corbusier, 186, 193–94, 202n5, 204n25; status of, 190, 200, 205n31; travel to Spain, 189–90, 204n25
settler colonial theory, 280, 281–84, 295
settler groups, 282–84
seven (number), 217
shade, 304, 310–11
Sharjah, United Arab Emirates, 117n19
Sheikh Zayed Road, Dubai, 104, 105–6
shipping: containerized, 226
Siedler, Eduard Jobst, 38

Siedlung Törten, Dessau, 217
Siegert, Bernhard, 228
Simpson and Neal (firm), 27
simulacra, 72, 99
Skidmore, Owings, and Merrill: Burj Khalifa, Dubai, 105
skyscrapers, 105
slavery, 20, 27–28, 29, 144
slave ships, 144
slave trade, 17, 20, 26–27, 29; broadside, 27, *28*
Smirke, Robert, 238
Smithson, James, 21
Smithsonian Institution, Washington, D.C. (Renwick), 17, 19–20, 21, 22–23, 25, 33, 34n3; architecture of, 20–21, 23, 25–26, *25*, 30, 33, 35n26; Board of Regents, 25, 30, 34n3, 35n26; construction, 27–28; exhibitions and engravings, 31; missions, 21, 22, 23, 25–26, 29–30, 33; scientific expeditions, 30–32, 33; site, 26
Smuts, Jan, 347
sociability. *See* community life
social classes, 263, 275, 284; elite/ruling, 101, 111, 283–84, 289, 290, 292, 294, 298n31, 349; lower, 85; middle class, 89, 90, 111–12; reification of, 107, 111–12, 113, 115, 117n26; segregation and, 101, 107, 111–12, 114, 115, 288, 290, 292, 298n24; working, 87, 89, 292
social reform, 21
society: disciplinary, 199, 213, 228; French revolutionary, 259
Sodré, Abreu, 86
Sota, Alejandro de la, 165, 176–80, 184n52; Delegación de Hacienda, La Coruña, 178–80; New Finance Headquarters Competition, Valencia, 177, *177*; New Headquarters for the Ministries of Industry and Commerce Competition, Madrid, *170*, 180
Soufflot, Jacques-Germain: Panthéon, 345
South America, 185–210; WWII diplomatic relationships, 202n9, 203n11
sovereignty, 9, 20, 21, 32, 33, 145, 259, 263, 275, 282, 334, 336, 348

spaces: class divisions within, 288; common, 275; compartmentalized, 99, 101, 107, 122, 123, 132, *133*, 134, 288, 290, 292; control/domination of, 123, 134, 135, 154–55, 199, 228, 330; experience of, 122, 123, 129, 130, 132, *133*, 134, 156, 192, 274, 287–88, 350; forced laborers and, 217; open, 92–93, 287, 310; prisoners of war and, 217; public/community, 87, 88, 91, 189, 321–22, 324, 326, 330, 350; race and, 217, 234, 288, 290, 291; scale of, 192, 226; shaded, 304, 310–11; servant, 288, 289; visualization of, 123, 132, *133*, 134, 135
Spain, 163–80; Air Force Ministry, 170; architectural competitions, 120, 176–80; building program, 175–76; developmentalism in, 167–68, 174; General Technical Secretary, 174; governance, 172–74; governmental control, 172–73; government offices and bureaucracy, 176–80; imperialism, 172, 180; Ministry of Finance, 175, 178; Ministry of Governance, 168; Ministry of Government, 175; modernization and, 167–68, 170–71, 173, 175, 179, 180; Official State Bulletin (BOE), 176; propaganda and, 171; student protests, 173. *See also* fascism (Spain); Franquismo
spatiality, 33, 130, 132, *133*, 134, 135, 226
spectatorship, 330
Speer, Albert, 8, 37, 39, 45, 54n8, 79n36, 120, 126, 127, 211–16, 221–26, 228; "Cathedral of Light," 226; concealed involvement in DUB project, 120, 220–21; construction and design background, 213, 214; Dortmunder Union-Brauerei (DUB) expansion plan, Dortmund, 212, 221–26, 225; "Haupstadt Germania," 212; imprisonment, 211, 219; New Reich Chancellery, Berlin, 37–53; relationship and collaboration with Neufert, 212, 213, 216, 220–26, 228; relationship with Neutra, 213–14
Speer, Albert, Jr., 214
Sprague, Mr., *291*

Stakely, J. Tracy, 150
standards and standardization, 212, 213, 214, 215, 216–19
standing man, 234, 324, *325*, 326–28, 330
standing woman, 324, 327
Stanley, John Mix, 31; *The Last of Their Race* (painting), 31, 33; *Old Fort Walla Walla* (painting), 32
steel, 218
Stevenson, Adlai, 58n71
Stieglitz, Christian: *Über altdeutsche Baukunst*, 245
stratification, 145
Study for the Buenos Aires Plan (EPBA), 193
subjectification, 275
subjectivities, 275, 278n48, 328, 329; fascist, 17, 18; of the multitudes, 275
sublime, 234, 323, 334, 336
suburbia, 89, 90, 91–92, 288, 298n31
Sueno arquitectonico para una exaltacion nacional (unbuilt monument) (Moya), 164
Sullivan, Louis, 280, 281
Sungur, Ceyda, 337n6
supply chains, 221
surveillance, 102, 110, 114, 115, 134, 146, 147, 213, 221
synthetics, 62

Tabanlıoğlu, Hayati: Atatürk Culture Center (AKM), Istanbul, 324
TAC, 234, 302, 303, 309, 310, *311*. See also Gropius, Walter
Tafuri, Manfredo, 8, 278n44; *Architecture and Utopia*, 8
Tahrir Square, Cairo, 321
Taksim Gezi Park, Istanbul, 322, 327, 330, 331, *335*, 336n2, 340n42. See also Taksim Gezi Park protests
Taksim Gezi Park protests, 234, 322–24, *322*, *325*, 326–29, *327*, 331–32, *335*, 336n2, 338n8; camaraderie at, 329; iconic imagery, 321–23, *325*, 337n6; injuries and deaths, 326, 336n2; LGBT bloc at, 329; occupiers, 329, 331–32; occupiers' politics, 332; performative acts, 322, 323, 331; police response, 322, *322*, 324, 336n2, 337n6; solidarity within, 329, 332–33; soundscapes, 323; survey of participants, 331–32. See also standing man; standing woman
Taksim Solidarity, 332
Taksim Square, Istanbul (Prost), 322, 324, 327, *335*, 335
Taney, Roger, 27
Tarchi, Angelo, 81n55
Tauriello, Sebastian, 295
Taylorism, 217
technocracy, 1, 7–8, 11, 119–20, 166, 173–74, 175, 180, 344, 349, 350
technocrats, 60, 62, 65, 66, 120, 173–74, 175
technology, 119–20, 163–64, 166, 178, 203n15, 350; autonomous, 7; Italy, 66; Middle East, 307
temporality, 32, 99, 125, 151, 154–55, 226
Temporary People (Unnikrishnan), 99
Ten Haeff, Ingeborg, 205n30
Tenreiro, Antonio: Delegación de Hacienda, La Coruña, 178–80
Tessenow, Heinrich, 211
textiles, 62
Thälmann, Ernst, 58n64
Thälmannplatz, East Berlin, 49, 52
The Architects Collaborative (TAC). See TAC
Thiers, Adolphe, 265
Thornton, William, 344
Tilton, Edward, 146, 15
timelessness, 66
Todt Organization, 214
Torres Clavé, Josep, 190, 202n1
totalitarianism, 3–5, 12n8, 155,
Town Planning and Associates (TPA), 186, 188–90, 193, 194, 196–97, 199–200, 201, 205n38, 208n57, 208n61, 208n63, 209n75, 209n77. See also Sert, José Luis; Wiener, Paul Lester
TPA. See Town Planning and Associates (TPA)

378   Index

"translation," 234, 300, 310, 313, 319n51
transportation, 91, 109
Treaty of Versailles, 55n36
Truman, Harry S., 179
Tuck, Richard, 9
Tumaco, Colombia, 193, 195, 208n63
Turkey, 234, 333–34; ban on Islamic headscarves, 328; governmental control, 234, 329–31, 336; government/police response to protesters, 322, 322, 324, 328, 335, 336n2, 337n6; heritage and, 330, 340n36; opposition to authoritarian government, 9, 332–33; privatization and, 330, 332; secularism, 328–29; social engineering, 329; urban transformation, 329–31. *See also* Taksim Gezi Park protests
Turner, Nat, 20
typologies, 192, 193, 201

UAE. *See* United Arab Emirates (UAE)
Über altdeutsche Baukunst (Stieglitz), 245
Ullastres, Alberto, 174
Uluğ, Özden Melis, 332
Unidad Vecinal No. 3 (UV3), Lima, 205n38
unionization, 88, 90, 213, 221, 226
United Arab Emirates (UAE), 18, 98–118; citizenship, 99, 101; demographics, 101; economy, 98, 101, 102–3, 109; expatriates, 18, 98, 99, 101, 102–3, 107–8; exurbs, 101, 108–13; GDP, 107, 117n27; health profile, 116n9; housing, 6, *100*; labor, 99, 102–3; nation-building, 99, 107, 114; parks, *100*; religion within, 116n13; residency, 98, 101, 107–11; residential enclaves, 6, 99, 100, 101, 103, 107, 108–13; restrictions on residents, 98, 102, 103, 114; rulership and ruling elite, 101–2, 114, 117n26; security and surveillance, 102, 110, 114–15; social services, 101; spatial strategies, 99, 101, 111, 113; urban planning, 99, 101, 111, 114; wealth, 101, 102, 113
United Nations, 164, 165
United Nations Secretariat, New York, 163–64, 165, 178, 179, 204n27, 347, 348

United States: Civil War, 33; Department of State, 186, 191, 200, 205n30; expansionism, 20, 29, 31–32, 179, 282; Fugitive Slave Act, 29; Homestead Act, 32; interest in Iraq and oil revenue, 306–7, 308, 313; invasion of Iraq, 299, 313, 315n1; Johnson–Reed Act, 142; McCarran–Walter Act, 155; military, 299, 315n3; Select Committee on the Smithsonian Bequest, 21
United States Capitol Building, Washington, D.C., 344
United States Embassy, Athens (Gropius), 10
Universal Negro Improvement Association (UNIA), 143
University of Baghdad, Iraq, 234, 299–302, *301*, *302*, 303–4, *305*, 306, 309–11, *311*, *312*, 313; corruption during building of, 318n45; dormitories, 304, 310, 318n46; Harvard experts consulted, 306–8; mosque, *305*, 309; plan participants, 304, 313, 316n17; plans for, *301*, *302*, 304, 309, 310; site plan, *301*; walkways, *302*
Unnikrishnan, Deepak: *Temporary People*, 99
urbanism, 11, 120, 199, 206, 329, 317n23, 346; Germany, 5; Turkey, 329–31; United Arab Emirates, 104, 117n19
urban planning, 189, 200, 204n21; Brazil, 188–89, 204nn18–19; CIAM and, 192, 193–94, 200, 201, 208n66; Colombia, 194–97, 198, 199, 208n57, 208nn62–63, 208n66; Latin America, 8, 120, 185–210; local input and, 192, 197, 199; local typologies and, 192, 193; National Socialist, 122; Peru, 190–92, 201, 205n38, 207n46; Soviet, 58n69; Spain, 202n1; United Arab Emirates, 99, 101, 111, 114
Üstel, Füsun: *"Makbul Vatandas" in Peşinde*, 334
utopias, 260–63, 274

Vágó, József, 346; League of Nations headquarters, Geneva, 346–47

Vallendar, Rhineland, 238, 240, 242, 244–49
Vargas, Getúlio, 188, 189, 204n20, 205n30
Vargas, Lutero, 205n30
vaulting, 67, 147, 244
Veblen, Thorstein, 7
Veja (journal), 87
Vendôme Column, Paris, 265
Venezuela, 200
ventilation, 224
Venturi, Robert, 349
Veracini, Lorenzo, 281, 282, 283, 295
Vergangenheitsbewaltigung, 5
Vieco, Hernán, 199
Villa de Vedette, Lausanne, 286
Villa Presidente Ríos, Talcahuano, Chile (Larraín and Duhart), 201, 209n77
villas, 101, 108, 110
violence, 207nn54–55; police, 322, 324, 336n2, 337n6; racial, 20, 29, 32, 33; state, 282
"Violencia, La," 207nn54–55
Viollet-le-Duc, Eugène Emmanuel, 258, 259–60, 268, 271; *Encyclopédie d'Architecture*, 268; *Mémoire sur la defense de Paris*, 257–59; Villa la Vedette, Lausanne, 286
Viollet-le-Duc, Eugène-Louis, 261
Virno, Paolo, 275
Visconti, Giselda, 91
Viscosuisse (firm), 225
visualizations: digital, 122, 132, 134, 135, 136n10; historical, 122
Vitellozzi, Annibale: Pavilion of Autarchy, Research, and Invention, MAMI, 68, *69*, 70
voids, 37–38, 196, *198*, 201, 335
Voßstraße, Berlin, 37, 40, 55n26
voting and voting booths, 343

Walter, Thomas Ustick, 345
wars, 8, 257–58, 314
Warsaw, Poland, 124
Washington, Booker T., 33, 152
Washington, D.C., 19; Black population of, 27; slave trade in, 26–27, *28*
Washington Canal, Washington, D.C., 26
water, 72, 80n48
Wawel Castle, Krakow, 124, 127, 128–29, 132, 138n31; administrative extension to, 130–31, *131*
wealth, 29, 33, 101, 102, 113
Weber, Max, 8
Weiss, Peter: *Die Ästhetik des Widerstands*, 338n8
Weissmann, Ernest, 202n5
Welles, Sumner, 203n11
Western–Oriental divide, 306, 307
Weyl, Glen, 102–3
What Is to Be Done? (Chernyshevsky), 260
What the Arabs Think (Polk), 307
whiteness, 27, 28–29, 30, 33, 140, 234, 279, 281, 283, 284, 286, 290, 292, 294–95, 297n15. *See also* identity
white supremacy, 27, 28, 279, 284
Whitwell, Thomas Stedman, 22, 23
Wie baut Amerika? (Neutra), 213
Wied, Maximilian, Prince of, 30
Wiener, Paul Lester, 120, 185–86, *187*, 188–91, 199, 203n17, 209n77; in Brazil, 188–89; lecture tours in South America, 186, 188, 191, 203n13, 209n75; marriage to ten Haeff, 205n30; partnership with Sert, 185–86, 189–91; political connections, 190, 205n30; status of, 200; United States Pavilion, Paris, 202n2; work for Le Corbusier, 190, 204n27
Wilhelmplatz, Berlin, 37, 39. *See also* Thälmannplatz, Berlin
Willems, Suzanne, 214
William H. William (firm), 27
Winner, Langdon, 7
Winter Evening Conversations among a Few Villagers by a Warm Oven, 249–51
Wohnhaus in Bagdad, Das (Reuter), 313
Wolf, Martin, 10, 102
Wolfe, Patrick, 281, 283, 295

women, 324, 327, 329; discrimination against, 328; transgender, 329
World Bank, 348, 351n15
World's Fair, New York: Brazilian pavilion, 185, 202n4
Wright, Frank Lloyd, 9, 234, 279–96; "A Home in a Prairie Town," 280; Prairie Style, 279, 280, 284–90, 292, 294–95, 296; race and, 9, 233, 286–87; writings, 280, 286–87, 294–95
Wyatt, Matthew Digby, 344

Zacka, Bernardo: *Political Theory and Architecture*, 3
Zuccotti Park, New York, 321